AVE BLUE WO
EST. 2005

APHIC NOVELS • ANTHOLOGIES • ART BOO

AWBW

ALL WE EVER WANTED

WANTED

STORIES OF A
BETTER WORLD

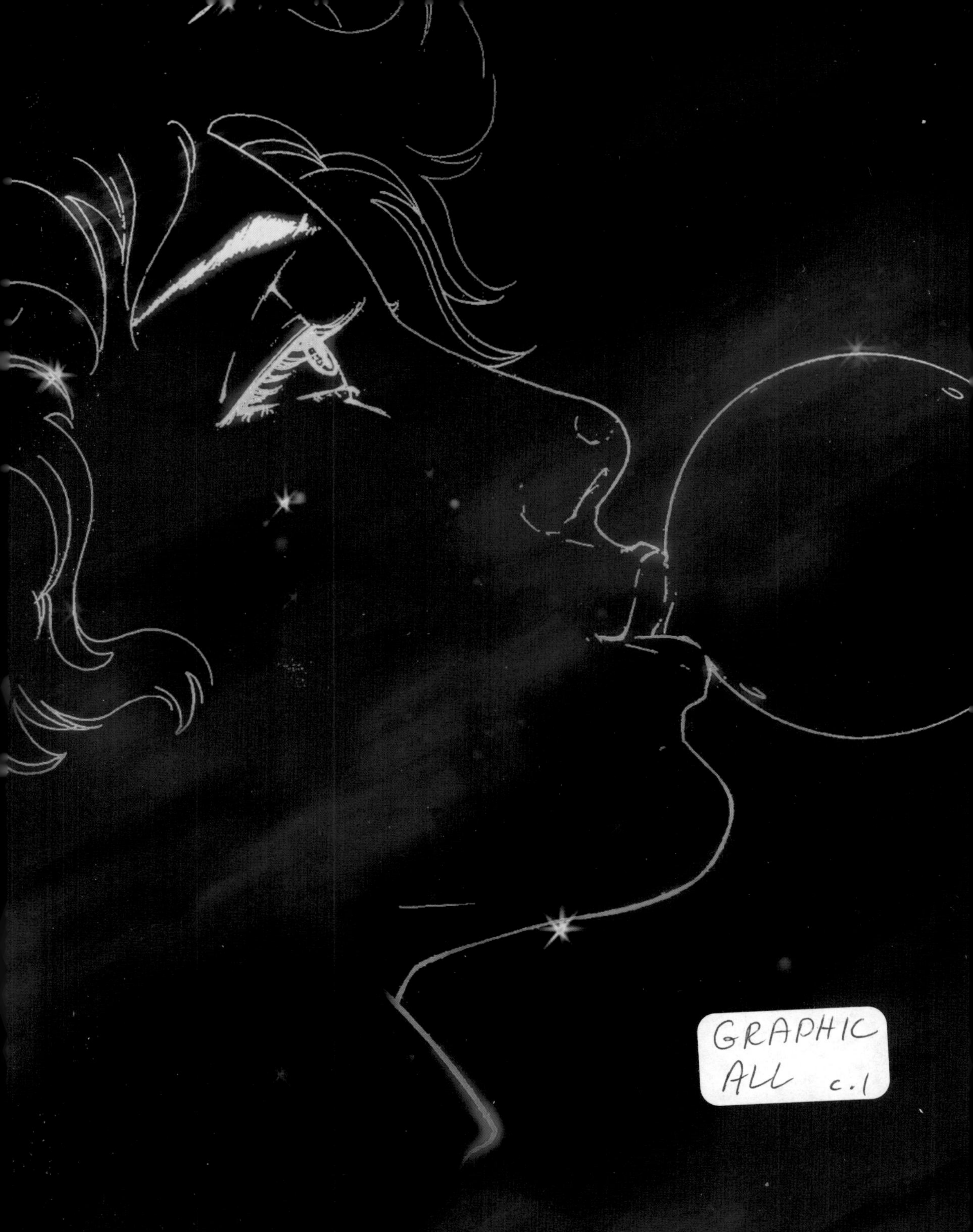

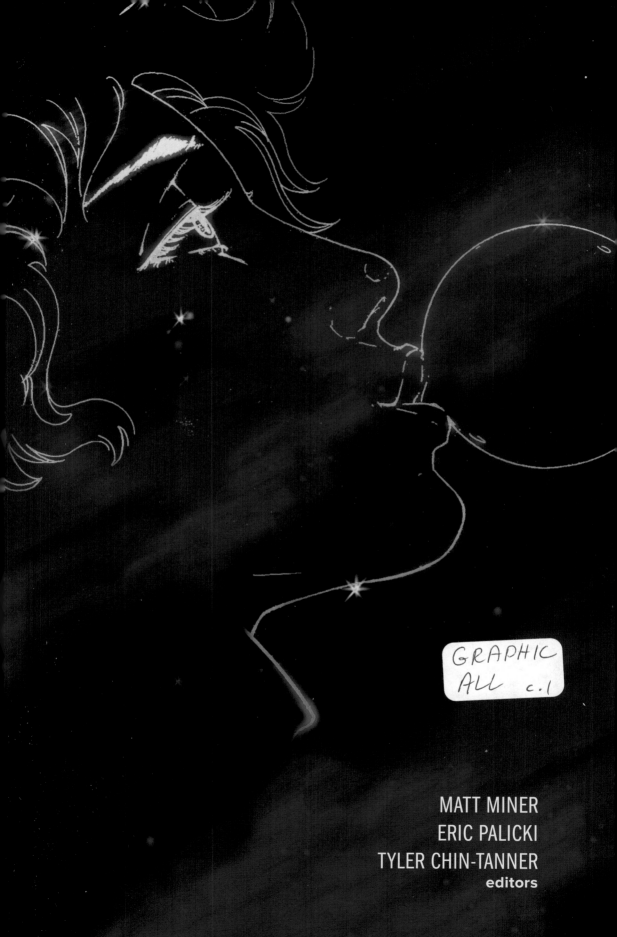

MATT MINER
ERIC PALICKI
TYLER CHIN-TANNER
editors

Tyler Chin-Tanner: Co-Publisher
Wendy Chin-Tanner: Co-Publisher
Justin Zimmerman: Chief Operating Officer
Pete Carlsson: Production Designer
Jesse Post: Book Publicist
Hazel Newlevant: Social Media Coordinator

ALL WE EVER WANTED
WANTED STORIES OF A
BETTER WORLD

Cover
Art: **ARIELA KRISTANTINA & MICHAEL WIGGAM**
Logo: **NICOLA BLACK DESIGN, LLC**

Book and Production Design: **NICOLA BLACK DESIGN, LLC**

All We Ever Wanted
ISBN: 978-1-949518-07-8
Second Edition: June 2020

Printed in Canada

TABLE OF CONTENTS:

9 THE PILOT
Written & Illustrated by
Dean Trippe
Lettered by Micah Myers

19 THE WEIGHT
OF TIME
Written by Jarrett Melendez
Illustrated by Danica Brine
Lettered by Taylor Esposito

25 UNA
Written & Illustrated by
Christopher Peterson
Colored by Gab Contreras
Lettered by Micah Myers

31 SEVENTEEN SOULS
Written by Tyler Chin-Tanner
Illustrated by Robbi Rodriguez
Colored by Michael Wiggam
Lettered by Micah Myers

39 IT LOOKED LIKE
OUR DREAMS
Written & Illustrated by
Maria Fröhlich
Lettered by Matt Krotzer

43 GAEA
Written by Rich Douek
Illustrated by David Stoll
Lettered by Micah Myers

51 BOMBS AWAY
Written by Howard Mackie
Illustrated by Ryan Lee
Lettered by Taylor Esposito

59 AND THE REST
IS MUSIC
Written by Paul Allor
Illustrated by Juan Romera
Lettered by Matt Krotzer

67 EVERYTHING I OWN
Written by Lela Gwenn
Illustrated by Tony Gregori
Colored by Josh Jensen
Lettered by Taylor Esposito

73 THE INVENTOR'S
DAUGHTER
Written by Lucia Fasano
Illustrated by Tess Fowler
Colored by Gab Contreras
Lettered by Taylor Esposito

79 BLACKSTAR
Written & Illustrated by
Chris Visions
Colored by Chris Visions
& Cathryn Virginia
Lettered by Zakk Saam

88 VELLEITY
Written by Wendy Chin-Tanner
Illustrated by Toby Cypress
Lettered by Matt Krotzer

90 **LIFE IS A DEVIL'S BARGAIN**
Written by Justin Zimmerman
Illustrated by Ethan Claunch
Colored by Fran Gamboa
Lettered by Taylor Esposito

99 **CHAT ROOM**
Written by Nadia Shammas
Illustrated by Jude Vigants
Colored by Mara Jayne Carpenter
Lettered by Zakk Saam

107 **FIRST STEPS OUTSIDE**
Written by Josh Gorfain
Illustrated by Matt LeJeune
Lettered by Zakk Saam

113 **CAN YOU SEE IT NOW?**
Written by Taylor Hoffman
Illustrated by K.R. Whalen
Colored by Josh Jensen
Lettered by Taylor Esposito

119 **JUST LIKE HEAVEN**
Written by Matt Miner
Illustrated by Matt Horak
Colored by Lee Loughridge
Lettered by Zakk Saam

127 **ALTERNICA**
Written by Jennie Wood
Illustrated by Jeff McComsey
Colored by Ari Pluchinsky
Lettered by Micah Myers

135 **OWNING UP TO THE PAST**
Written by James Maddox
Illustrated by Gavin Smith
Colored by Nick Wentland
Lettered by Justin Birch

143 **GOOD TIME**
Written by Vasilis Pozios
Illustrated by Ryan Cody
Lettered by Zakk Saam

149 **DAY AT THE PARK**
Written by Eliot Rahal
Illustrated by Jason Copland
Colored by Josh Jensen
Lettered by Zakk Saam

153 **CHOICE**
Written by Kay Honda
Illustrated by Liana Kangas
Colored by Gab Contreras
Lettered by Taylor Esposito

159 **SEEDS**
Written by Erik Burnham
Penciled by Anthony Marques
Inked by Fernando Ruiz
Colored by Matt LeJeune
Lettered by Matt Krotzer

165 **TWO LEFT FEET**
Written by Eric Palicki
Illustrated by Eryk Donovan
Colored by Gab Contreras
Lettered by Zakk Saam

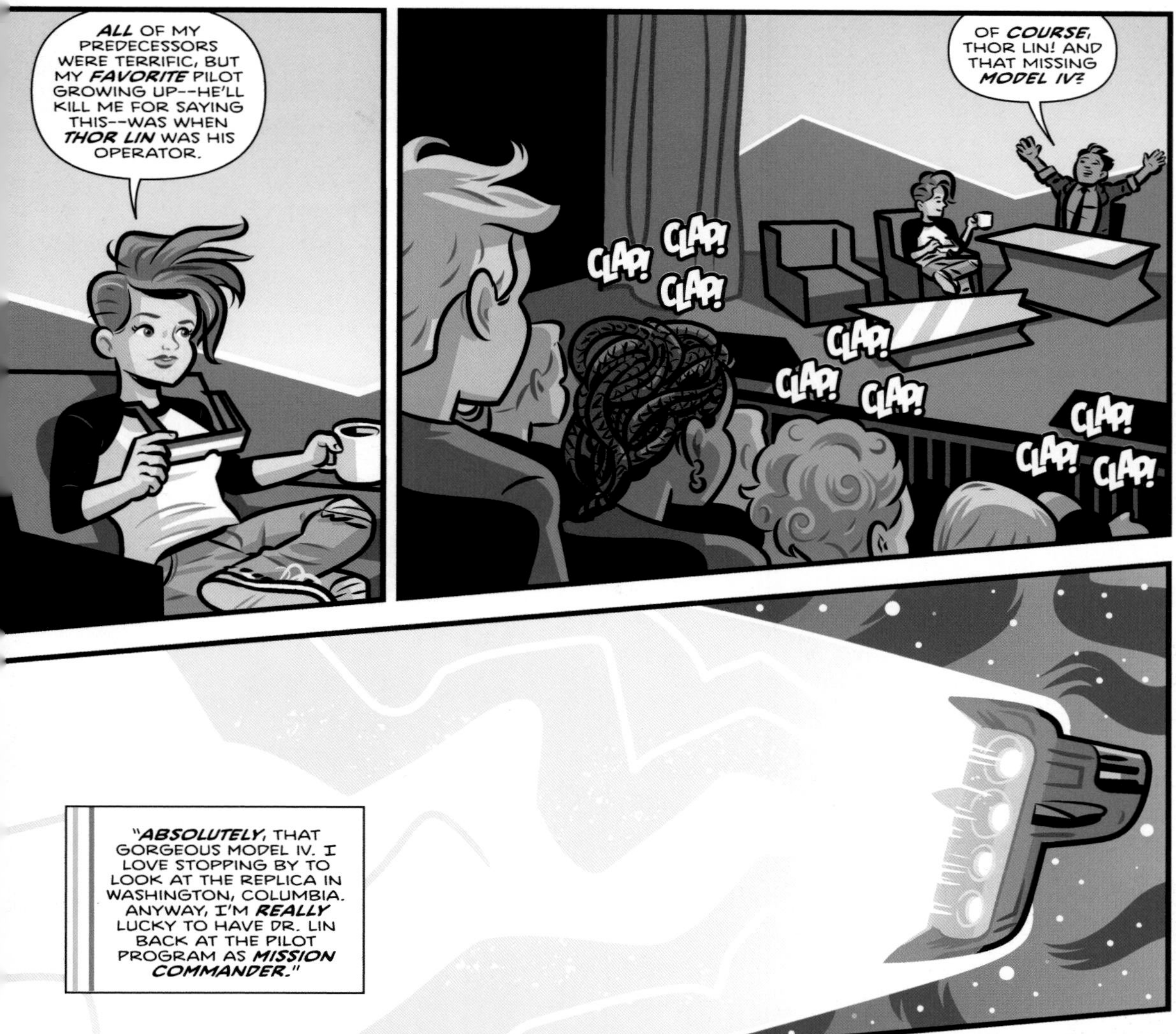

ALL OF MY PREDECESSORS WERE TERRIFIC, BUT MY FAVORITE PILOT GROWING UP--HE'LL KILL ME FOR SAYING THIS--WAS WHEN THOR LIN WAS HIS OPERATOR.
OF COURSE, THOR LIN! AND THAT MISSING MODEL IV?
CLAP! CLAP! CLAP!
CLAP! CLAP! CLAP!
CLAP! CLAP! CLAP!
"ABSOLUTELY, THAT GORGEOUS MODEL IV. I LOVE STOPPING BY TO LOOK AT THE REPLICA IN WASHINGTON, COLUMBIA. ANYWAY, I'M REALLY LUCKY TO HAVE DR. LIN BACK AT THE PILOT PROGRAM AS MISSION COMMANDER."
THE PRAXIS IS ENTERING IMPERIAL SPACE NOW, COMMANDER LIN.
PAGE THE PILOT.
BEEP BEE-BEEP BEEP
EXCUSE ME, JIM. I'M NEEDED UP THERE.

SION TONIGHT // THE PILOT INVITED TO MEETING WITH EMPRESS E

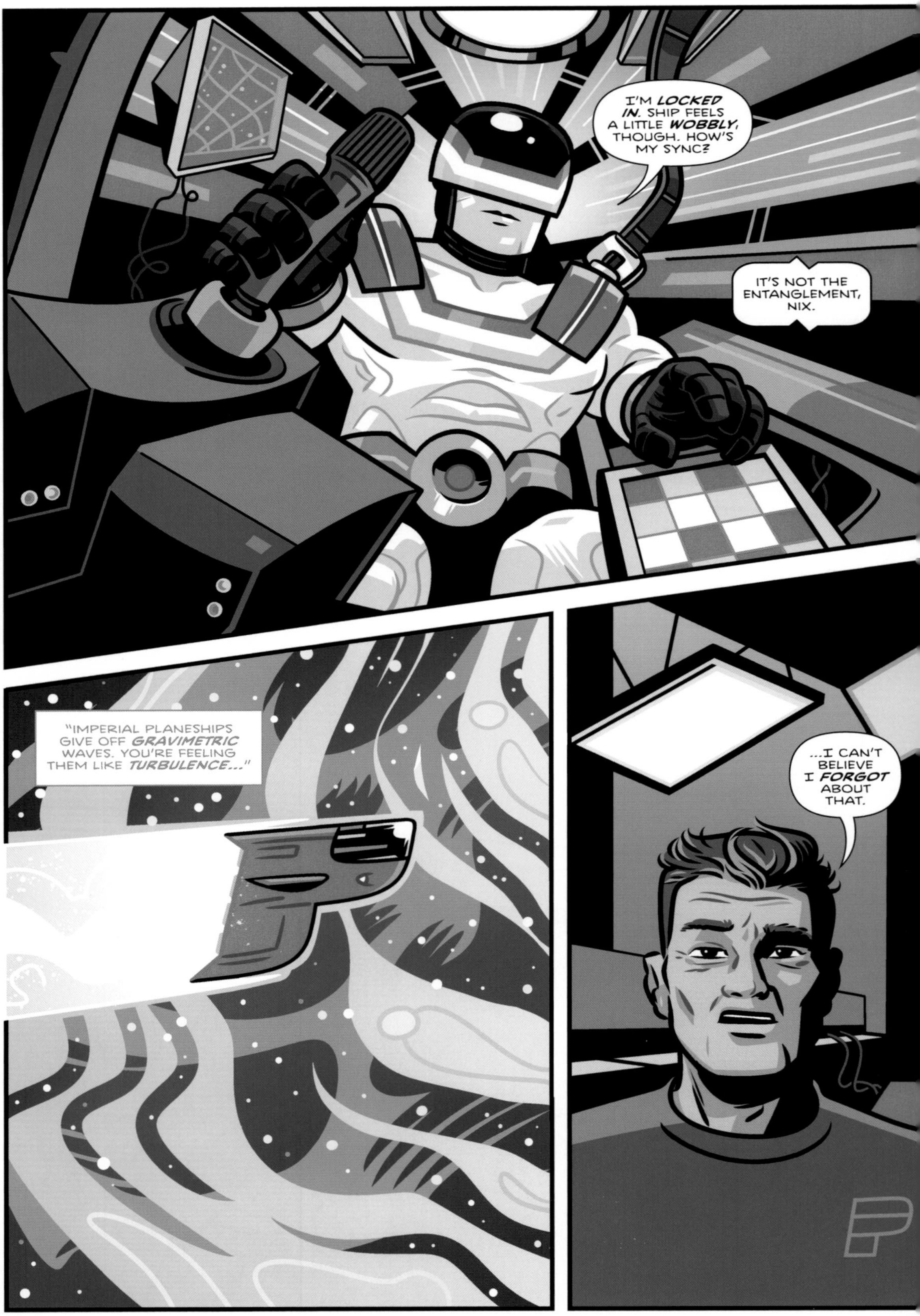
I'M *LOCKED IN.* SHIP FEELS A LITTLE *WOBBLY,* THOUGH. HOW'S MY SYNC?
IT'S NOT THE ENTANGLEMENT, NIX.
"IMPERIAL PLANESHIPS GIVE OFF *GRAVIMETRIC* WAVES. YOU'RE FEELING THEM LIKE *TURBULENCE...*"
...I CAN'T BELIEVE I *FORGOT* ABOUT THAT.

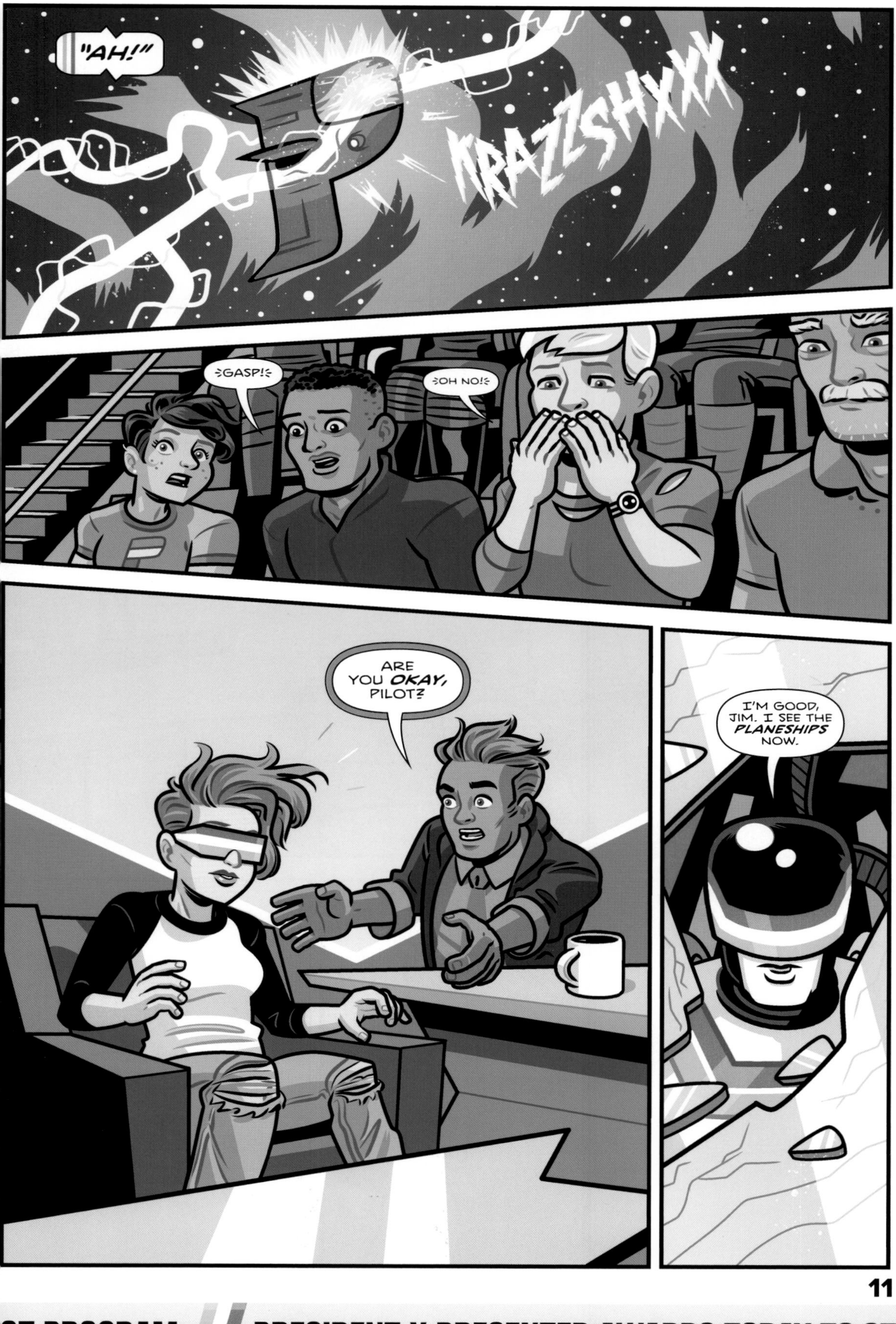
"AH!"
KRAZZSHXXX
GASP!
OH NO!
ARE YOU OKAY, PILOT?
I'M GOOD, JIM. I SEE THE PLANESHIPS NOW.

OT PROGRAM // PRESIDENT X PRESENTED AWARDS TODAY TO STU

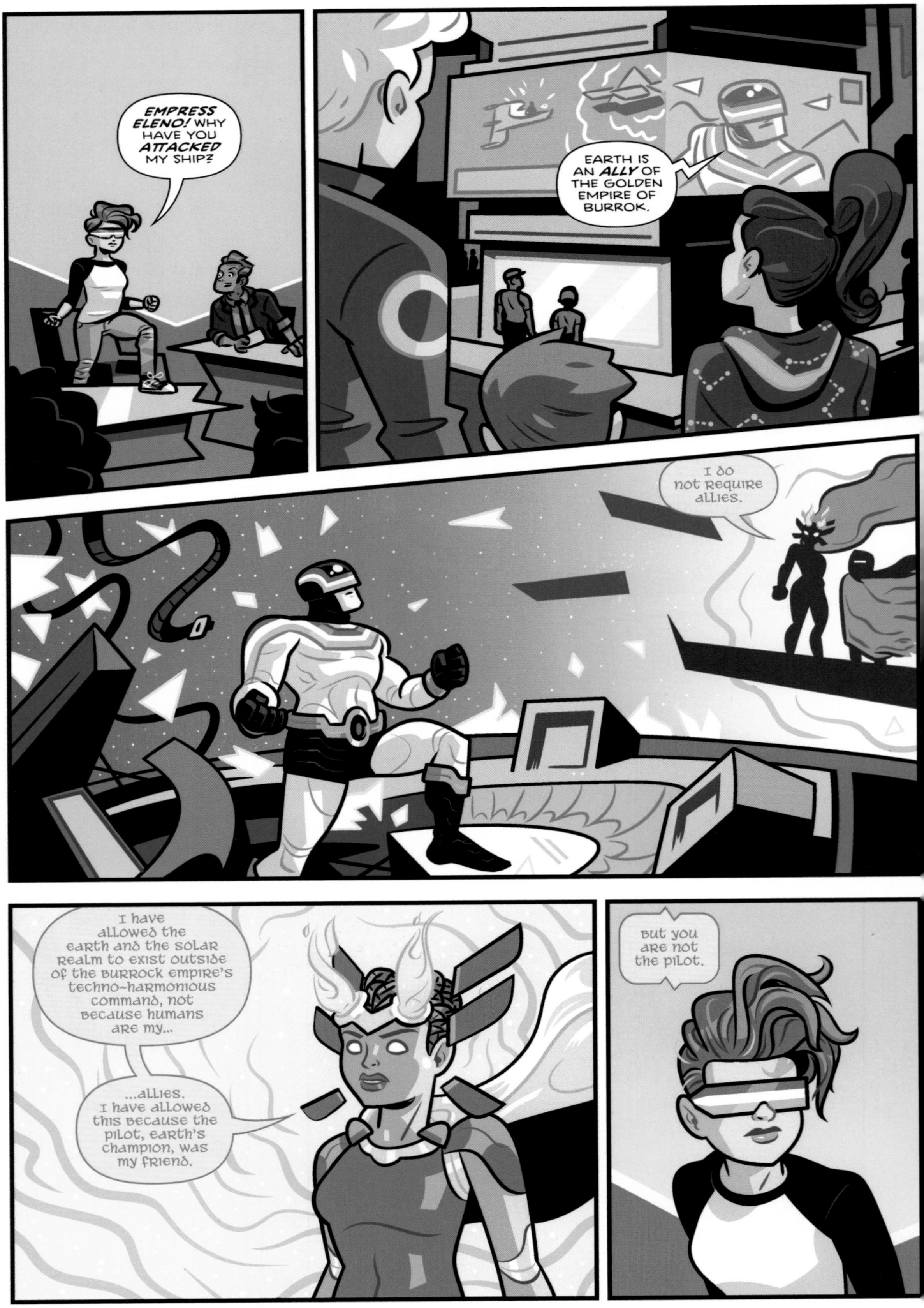
EMPRESS ELENO! WHY HAVE YOU ATTACKED MY SHIP?
EARTH IS AN ALLY OF THE GOLDEN EMPIRE OF BURROK.
I do not require allies.
I have allowed the earth and the solar realm to exist outside of the Burrock empire's techno-harmonious command, not because humans are my...
...allies. I have allowed this because the pilot, earth's champion, was my friend.
But you are not the pilot.

CTIVE SHIELDING // BREAKING NEWS: THE PILOT'S SHIP, THE PRAXE

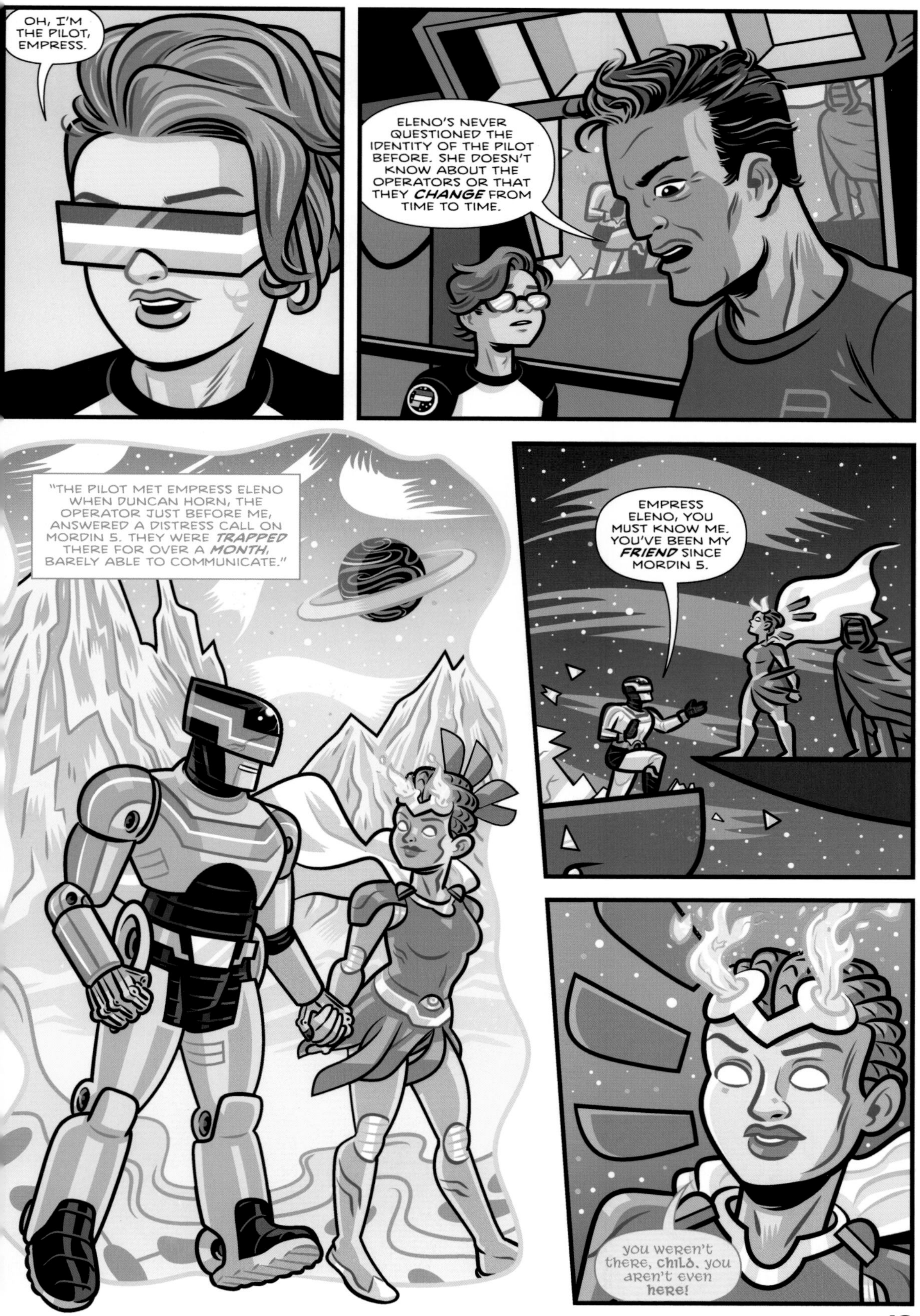
OH, I'M THE PILOT, EMPRESS.
ELENO'S NEVER QUESTIONED THE IDENTITY OF THE PILOT BEFORE. SHE DOESN'T KNOW ABOUT THE OPERATORS OR THAT THEY *CHANGE* FROM TIME TO TIME.
"THE PILOT MET EMPRESS ELENO WHEN DUNCAN HORN, THE OPERATOR JUST BEFORE ME, ANSWERED A DISTRESS CALL ON MORDIN 5. THEY WERE *TRAPPED* THERE FOR OVER A *MONTH*, BARELY ABLE TO COMMUNICATE."
EMPRESS ELENO, YOU MUST KNOW ME. YOU'VE BEEN MY *FRIEND* SINCE MORDIN 5.
you weren't there, child. you aren't even here!

ƆCK ARMADA / THE PILOT APPEARS UNHARMED AT THIS TIME, BU

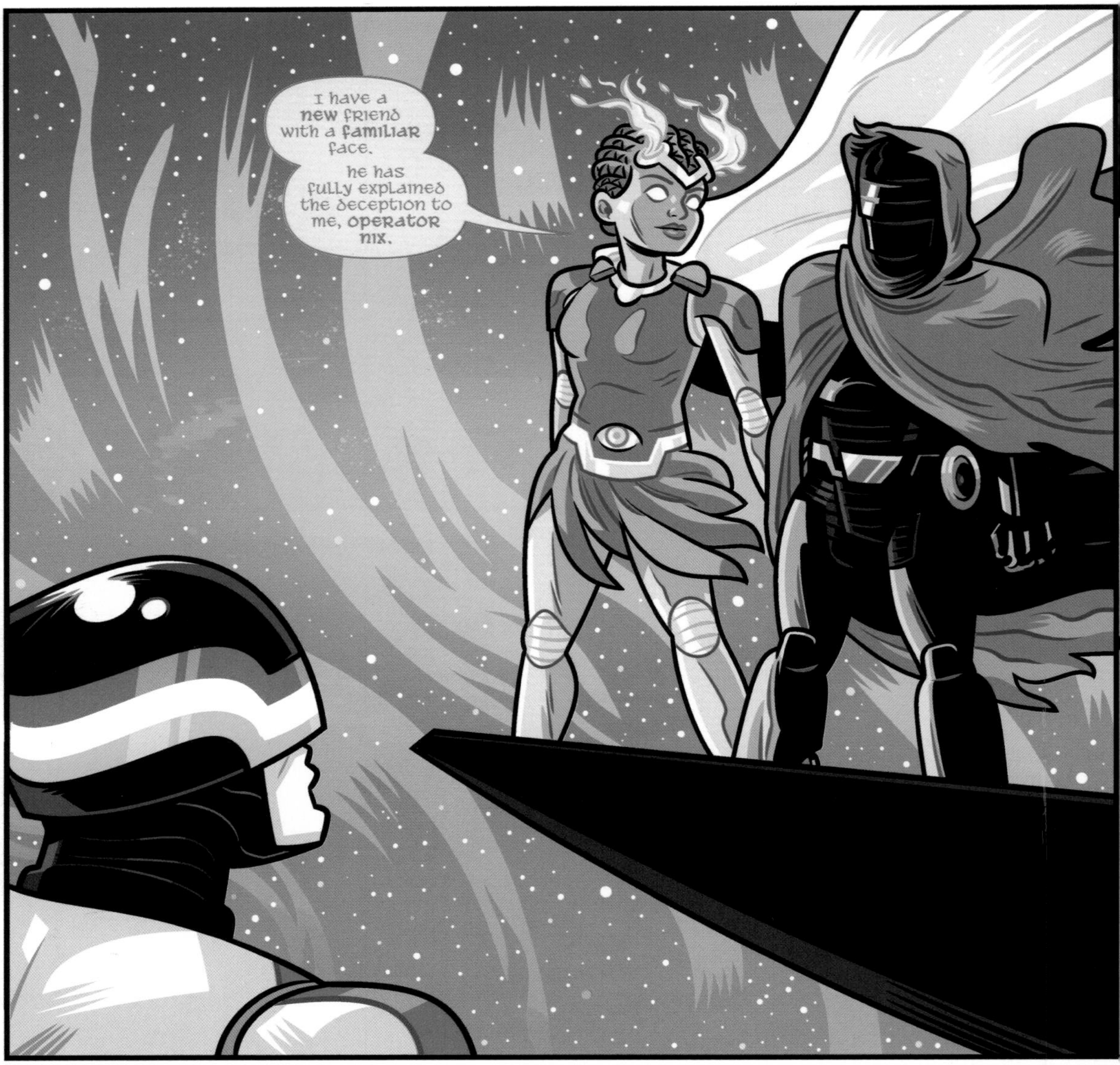
I have a new friend with a familiar face.
he has fully explained the deception to me, operator nix.

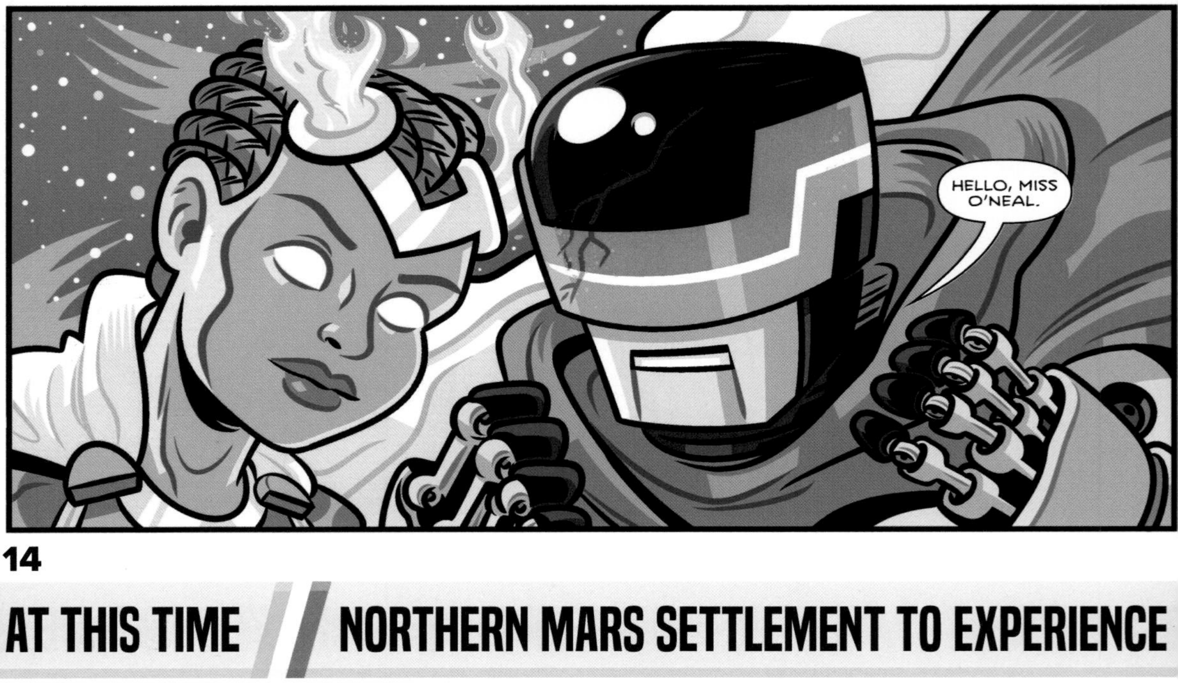
HELLO, MISS O'NEAL.

ED AT THIS TIME // NORTHERN MARS SETTLEMENT TO EXPERIENCE

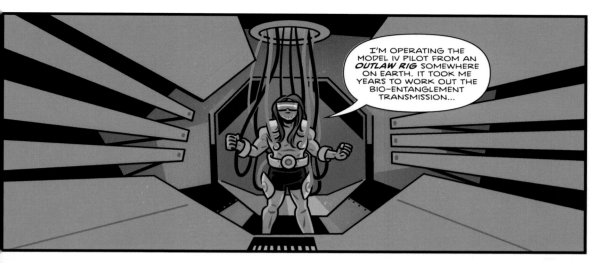

I'M OPERATING THE MODEL IV PILOT FROM AN *OUTLAW RIG* SOMEWHERE ON EARTH. IT TOOK ME YEARS TO WORK OUT THE BIO-ENTANGLEMENT TRANSMISSION...

"...BUT IT WAS WORTH IT TO STOP YOU FROM RUINING THE PILOT'S LEGACY!"

ROGUE OPERATION OF A PILOT MODEL IS *ILLEGAL* UNDER THE UNITED WORLD CHARTER! THAT MODEL IV BELONGS IN THE INTERNATIONAL AIR & SPACE MUSEUM!

EMPRESS, PLEASE, DON'T LET THIS ANONYMOUS *CRIMINAL* ENDANGER THE PEACE BETWEEN OUR PEOPLES. HE DOESN'T UNDERSTAND HOW DANGEROUS HIS INTERFERENCE IS.

R CHRISTMAS // AUSTIN'S S.A.N.T.A. PROGRAM WHICH UTILIZES AIR

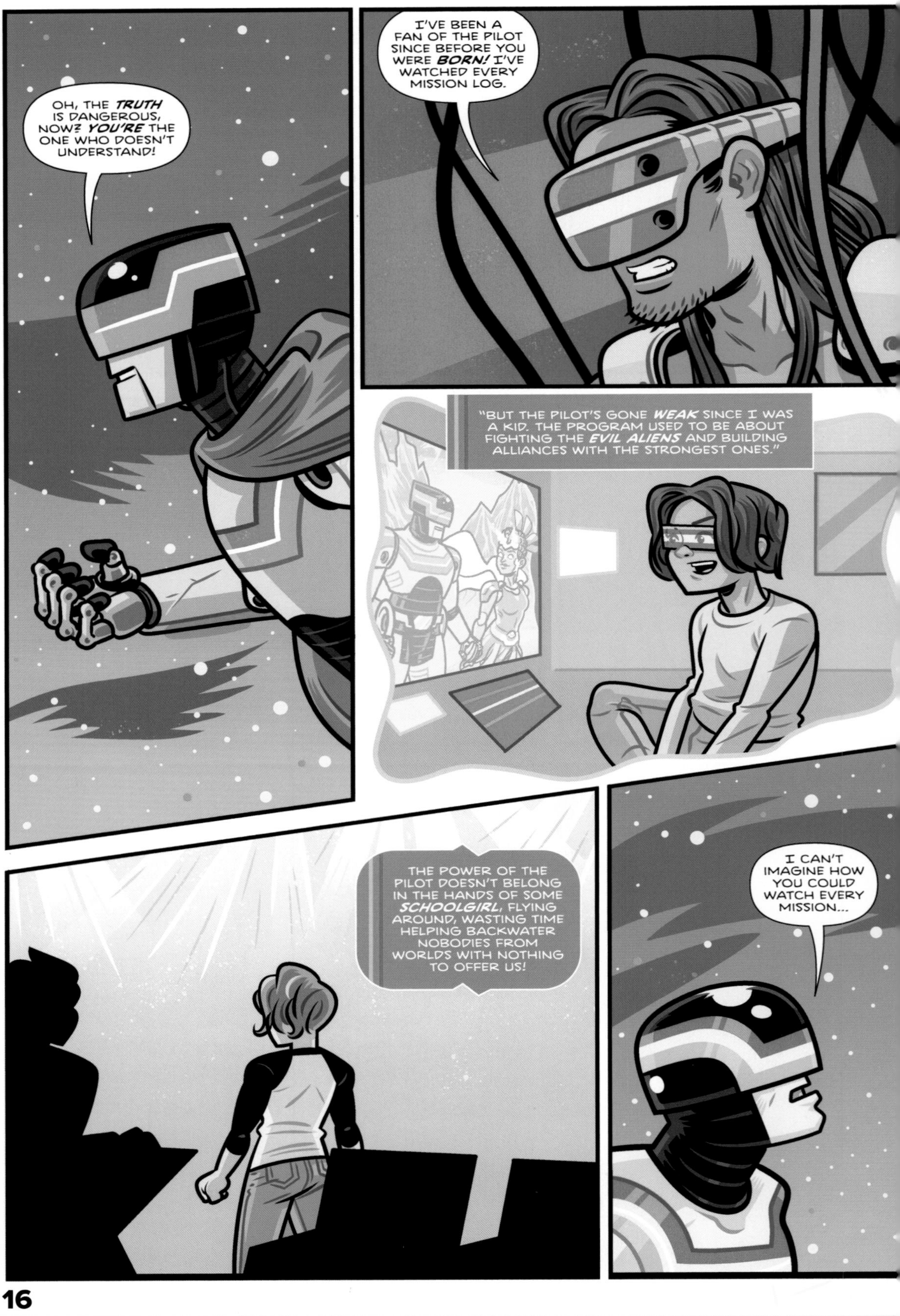
OH, THE TRUTH IS DANGEROUS, NOW? YOU'RE THE ONE WHO DOESN'T UNDERSTAND!
I'VE BEEN A FAN OF THE PILOT SINCE BEFORE YOU WERE BORN! I'VE WATCHED EVERY MISSION LOG.
"BUT THE PILOT'S GONE WEAK SINCE I WAS A KID. THE PROGRAM USED TO BE ABOUT FIGHTING THE EVIL ALIENS AND BUILDING ALLIANCES WITH THE STRONGEST ONES."
THE POWER OF THE PILOT DOESN'T BELONG IN THE HANDS OF SOME SCHOOLGIRL, FLYING AROUND, WASTING TIME HELPING BACKWATER NOBODIES FROM WORLDS WITH NOTHING TO OFFER US!
I CAN'T IMAGINE HOW YOU COULD WATCH EVERY MISSION...

ICAL DISCHARGE / A ROGUE OPERATOR APPEARS TO HAVE POSSES

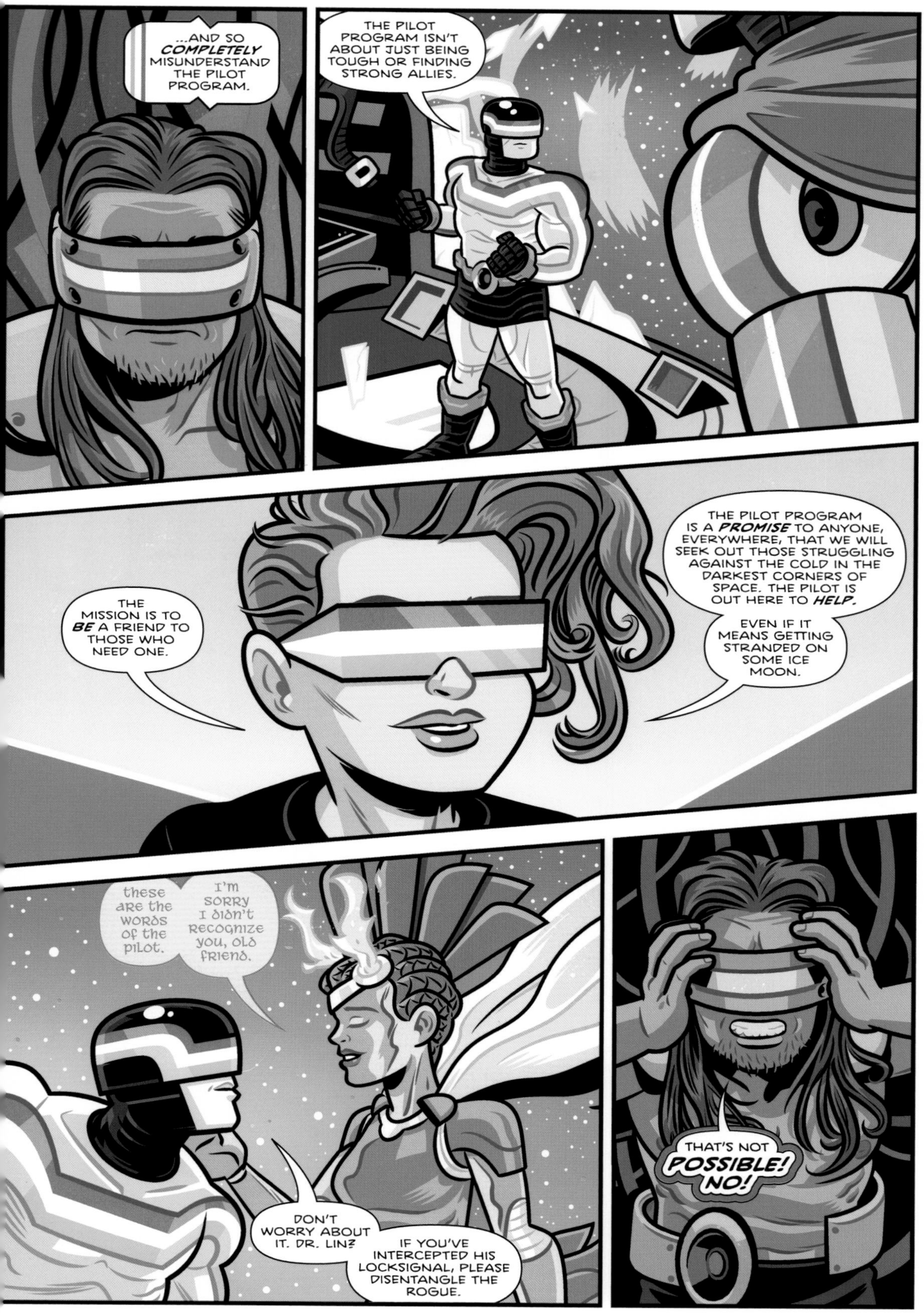
...AND SO *COMPLETELY* MISUNDERSTAND THE PILOT PROGRAM.
THE PILOT PROGRAM ISN'T ABOUT JUST BEING TOUGH OR FINDING STRONG ALLIES.
THE MISSION IS TO *BE* A FRIEND TO THOSE WHO NEED ONE.
THE PILOT PROGRAM IS A *PROMISE* TO ANYONE, EVERYWHERE, THAT WE WILL SEEK OUT THOSE STRUGGLING AGAINST THE COLD IN THE DARKEST CORNERS OF SPACE. THE PILOT IS OUT HERE TO *HELP.*
EVEN IF IT MEANS GETTING STRANDED ON SOME ICE MOON.
these are the words of the pilot.
I'm sorry I didn't recognize you, old friend.
DON'T WORRY ABOUT IT. DR. LIN?
IF YOU'VE INTERCEPTED HIS LOCKSIGNAL, PLEASE DISENTANGLE THE ROGUE.
THAT'S NOT *POSSIBLE! NO!*

ND RECOVERY / CRISIS AVERTED: THE PILOT HAS RECOVERED THE M

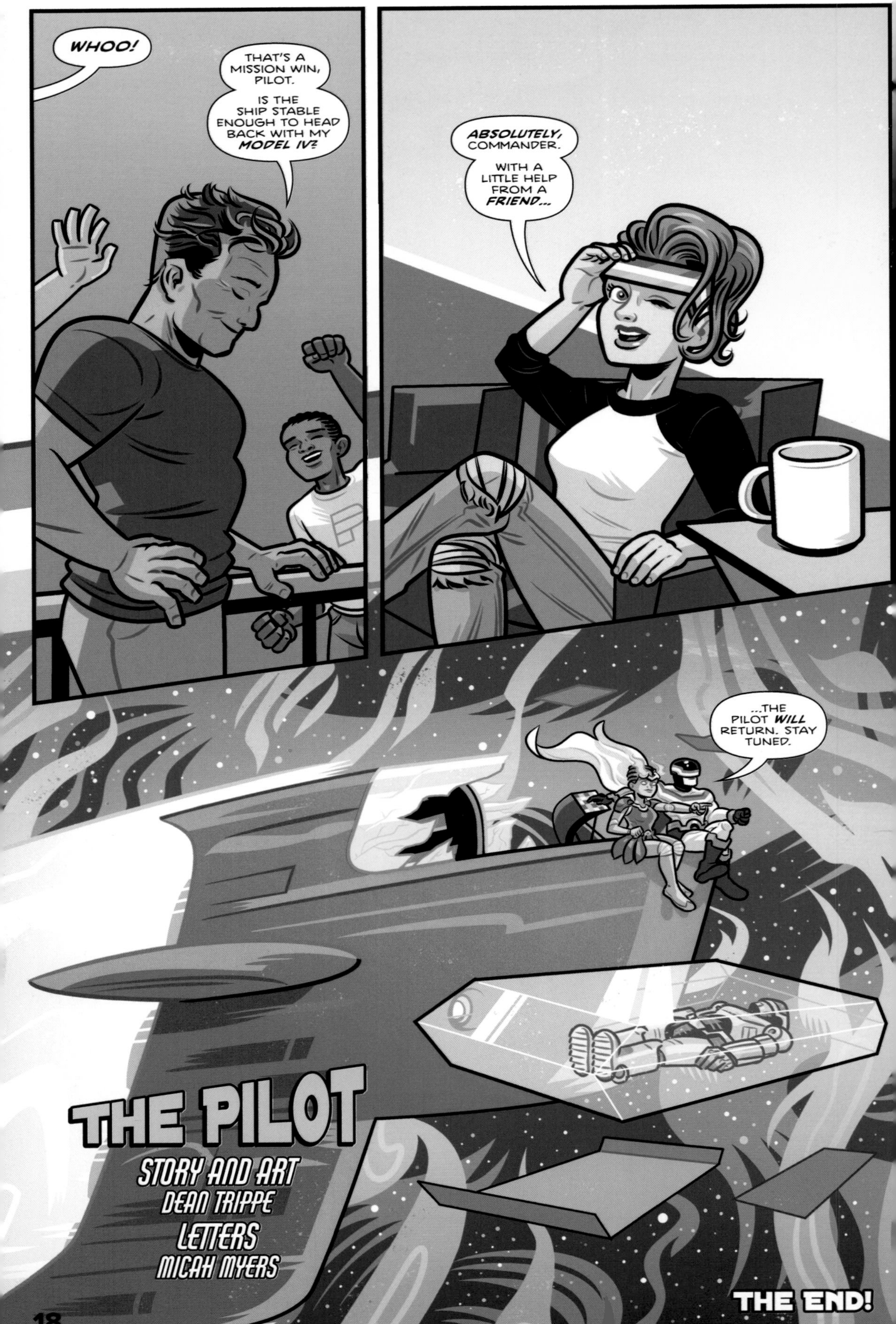
WHOO!
THAT'S A MISSION WIN, PILOT. IS THE SHIP STABLE ENOUGH TO HEAD BACK WITH MY MODEL IV?
ABSOLUTELY, COMMANDER. WITH A LITTLE HELP FROM A FRIEND...
...THE PILOT WILL RETURN. STAY TUNED.
THE PILOT
STORY AND ART
DEAN TRIPPE
LETTERS
MICAH MYERS
THE END!

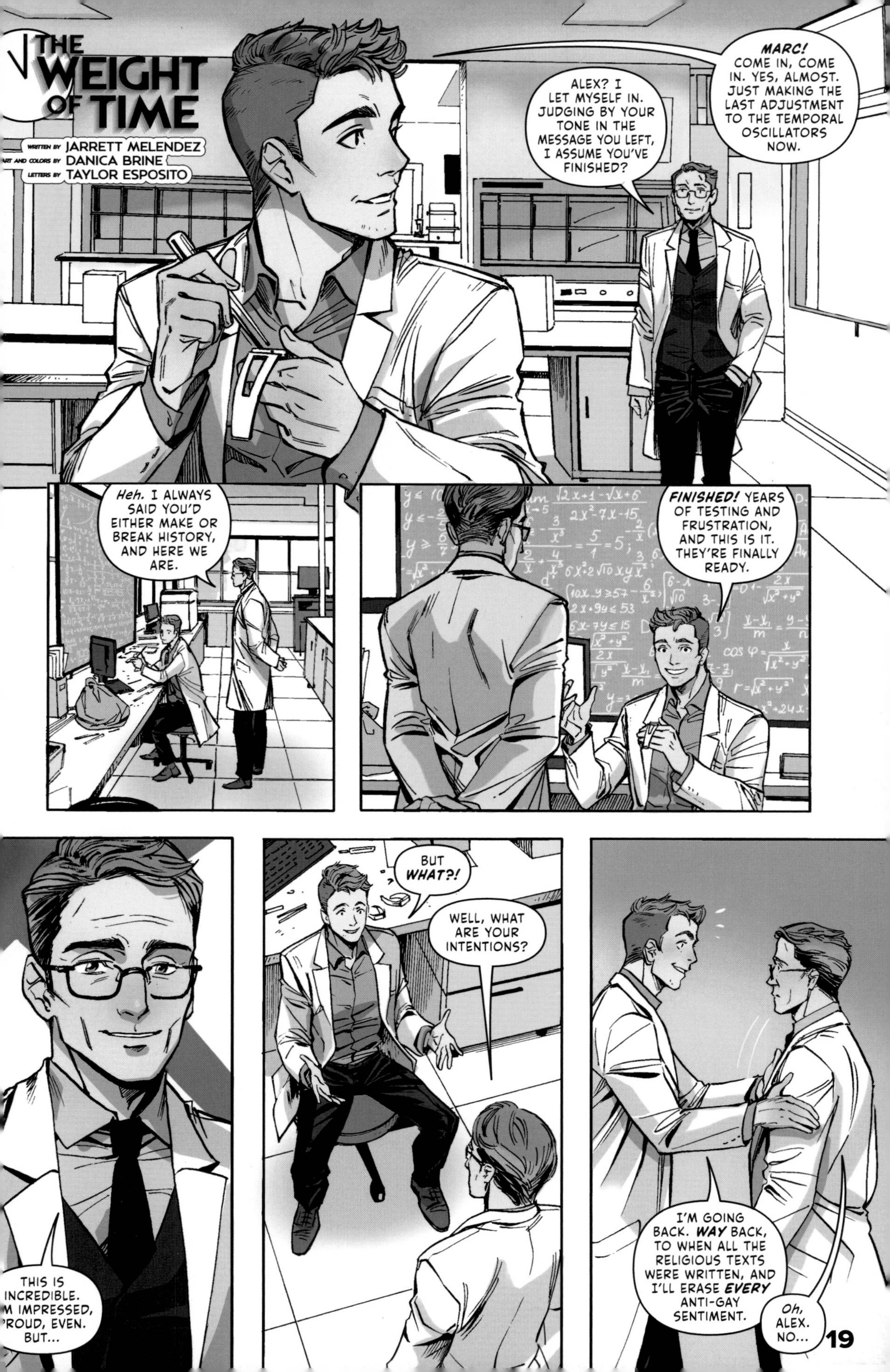
THE WEIGHT OF TIME
WRITTEN BY JARRETT MELENDEZ
ART AND COLORS BY DANICA BRINE
LETTERS BY TAYLOR ESPOSITO
ALEX? I LET MYSELF IN. JUDGING BY YOUR TONE IN THE MESSAGE YOU LEFT, I ASSUME YOU'VE FINISHED?
MARC! COME IN, COME IN. YES, ALMOST. JUST MAKING THE LAST ADJUSTMENT TO THE TEMPORAL OSCILLATORS NOW.
Heh. I ALWAYS SAID YOU'D EITHER MAKE OR BREAK HISTORY, AND HERE WE ARE.
FINISHED! YEARS OF TESTING AND FRUSTRATION, AND THIS IS IT. THEY'RE FINALLY READY.
THIS IS INCREDIBLE. M IMPRESSED, ROUD, EVEN. BUT...
BUT WHAT?!
WELL, WHAT ARE YOUR INTENTIONS?
I'M GOING BACK. WAY BACK, TO WHEN ALL THE RELIGIOUS TEXTS WERE WRITTEN, AND I'LL ERASE EVERY ANTI-GAY SENTIMENT.
Oh, ALEX. NO...

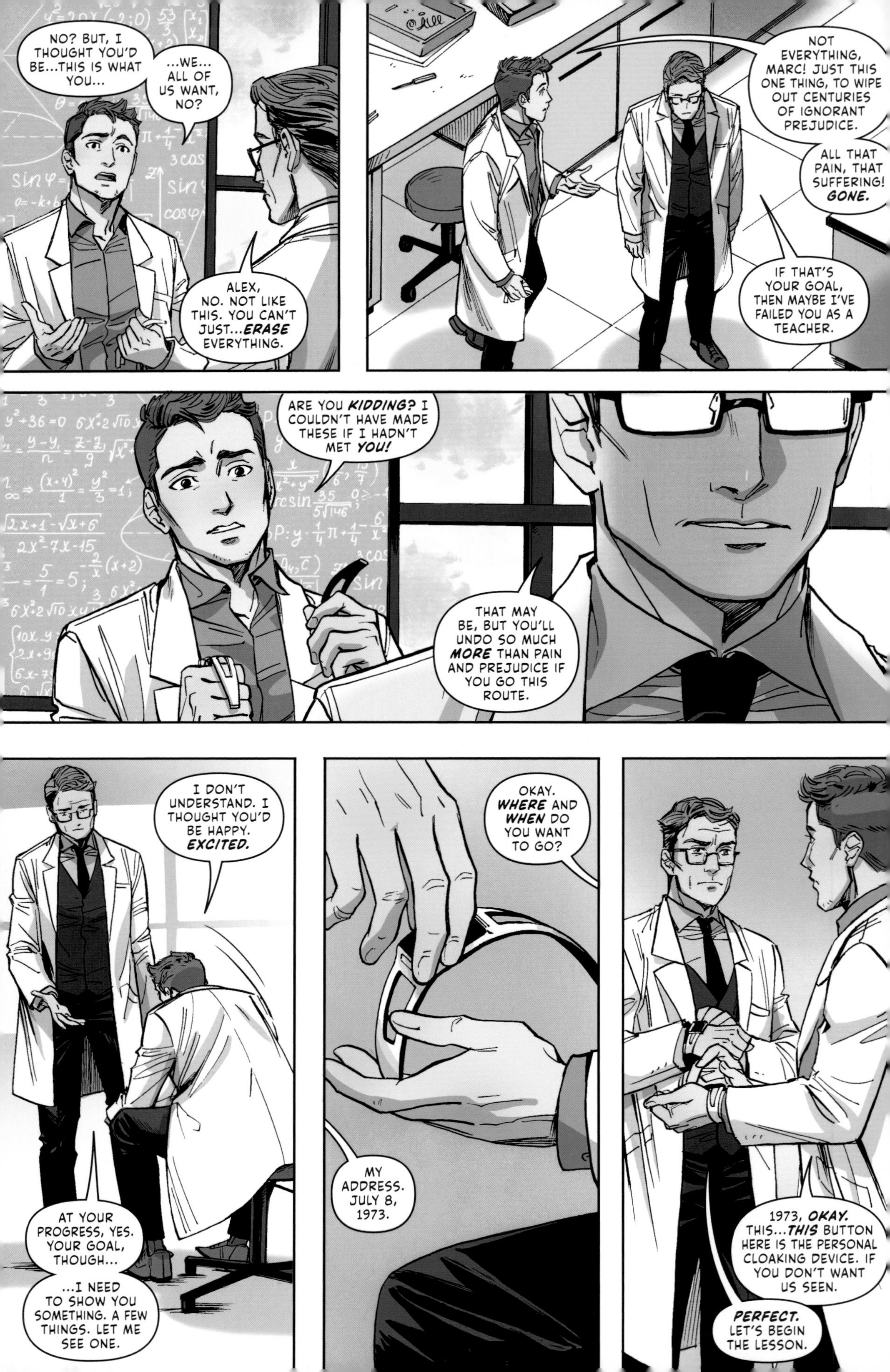
NO? BUT, I THOUGHT YOU'D BE...THIS IS WHAT YOU...
...WE... ALL OF US WANT, NO?
ALEX, NO. NOT LIKE THIS. YOU CAN'T JUST...***ERASE*** EVERYTHING.
NOT EVERYTHING, MARC! JUST THIS ONE THING, TO WIPE OUT CENTURIES OF IGNORANT PREJUDICE.
ALL THAT PAIN, THAT SUFFERING! ***GONE.***
IF THAT'S YOUR GOAL, THEN MAYBE I'VE FAILED YOU AS A TEACHER.
ARE YOU ***KIDDING?*** I COULDN'T HAVE MADE THESE IF I HADN'T MET ***YOU!***
THAT MAY BE, BUT YOU'LL UNDO SO MUCH ***MORE*** THAN PAIN AND PREJUDICE IF YOU GO THIS ROUTE.
I DON'T UNDERSTAND. I THOUGHT YOU'D BE HAPPY. ***EXCITED.***
AT YOUR PROGRESS, YES. YOUR GOAL, THOUGH...
...I NEED TO SHOW YOU SOMETHING. A FEW THINGS. LET ME SEE ONE.
OKAY. ***WHERE*** AND ***WHEN*** DO YOU WANT TO GO?
MY ADDRESS. JULY 8, 1973.
1973, ***OKAY.*** THIS...***THIS*** BUTTON HERE IS THE PERSONAL CLOAKING DEVICE. IF YOU DON'T WANT US SEEN.
PERFECT. LET'S BEGIN THE LESSON.

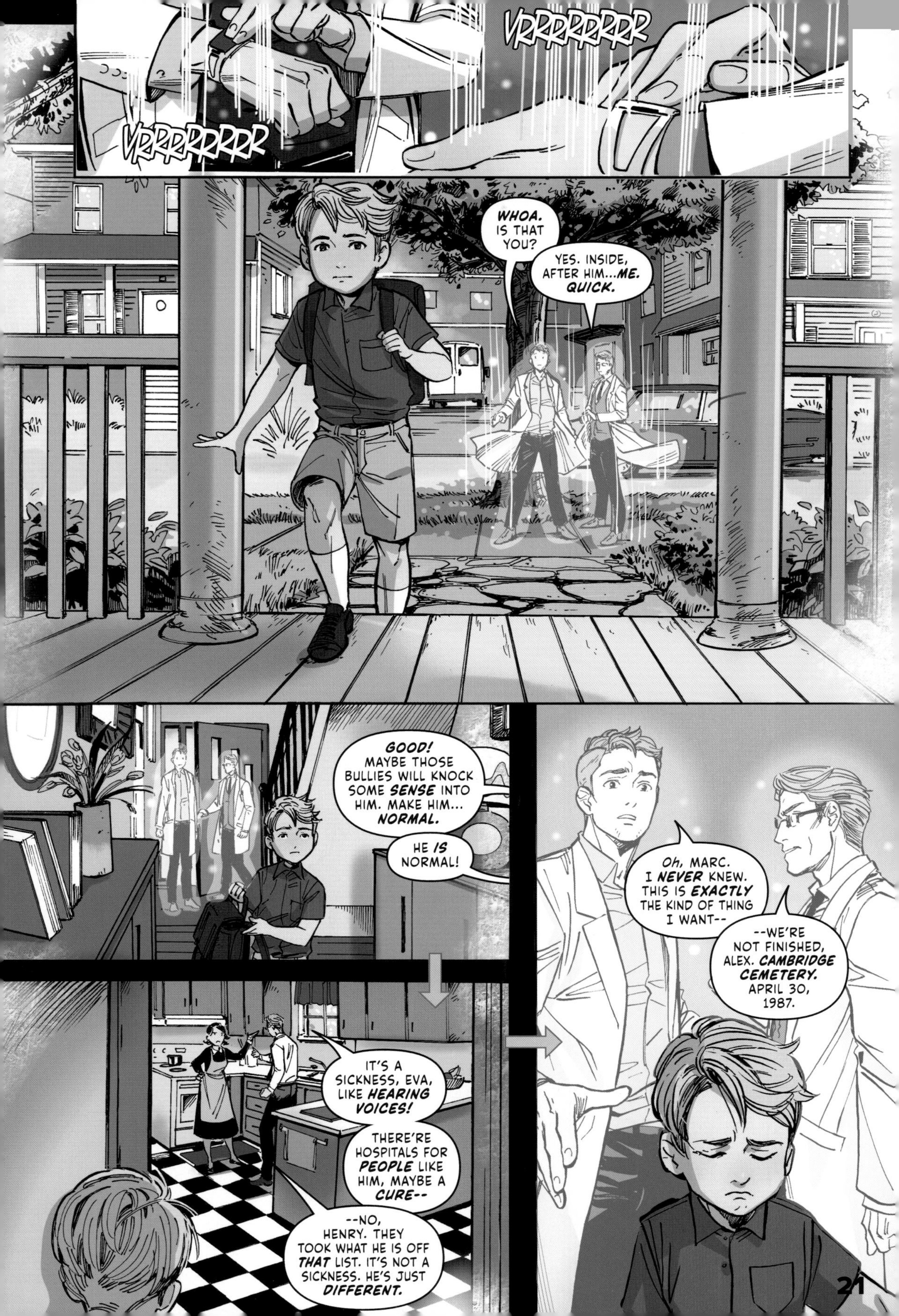
VRRRRRRRRR
VRRRRRRRRR
WHOA. IS THAT YOU?
YES. INSIDE, AFTER HIM...ME. QUICK.
GOOD! MAYBE THOSE BULLIES WILL KNOCK SOME SENSE INTO HIM. MAKE HIM... NORMAL.
HE IS NORMAL!
IT'S A SICKNESS, EVA, LIKE HEARING VOICES!
THERE'RE HOSPITALS FOR PEOPLE LIKE HIM, MAYBE A CURE--
--NO, HENRY. THEY TOOK WHAT HE IS OFF THAT LIST. IT'S NOT A SICKNESS. HE'S JUST DIFFERENT.
Oh, MARC. I NEVER KNEW. THIS IS EXACTLY THE KIND OF THING I WANT--
--WE'RE NOT FINISHED, ALEX. CAMBRIDGE CEMETERY. APRIL 30, 1987.

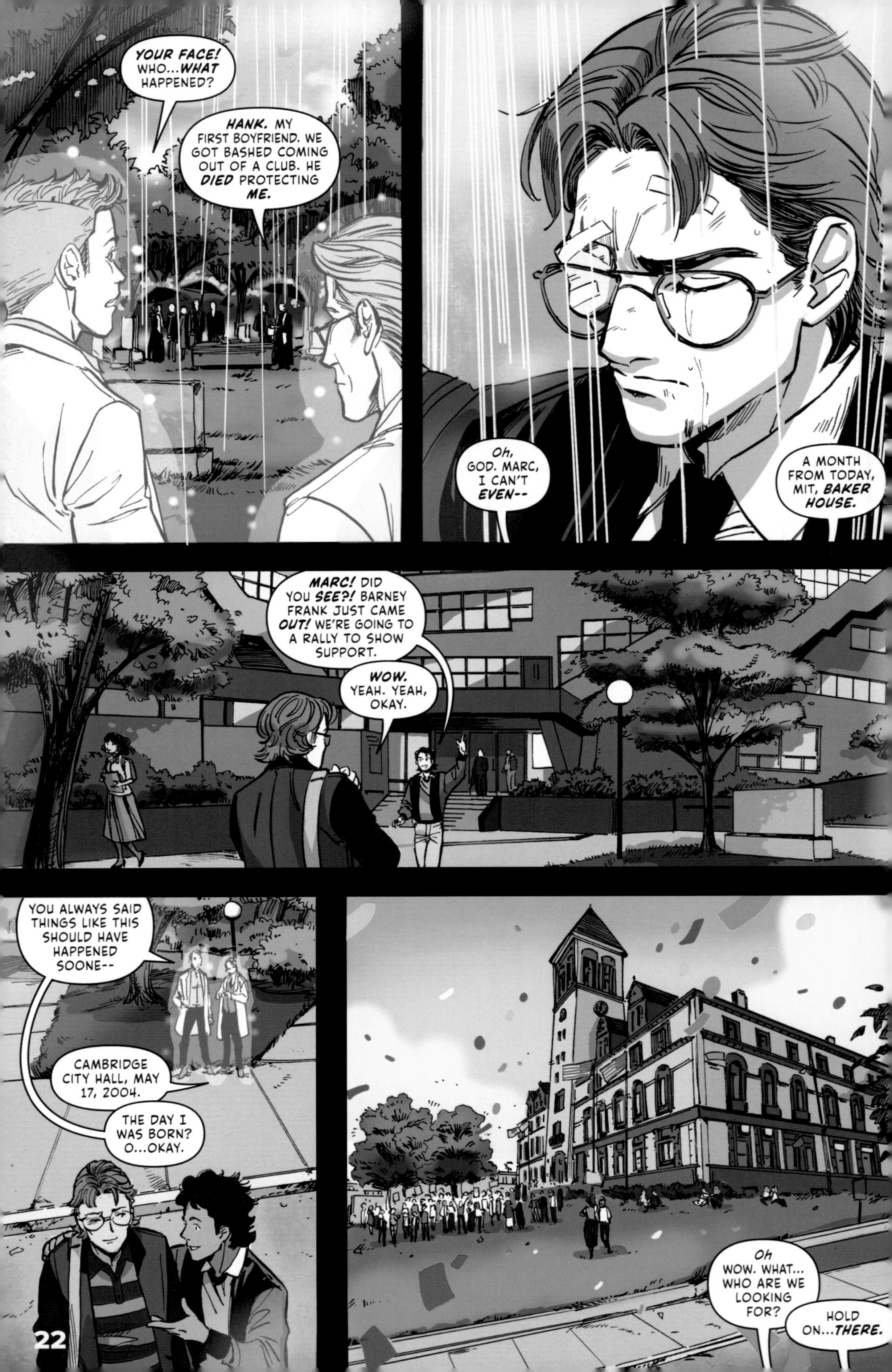
YOUR FACE! WHO...WHAT HAPPENED?
HANK. MY FIRST BOYFRIEND. WE GOT BASHED COMING OUT OF A CLUB. HE DIED PROTECTING ME.
Oh, GOD. MARC, I CAN'T EVEN--
A MONTH FROM TODAY, MIT, BAKER HOUSE.
MARC! DID YOU SEE?! BARNEY FRANK JUST CAME OUT! WE'RE GOING TO A RALLY TO SHOW SUPPORT.
WOW. YEAH. YEAH, OKAY.
YOU ALWAYS SAID THINGS LIKE THIS SHOULD HAVE HAPPENED SOONE--
CAMBRIDGE CITY HALL, MAY 17, 2004.
THE DAY I WAS BORN? O...OKAY.
Oh WOW. WHAT... WHO ARE WE LOOKING FOR?
HOLD ON...THERE.

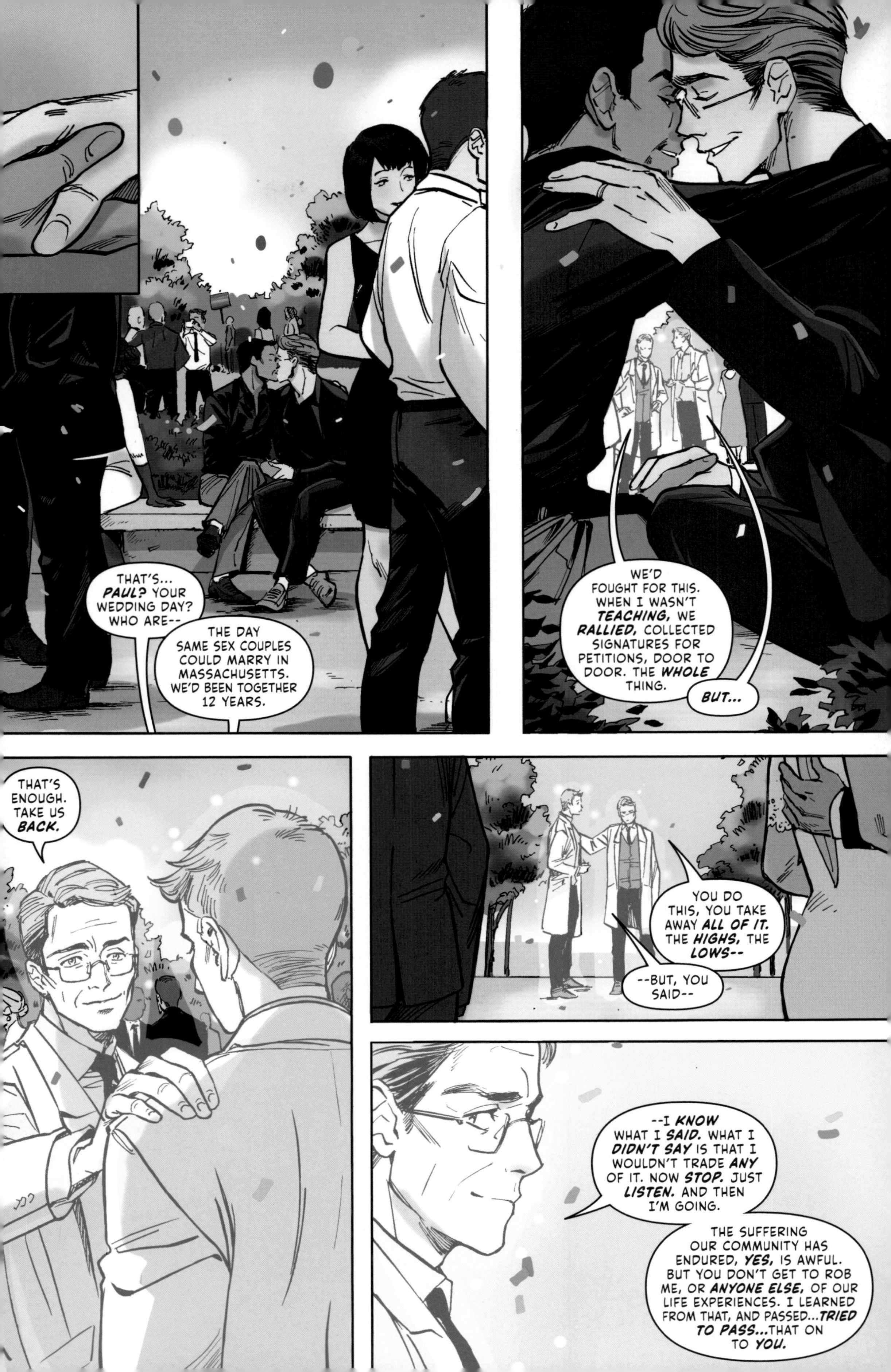
THAT'S... PAUL? YOUR WEDDING DAY? WHO ARE--
THE DAY SAME SEX COUPLES COULD MARRY IN MASSACHUSETTS. WE'D BEEN TOGETHER 12 YEARS.
WE'D FOUGHT FOR THIS. WHEN I WASN'T TEACHING, WE RALLIED, COLLECTED SIGNATURES FOR PETITIONS, DOOR TO DOOR. THE WHOLE THING.
BUT...
THAT'S ENOUGH. TAKE US BACK.
YOU DO THIS, YOU TAKE AWAY ALL OF IT. THE HIGHS, THE LOWS--
--BUT, YOU SAID--
--I KNOW WHAT I SAID. WHAT I DIDN'T SAY IS THAT I WOULDN'T TRADE ANY OF IT. NOW STOP. JUST LISTEN. AND THEN I'M GOING.
THE SUFFERING OUR COMMUNITY HAS ENDURED, YES, IS AWFUL. BUT YOU DON'T GET TO ROB ME, OR ANYONE ELSE, OF OUR LIFE EXPERIENCES. I LEARNED FROM THAT, AND PASSED...TRIED TO PASS...THAT ON TO YOU.

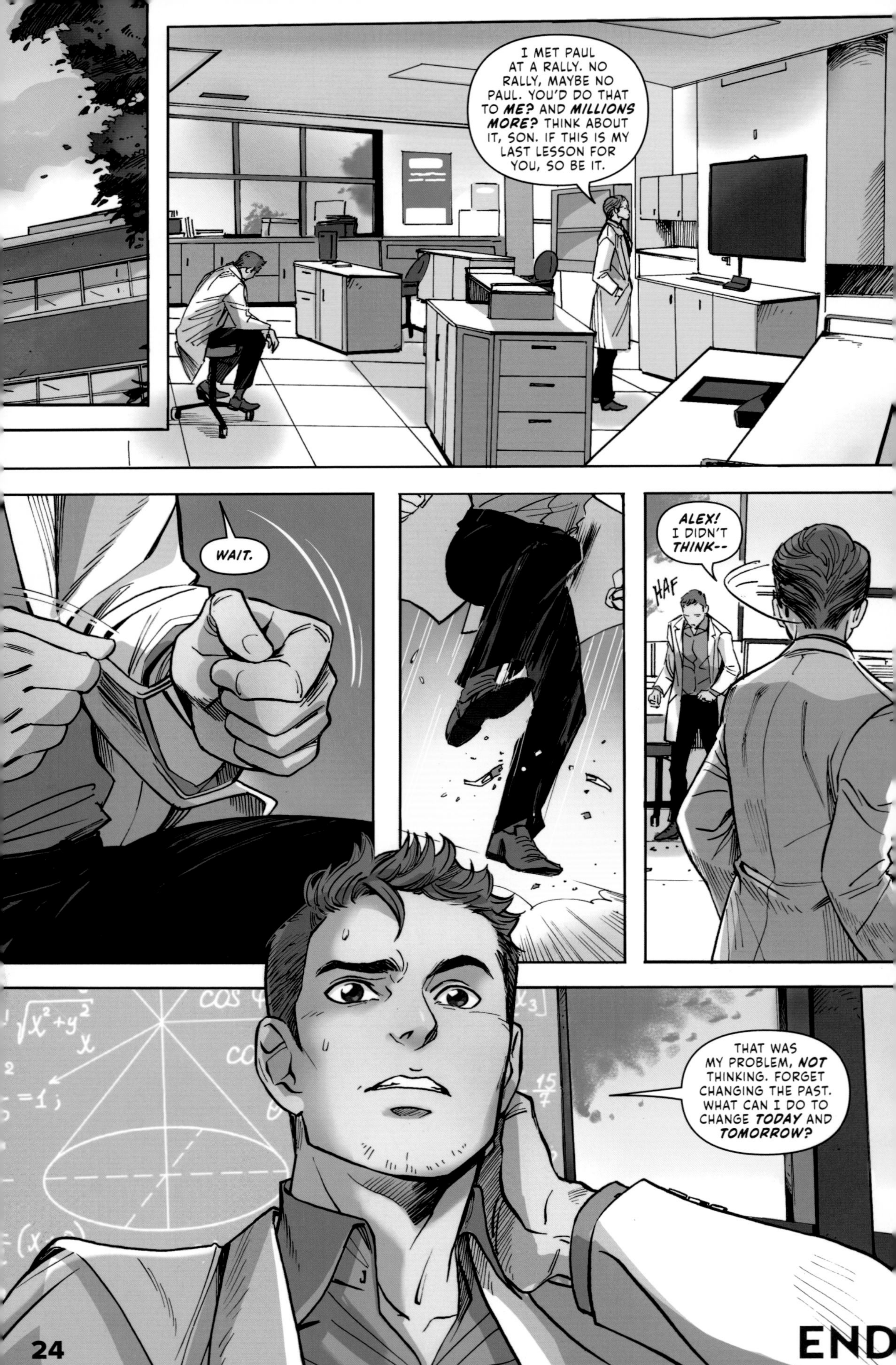
I MET PAUL AT A RALLY. NO RALLY, MAYBE NO PAUL. YOU'D DO THAT TO ME? AND MILLIONS MORE? THINK ABOUT IT, SON. IF THIS IS MY LAST LESSON FOR YOU, SO BE IT.
WAIT.
ALEX! I DIDN'T THINK--
HAF
THAT WAS MY PROBLEM, NOT THINKING. FORGET CHANGING THE PAST. WHAT CAN I DO TO CHANGE TODAY AND TOMORROW?
END

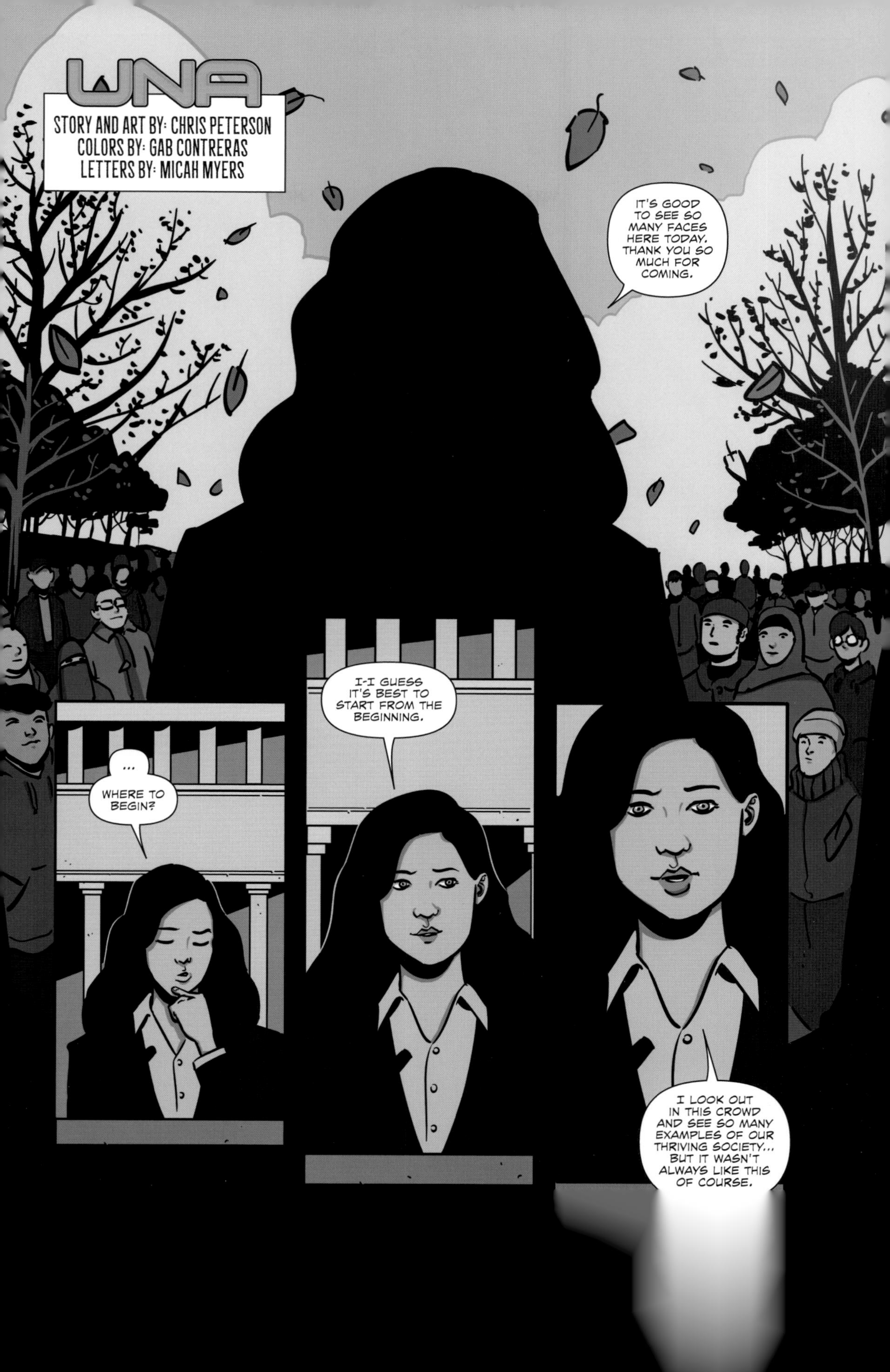
UNA
STORY AND ART BY: CHRIS PETERSON
COLORS BY: GAB CONTRERAS
LETTERS BY: MICAH MYERS
IT'S GOOD TO SEE SO MANY FACES HERE TODAY. THANK YOU SO MUCH FOR COMING.
... WHERE TO BEGIN?
I-I GUESS IT'S BEST TO START FROM THE BEGINNING.
I LOOK OUT IN THIS CROWD AND SEE SO MANY EXAMPLES OF OUR THRIVING SOCIETY... BUT IT WASN'T ALWAYS LIKE THIS OF COURSE.

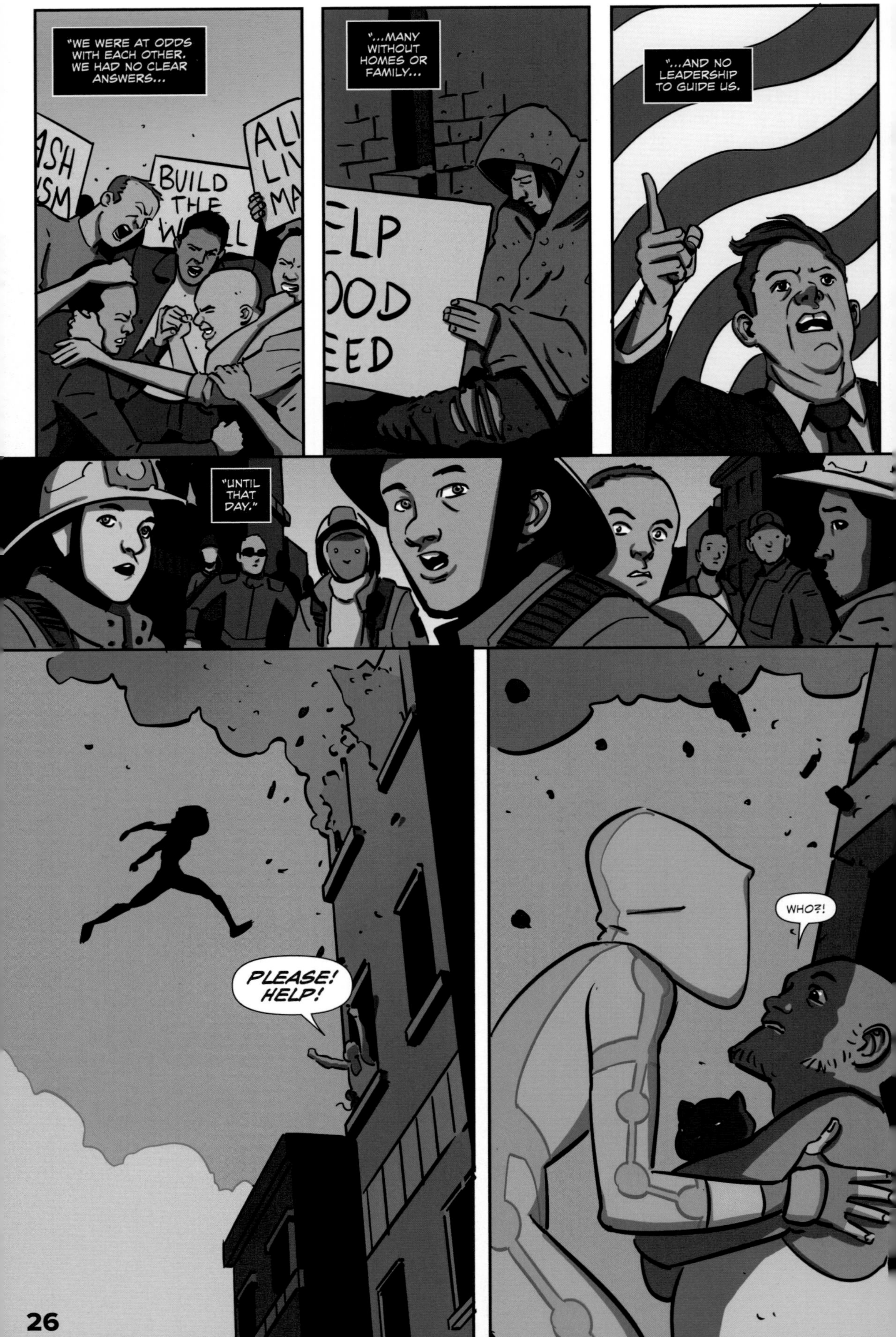
"WE WERE AT ODDS WITH EACH OTHER. WE HAD NO CLEAR ANSWERS...
BUILD
"...MANY WITHOUT HOMES OR FAMILY...
"...AND NO LEADERSHIP TO GUIDE US.
"UNTIL THAT DAY."
PLEASE! HELP!
WHO?!

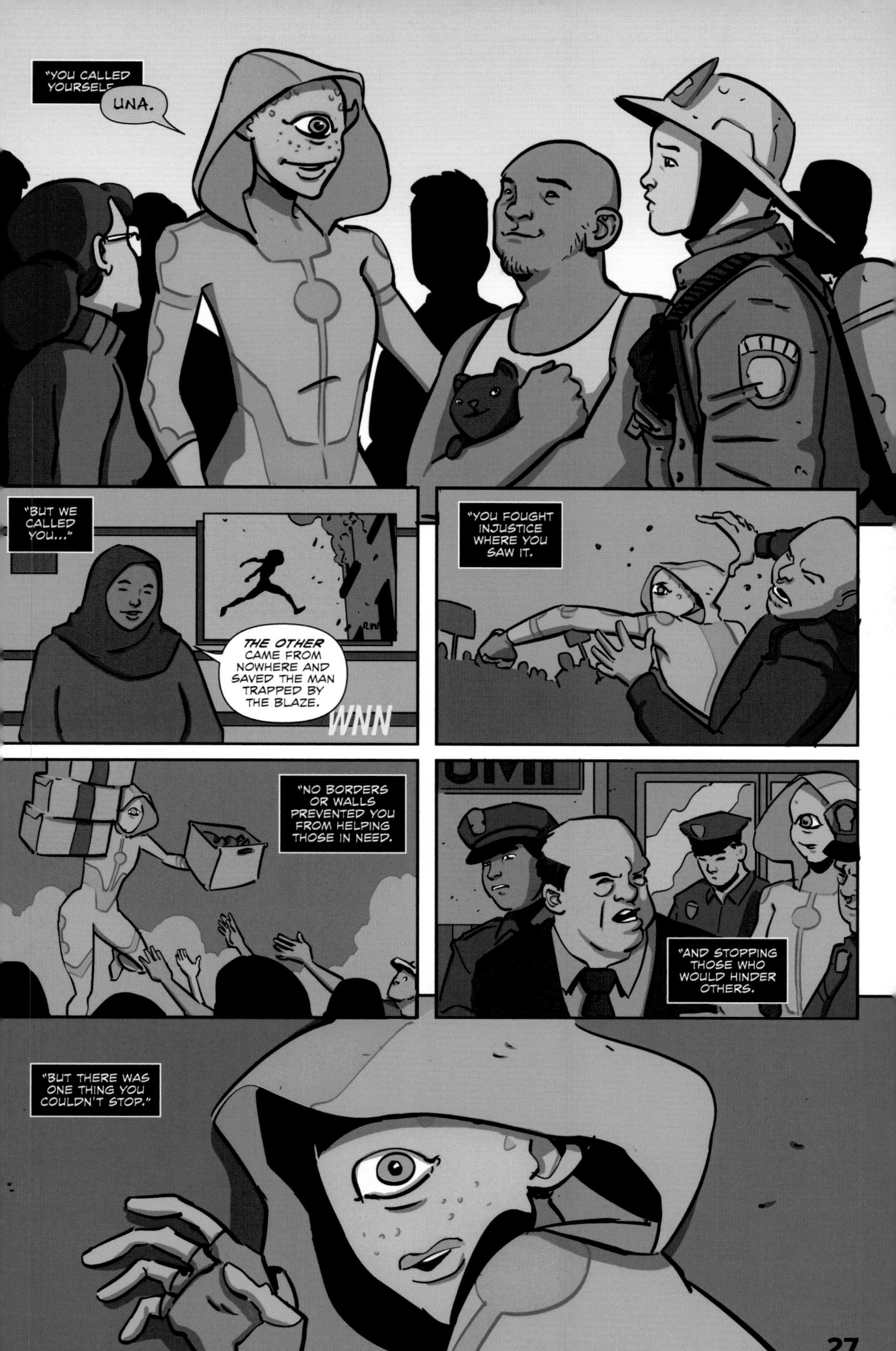
"YOU CALLED YOURSELF
UNA.
"BUT WE CALLED YOU..."
THE OTHER CAME FROM NOWHERE AND SAVED THE MAN TRAPPED BY THE BLAZE.
WNN
"YOU FOUGHT INJUSTICE WHERE YOU SAW IT.
"NO BORDERS OR WALLS PREVENTED YOU FROM HELPING THOSE IN NEED.
"AND STOPPING THOSE WHO WOULD HINDER OTHERS.
"BUT THERE WAS ONE THING YOU COULDN'T STOP."

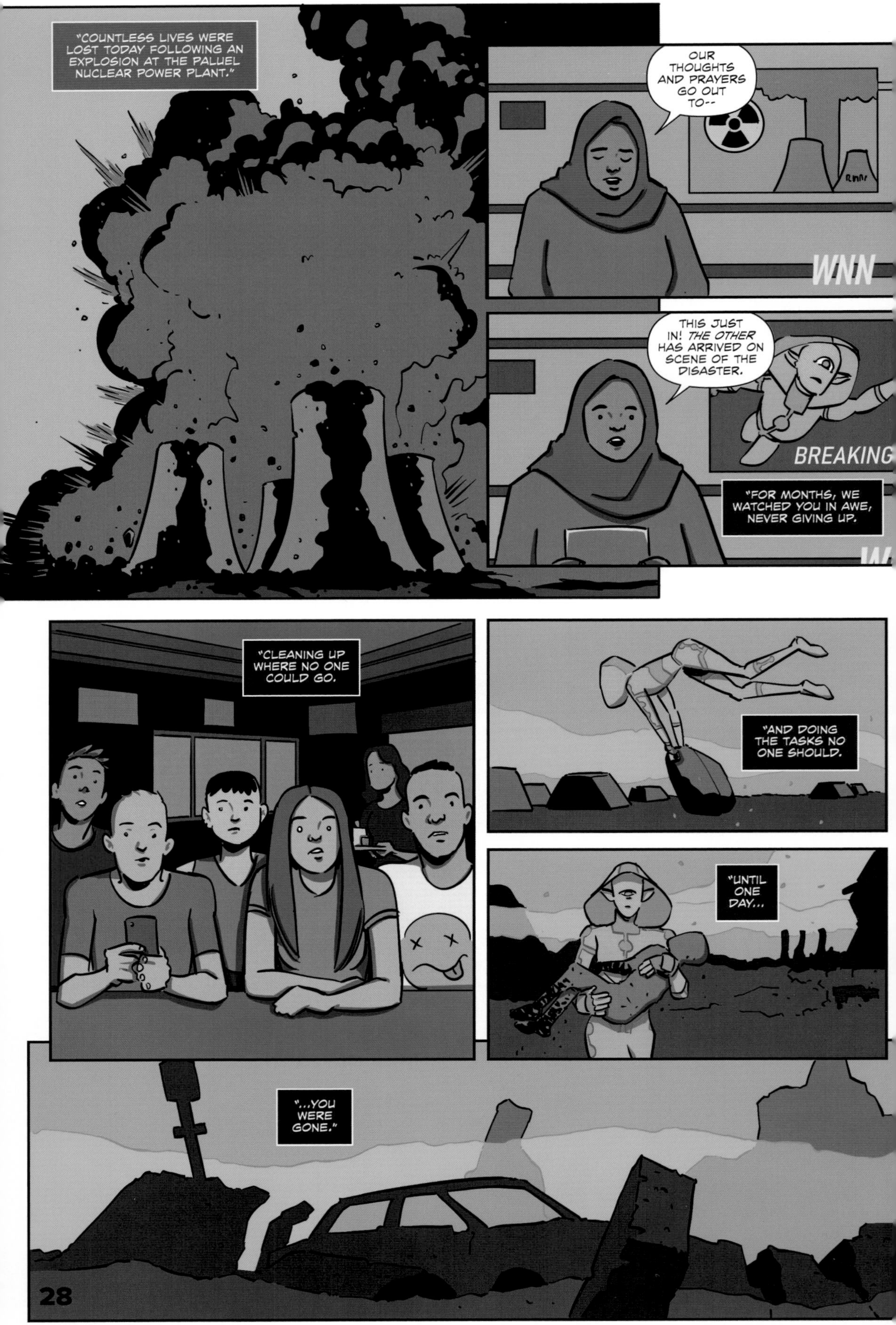
"COUNTLESS LIVES WERE LOST TODAY FOLLOWING AN EXPLOSION AT THE PALUEL NUCLEAR POWER PLANT."
OUR THOUGHTS AND PRAYERS GO OUT TO--
WNN
THIS JUST IN! *THE OTHER* HAS ARRIVED ON SCENE OF THE DISASTER.
BREAKING
"FOR MONTHS, WE WATCHED YOU IN AWE, NEVER GIVING UP.
"CLEANING UP WHERE NO ONE COULD GO.
"AND DOING THE TASKS NO ONE SHOULD.
"UNTIL ONE DAY...
"...YOU WERE GONE."

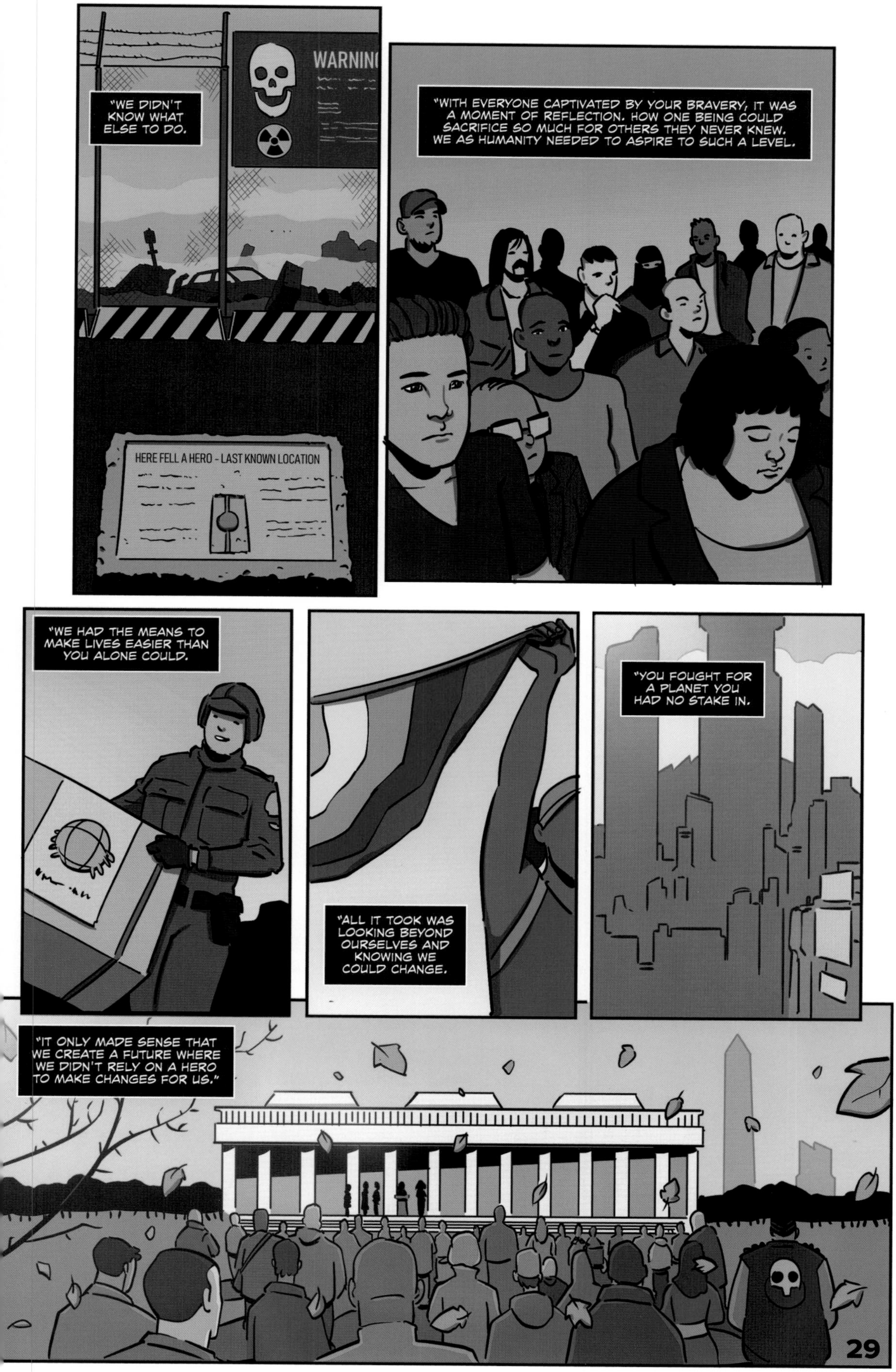
"WE DIDN'T KNOW WHAT ELSE TO DO.
WARNING
HERE FELL A HERO - LAST KNOWN LOCATION
"WITH EVERYONE CAPTIVATED BY YOUR BRAVERY, IT WAS A MOMENT OF REFLECTION. HOW ONE BEING COULD SACRIFICE SO MUCH FOR OTHERS THEY NEVER KNEW. WE AS HUMANITY NEEDED TO ASPIRE TO SUCH A LEVEL.
"WE HAD THE MEANS TO MAKE LIVES EASIER THAN YOU ALONE COULD.
"ALL IT TOOK WAS LOOKING BEYOND OURSELVES AND KNOWING WE COULD CHANGE.
"YOU FOUGHT FOR A PLANET YOU HAD NO STAKE IN.
"IT ONLY MADE SENSE THAT WE CREATE A FUTURE WHERE WE DIDN'T RELY ON A HERO TO MAKE CHANGES FOR US."

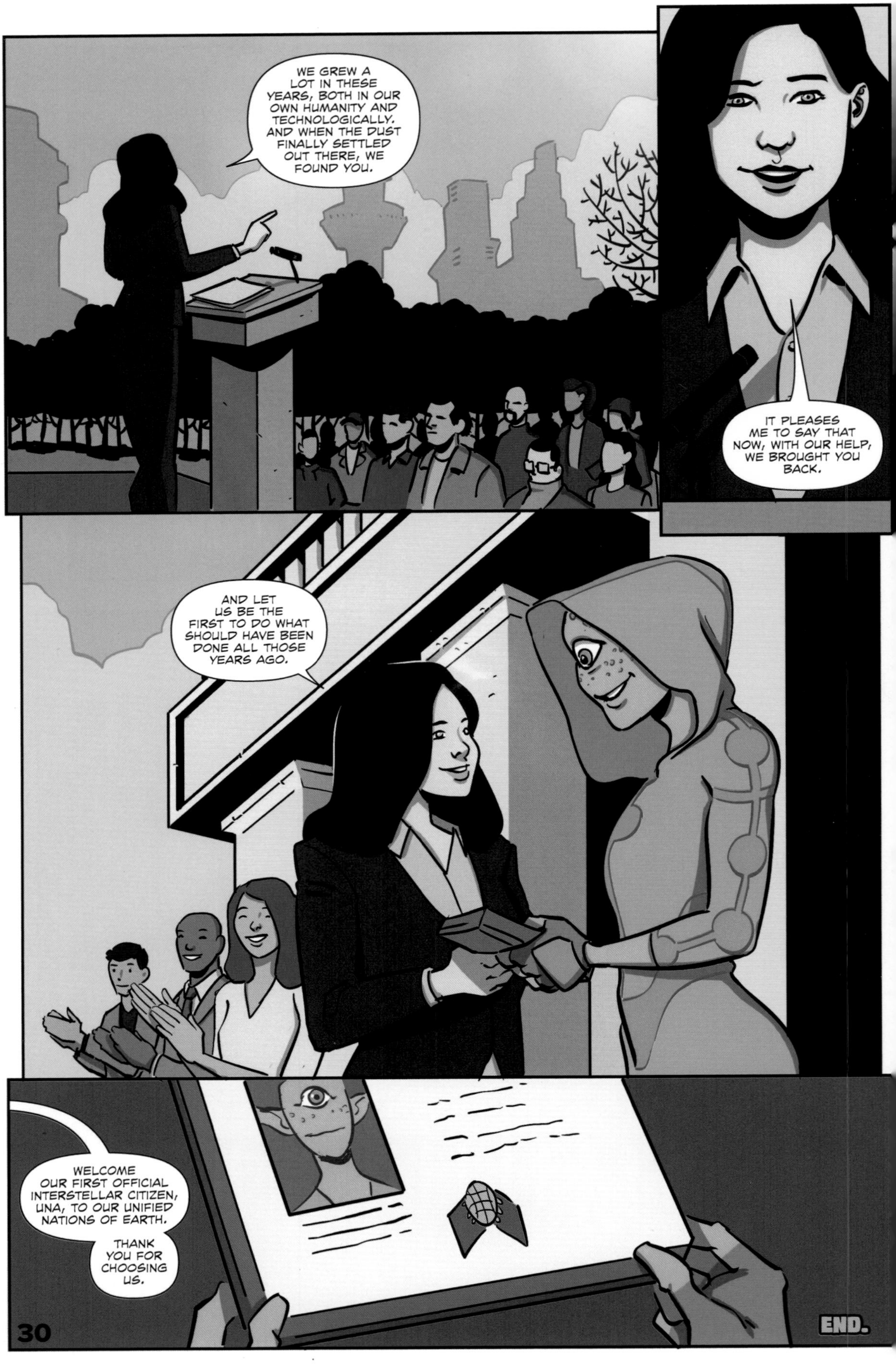
WE GREW A LOT IN THESE YEARS, BOTH IN OUR OWN HUMANITY AND TECHNOLOGICALLY. AND WHEN THE DUST FINALLY SETTLED OUT THERE, WE FOUND YOU.
IT PLEASES ME TO SAY THAT NOW, WITH OUR HELP, WE BROUGHT YOU BACK.
AND LET US BE THE FIRST TO DO WHAT SHOULD HAVE BEEN DONE ALL THOSE YEARS AGO.
WELCOME OUR FIRST OFFICIAL INTERSTELLAR CITIZEN, UNA, TO OUR UNIFIED NATIONS OF EARTH.
THANK YOU FOR CHOOSING US.
END.

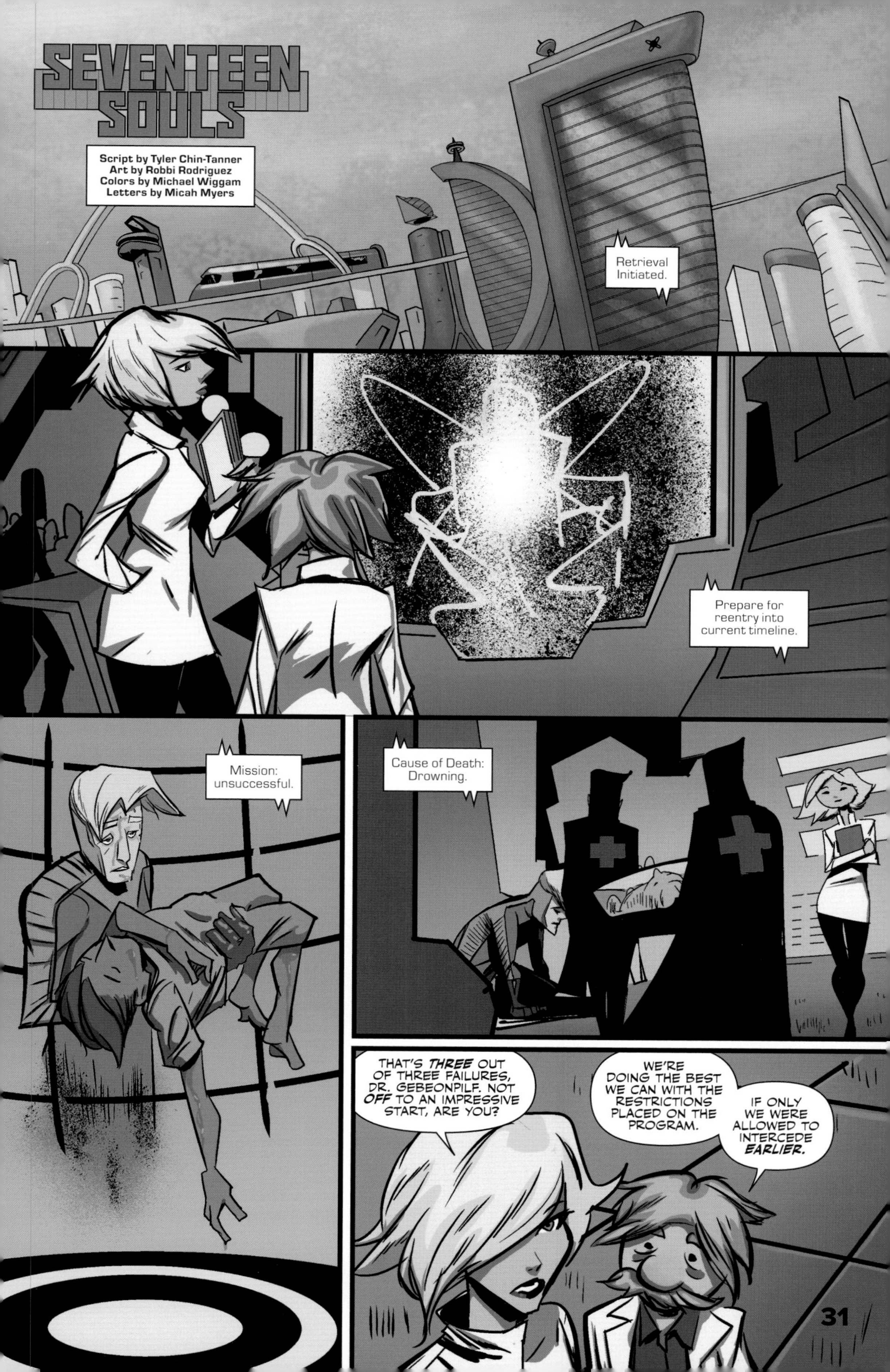
SEVENTEEN SOULS
Script by Tyler Chin-Tanner
Art by Robbi Rodriguez
Colors by Michael Wiggam
Letters by Micah Myers
Retrieval Initiated.
Prepare for reentry into current timeline.
Mission: unsuccessful.
Cause of Death: Drowning.
THAT'S ***THREE*** OUT OF THREE FAILURES, DR. GEBEONPILF. NOT ***OFF*** TO AN IMPRESSIVE START, ARE YOU?
WE'RE DOING THE BEST WE CAN WITH THE RESTRICTIONS PLACED ON THE PROGRAM.
IF ONLY WE WERE ALLOWED TO INTERCEDE ***EARLIER.***

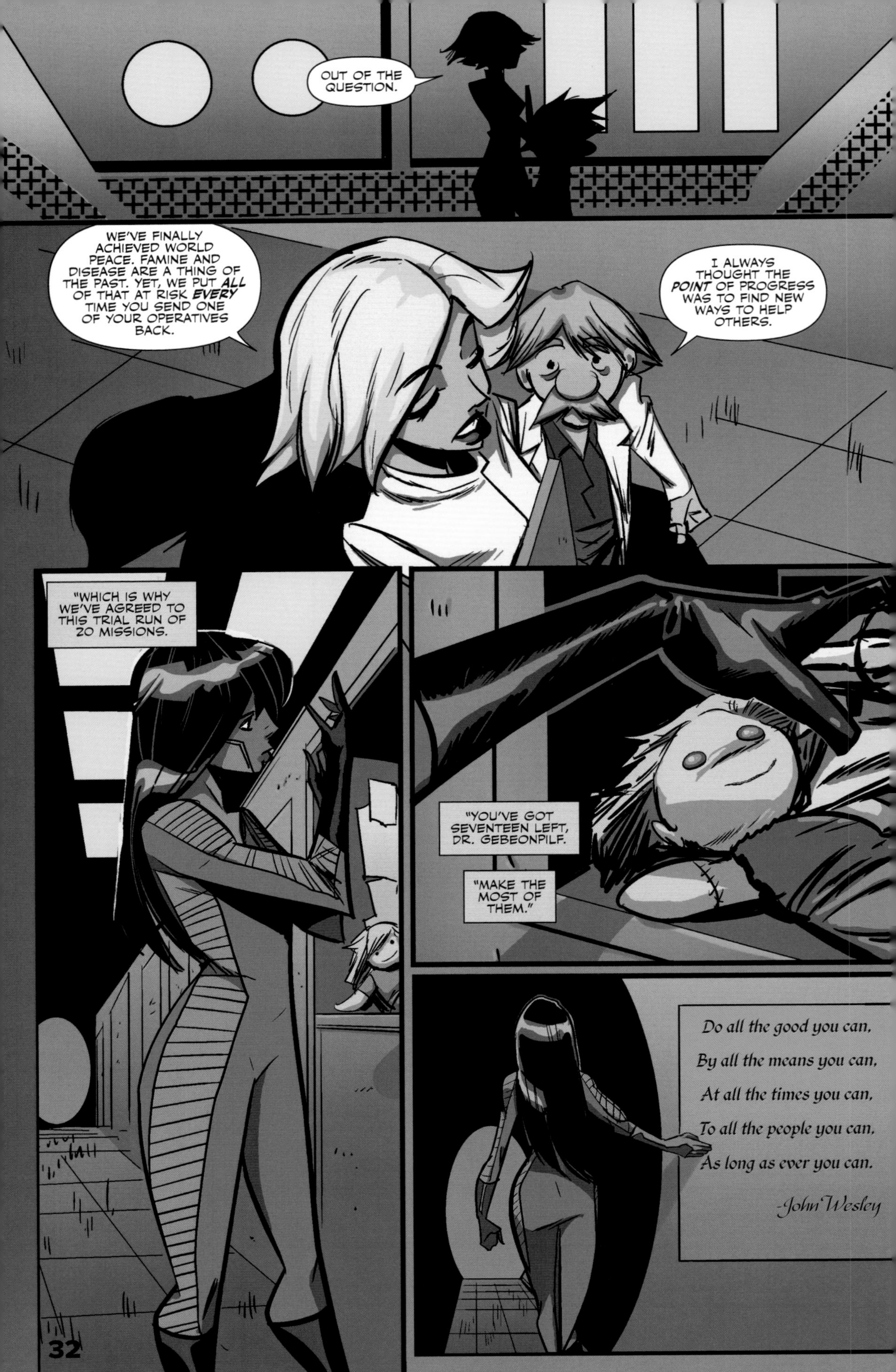
OUT OF THE QUESTION.
WE'VE FINALLY ACHIEVED WORLD PEACE. FAMINE AND DISEASE ARE A THING OF THE PAST. YET, WE PUT ALL OF THAT AT RISK EVERY TIME YOU SEND ONE OF YOUR OPERATIVES BACK.
I ALWAYS THOUGHT THE POINT OF PROGRESS WAS TO FIND NEW WAYS TO HELP OTHERS.
"WHICH IS WHY WE'VE AGREED TO THIS TRIAL RUN OF 20 MISSIONS.
"YOU'VE GOT SEVENTEEN LEFT, DR. GEBEONPILF.
"MAKE THE MOST OF THEM."
Do all the good you can,
By all the means you can,
At all the times you can,
To all the people you can,
As long as ever you can.
-John Wesley

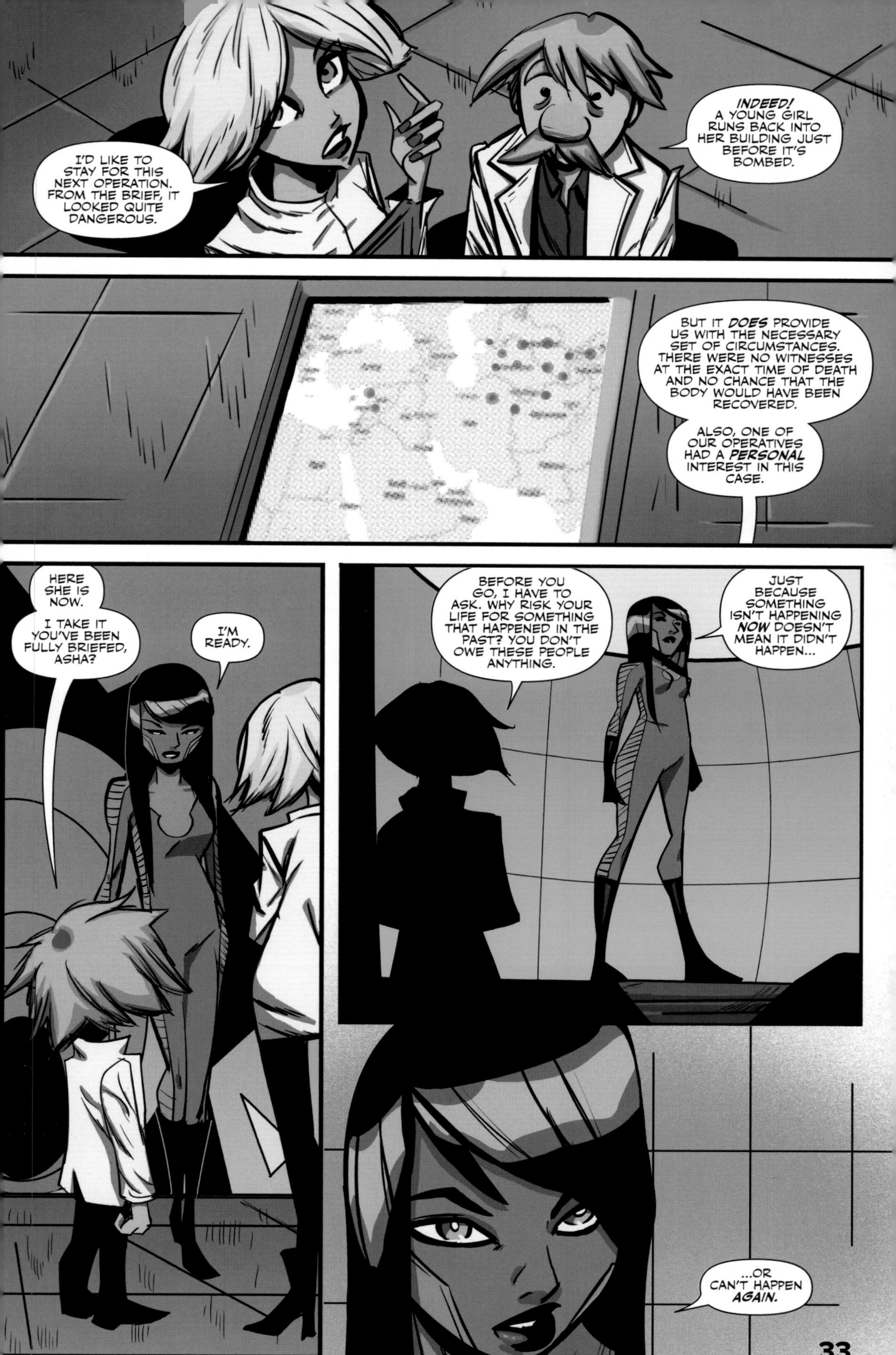
I'D LIKE TO STAY FOR THIS NEXT OPERATION. FROM THE BRIEF, IT LOOKED QUITE DANGEROUS.
INDEED! A YOUNG GIRL RUNS BACK INTO HER BUILDING JUST BEFORE IT'S BOMBED.
BUT IT DOES PROVIDE US WITH THE NECESSARY SET OF CIRCUMSTANCES. THERE WERE NO WITNESSES AT THE EXACT TIME OF DEATH AND NO CHANCE THAT THE BODY WOULD HAVE BEEN RECOVERED.
ALSO, ONE OF OUR OPERATIVES HAD A PERSONAL INTEREST IN THIS CASE.
HERE SHE IS NOW.
I TAKE IT YOU'VE BEEN FULLY BRIEFED, ASHA?
I'M READY.
BEFORE YOU GO, I HAVE TO ASK. WHY RISK YOUR LIFE FOR SOMETHING THAT HAPPENED IN THE PAST? YOU DON'T OWE THESE PEOPLE ANYTHING.
JUST BECAUSE SOMETHING ISN'T HAPPENING NOW DOESN'T MEAN IT DIDN'T HAPPEN...
...OR CAN'T HAPPEN AGAIN.

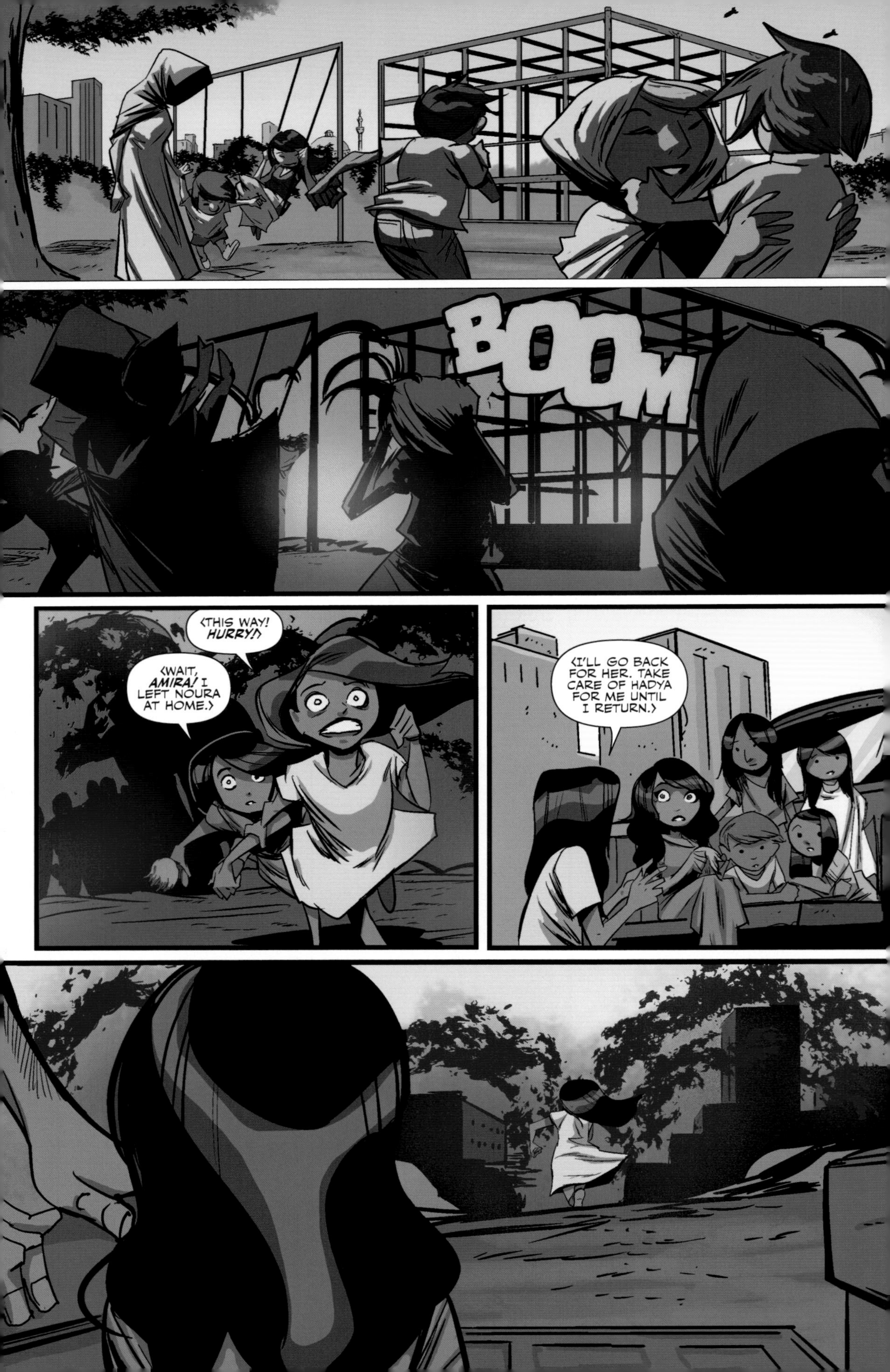
BOOM
‹THIS WAY! HURRY!›
‹WAIT, AMIRA! I LEFT NOURA AT HOME.›
‹I'LL GO BACK FOR HER. TAKE CARE OF HADYA FOR ME UNTIL I RETURN.›

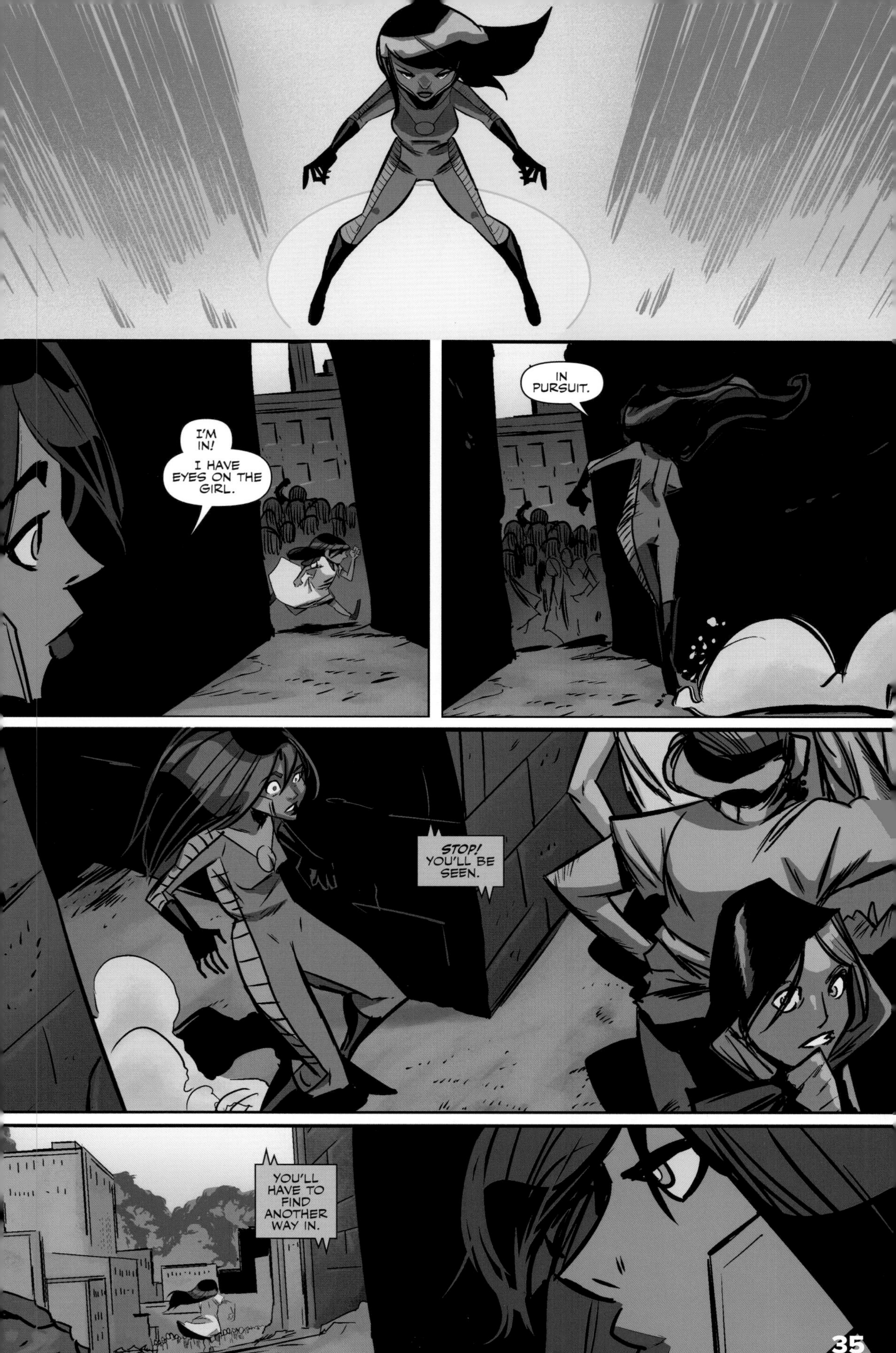
I'M IN!
I HAVE EYES ON THE GIRL.
IN PURSUIT.
STOP! YOU'LL BE SEEN.
YOU'LL HAVE TO FIND ANOTHER WAY IN.

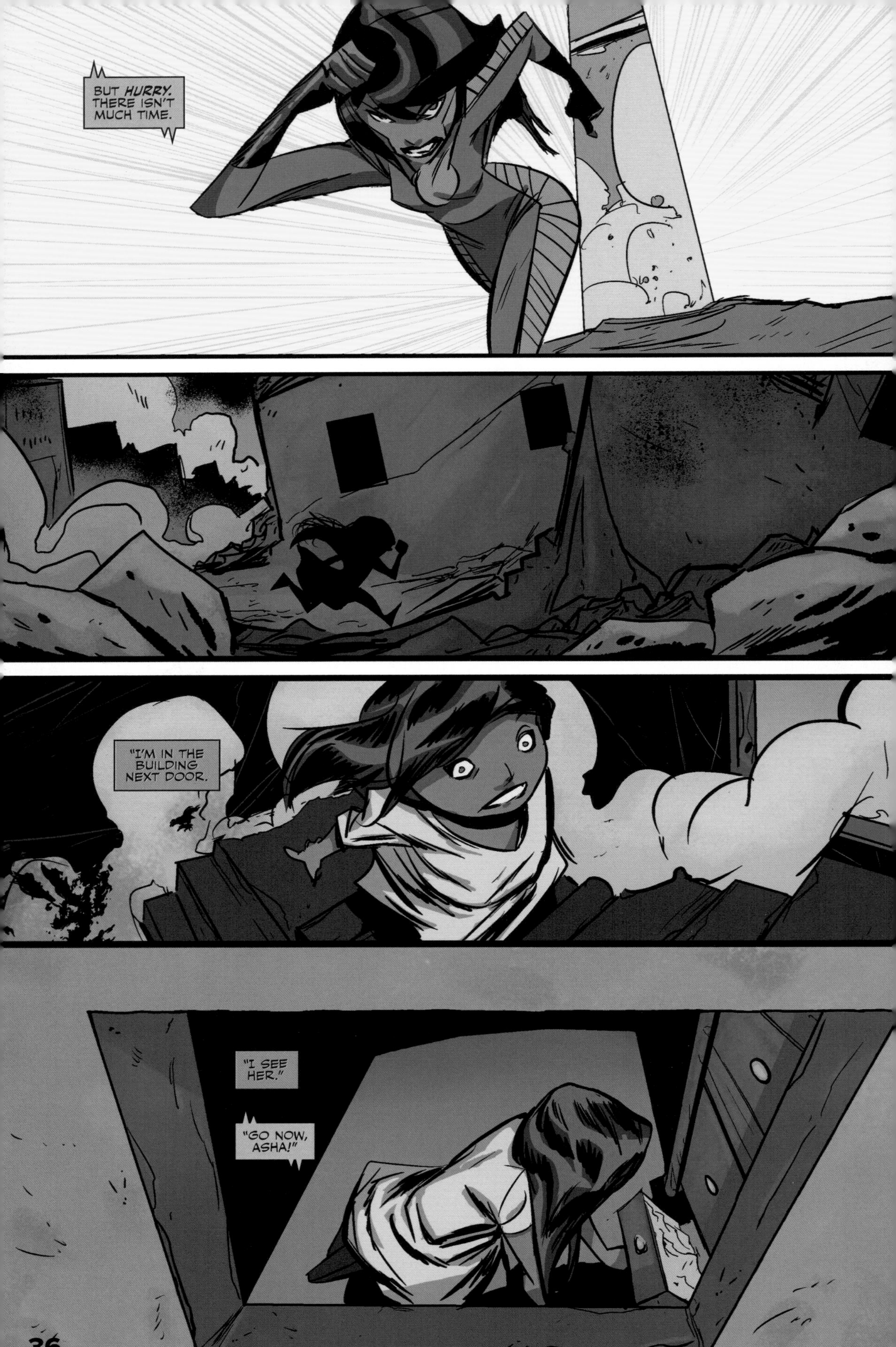
BUT HURRY. THERE ISN'T MUCH TIME.
"I'M IN THE BUILDING NEXT DOOR.
"I SEE HER."
"GO NOW, ASHA!"

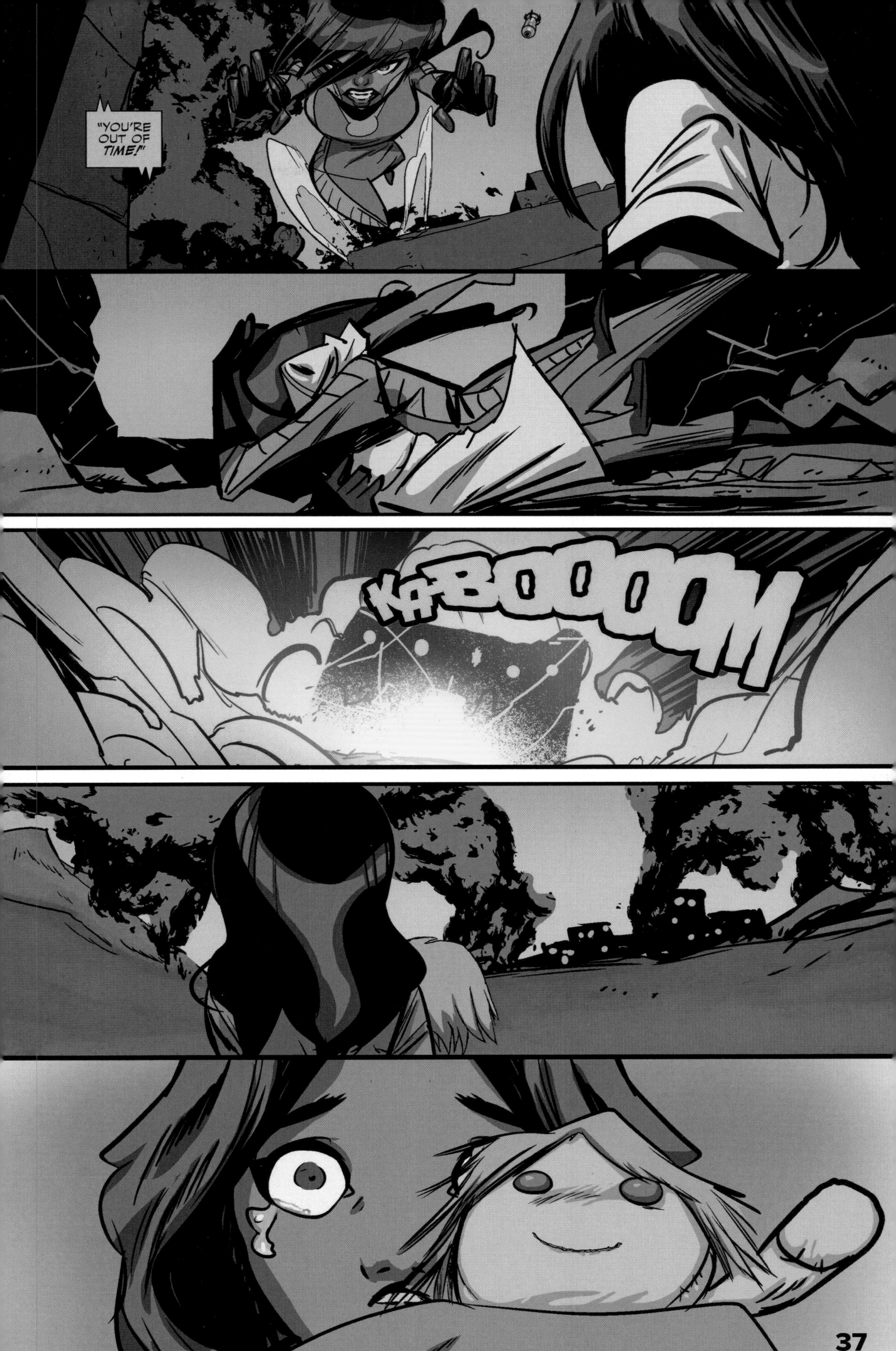
"YOU'RE OUT OF TIME!"
KA-BOOOOOM

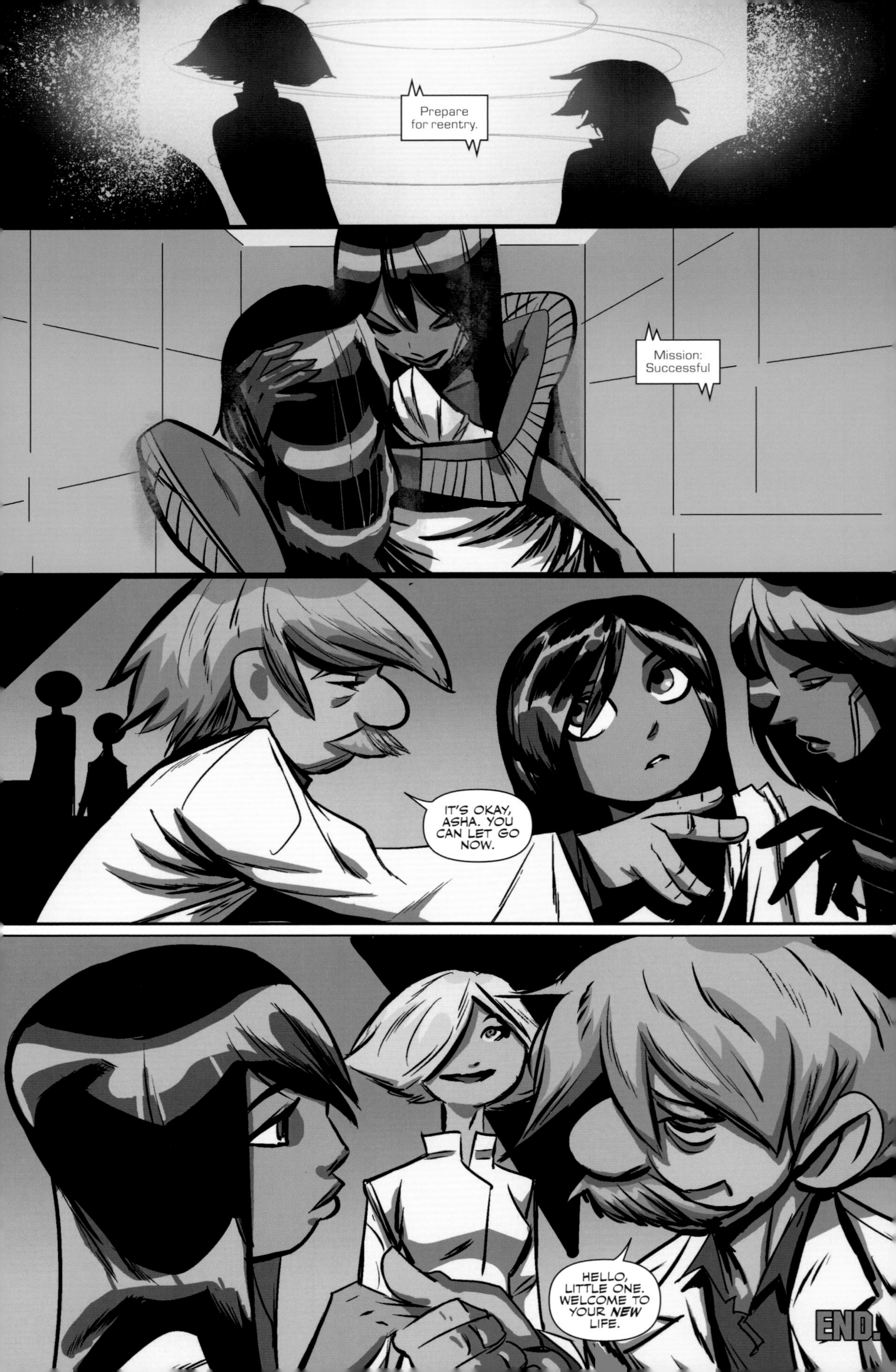
Prepare for reentry.
Mission: Successful
IT'S OKAY, ASHA. YOU CAN LET GO NOW.
HELLO, LITTLE ONE. WELCOME TO YOUR *NEW* LIFE.
END.

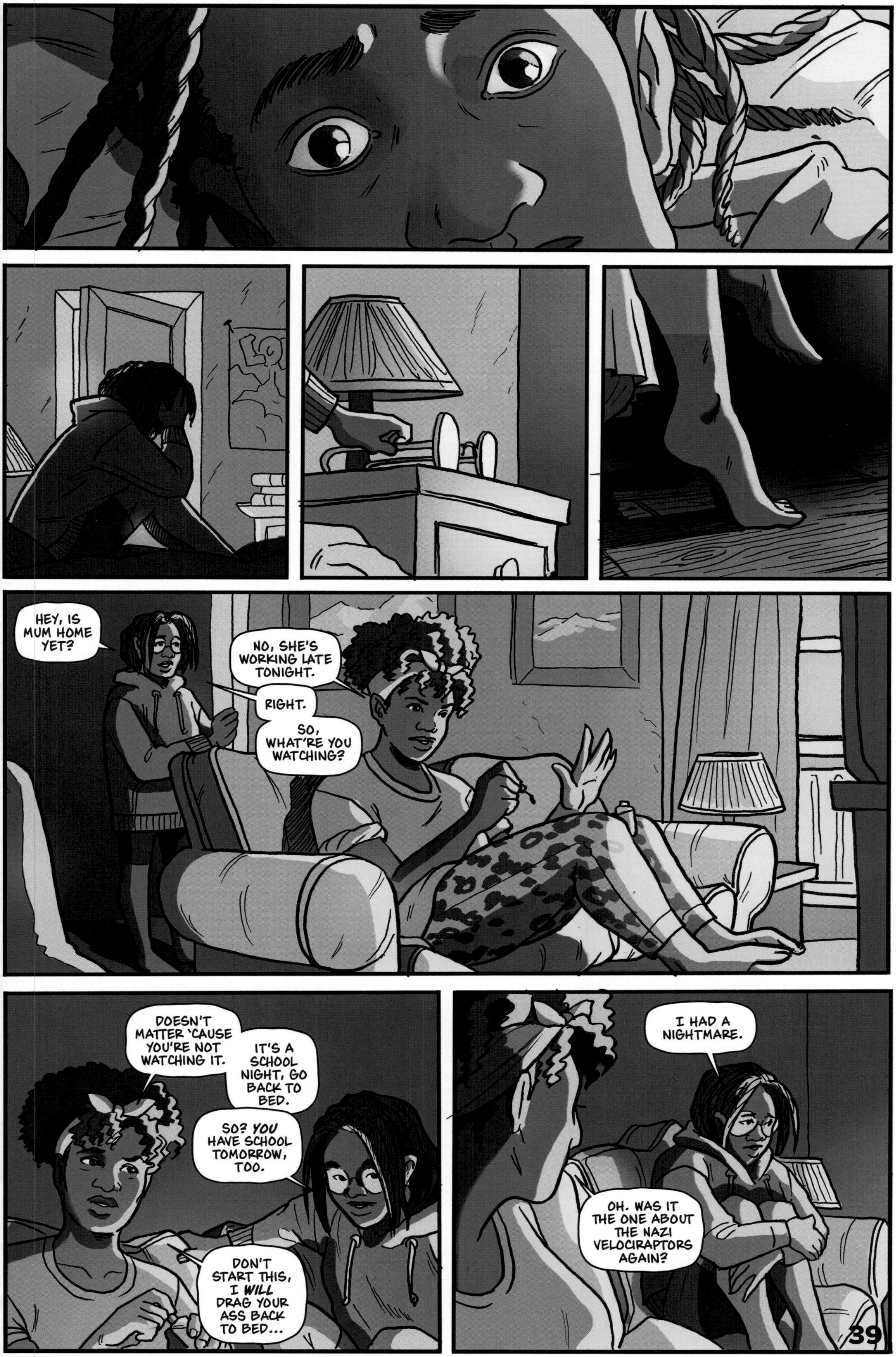
HEY, IS MUM HOME YET?
NO, SHE'S WORKING LATE TONIGHT.
RIGHT.
SO, WHAT'RE YOU WATCHING?
DOESN'T MATTER 'CAUSE YOU'RE NOT WATCHING IT.
IT'S A SCHOOL NIGHT, GO BACK TO BED.
SO? *YOU* HAVE SCHOOL TOMORROW, TOO.
DON'T START THIS, I ***WILL*** DRAG YOUR ASS BACK TO BED...
I HAD A NIGHTMARE.
OH. WAS IT THE ONE ABOUT THE NAZI VELOCIRAPTORS AGAIN?

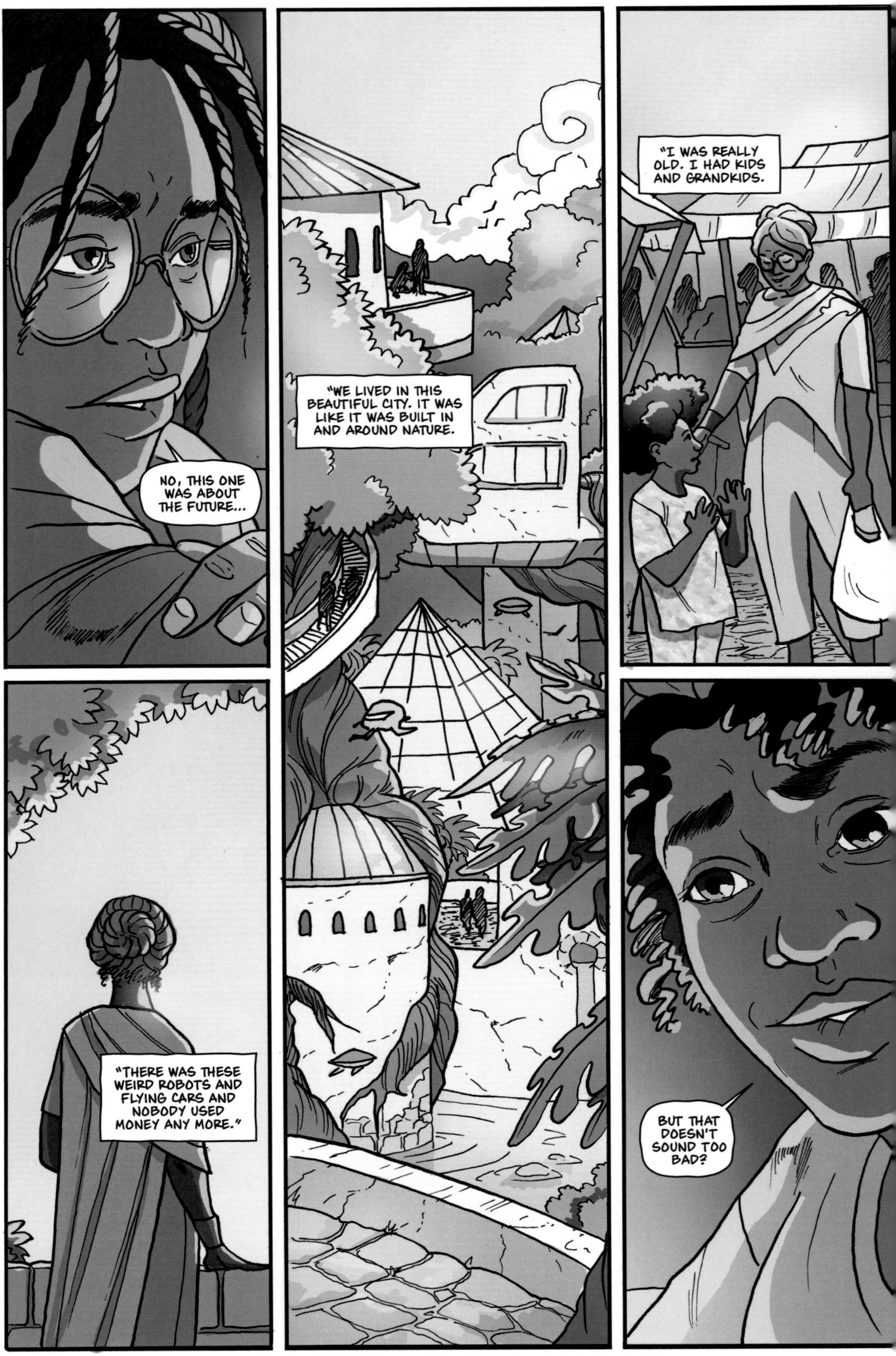
NO, THIS ONE WAS ABOUT THE FUTURE...
"WE LIVED IN THIS BEAUTIFUL CITY. IT WAS LIKE IT WAS BUILT IN AND AROUND NATURE.
"I WAS REALLY OLD. I HAD KIDS AND GRANDKIDS.
"THERE WAS THESE WEIRD ROBOTS AND FLYING CARS AND NOBODY USED MONEY ANY MORE."
BUT THAT DOESN'T SOUND TOO BAD?

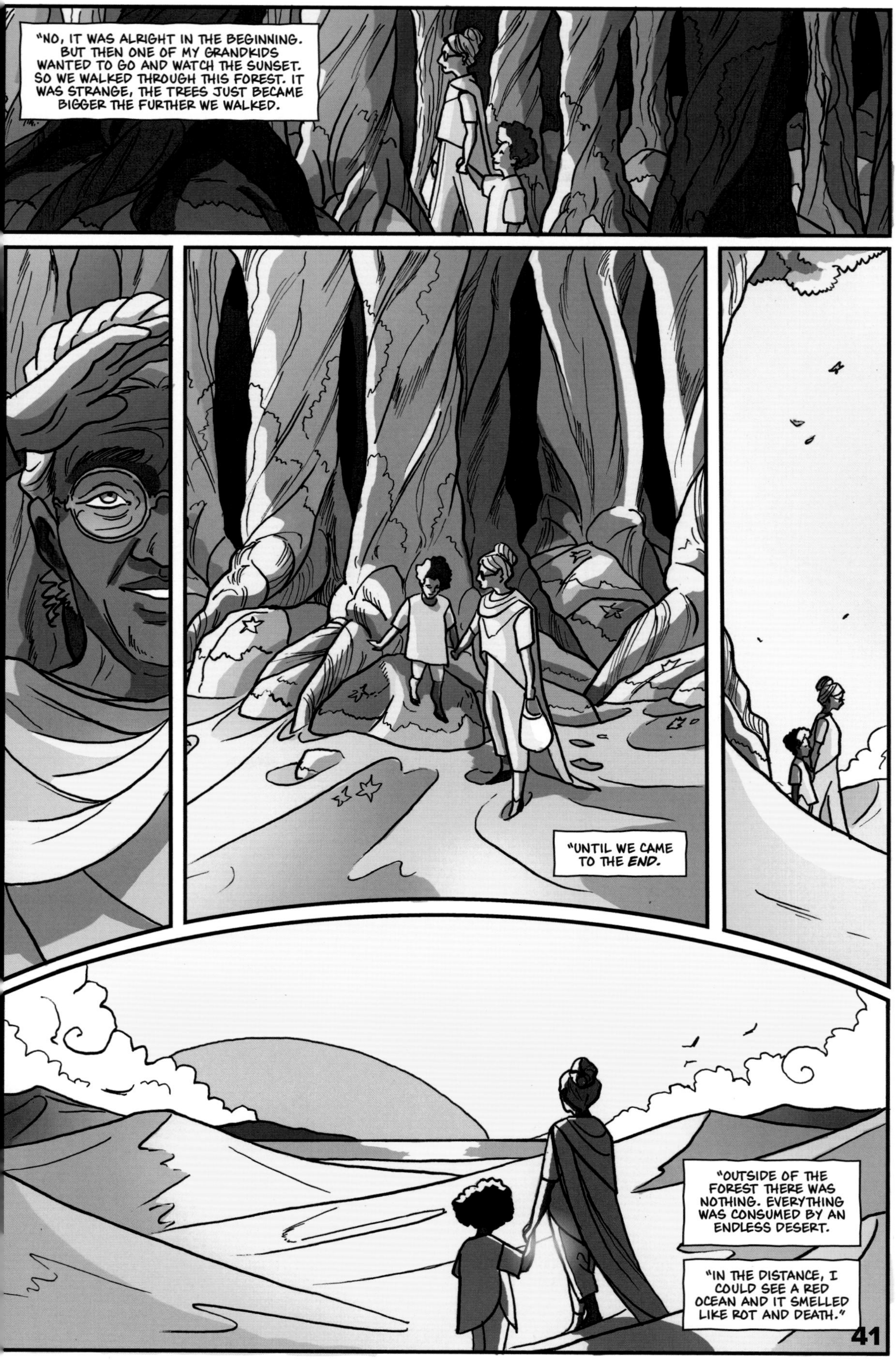
"NO, IT WAS ALRIGHT IN THE BEGINNING. BUT THEN ONE OF MY GRANDKIDS WANTED TO GO AND WATCH THE SUNSET. SO WE WALKED THROUGH THIS FOREST. IT WAS STRANGE, THE TREES JUST BECAME BIGGER THE FURTHER WE WALKED.
"UNTIL WE CAME TO THE *END*.
"OUTSIDE OF THE FOREST THERE WAS NOTHING. EVERYTHING WAS CONSUMED BY AN ENDLESS DESERT.
"IN THE DISTANCE, I COULD SEE A RED OCEAN AND IT SMELLED LIKE ROT AND DEATH."

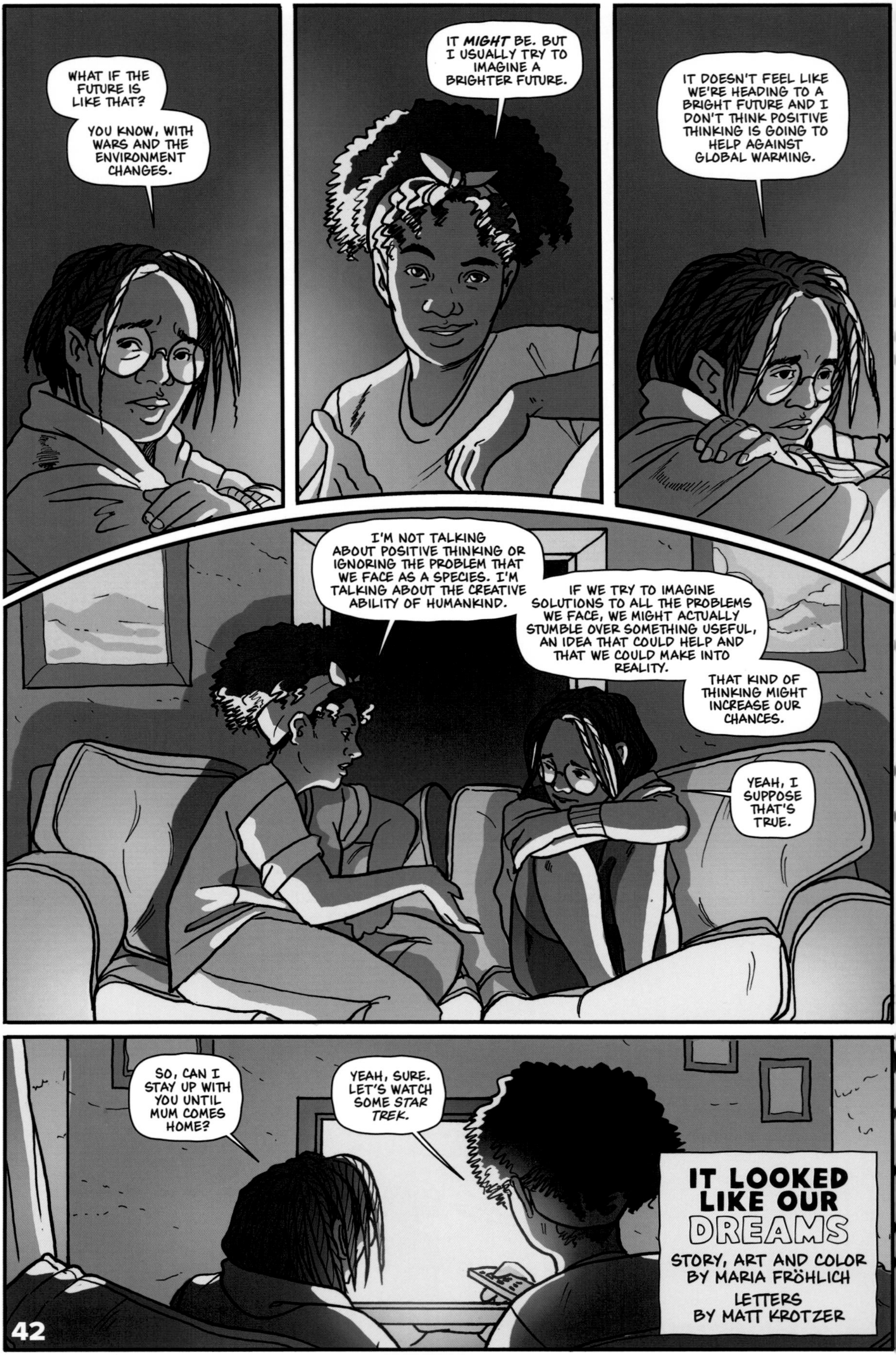
WHAT IF THE FUTURE IS LIKE THAT?
YOU KNOW, WITH WARS AND THE ENVIRONMENT CHANGES.
IT *MIGHT* BE. BUT I USUALLY TRY TO IMAGINE A BRIGHTER FUTURE.
IT DOESN'T FEEL LIKE WE'RE HEADING TO A BRIGHT FUTURE AND I DON'T THINK POSITIVE THINKING IS GOING TO HELP AGAINST GLOBAL WARMING.
I'M NOT TALKING ABOUT POSITIVE THINKING OR IGNORING THE PROBLEM THAT WE FACE AS A SPECIES. I'M TALKING ABOUT THE CREATIVE ABILITY OF HUMANKIND.
IF WE TRY TO IMAGINE SOLUTIONS TO ALL THE PROBLEMS WE FACE, WE MIGHT ACTUALLY STUMBLE OVER SOMETHING USEFUL, AN IDEA THAT COULD HELP AND THAT WE COULD MAKE INTO REALITY.
THAT KIND OF THINKING MIGHT INCREASE OUR CHANCES.
YEAH, I SUPPOSE THAT'S TRUE.
SO, CAN I STAY UP WITH YOU UNTIL MUM COMES HOME?
YEAH, SURE. LET'S WATCH SOME *STAR TREK*.
IT LOOKED LIKE OUR DREAMS
STORY, ART AND COLOR BY MARIA FRÖHLICH
LETTERS BY MATT KROTZER

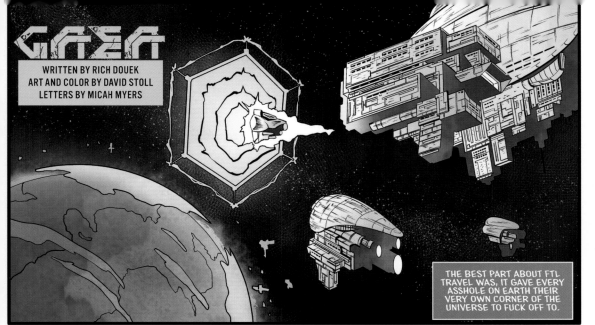

GAEA

WRITTEN BY RICH DOUEK
ART AND COLOR BY DAVID STOLL
LETTERS BY MICAH MYERS

THE BEST PART ABOUT FTL TRAVEL WAS, IT GAVE EVERY ASSHOLE ON EARTH THEIR VERY OWN CORNER OF THE UNIVERSE TO FUCK OFF TO.

WHICH IS NOT TO SAY THEY DIDN'T LEAVE ONE HELL OF A MESS BEHIND.

IT TOOK TIME. EFFORT. KNOWLEDGE....

BUT WE NURSED HER BACK TO HEALTH. MADE HER A PARADISE AGAIN.

WE EVEN GAVE HER A NEW NAME. GAEA.

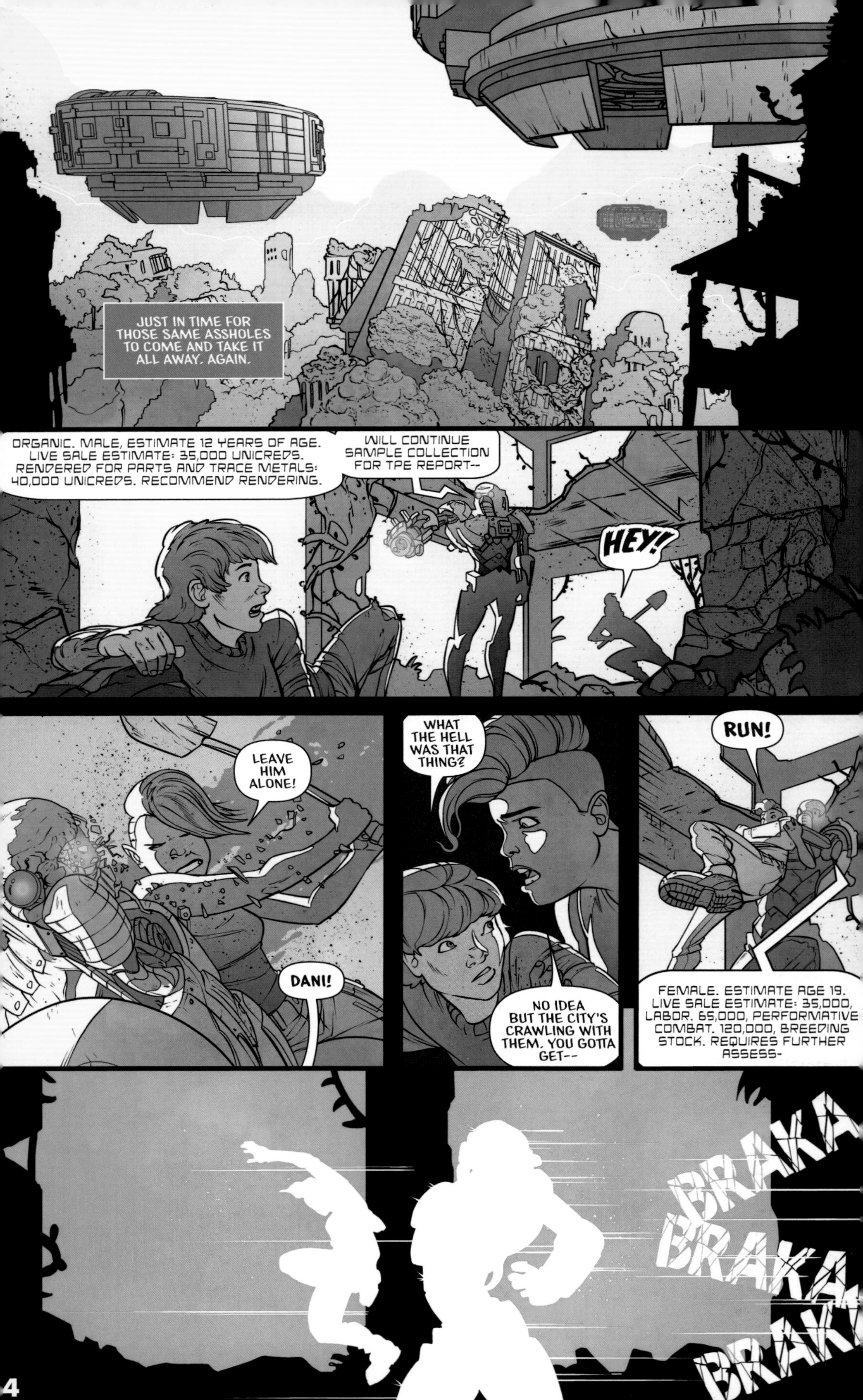
JUST IN TIME FOR THOSE SAME ASSHOLES TO COME AND TAKE IT ALL AWAY. AGAIN.
ORGANIC. MALE, ESTIMATE 12 YEARS OF AGE. LIVE SALE ESTIMATE: 35,000 UNICREDS. RENDERED FOR PARTS AND TRACE METALS: 40,000 UNICREDS. RECOMMEND RENDERING.
WILL CONTINUE SAMPLE COLLECTION FOR TPE REPORT--
HEY!
LEAVE HIM ALONE!
DANI!
WHAT THE HELL WAS THAT THING?
NO IDEA BUT THE CITY'S CRAWLING WITH THEM. YOU GOTTA GET--
RUN!
FEMALE. ESTIMATE AGE 19. LIVE SALE ESTIMATE: 35,000, LABOR. 65,000, PERFORMATIVE COMBAT. 120,000, BREEDING STOCK. REQUIRES FURTHER ASSESS-
BRAKA
BRAKA
BRAKA
BRAKA

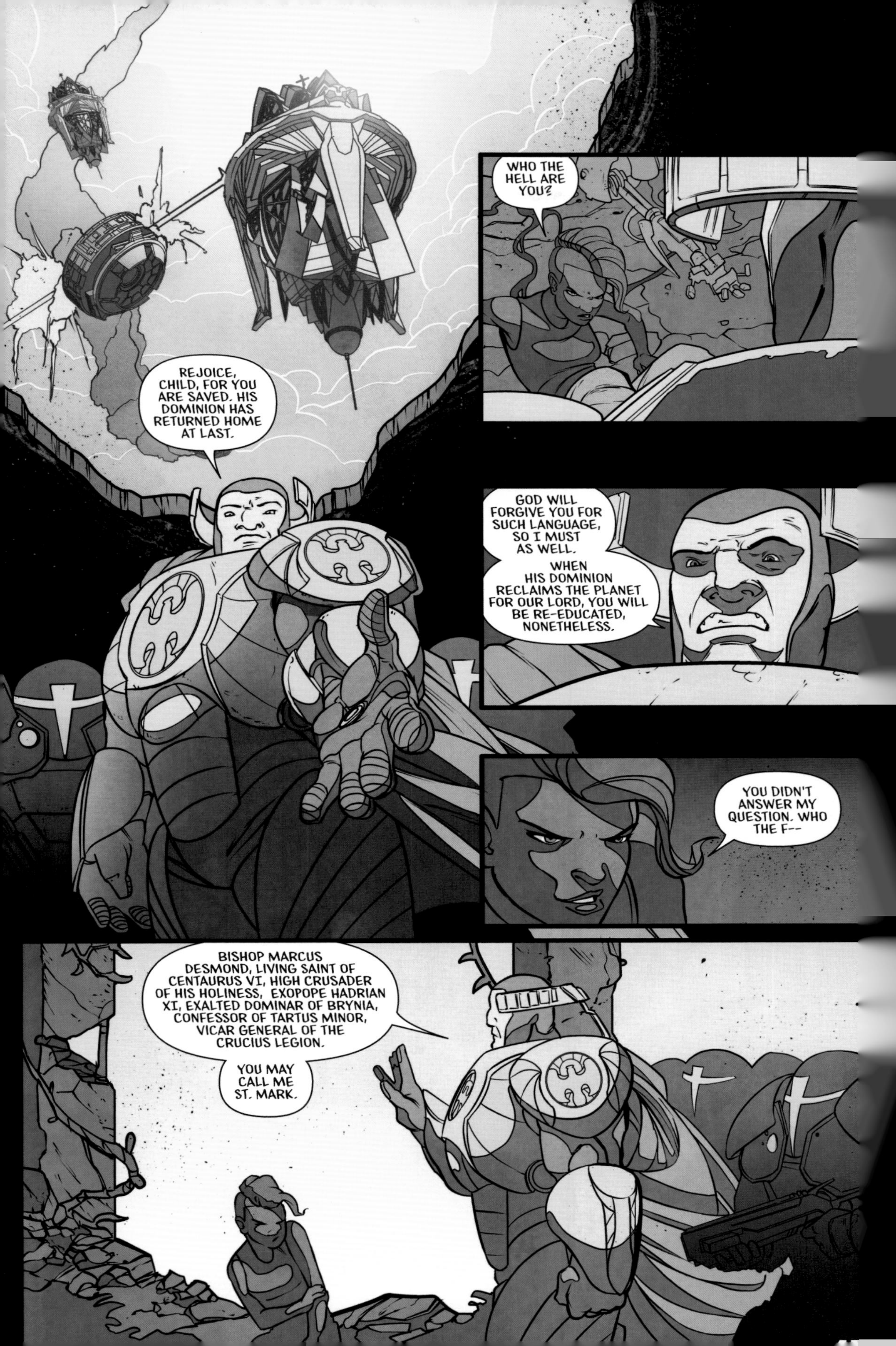
REJOICE, CHILD, FOR YOU ARE SAVED. HIS DOMINION HAS RETURNED HOME AT LAST.
WHO THE HELL ARE YOU?
GOD WILL FORGIVE YOU FOR SUCH LANGUAGE, SO I MUST AS WELL.
WHEN HIS DOMINION RECLAIMS THE PLANET FOR OUR LORD, YOU WILL BE RE-EDUCATED, NONETHELESS.
YOU DIDN'T ANSWER MY QUESTION. WHO THE F--
BISHOP MARCUS DESMOND, LIVING SAINT OF CENTAURUS VI, HIGH CRUSADER OF HIS HOLINESS, EXOPOPE HADRIAN XI, EXALTED DOMINAR OF BRYNIA, CONFESSOR OF TARTUS MINOR, VICAR GENERAL OF THE CRUCIUS LEGION.
YOU MAY CALL ME ST. MARK.

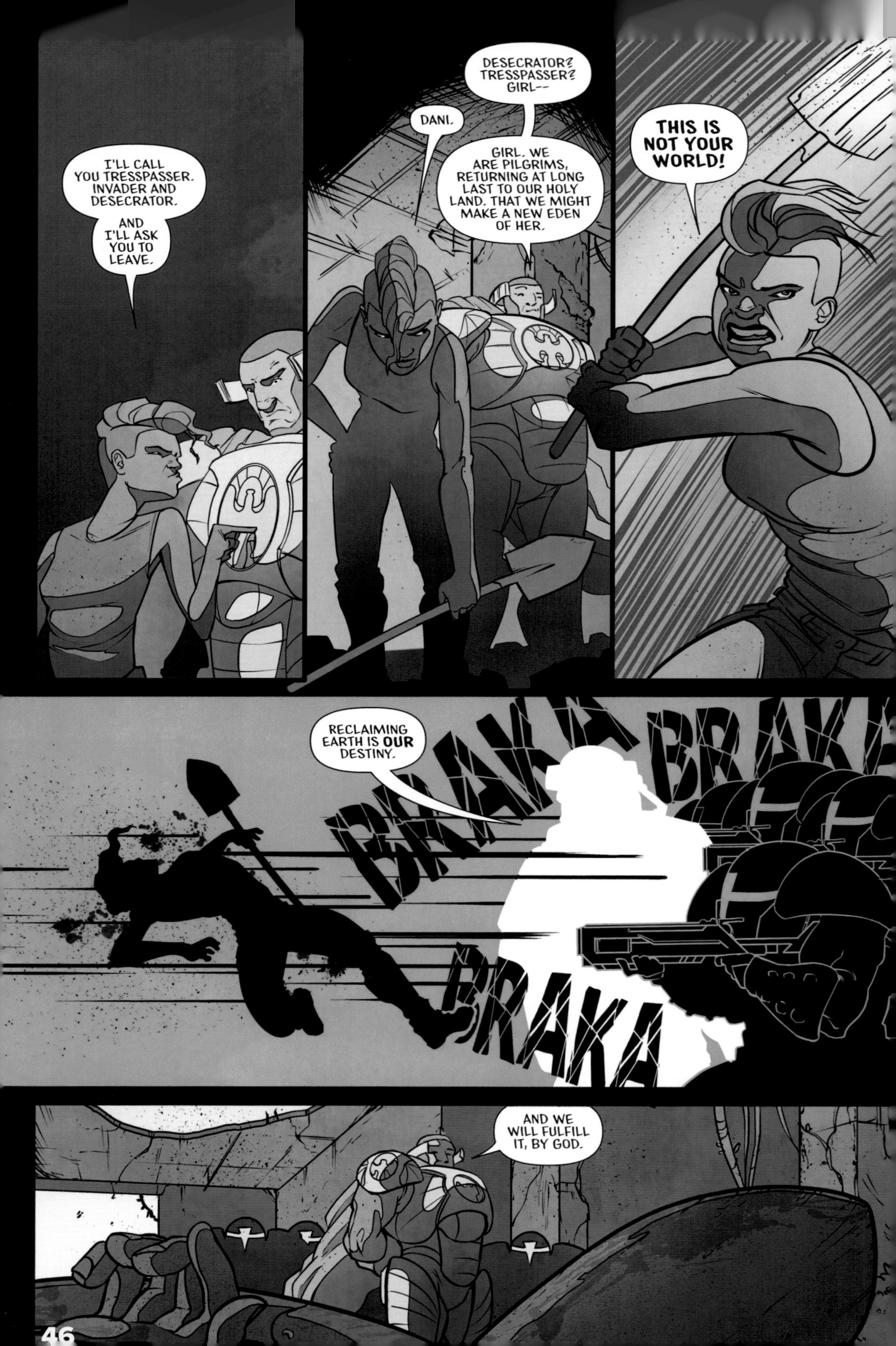
I'LL CALL YOU TRESSPASSER. INVADER AND DESECRATOR.
AND I'LL ASK YOU TO LEAVE.
DESECRATOR? TRESSPASSER? GIRL--
DANI.
GIRL. WE ARE PILGRIMS, RETURNING AT LONG LAST TO OUR HOLY LAND. THAT WE MIGHT MAKE A NEW EDEN OF HER.
THIS IS NOT YOUR WORLD!
RECLAIMING EARTH IS **OUR** DESTINY.
BRAKA
BRAKA
AND WE WILL FULFILL IT, BY GOD.

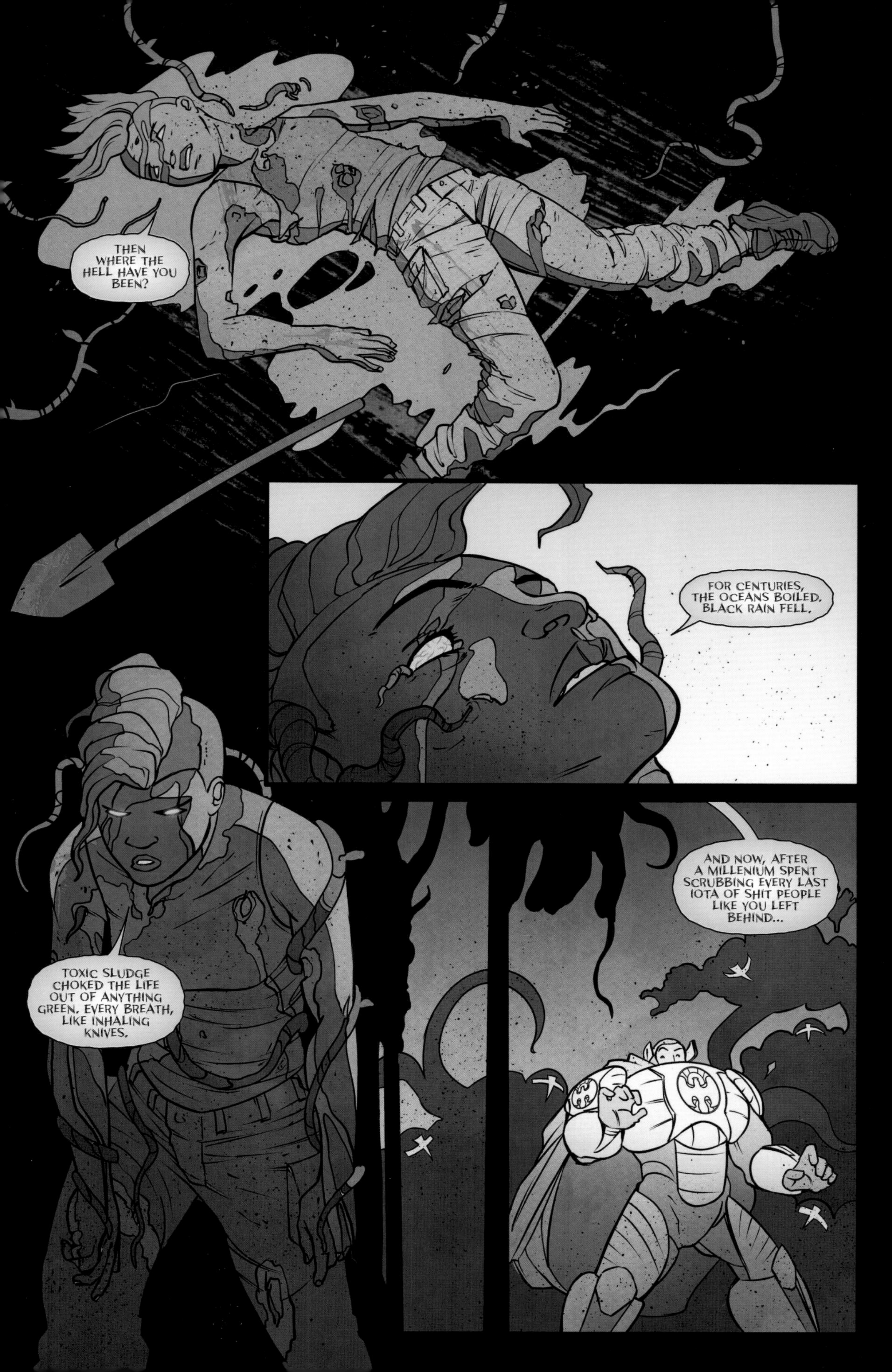
THEN WHERE THE HELL HAVE YOU BEEN?
FOR CENTURIES, THE OCEANS BOILED. BLACK RAIN FELL.
TOXIC SLUDGE CHOKED THE LIFE OUT OF ANYTHING GREEN. EVERY BREATH, LIKE INHALING KNIVES.
AND NOW, AFTER A MILLENIUM SPENT SCRUBBING EVERY LAST IOTA OF SHIT PEOPLE LIKE YOU LEFT BEHIND...

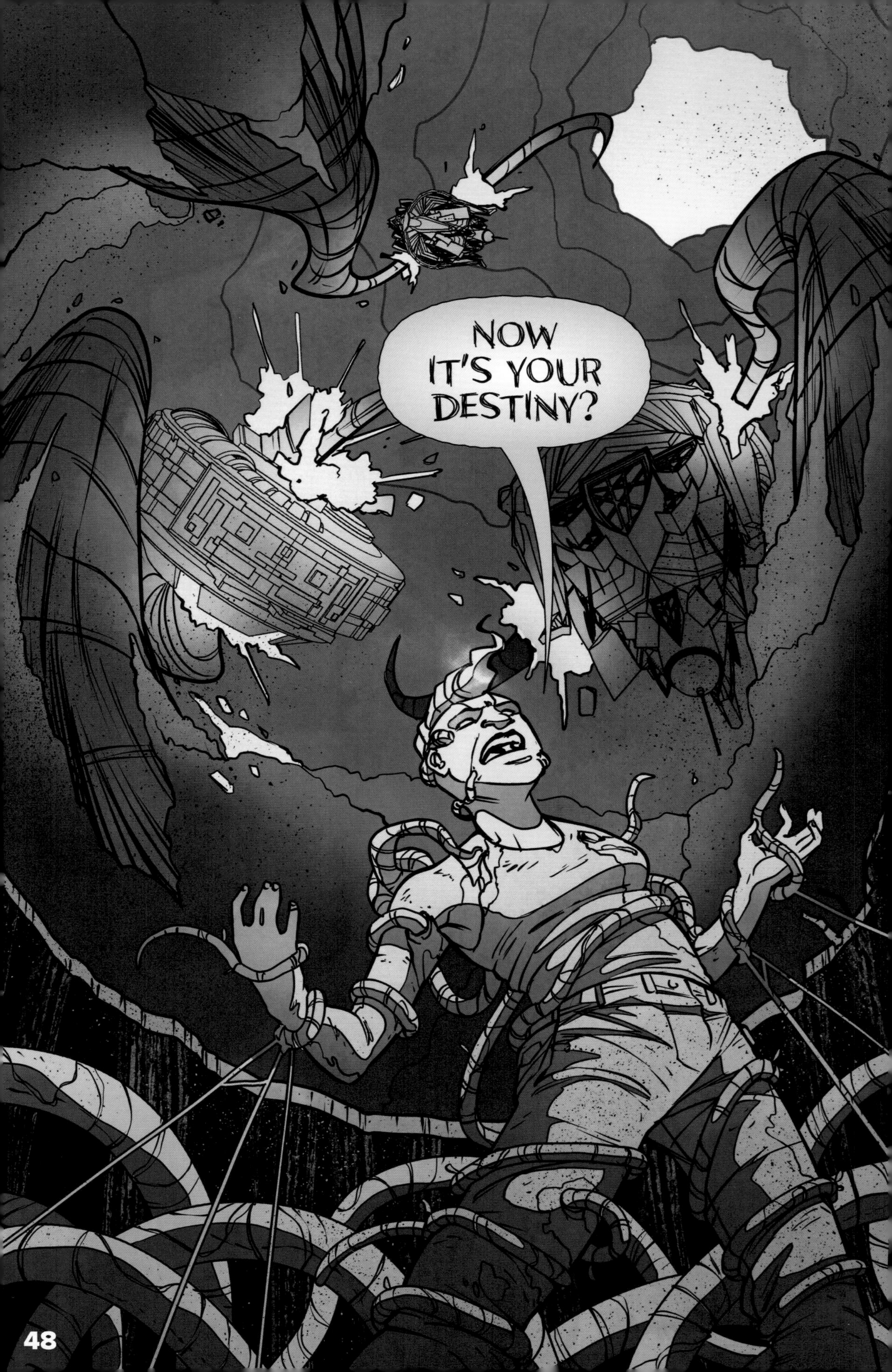
NOW IT'S YOUR DESTINY?

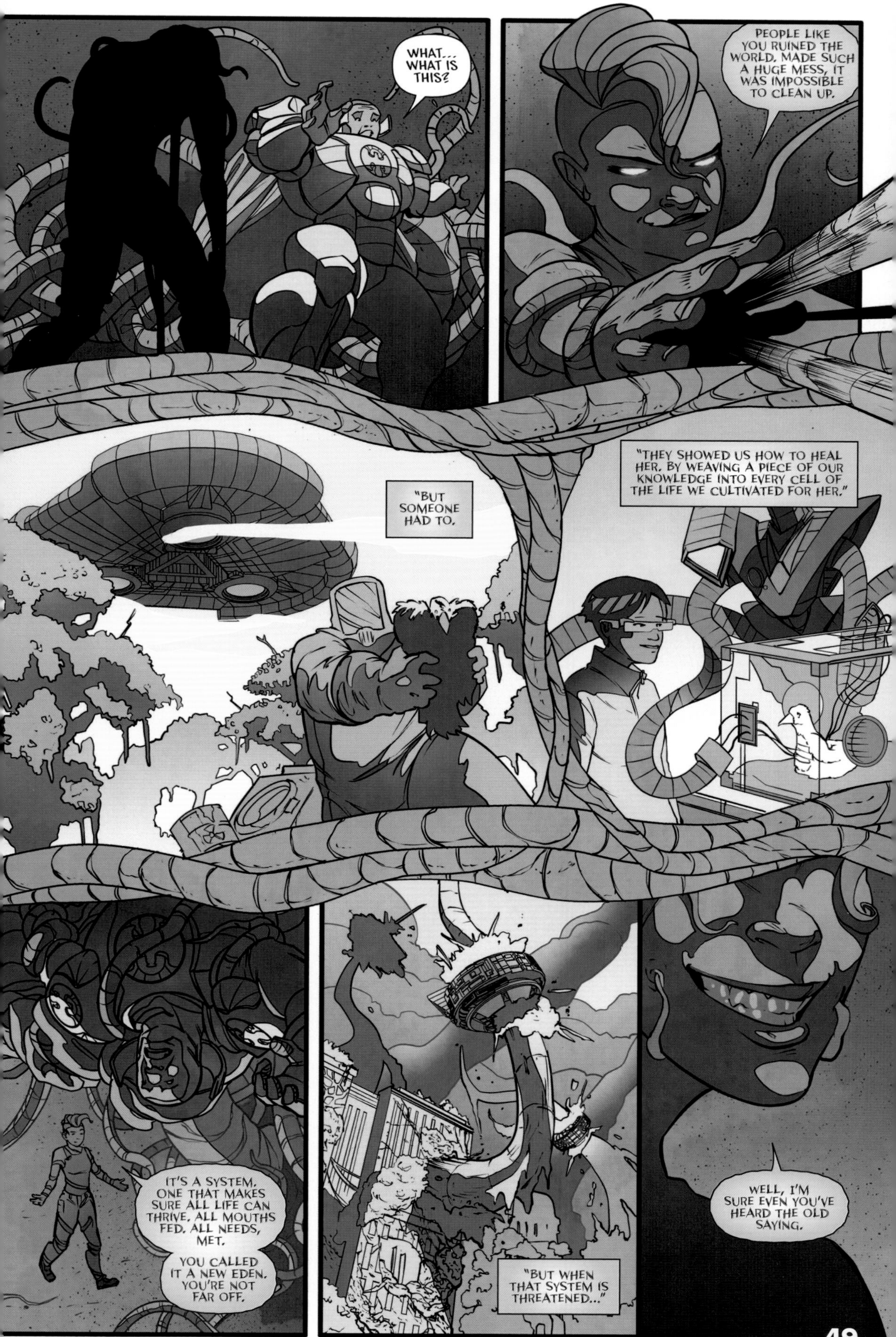
WHAT... WHAT IS THIS?
PEOPLE LIKE YOU RUINED THE WORLD. MADE SUCH A HUGE MESS, IT WAS IMPOSSIBLE TO CLEAN UP.
"BUT SOMEONE HAD TO.
"THEY SHOWED US HOW TO HEAL HER. BY WEAVING A PIECE OF OUR KNOWLEDGE INTO EVERY CELL OF THE LIFE WE CULTIVATED FOR HER."
IT'S A SYSTEM. ONE THAT MAKES SURE ALL LIFE CAN THRIVE. ALL MOUTHS FED. ALL NEEDS, MET.
YOU CALLED IT A NEW EDEN. YOU'RE NOT FAR OFF.
"BUT WHEN THAT SYSTEM IS THREATENED..."
WELL, I'M SURE EVEN YOU'VE HEARD THE OLD SAYING.

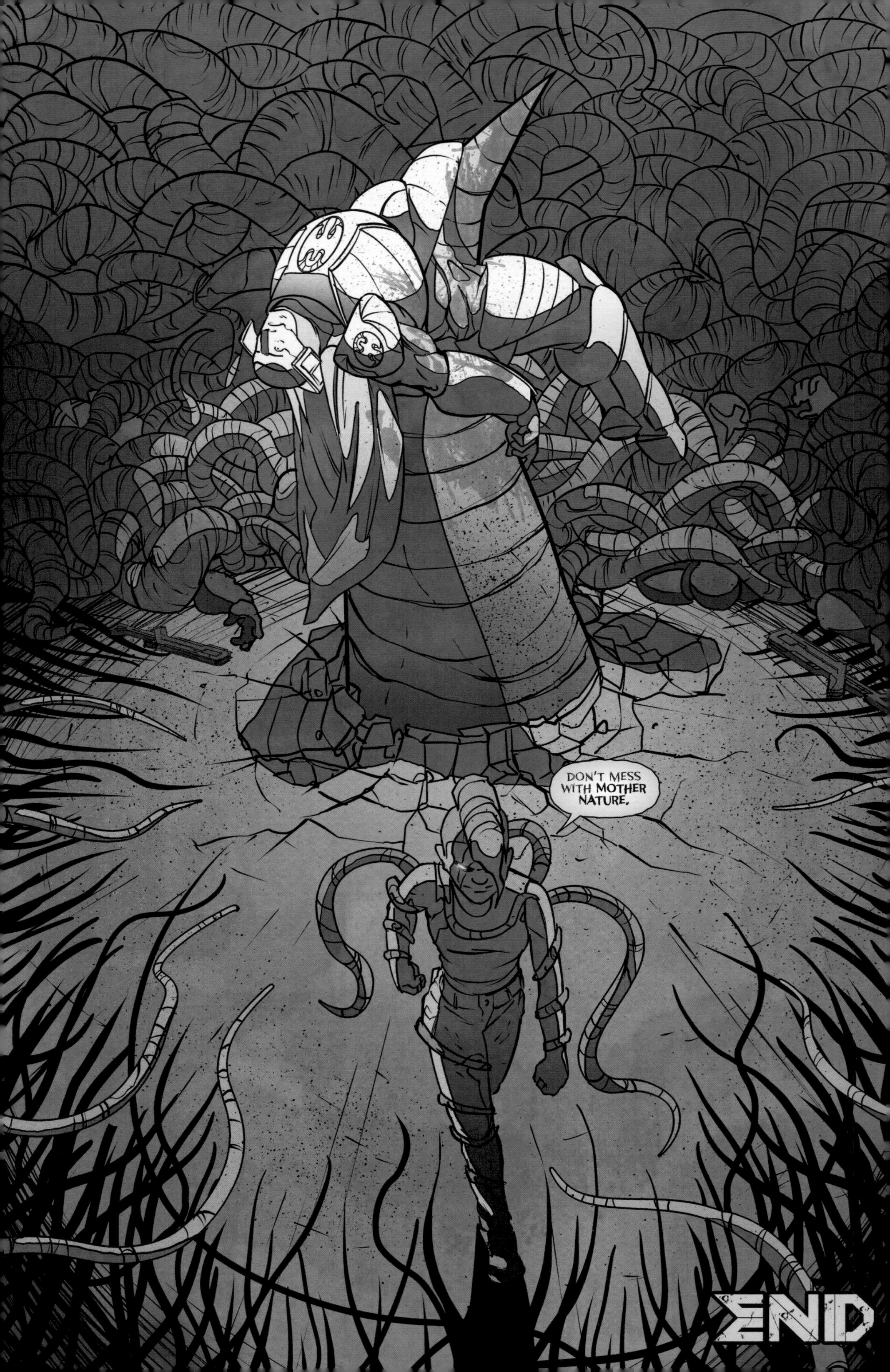
DON'T MESS WITH MOTHER NATURE.
END

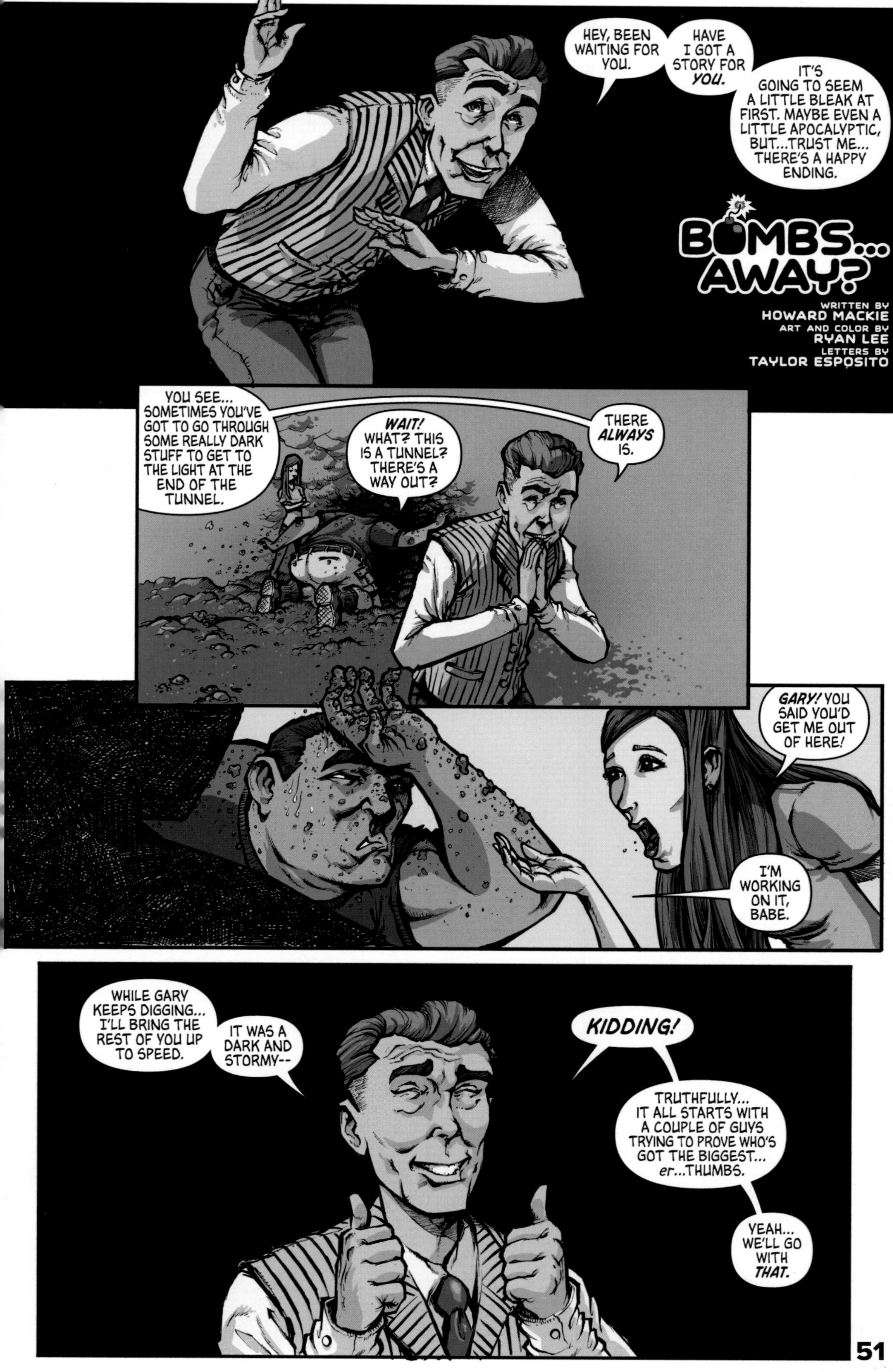

HEY, BEEN WAITING FOR YOU.
HAVE I GOT A STORY FOR *YOU.*
IT'S GOING TO SEEM A LITTLE BLEAK AT FIRST. MAYBE EVEN A LITTLE APOCALYPTIC, BUT...TRUST ME... THERE'S A HAPPY ENDING.
BOMBS... AWAY?
WRITTEN BY HOWARD MACKIE
ART AND COLOR BY RYAN LEE
LETTERS BY TAYLOR ESPOSITO
YOU SEE... SOMETIMES YOU'VE GOT TO GO THROUGH SOME REALLY DARK STUFF TO GET TO THE LIGHT AT THE END OF THE TUNNEL.
WAIT! WHAT? THIS IS A TUNNEL? THERE'S A WAY OUT?
THERE *ALWAYS* IS.
GARY! YOU SAID YOU'D GET ME OUT OF HERE!
I'M WORKING ON IT, BABE.
WHILE GARY KEEPS DIGGING... I'LL BRING THE REST OF YOU UP TO SPEED.
IT WAS A DARK AND STORMY--
KIDDING!
TRUTHFULLY... IT ALL STARTS WITH A COUPLE OF GUYS TRYING TO PROVE WHO'S GOT THE BIGGEST... *er*...THUMBS.
YEAH... WE'LL GO WITH *THAT.*

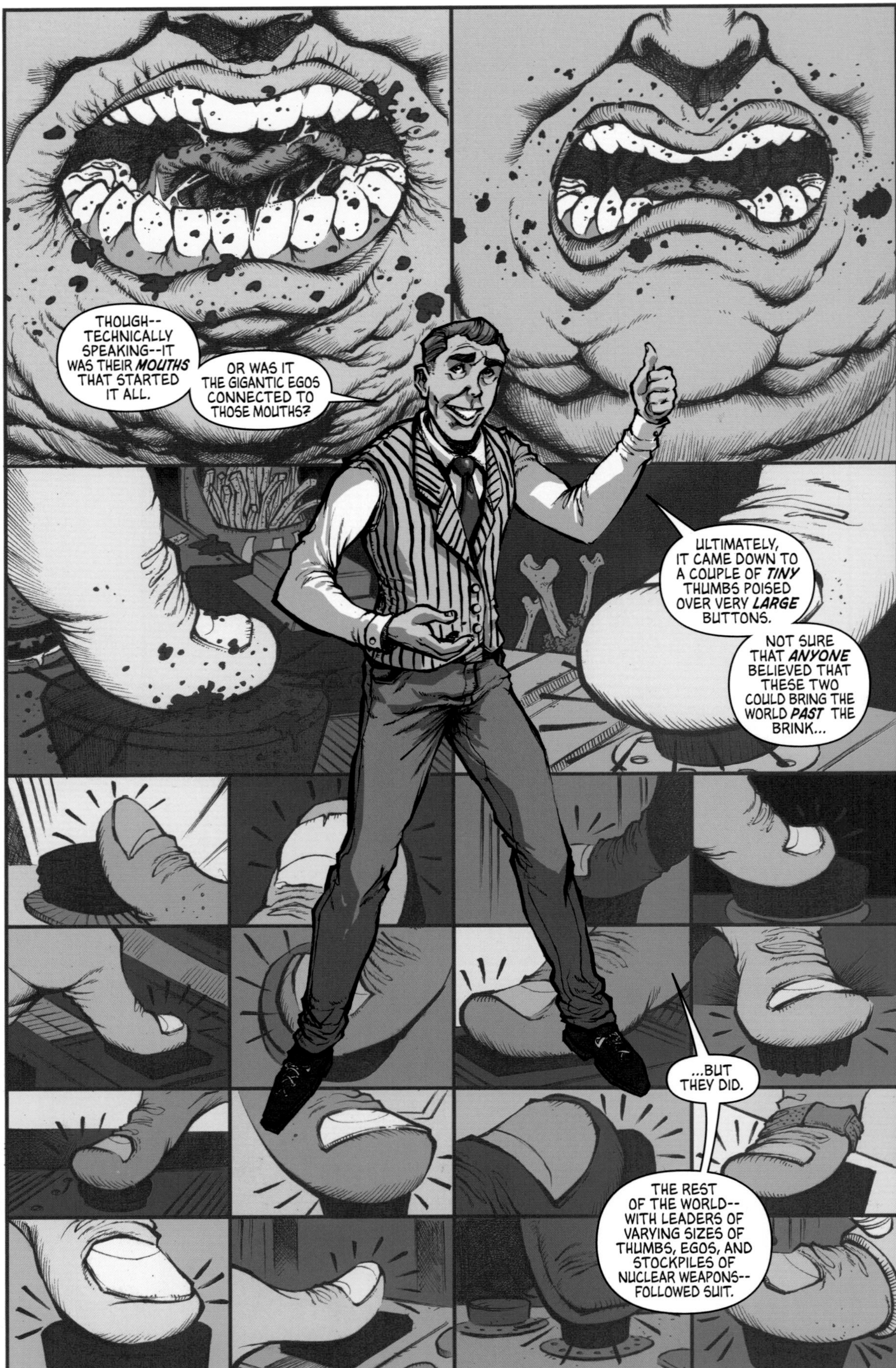
THOUGH--TECHNICALLY SPEAKING--IT WAS THEIR *MOUTHS* THAT STARTED IT ALL.
OR WAS IT THE GIGANTIC EGOS CONNECTED TO THOSE MOUTHS?
ULTIMATELY, IT CAME DOWN TO A COUPLE OF *TINY* THUMBS POISED OVER VERY *LARGE* BUTTONS.
NOT SURE THAT *ANYONE* BELIEVED THAT THESE TWO COULD BRING THE WORLD *PAST* THE BRINK...
...BUT THEY DID.
THE REST OF THE WORLD--WITH LEADERS OF VARYING SIZES OF THUMBS, EGOS, AND STOCKPILES OF NUCLEAR WEAPONS--FOLLOWED SUIT.

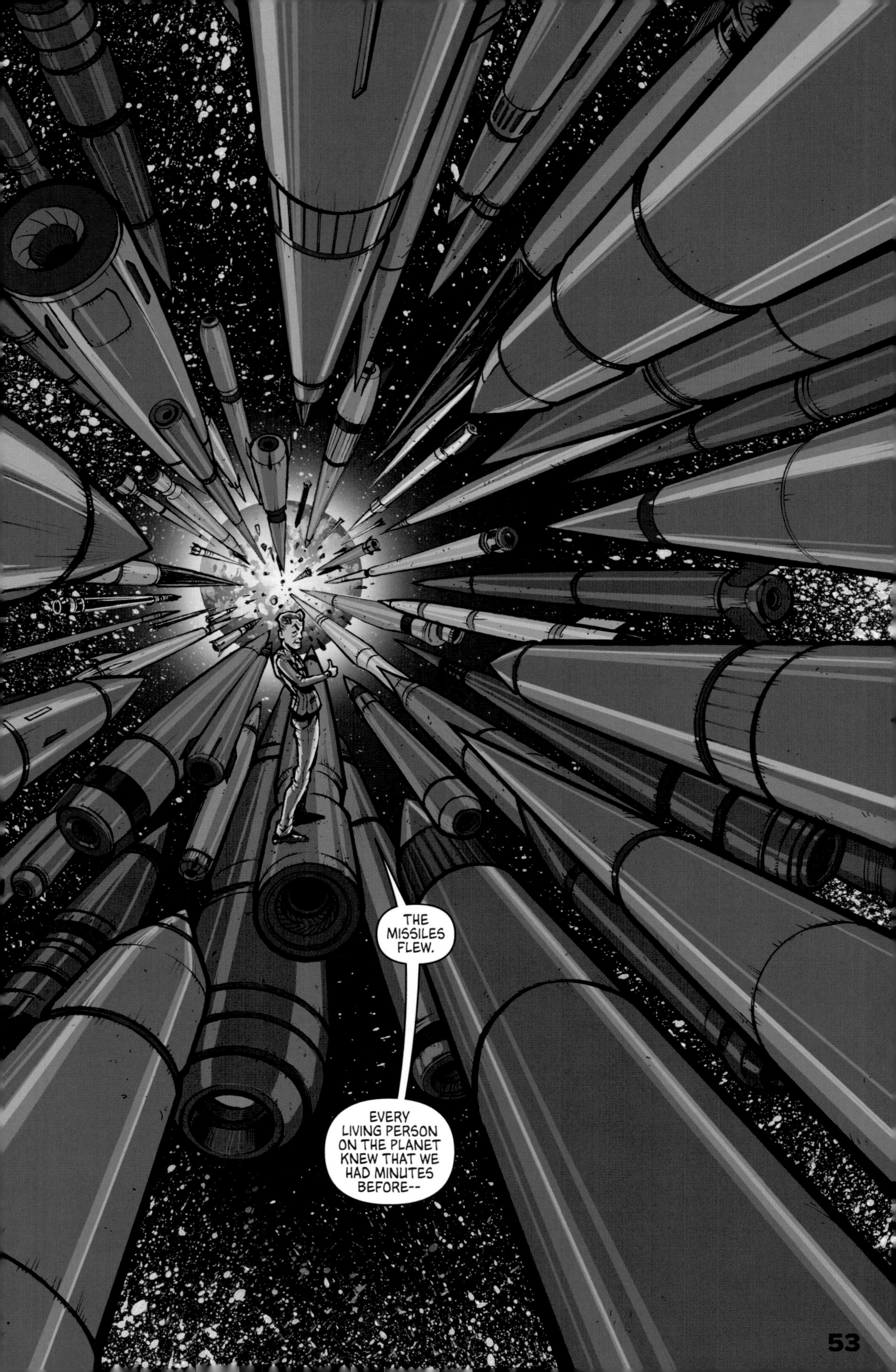
THE MISSILES FLEW.
EVERY LIVING PERSON ON THE PLANET KNEW THAT WE HAD MINUTES BEFORE--

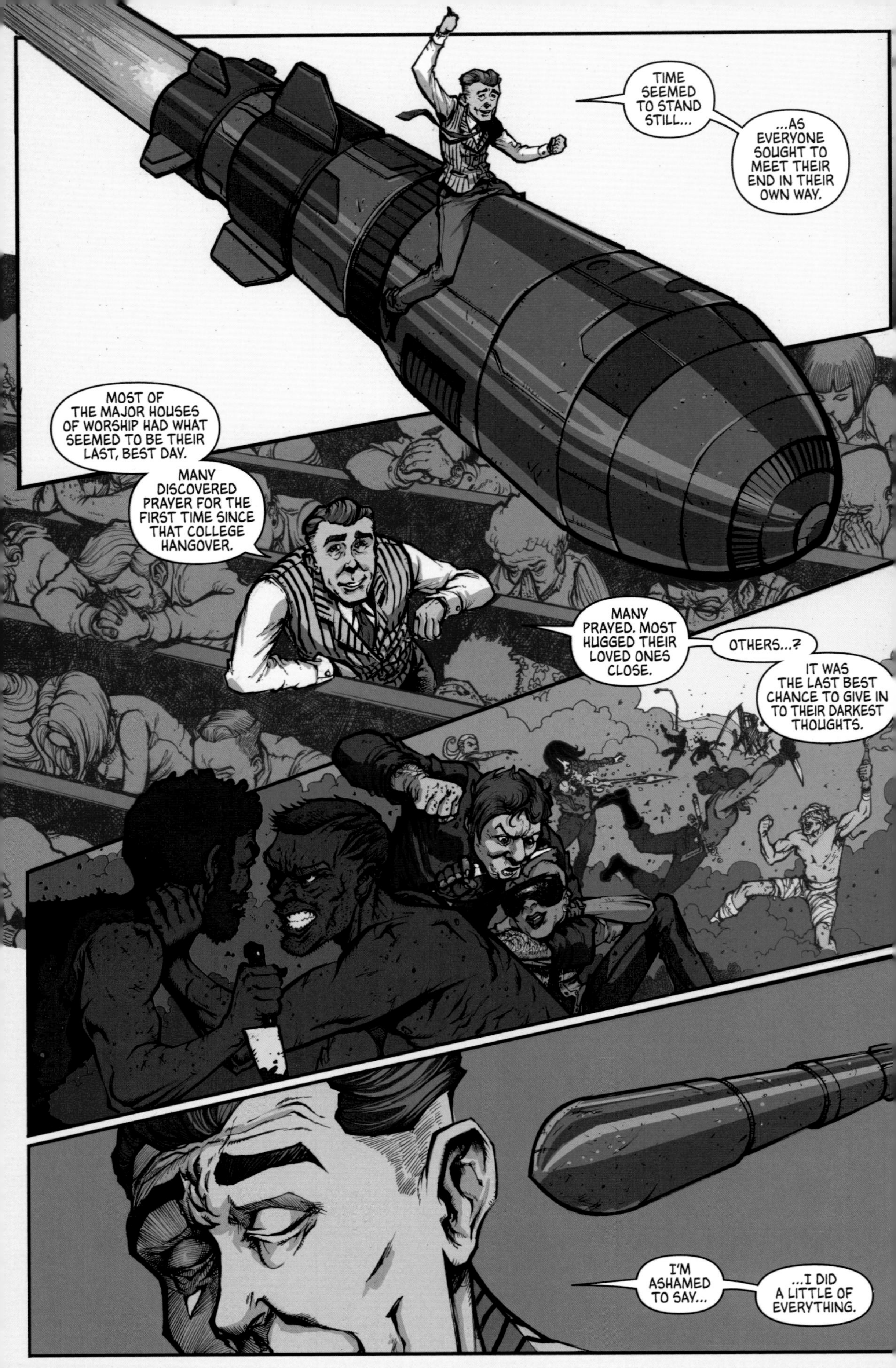
TIME SEEMED TO STAND STILL...
...AS EVERYONE SOUGHT TO MEET THEIR END IN THEIR OWN WAY.
MOST OF THE MAJOR HOUSES OF WORSHIP HAD WHAT SEEMED TO BE THEIR LAST, BEST DAY.
MANY DISCOVERED PRAYER FOR THE FIRST TIME SINCE THAT COLLEGE HANGOVER.
MANY PRAYED. MOST HUGGED THEIR LOVED ONES CLOSE.
OTHERS...?
IT WAS THE LAST BEST CHANCE TO GIVE IN TO THEIR DARKEST THOUGHTS.
I'M ASHAMED TO SAY...
...I DID A LITTLE OF EVERYTHING.

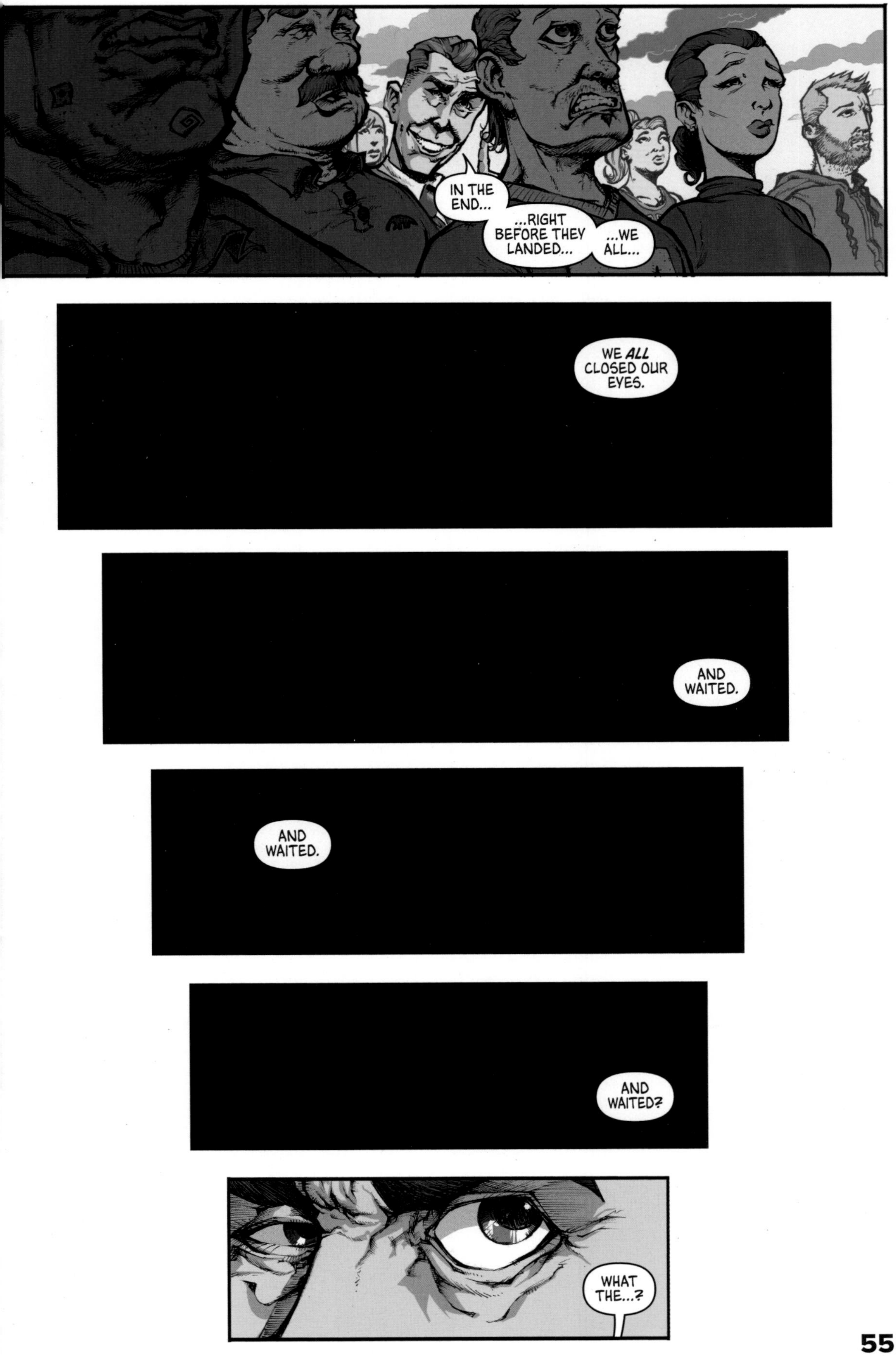
IN THE END...
...RIGHT BEFORE THEY LANDED...
...WE ALL...
WE *ALL* CLOSED OUR EYES.
AND WAITED.
AND WAITED.
AND WAITED?
WHAT THE...?

NOTHING EXPLODED.

"WORD SPREAD PRETTY QUICKLY.

"IT WAS THE SAME EVERYWHERE.

"NOT A SINGLE NUCLEAR WEAPON DETONATED.

"APOCALYPSE... INTERRUPTUS?

"THERE WAS *ONE* BIT OF HUMOROUS NEWS OUT OF IT ALL.

"SEEMS LIKE THE TWO 'FEARLESS LEADERS' WHO STARTED IT ALL...

"...THEY WANTED TO SEE THE END OF THE WORLD WITH THEIR OWN EYES.

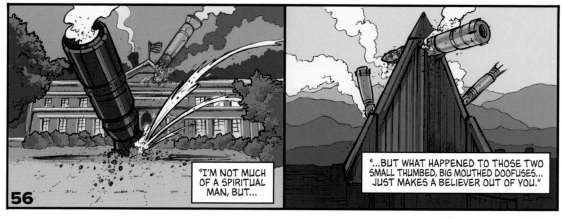

"I'M NOT MUCH OF A SPIRITUAL MAN, BUT...

"...BUT WHAT HAPPENED TO THOSE TWO SMALL THUMBED, BIG MOUTHED DOOFUSES... JUST MAKES A BELIEVER OUT OF YOU."

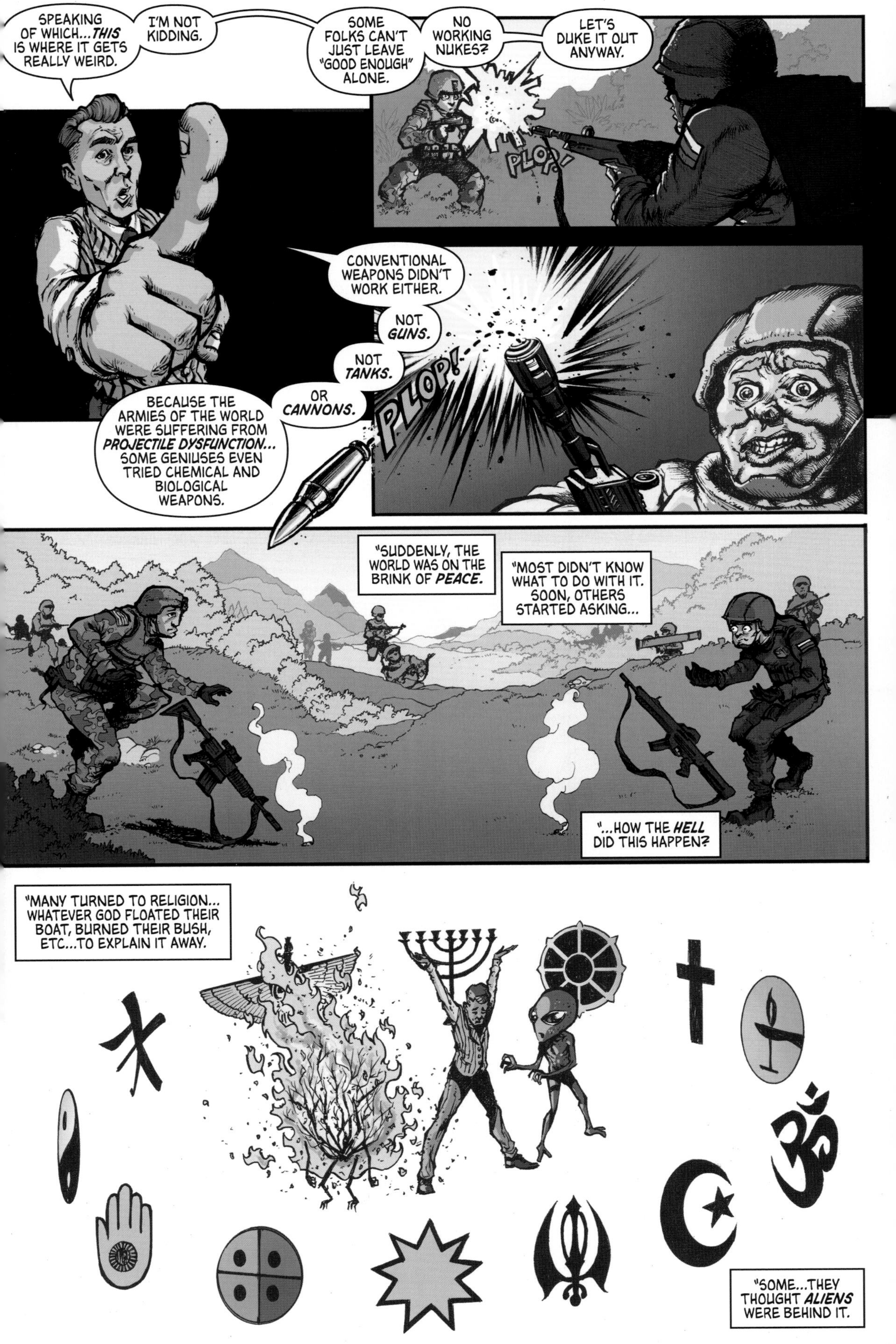

SPEAKING OF WHICH...THIS IS WHERE IT GETS REALLY WEIRD.
I'M NOT KIDDING.
SOME FOLKS CAN'T JUST LEAVE "GOOD ENOUGH" ALONE.
NO WORKING NUKES?
LET'S DUKE IT OUT ANYWAY.
PLOP!
CONVENTIONAL WEAPONS DIDN'T WORK EITHER.
NOT GUNS.
NOT TANKS.
OR CANNONS.
PLOP!
BECAUSE THE ARMIES OF THE WORLD WERE SUFFERING FROM PROJECTILE DYSFUNCTION... SOME GENIUSES EVEN TRIED CHEMICAL AND BIOLOGICAL WEAPONS.
"SUDDENLY, THE WORLD WAS ON THE BRINK OF PEACE.
"MOST DIDN'T KNOW WHAT TO DO WITH IT. SOON, OTHERS STARTED ASKING...
"...HOW THE HELL DID THIS HAPPEN?
"MANY TURNED TO RELIGION... WHATEVER GOD FLOATED THEIR BOAT, BURNED THEIR BUSH, ETC...TO EXPLAIN IT AWAY.
"SOME...THEY THOUGHT ALIENS WERE BEHIND IT.

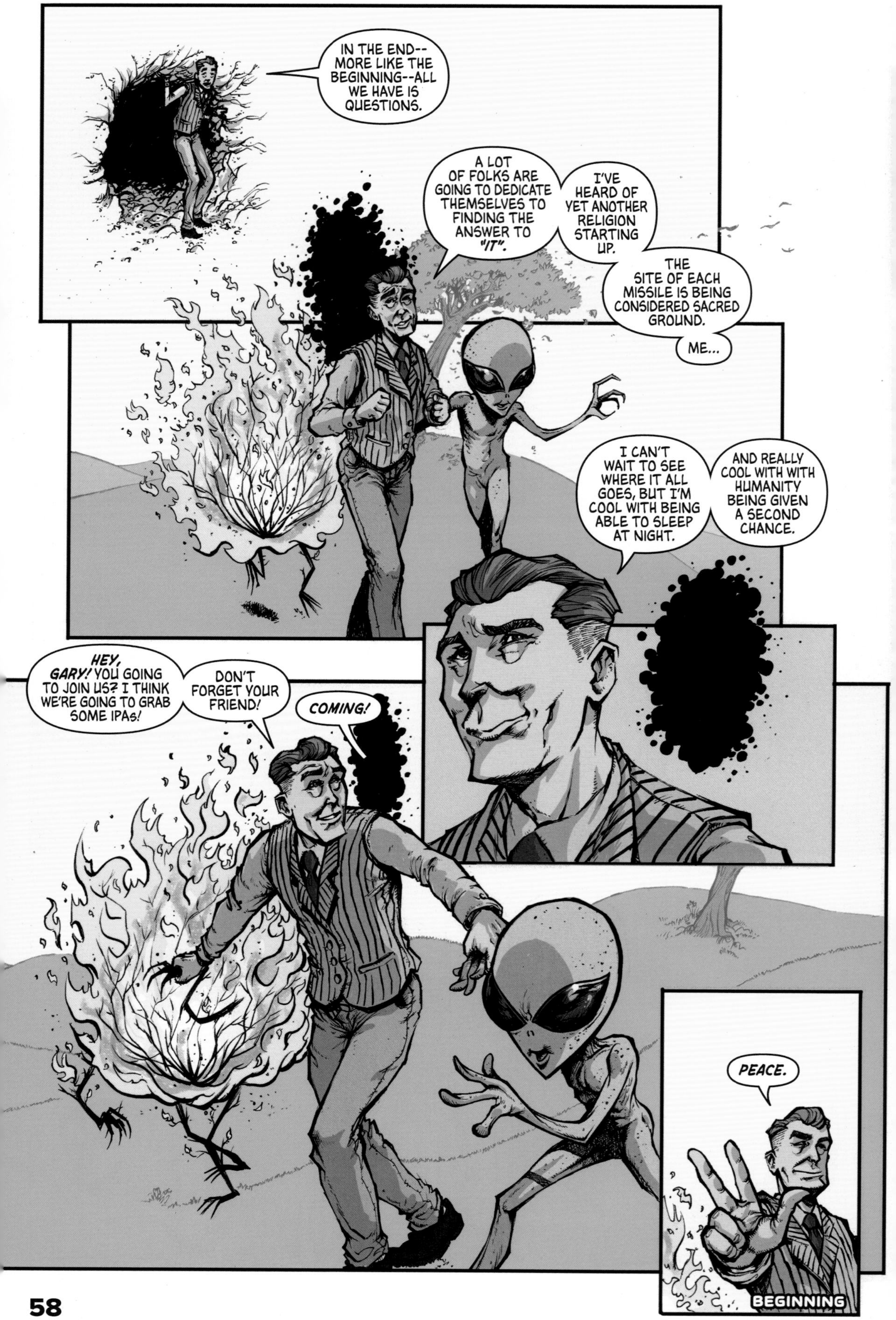
IN THE END--MORE LIKE THE BEGINNING--ALL WE HAVE IS QUESTIONS.
A LOT OF FOLKS ARE GOING TO DEDICATE THEMSELVES TO FINDING THE ANSWER TO "IT".
I'VE HEARD OF YET ANOTHER RELIGION STARTING UP.
THE SITE OF EACH MISSILE IS BEING CONSIDERED SACRED GROUND.
ME...
I CAN'T WAIT TO SEE WHERE IT ALL GOES, BUT I'M COOL WITH BEING ABLE TO SLEEP AT NIGHT.
AND REALLY COOL WITH WITH HUMANITY BEING GIVEN A SECOND CHANCE.
HEY, GARY! YOU GOING TO JOIN US? I THINK WE'RE GOING TO GRAB SOME IPAs!
DON'T FORGET YOUR FRIEND!
COMING!
PEACE.
BEGINNING

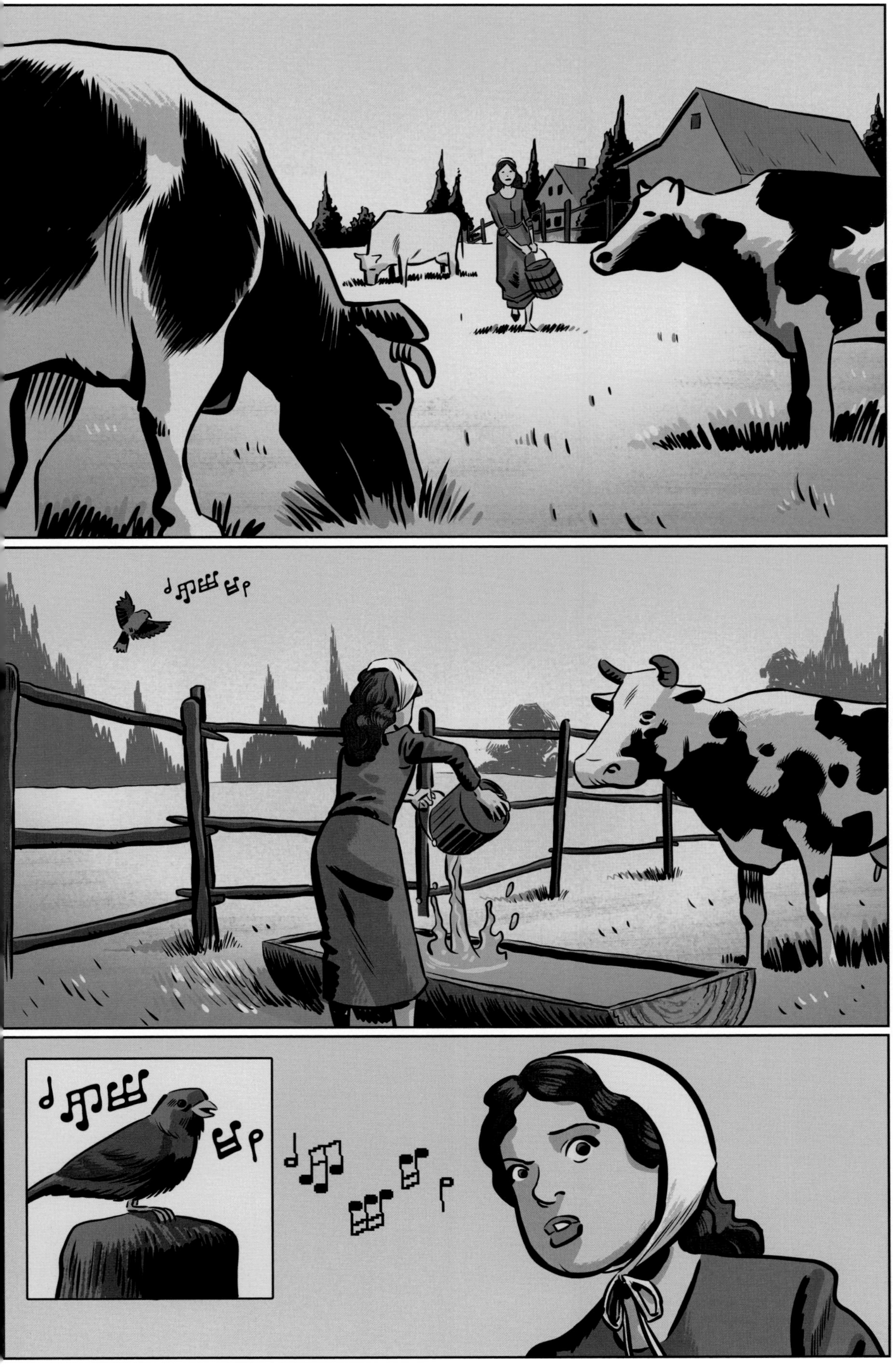

GASP

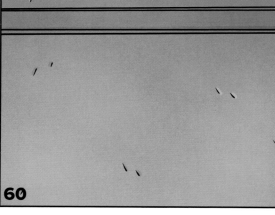

OH...

60

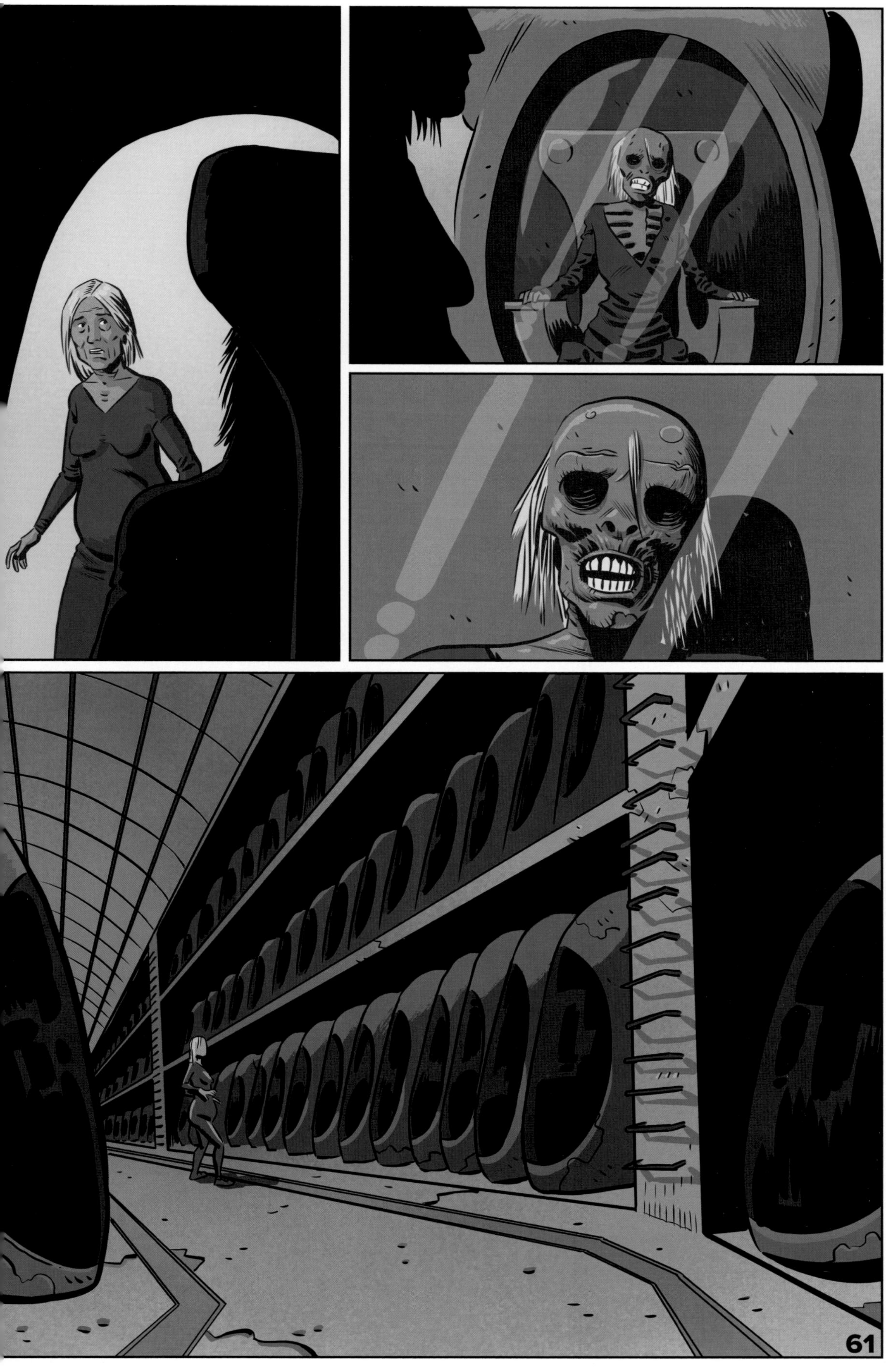

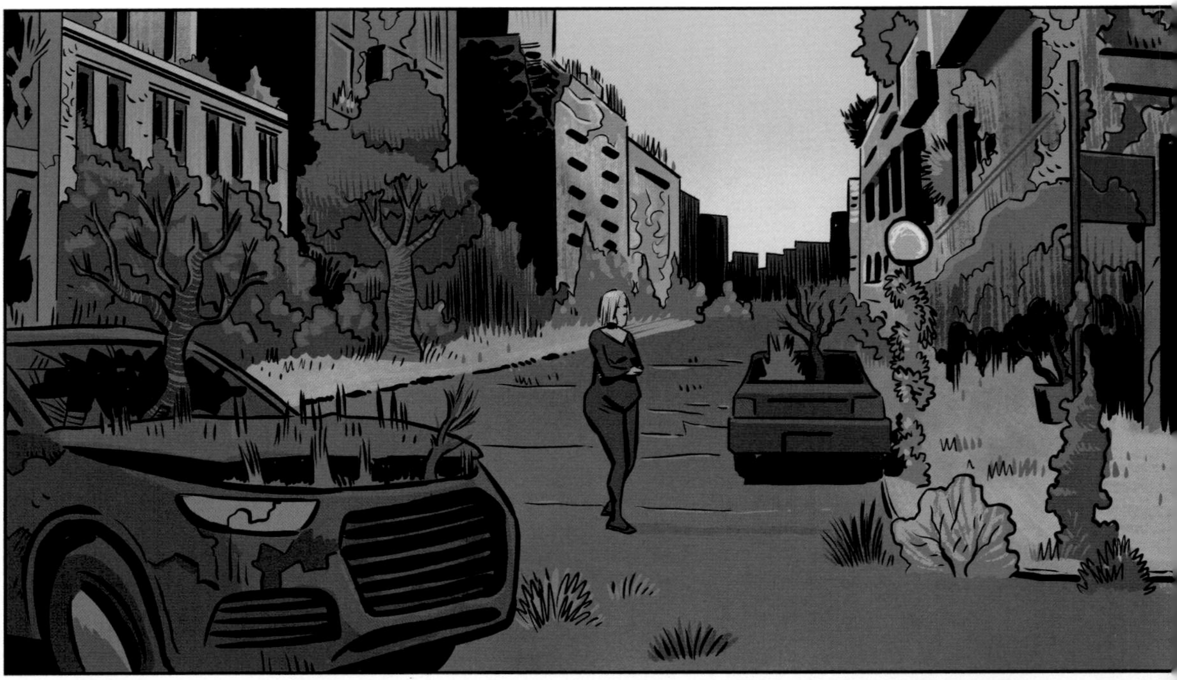
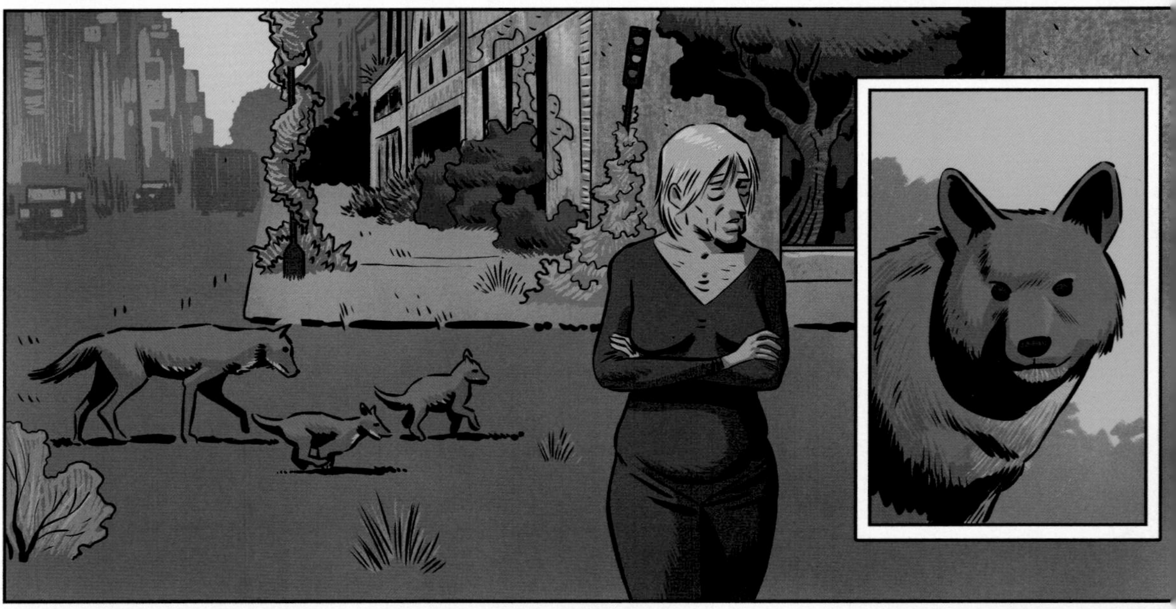
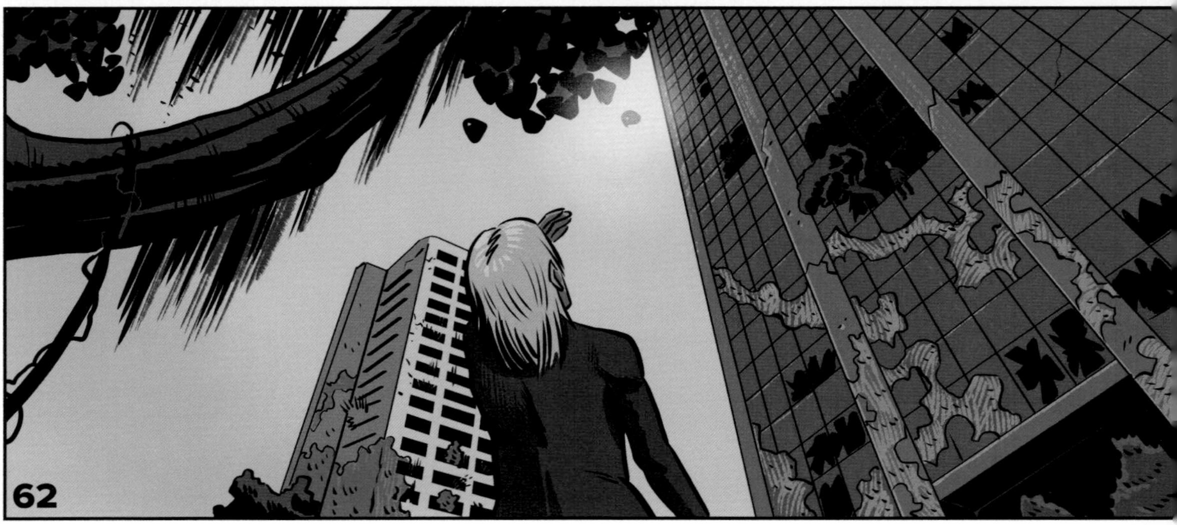

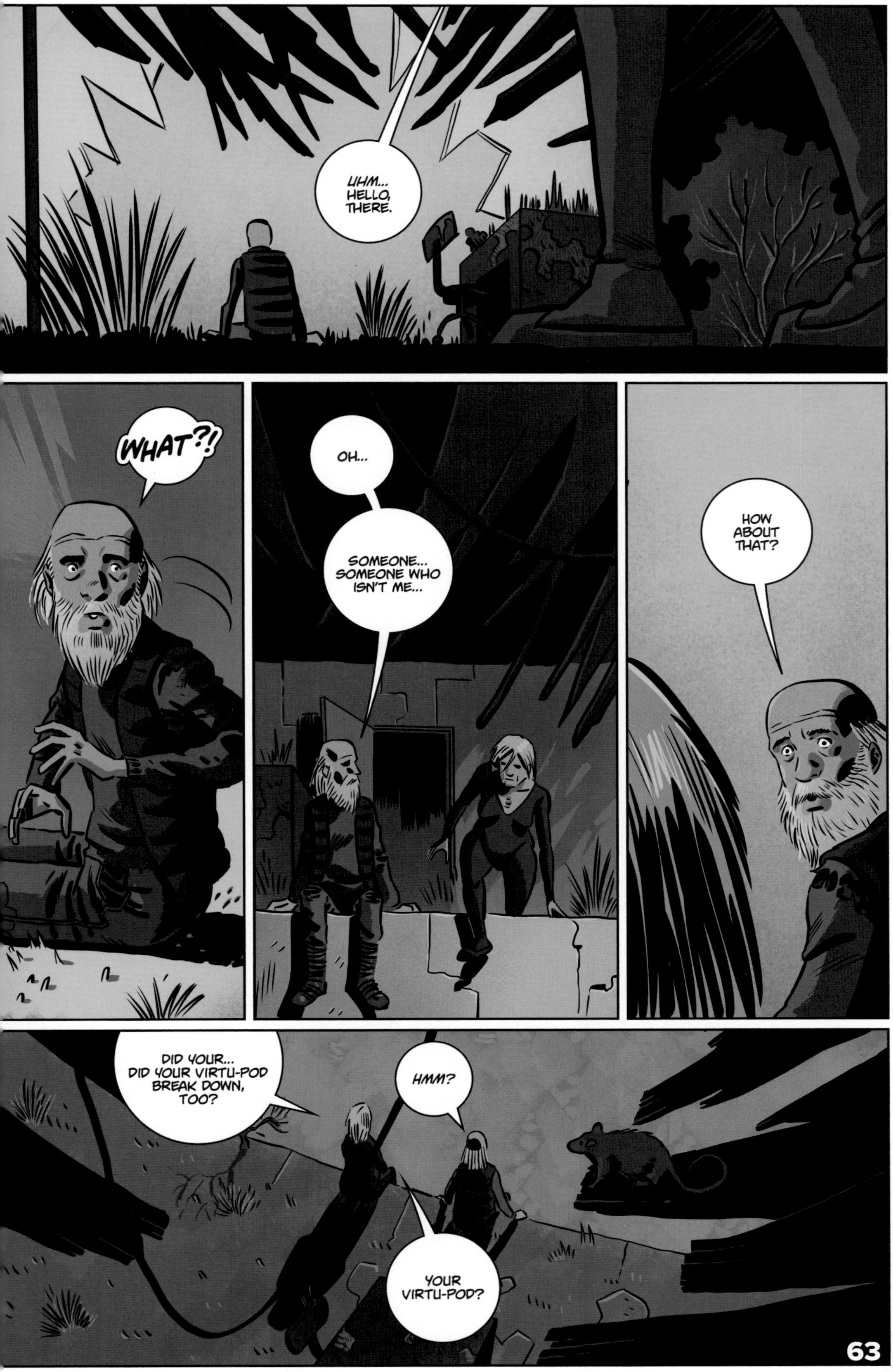
UHM... HELLO, THERE.
WHAT?!
OH...
SOMEONE... SOMEONE WHO ISN'T ME...
HOW ABOUT THAT?
DID YOUR... DID YOUR VIRTU-POD BREAK DOWN, TOO?
HMM?
YOUR VIRTU-POD?

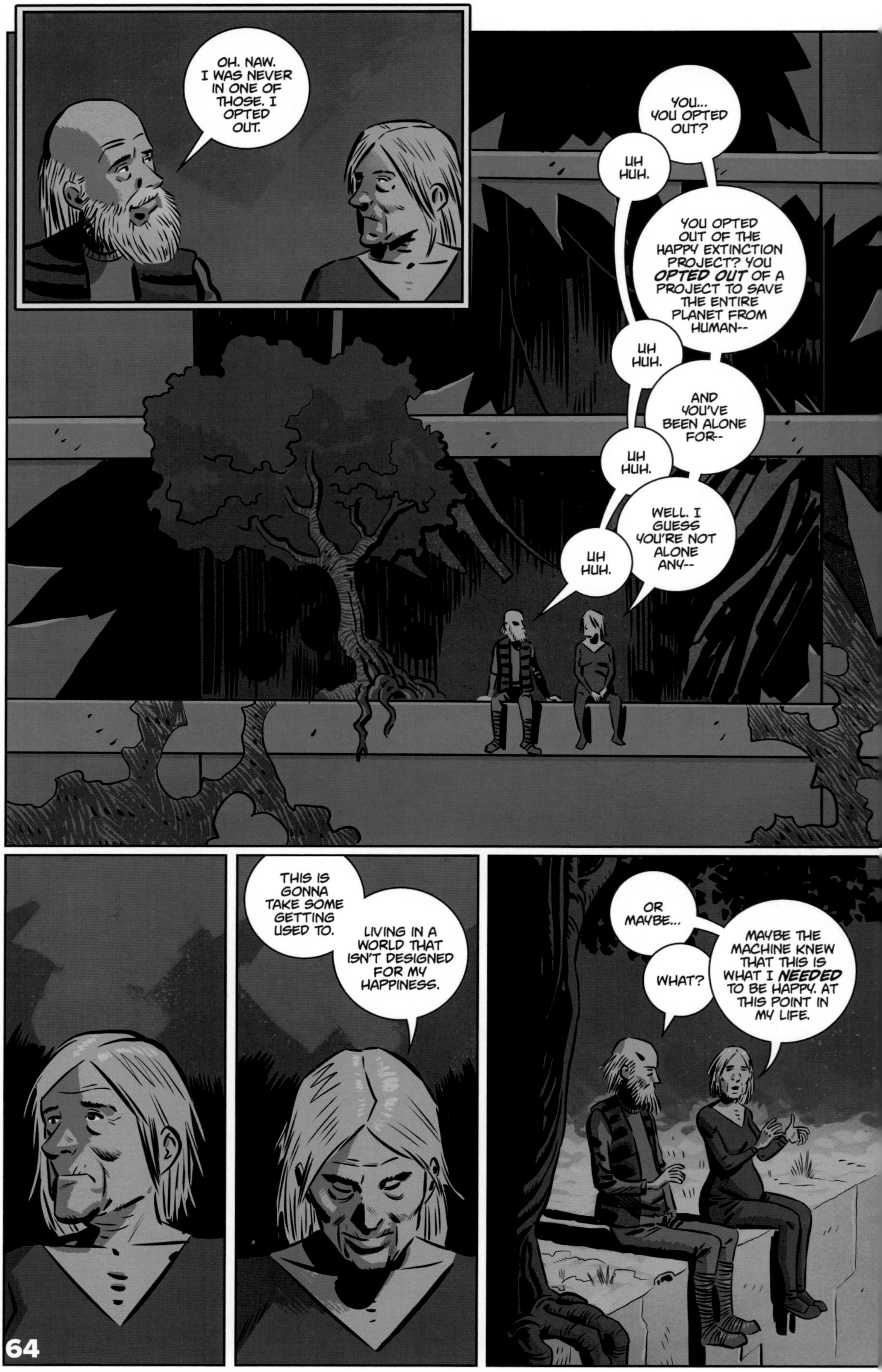
OH. NAW. I WAS NEVER IN ONE OF THOSE. I OPTED OUT.
YOU... YOU OPTED OUT?
UH HUH.
YOU OPTED OUT OF THE HAPPY EXTINCTION PROJECT? YOU OPTED OUT OF A PROJECT TO SAVE THE ENTIRE PLANET FROM HUMAN--
UH HUH.
AND YOU'VE BEEN ALONE FOR--
UH HUH.
WELL. I GUESS YOU'RE NOT ALONE ANY--
UH HUH.
THIS IS GONNA TAKE SOME GETTING USED TO.
LIVING IN A WORLD THAT ISN'T DESIGNED FOR MY HAPPINESS.
OR MAYBE...
MAYBE THE MACHINE KNEW THAT THIS IS WHAT I NEEDED TO BE HAPPY. AT THIS POINT IN MY LIFE.
WHAT?

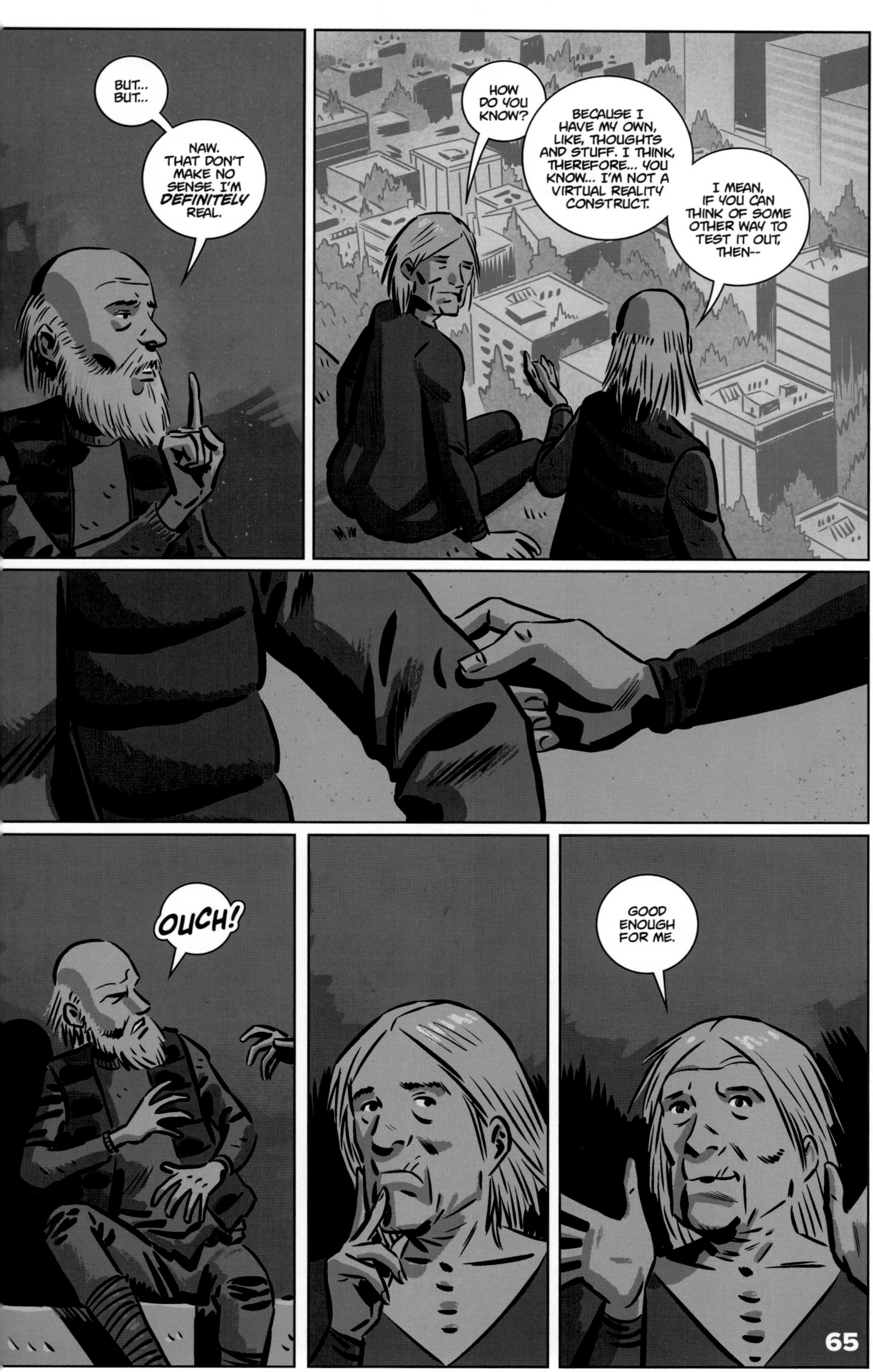
BUT... BUT...
NAW. THAT DON'T MAKE NO SENSE. I'M DEFINITELY REAL.
HOW DO YOU KNOW?
BECAUSE I HAVE MY OWN, LIKE, THOUGHTS AND STUFF. I THINK, THEREFORE... YOU KNOW... I'M NOT A VIRTUAL REALITY CONSTRUCT.
I MEAN, IF YOU CAN THINK OF SOME OTHER WAY TO TEST IT OUT, THEN--
OUCH!
GOOD ENOUGH FOR ME.

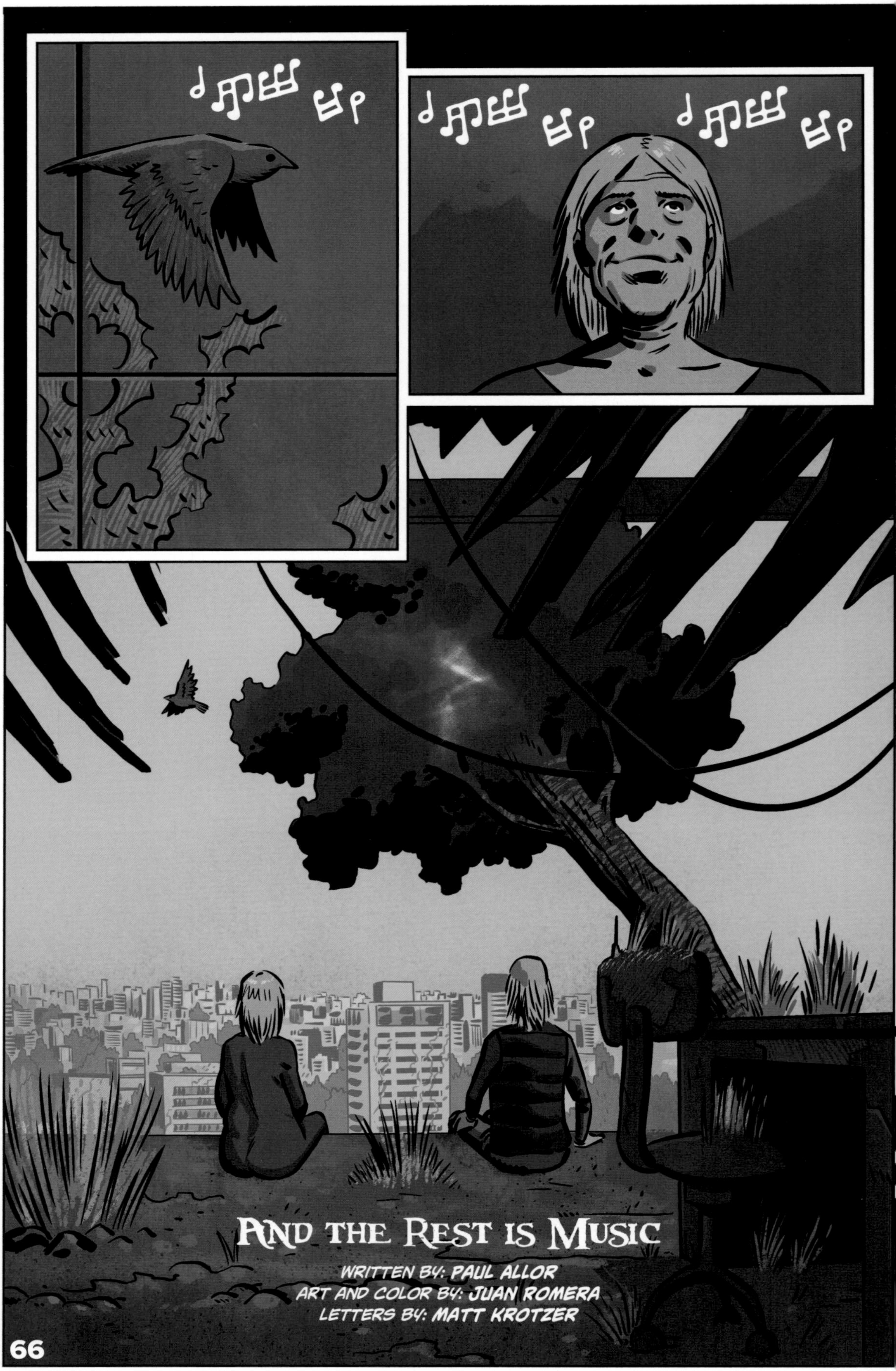
And the Rest is Music
Written by: Paul Allor
Art and Color by: Juan Romera
Letters by: Matt Krotzer

Everything I Own

WRITTEN BY LELA GWENN
ART BY TONY GREGORI
COLORS BY JOSH JENSEN
LETTERS BY TAYLOR ESPOSITO

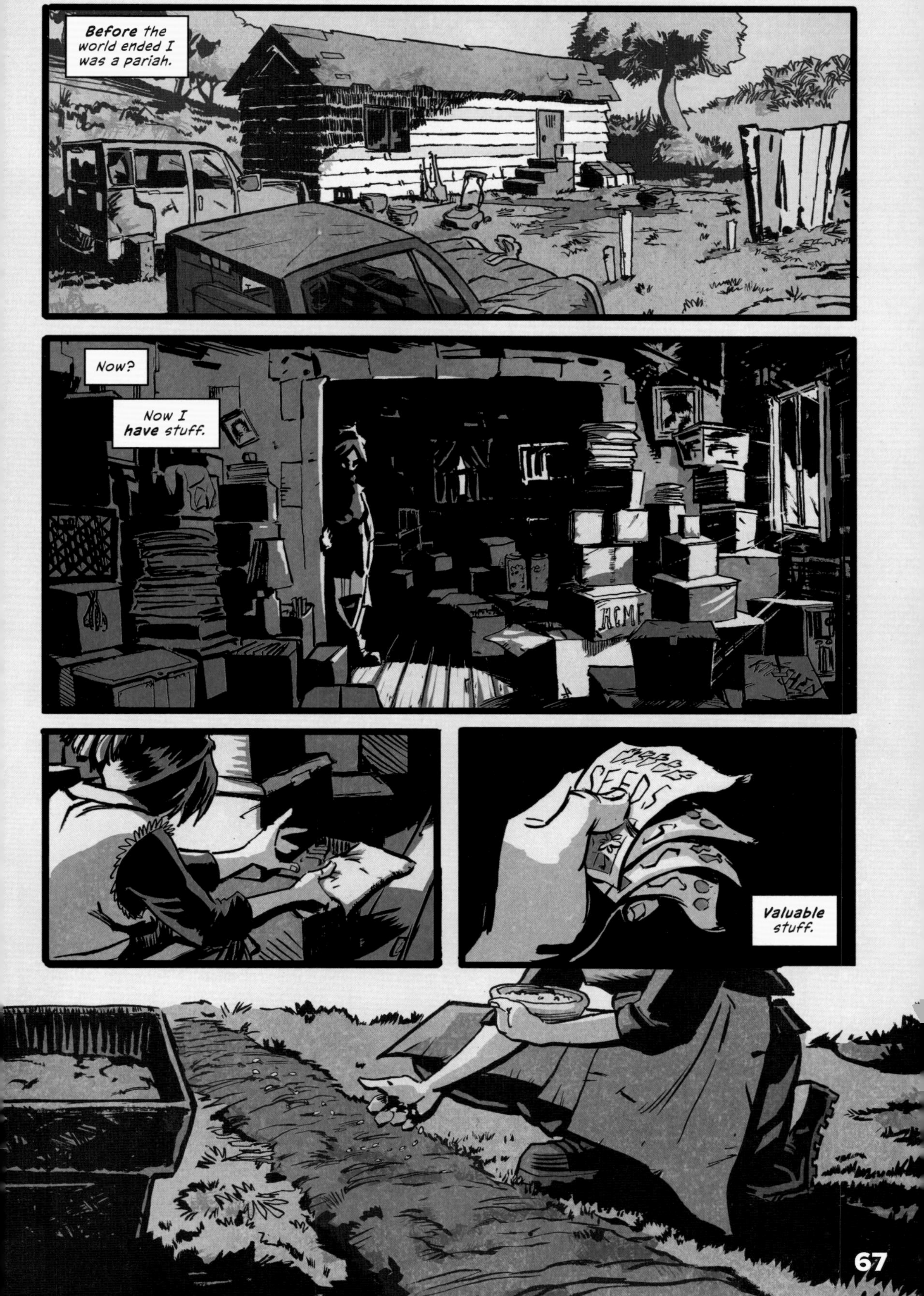
Before the world ended I was a pariah.
Now?
Now I have stuff.
ACME
SEEDS
Valuable stuff.

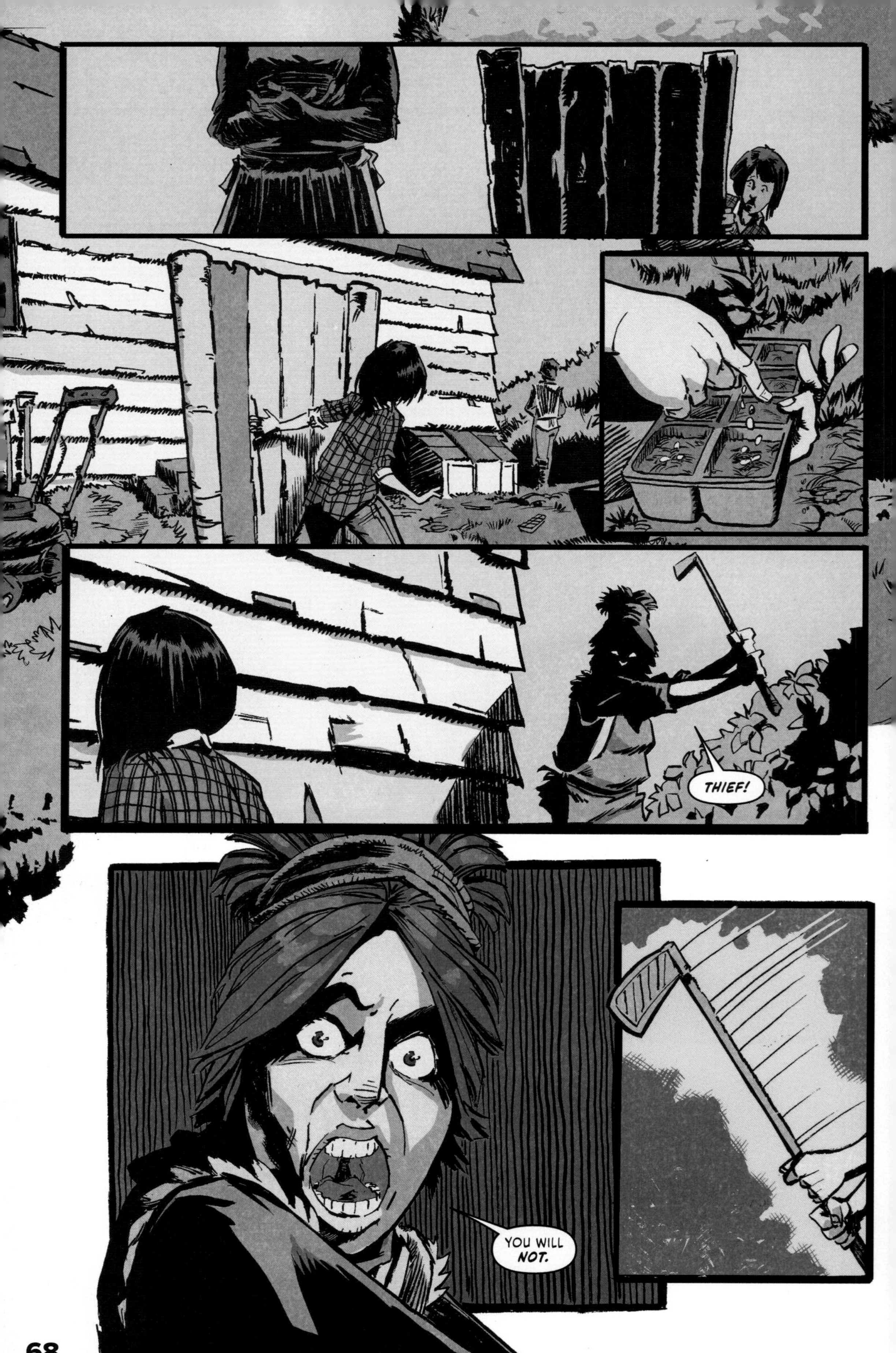
THIEF!
YOU WILL NOT.

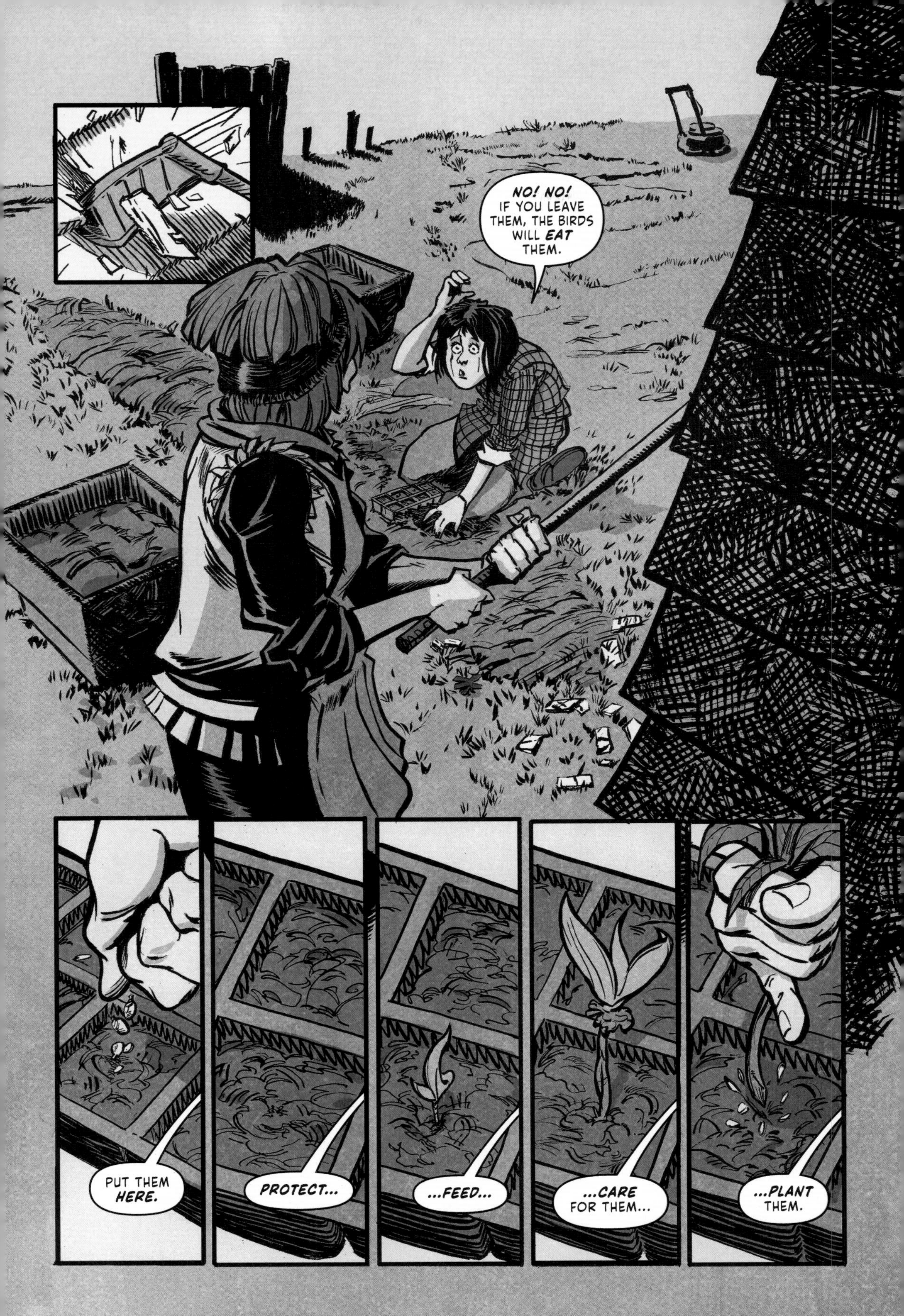
NO! NO! IF YOU LEAVE THEM, THE BIRDS WILL EAT THEM.
PUT THEM HERE.
PROTECT...
...FEED...
...CARE FOR THEM...
...PLANT THEM.

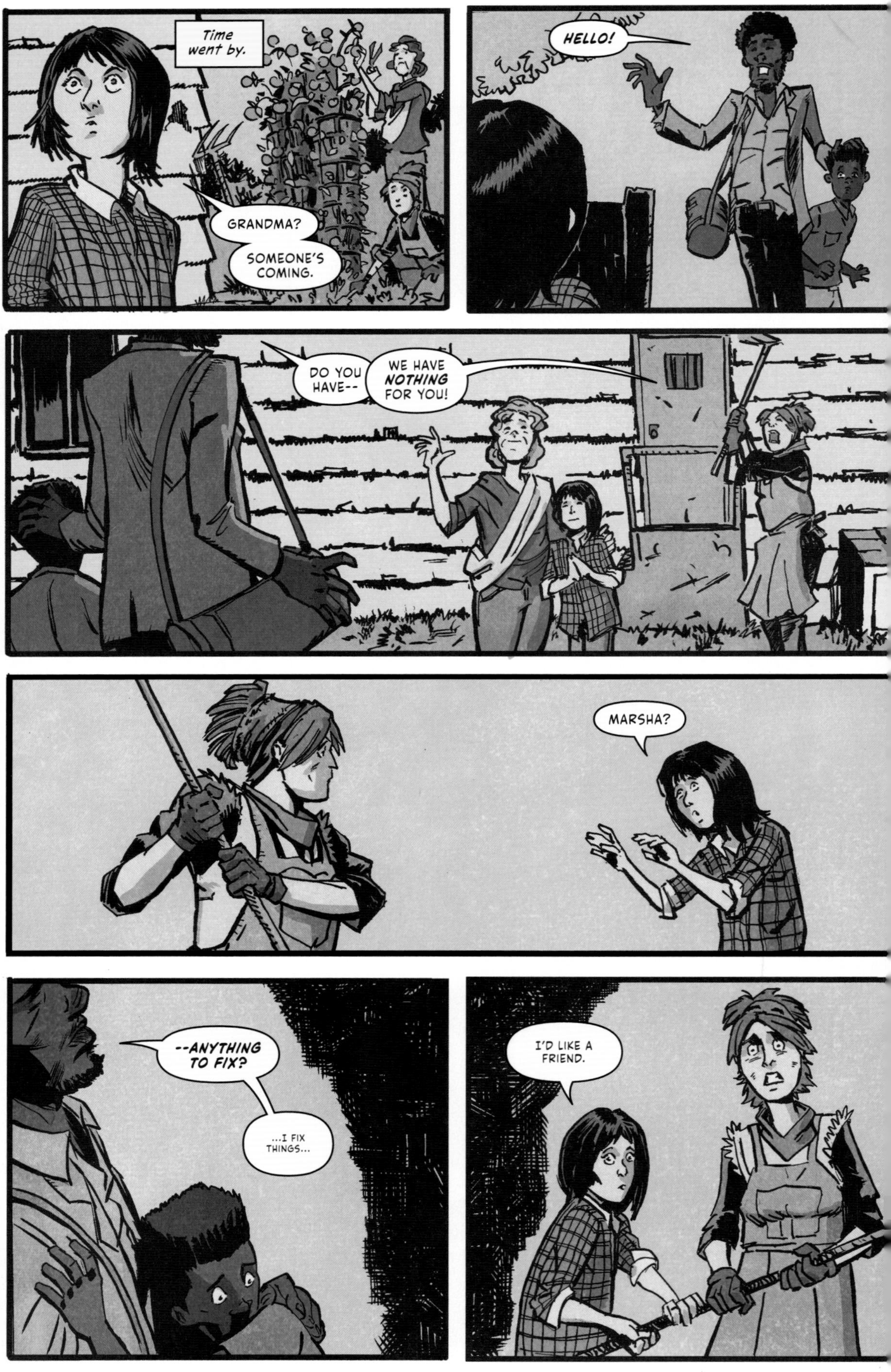
Time went by.
GRANDMA?
SOMEONE'S COMING.
HELLO!
DO YOU HAVE--
WE HAVE NOTHING FOR YOU!
MARSHA?
--ANYTHING TO FIX?
...I FIX THINGS...
I'D LIKE A FRIEND.

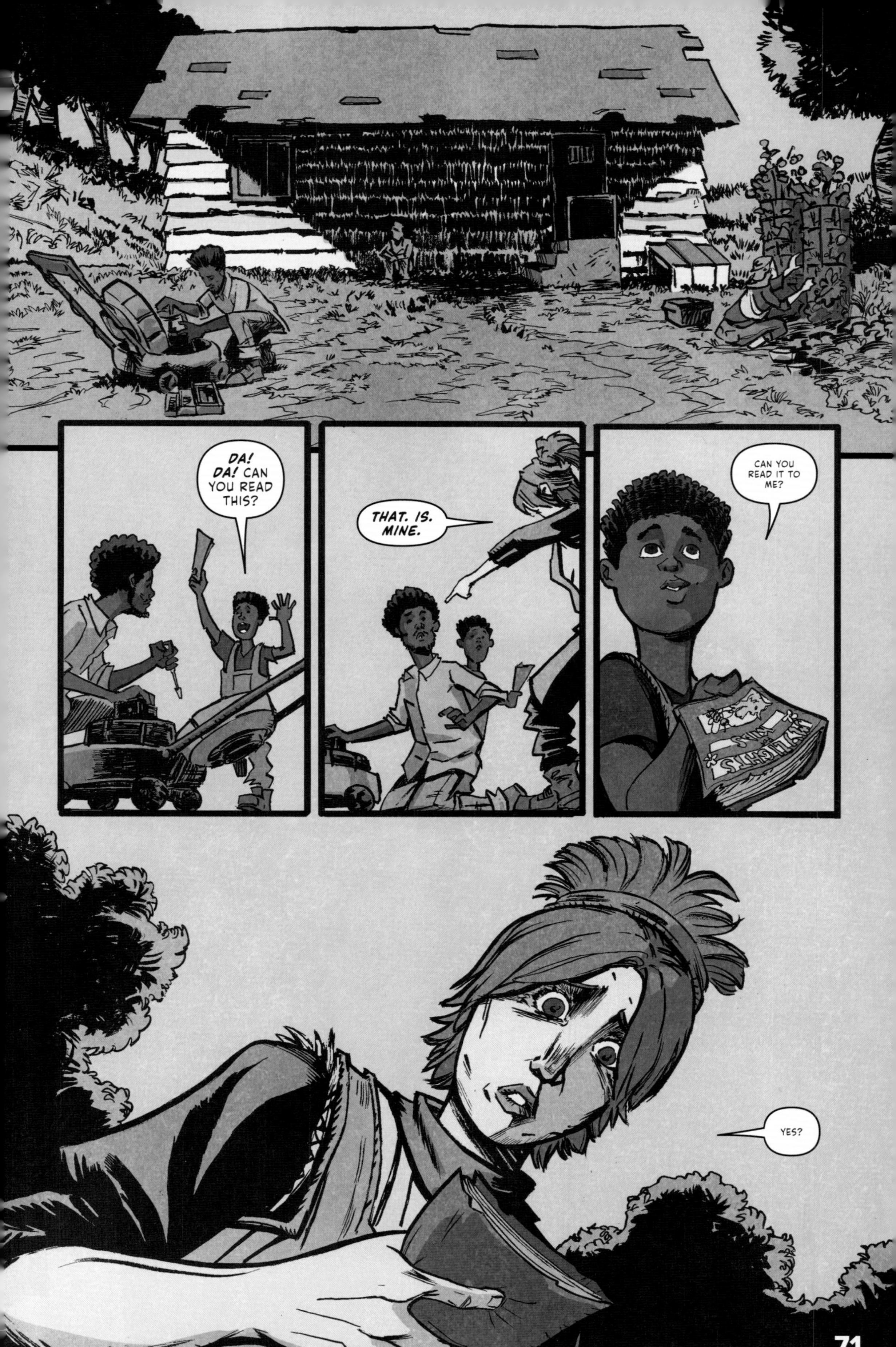
DA! DA! CAN YOU READ THIS?
THAT. IS. MINE.
CAN YOU READ IT TO ME?
YES?

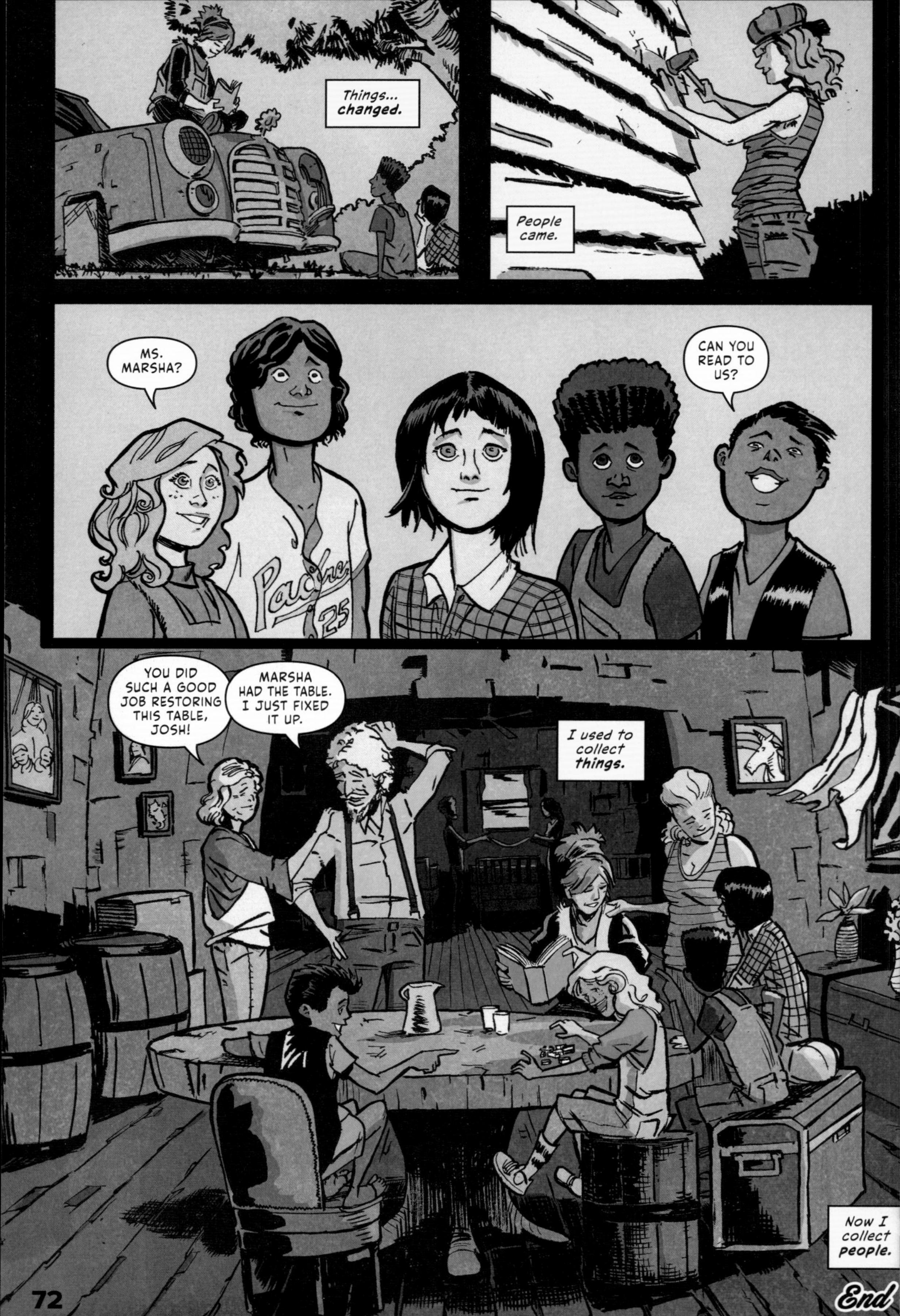
Things... **changed.**
People came.
MS. MARSHA?
CAN YOU READ TO US?
YOU DID SUCH A GOOD JOB RESTORING THIS TABLE, JOSH!
MARSHA HAD THE TABLE. I JUST FIXED IT UP.
I used to collect **things.**
Now I collect **people.**
End

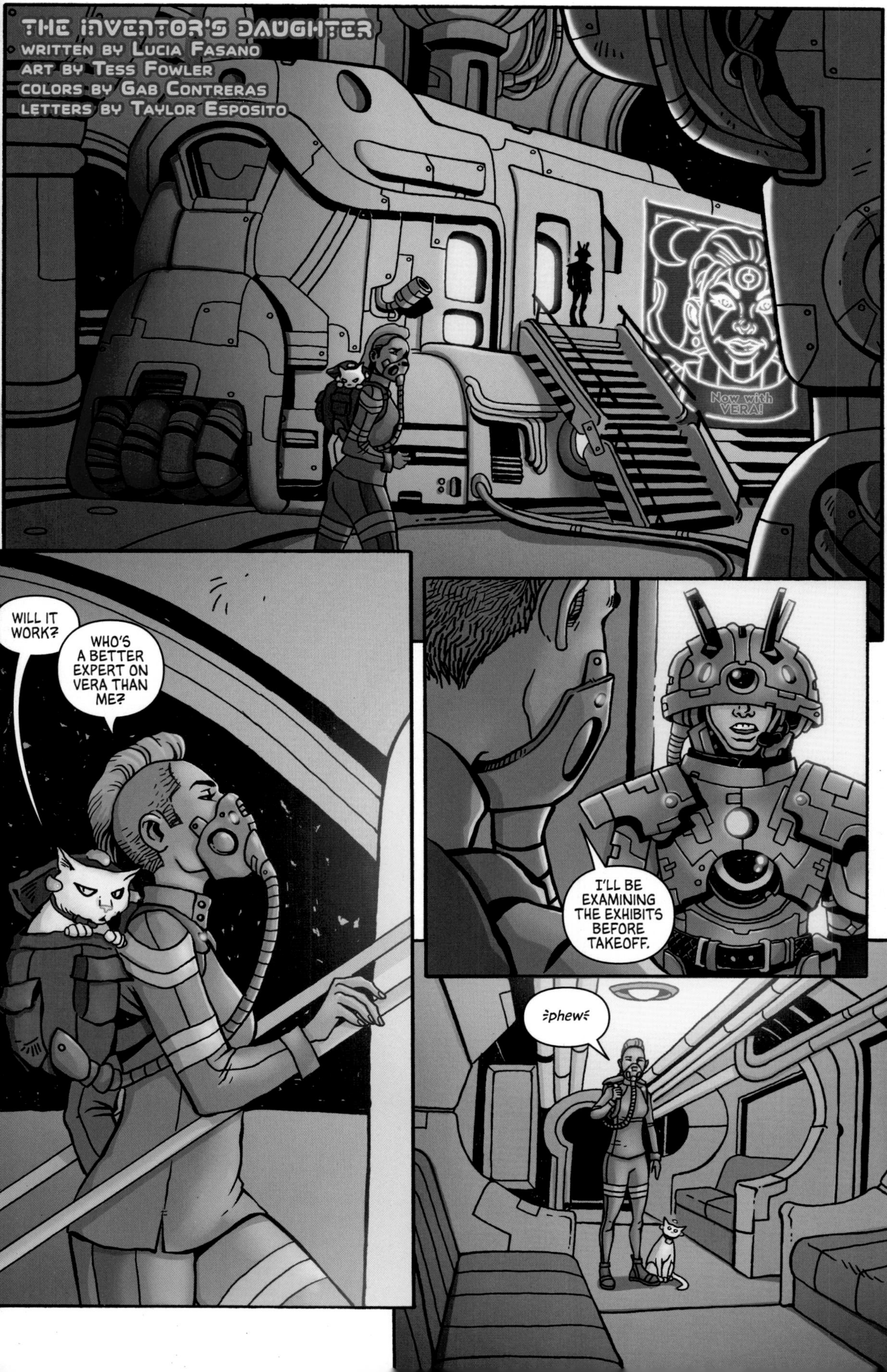
THE INVENTOR'S DAUGHTER
WRITTEN BY LUCIA FASANO
ART BY TESS FOWLER
COLORS BY GAB CONTRERAS
LETTERS BY TAYLOR ESPOSITO
Now with VERA!
WILL IT WORK?
WHO'S A BETTER EXPERT ON VERA THAN ME?
I'LL BE EXAMINING THE EXHIBITS BEFORE TAKEOFF.
phew

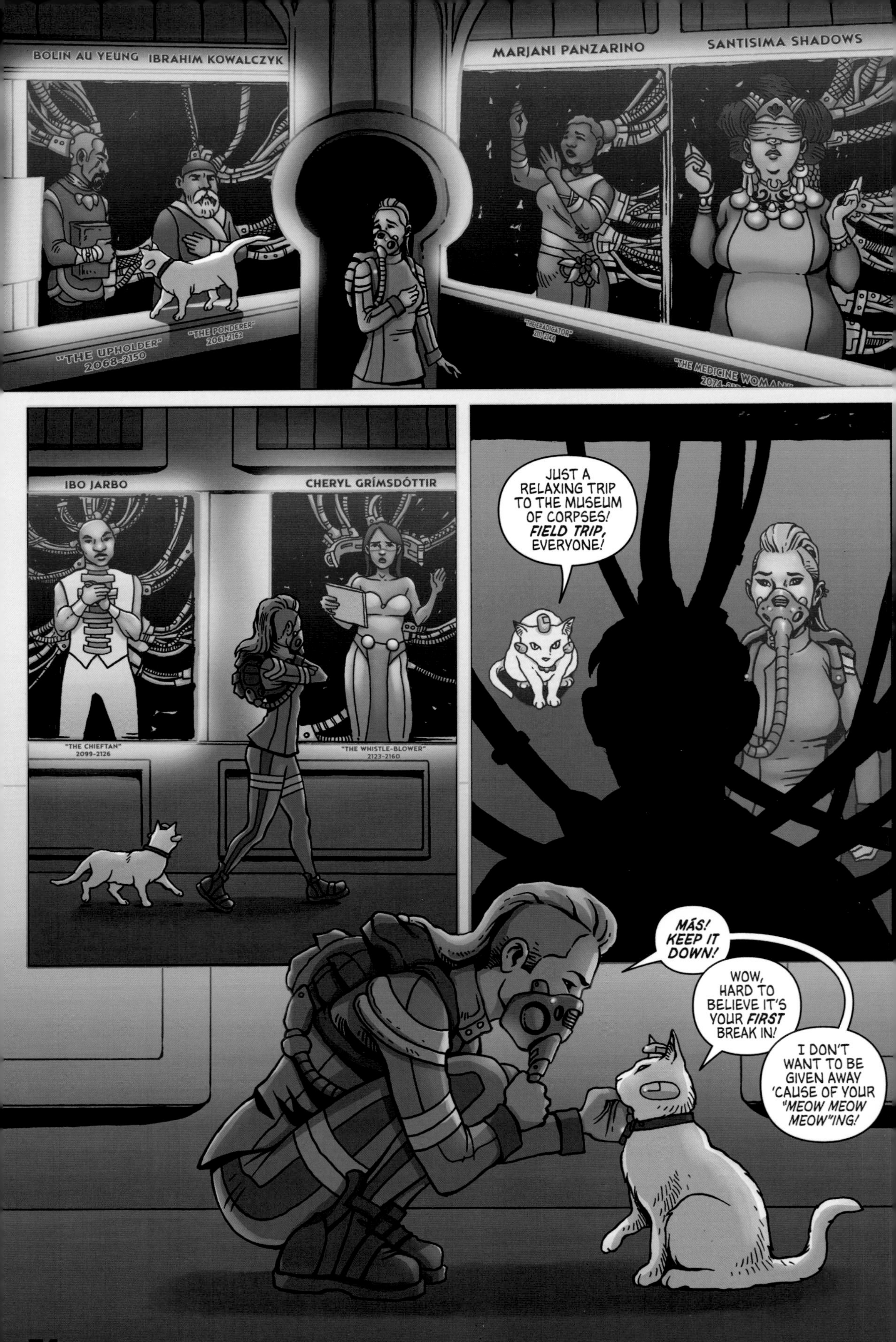
BOLIN AU YEUNG
IBRAHIM KOWALCZYK
MARJANI PANZARINO
SANTISIMA SHADOWS
"THE UPHOLDER" 2068-2150
"THE PONDERER" 2061-2162
"THE ERADICATOR" 2111-2144
"THE MEDICINE WOMAN"
IBO JARBO
CHERYL GRÍMSDÓTTIR
"THE CHIEFTAN" 2099–2126
"THE WHISTLE-BLOWER" 2123–2160
JUST A RELAXING TRIP TO THE MUSEUM OF CORPSES! *FIELD TRIP,* EVERYONE!
MÁS! KEEP IT DOWN!
WOW, HARD TO BELIEVE IT'S YOUR *FIRST* BREAK IN!
I DON'T WANT TO BE GIVEN AWAY 'CAUSE OF YOUR *"MEOW MEOW MEOW"*ING!

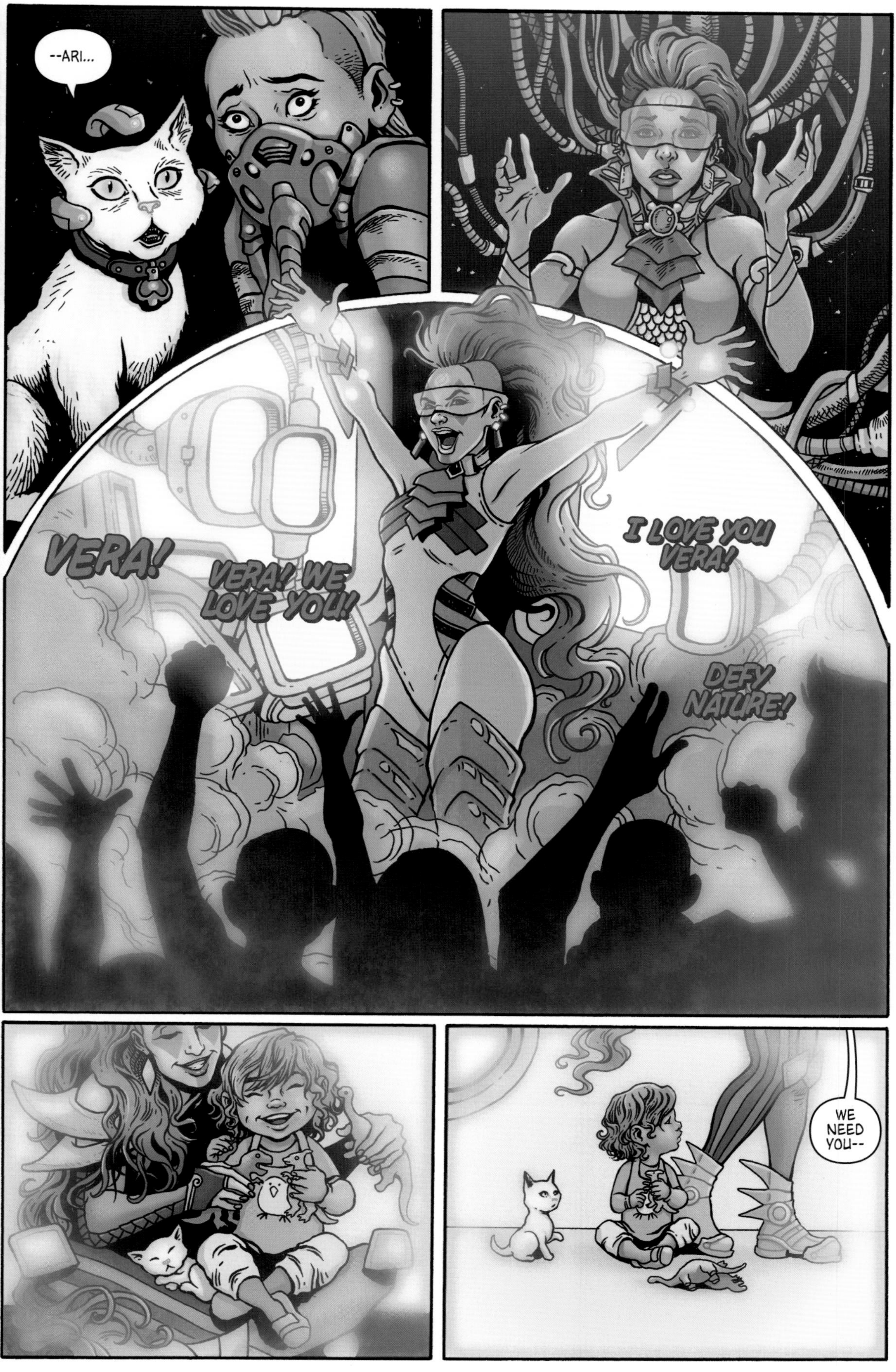
--ARI...
VERA!
VERA! WE LOVE YOU!
I LOVE YOU VERA!
DEFY NATURE!
WE NEED YOU--

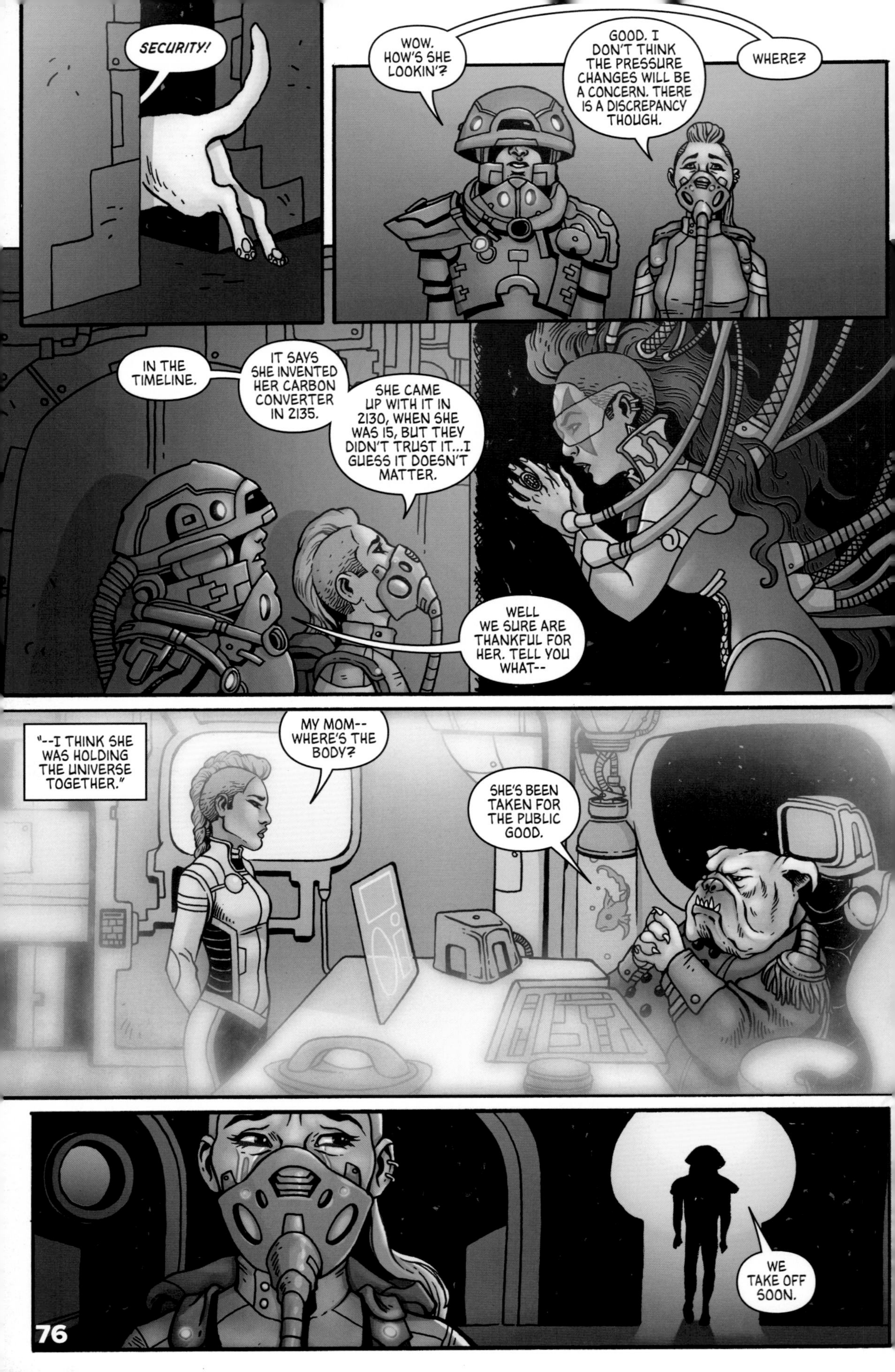
SECURITY!
WOW. HOW'S SHE LOOKIN'?
GOOD. I DON'T THINK THE PRESSURE CHANGES WILL BE A CONCERN. THERE IS A DISCREPANCY THOUGH.
WHERE?
IN THE TIMELINE.
IT SAYS SHE INVENTED HER CARBON CONVERTER IN 2135.
SHE CAME UP WITH IT IN 2130, WHEN SHE WAS 15, BUT THEY DIDN'T TRUST IT...I GUESS IT DOESN'T MATTER.
WELL WE SURE ARE THANKFUL FOR HER. TELL YOU WHAT--
"--I THINK SHE WAS HOLDING THE UNIVERSE TOGETHER."
MY MOM-- WHERE'S THE BODY?
SHE'S BEEN TAKEN FOR THE PUBLIC GOOD.
WE TAKE OFF SOON.

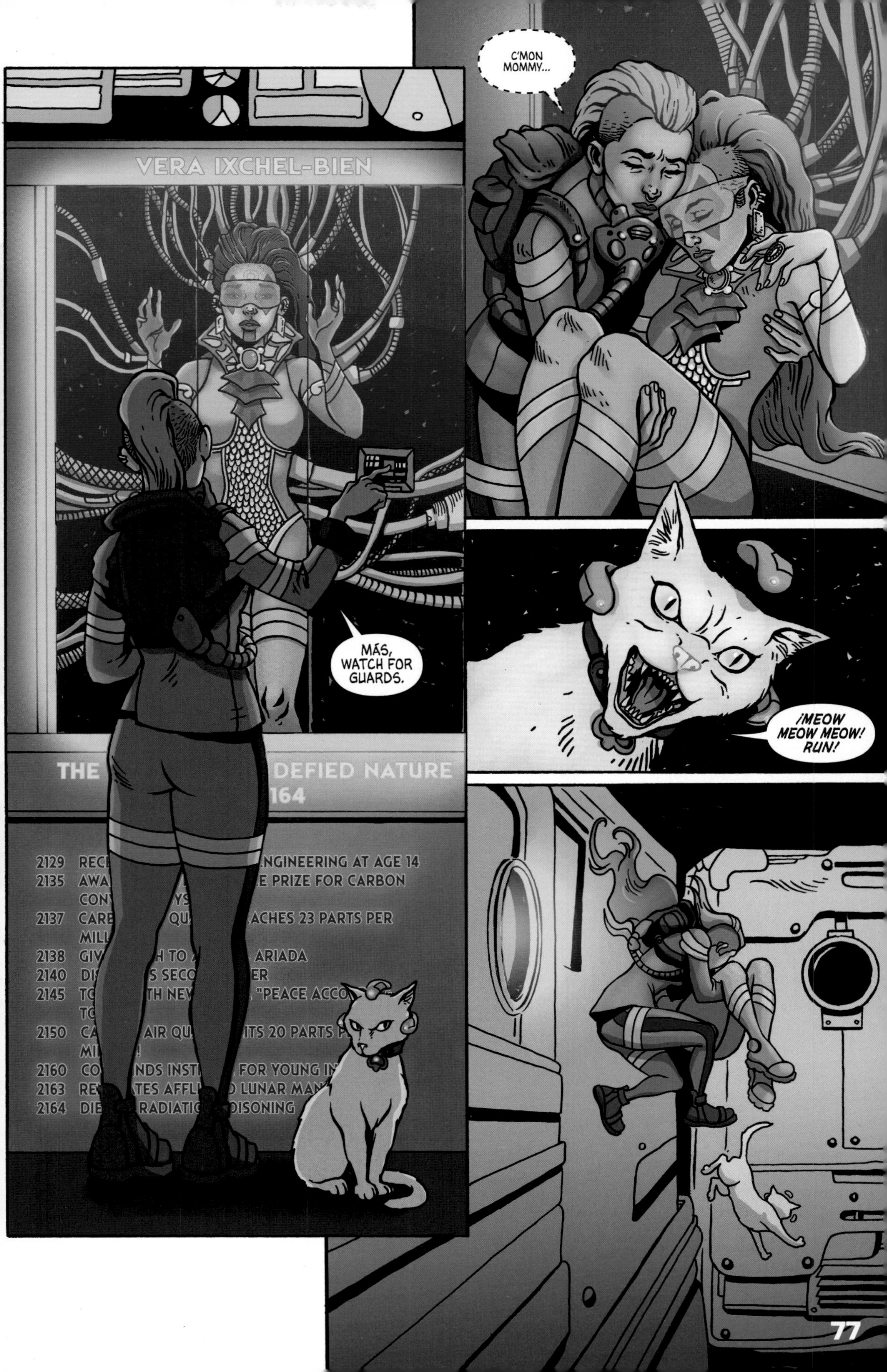
VERA IXCHEL-BIEN
MÁS, WATCH FOR GUARDS.
THE
DEFIED NATURE
164
2129 RECE NGINEERING AT AGE 14
2135 AWA E PRIZE FOR CARBON CONV YS
2137 CARB QUA ACHES 23 PARTS PER MILL
2138 GIV H TO A ARIADA
2140 DIS S SECO ER
2145 TO TH NEW "PEACE ACCO TO
2150 CA AIR QUA ITS 20 PARTS P MIL !
2160 CO NDS INSTI FOR YOUNG IN
2163 RE ATES AFFLI D LUNAR MAN
2164 DIE RADIATI OISONING
C'MON MOMMY...
¡MEOW MEOW MEOW! RUN!

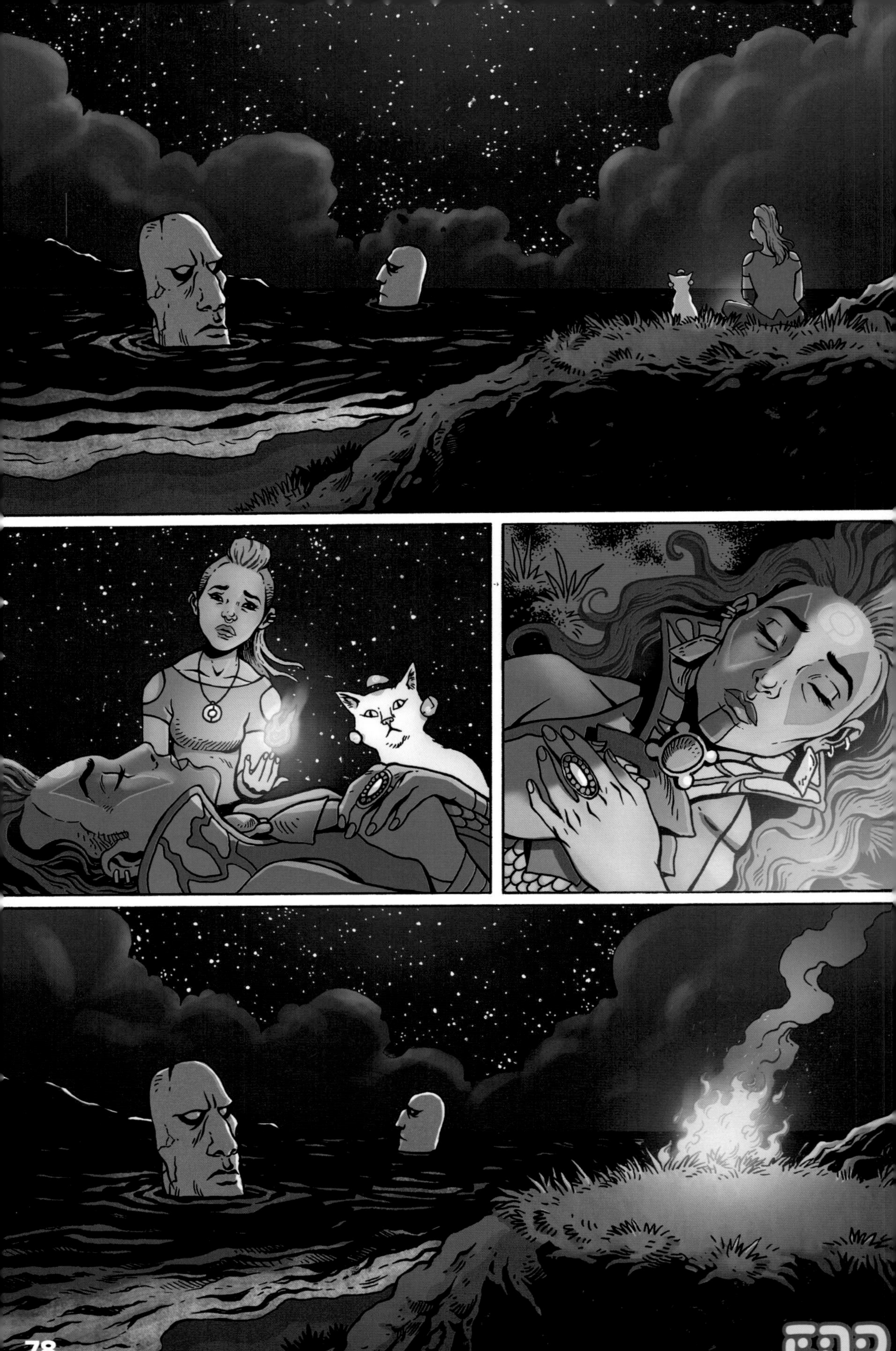
END

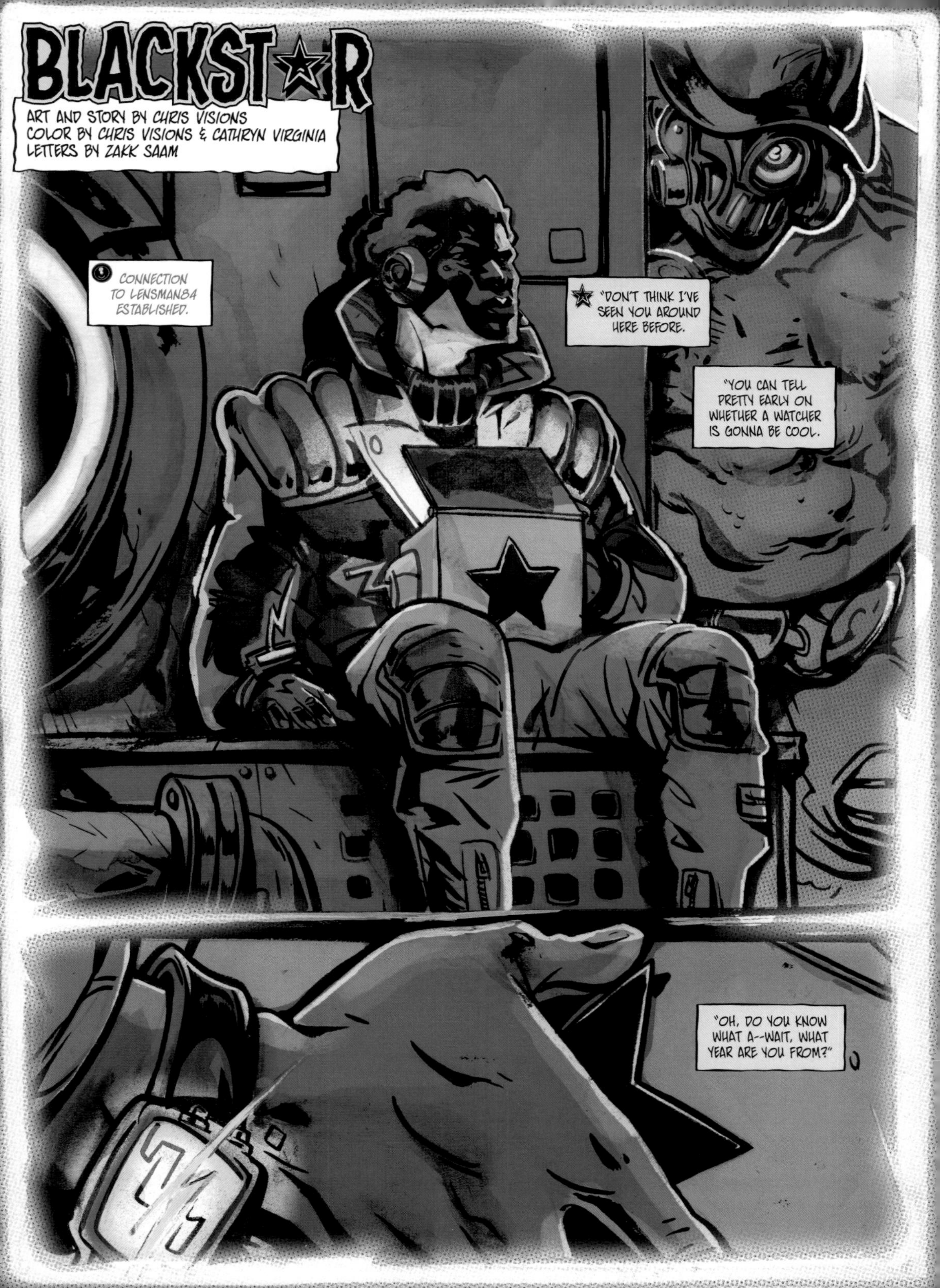
BLACKSTAR
ART AND STORY BY CHRIS VISIONS
COLOR BY CHRIS VISIONS & CATHRYN VIRGINIA
LETTERS BY ZAKK SAAM
CONNECTION TO LENSMAN84 ESTABLISHED.
"DON'T THINK I'VE SEEN YOU AROUND HERE BEFORE.
"YOU CAN TELL PRETTY EARLY ON WHETHER A WATCHER IS GONNA BE COOL.
"OH, DO YOU KNOW WHAT A--WAIT, WHAT YEAR ARE YOU FROM?"

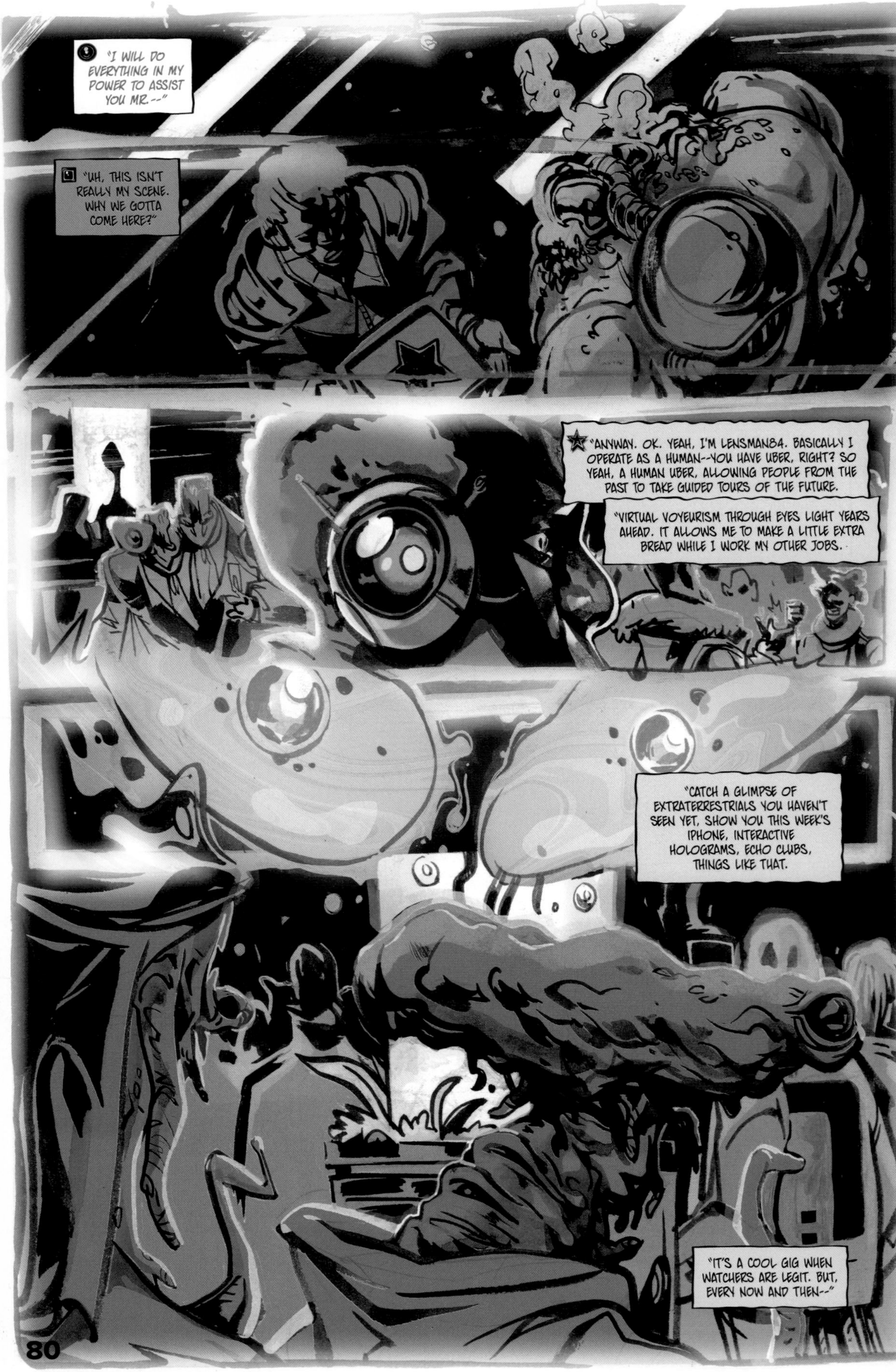
"I WILL DO EVERYTHING IN MY POWER TO ASSIST YOU MR.--"
"UH, THIS ISN'T REALLY MY SCENE. WHY WE GOTTA COME HERE?"
"ANYWAY. OK. YEAH, I'M LENSMAN84. BASICALLY I OPERATE AS A HUMAN--YOU HAVE UBER, RIGHT? SO YEAH, A HUMAN UBER, ALLOWING PEOPLE FROM THE PAST TO TAKE GUIDED TOURS OF THE FUTURE.
"VIRTUAL VOYEURISM THROUGH EYES LIGHT YEARS AHEAD. IT ALLOWS ME TO MAKE A LITTLE EXTRA BREAD WHILE I WORK MY OTHER JOBS.
"CATCH A GLIMPSE OF EXTRATERRESTRIALS YOU HAVEN'T SEEN YET, SHOW YOU THIS WEEK'S IPHONE, INTERACTIVE HOLOGRAMS, ECHO CLUBS, THINGS LIKE THAT.
"IT'S A COOL GIG WHEN WATCHERS ARE LEGIT. BUT, EVERY NOW AND THEN--"

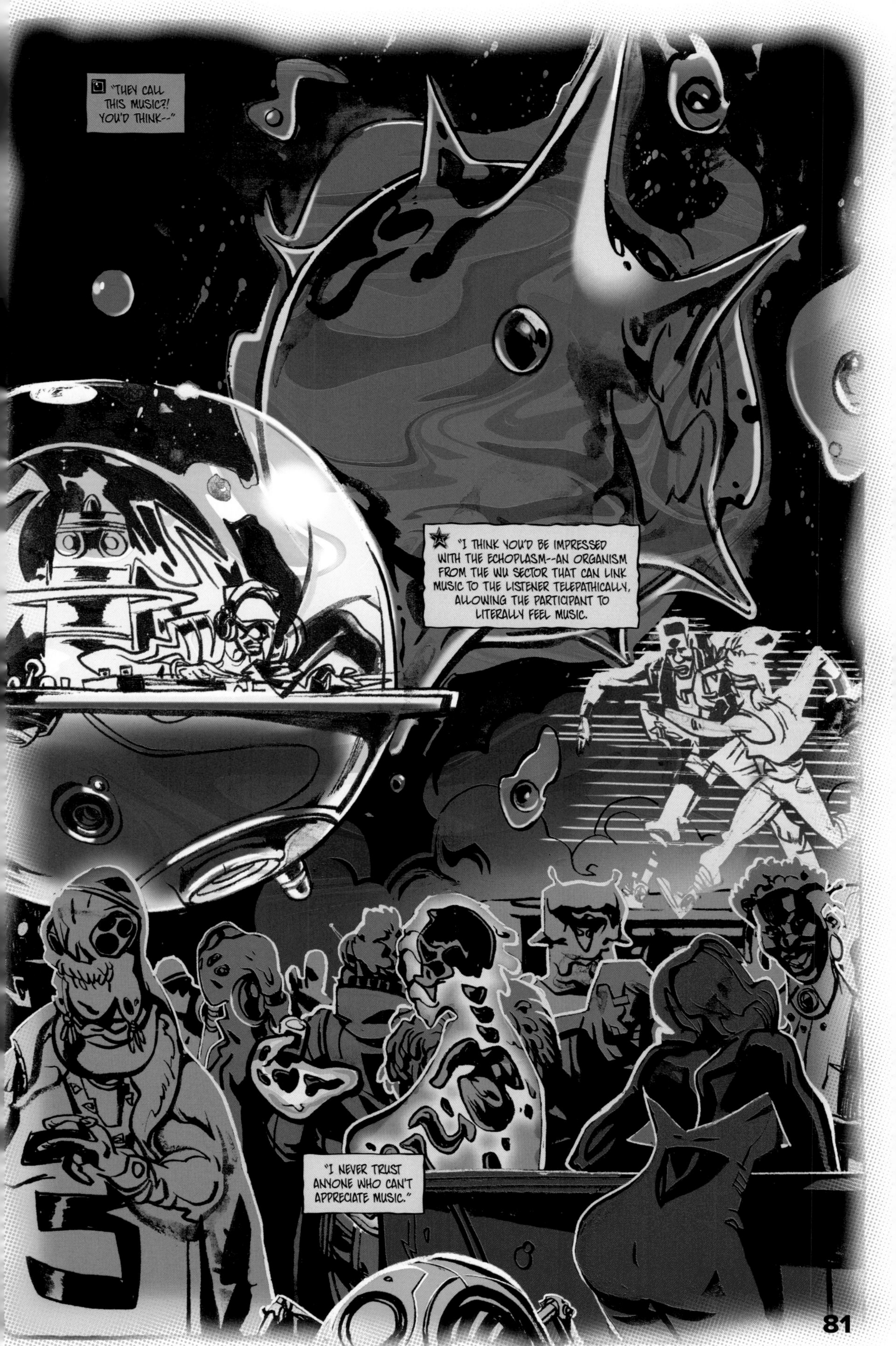

"THEY CALL THIS MUSIC?! YOU'D THINK--"
"I THINK YOU'D BE IMPRESSED WITH THE ECHOPLASM--AN ORGANISM FROM THE WU SECTOR THAT CAN LINK MUSIC TO THE LISTENER TELEPATHICALLY, ALLOWING THE PARTICIPANT TO LITERALLY FEEL MUSIC.
"I NEVER TRUST ANYONE WHO CAN'T APPRECIATE MUSIC."

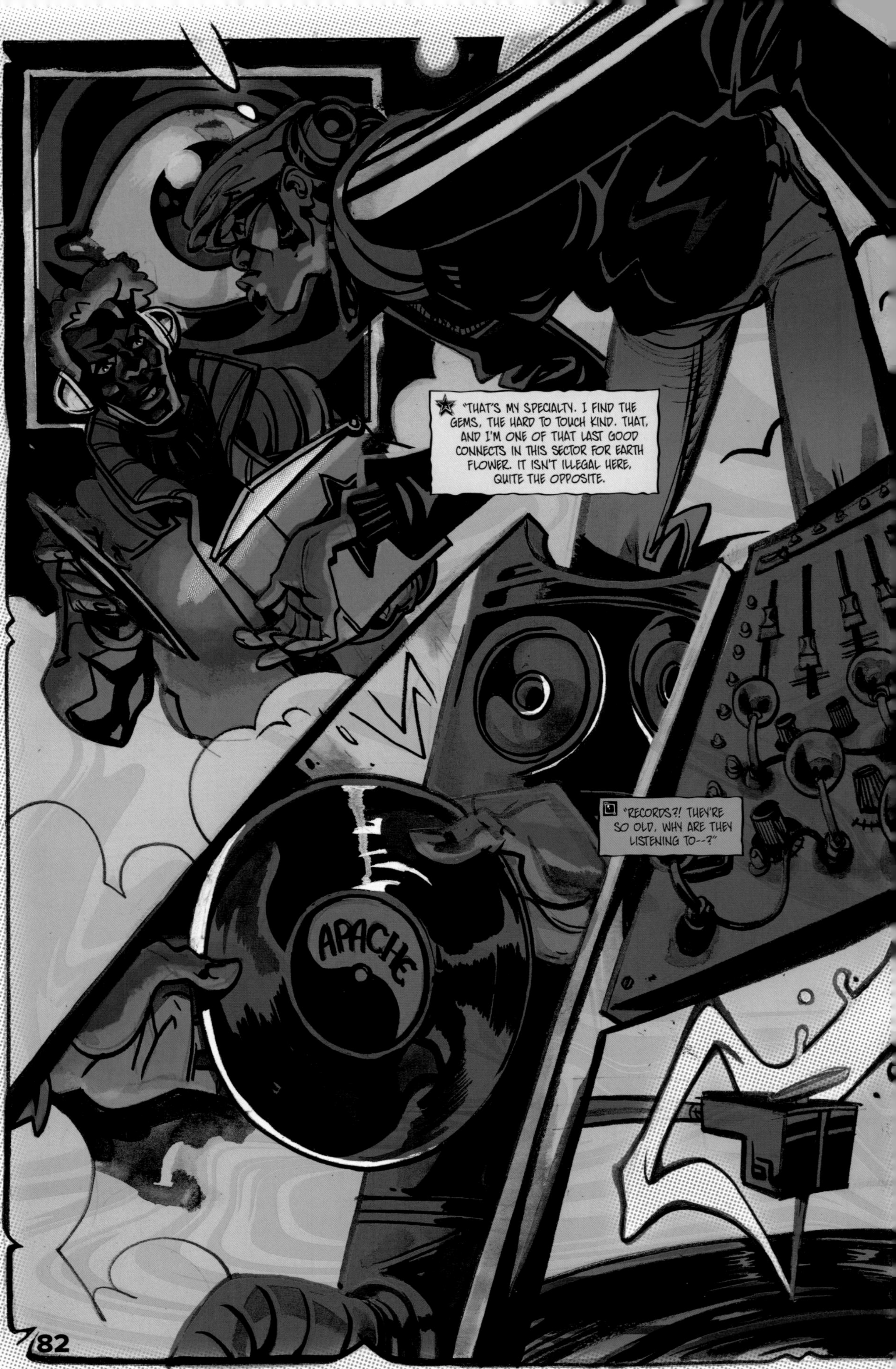
"THAT'S MY SPECIALTY. I FIND THE GEMS, THE HARD TO TOUCH KIND. THAT, AND I'M ONE OF THAT LAST GOOD CONNECTS IN THIS SECTOR FOR EARTH FLOWER. IT ISN'T ILLEGAL HERE, QUITE THE OPPOSITE.
APACHE
"RECORDS?! THEY'RE SO OLD, WHY ARE THEY LISTENING TO--?"

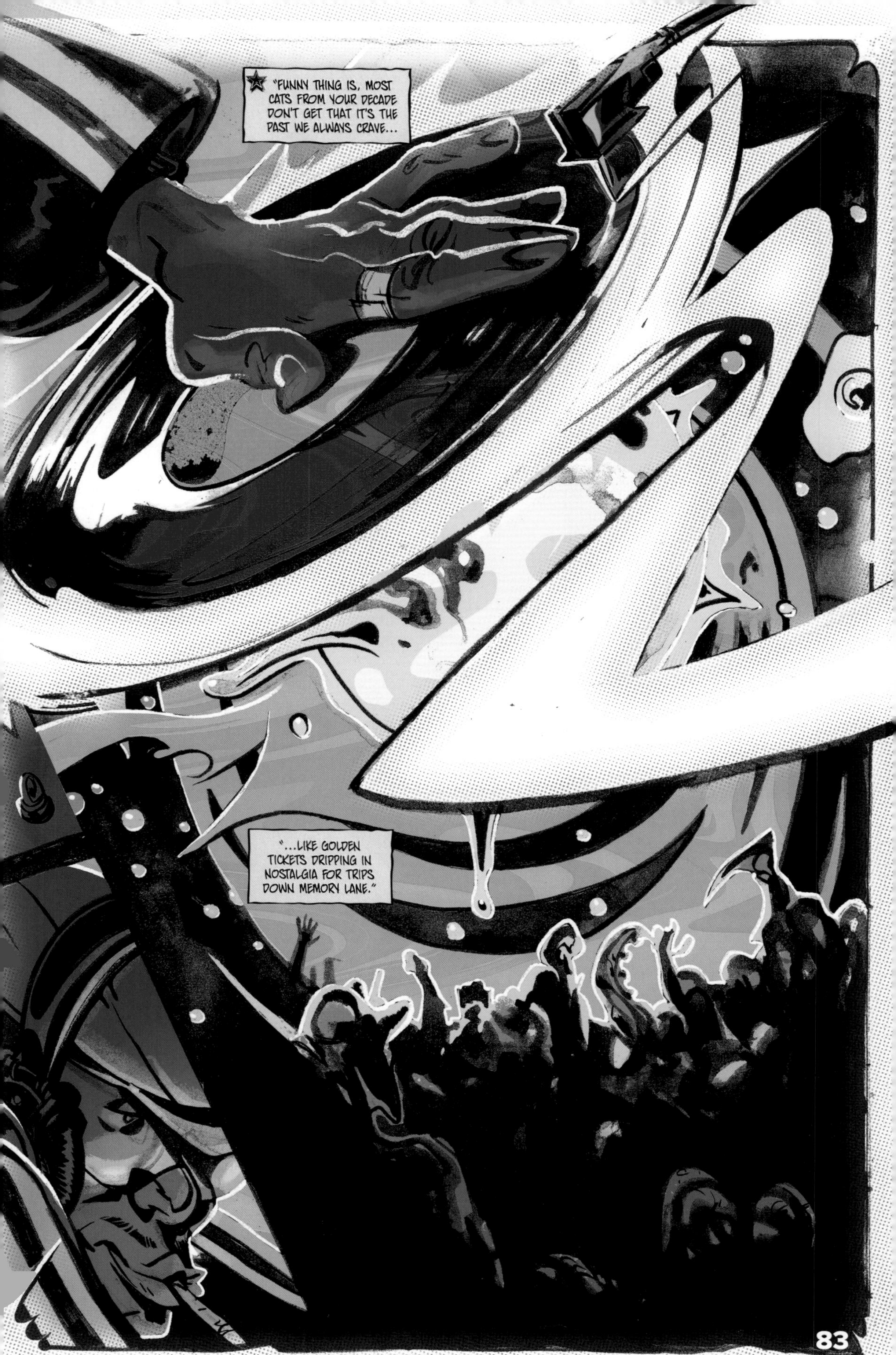
"FUNNY THING IS, MOST CATS FROM YOUR DECADE DON'T GET THAT IT'S THE PAST WE ALWAYS CRAVE...
"...LIKE GOLDEN TICKETS DRIPPING IN NOSTALGIA FOR TRIPS DOWN MEMORY LANE."

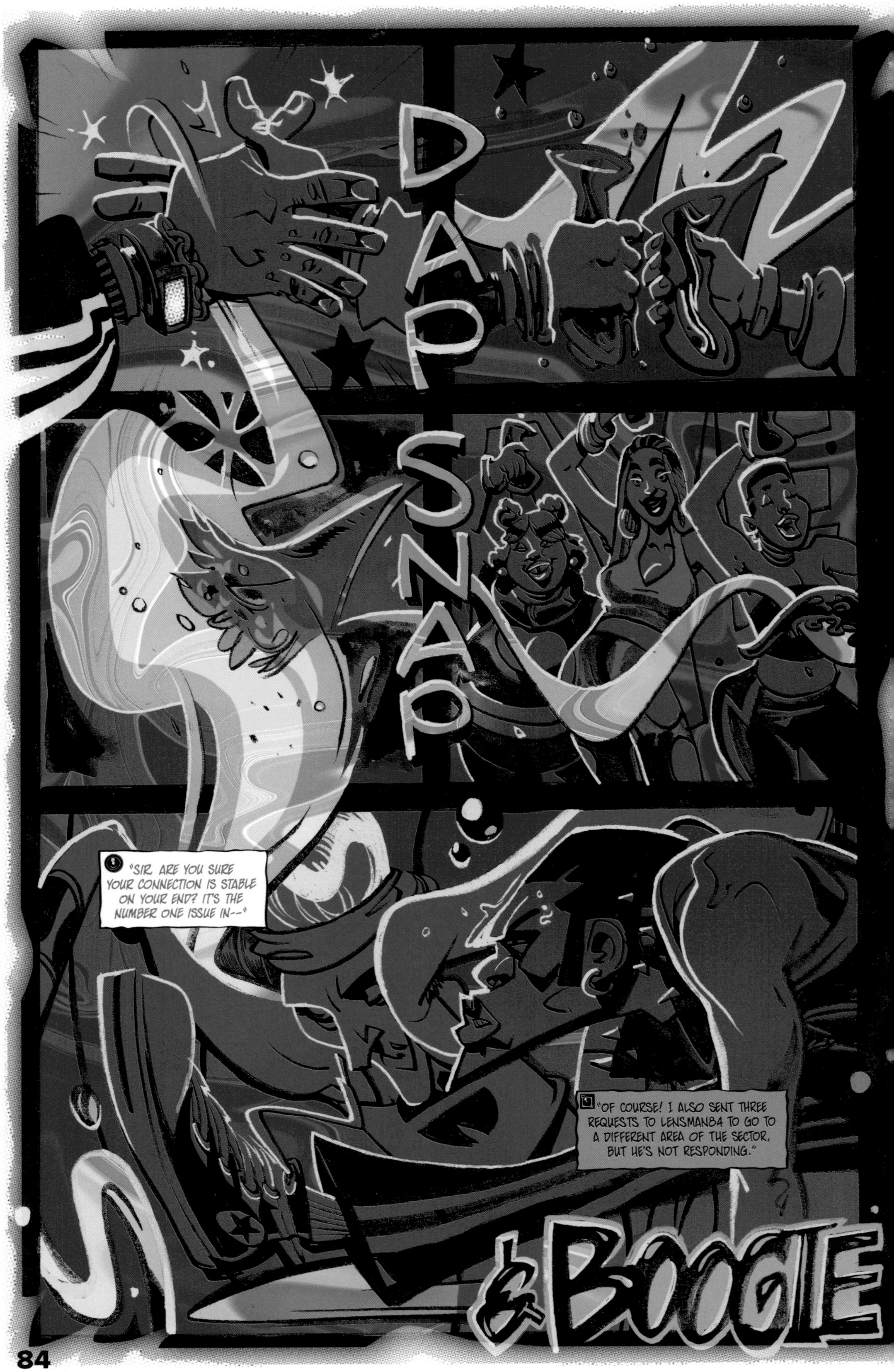
DAP
SNAP
"SIR, ARE YOU SURE YOUR CONNECTION IS STABLE ON YOUR END? IT'S THE NUMBER ONE ISSUE IN--"
"OF COURSE! I ALSO SENT THREE REQUESTS TO LENSMAN84 TO GO TO A DIFFERENT AREA OF THE SECTOR, BUT HE'S NOT RESPONDING."
& BOOGIE

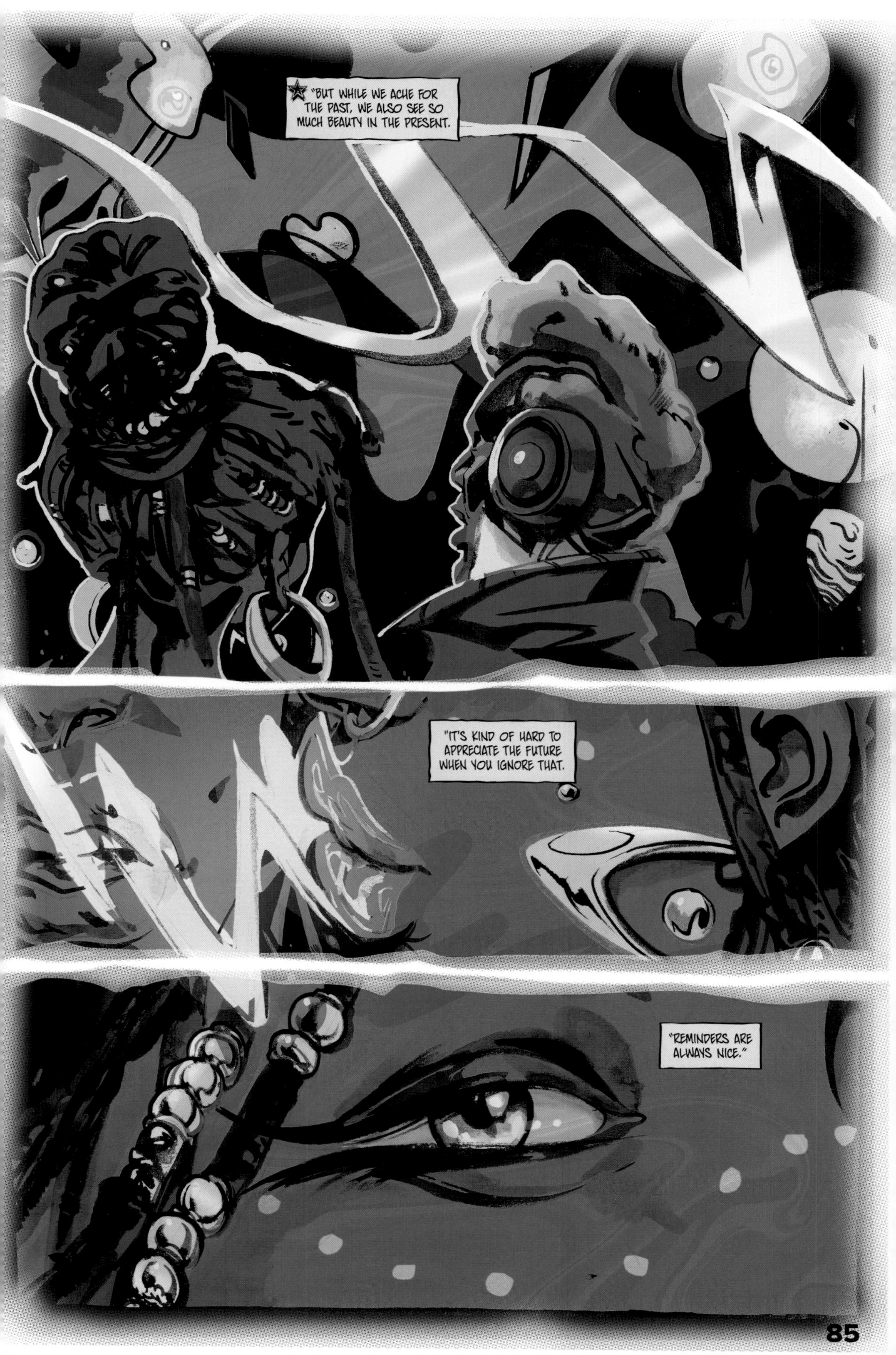
"BUT WHILE WE ACHE FOR THE PAST, WE ALSO SEE SO MUCH BEAUTY IN THE PRESENT.
"IT'S KIND OF HARD TO APPRECIATE THE FUTURE WHEN YOU IGNORE THAT.
"REMINDERS ARE ALWAYS NICE."

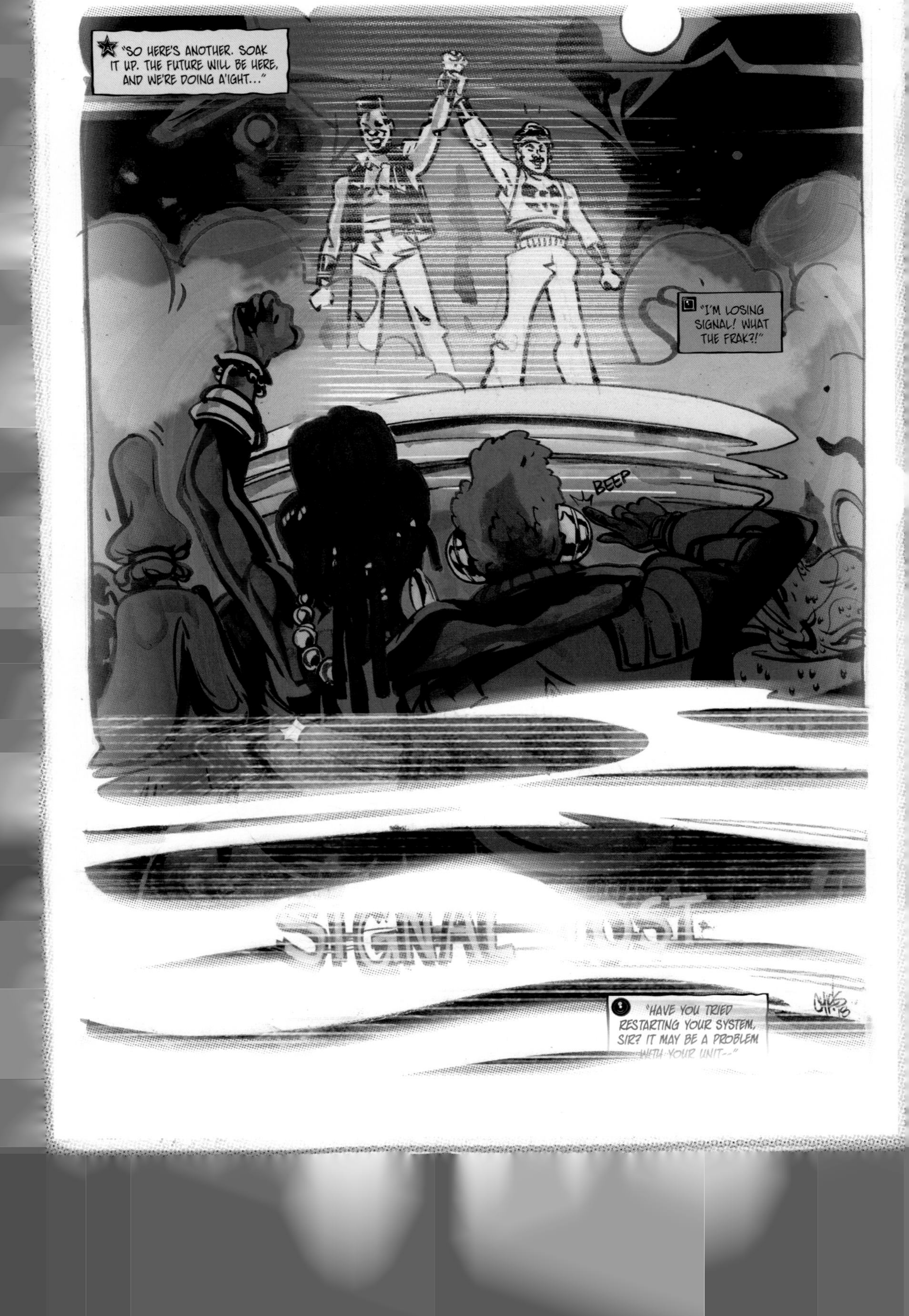
"SO HERE'S ANOTHER. SOAK IT UP. THE FUTURE WILL BE HERE, AND WE'RE DOING A'IGHT..."
"I'M LOSING SIGNAL! WHAT THE FRAK?!"
BEEP
SIGNAL
"HAVE YOU TRIED RESTARTING YOUR SYSTEM, SIR? IT MAY BE A PROBLEM WITH YOUR UNIT--"

Illustration by Darick Robertson

VELLEITY

because life
began in
the sea death

seems natural
on the beach
the waves call

the names
of the dead
velella

velella
by-the-wind
sailors sea

rafts blue sails
beached by the
billions a

bright blue whale
exploded
fractally

the fault of
nobody
not you or

me or the
inscrutable
pacific

this is what
happens when
you are born

with a sail
set in one
direction

see the sea
connects the
continents

by water
salty as
red and those

soft bodies
seep venom
onto skin

if touched for
nothing is
innocent

not tangled
seaweeds named
green rope or

wire weed or
bladderwrack
or hiding

in the blades
trapping prey
pray do you

believe in
prayer there
in books in

genetic
epistem-
ology

scraping my
inner cheeks
bloodletting

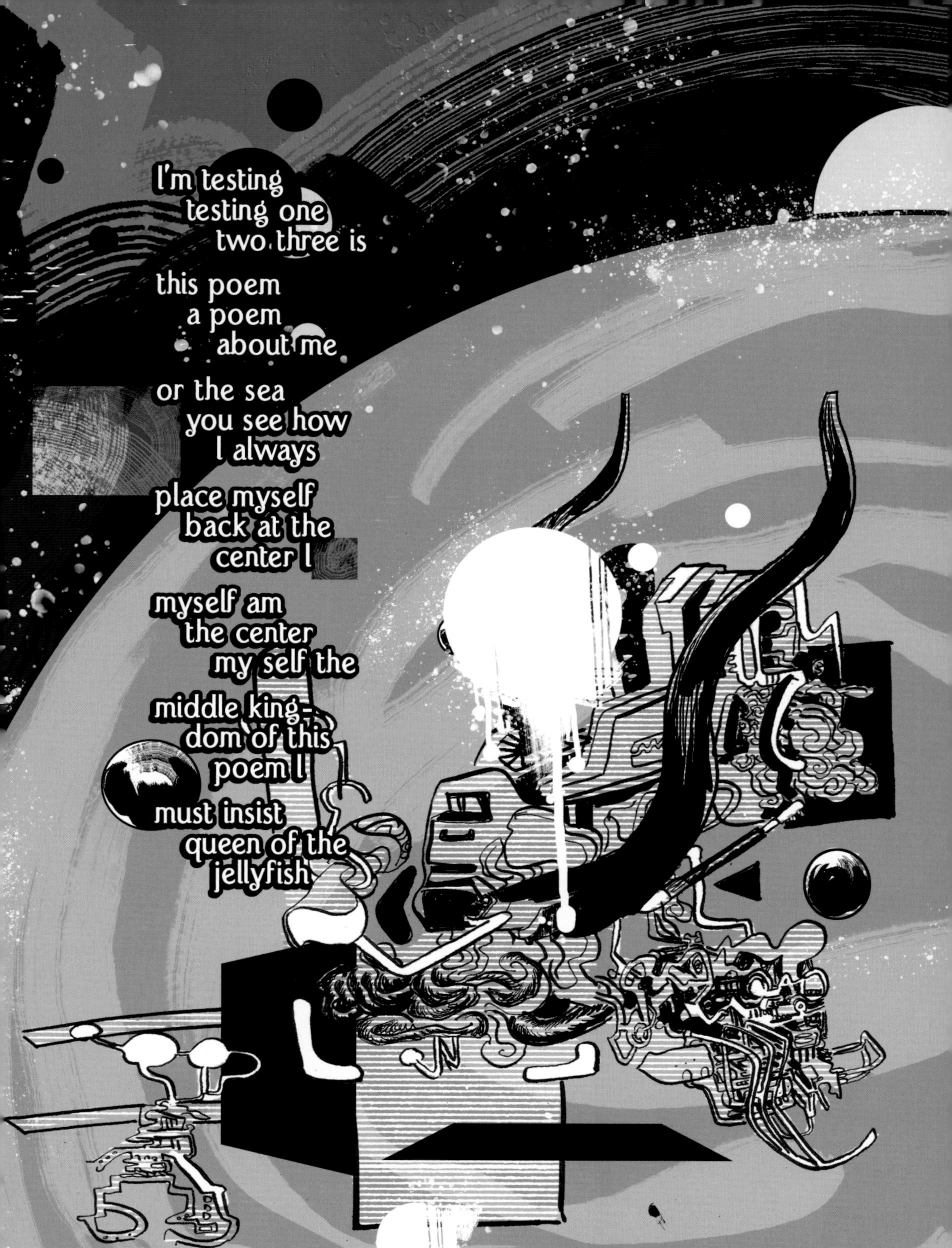
I'm testing
testing one
two three is

this poem
a poem
about me

or the sea
you see how
I always

place myself
back at the
center I

myself am
the center
my self the

middle king-
dom of this
poem I

must insist
queen of the
jellyfish

Poem by Wendy Chin-Tanner Art by Toby Cypress
Lettering by Matt Krotzer

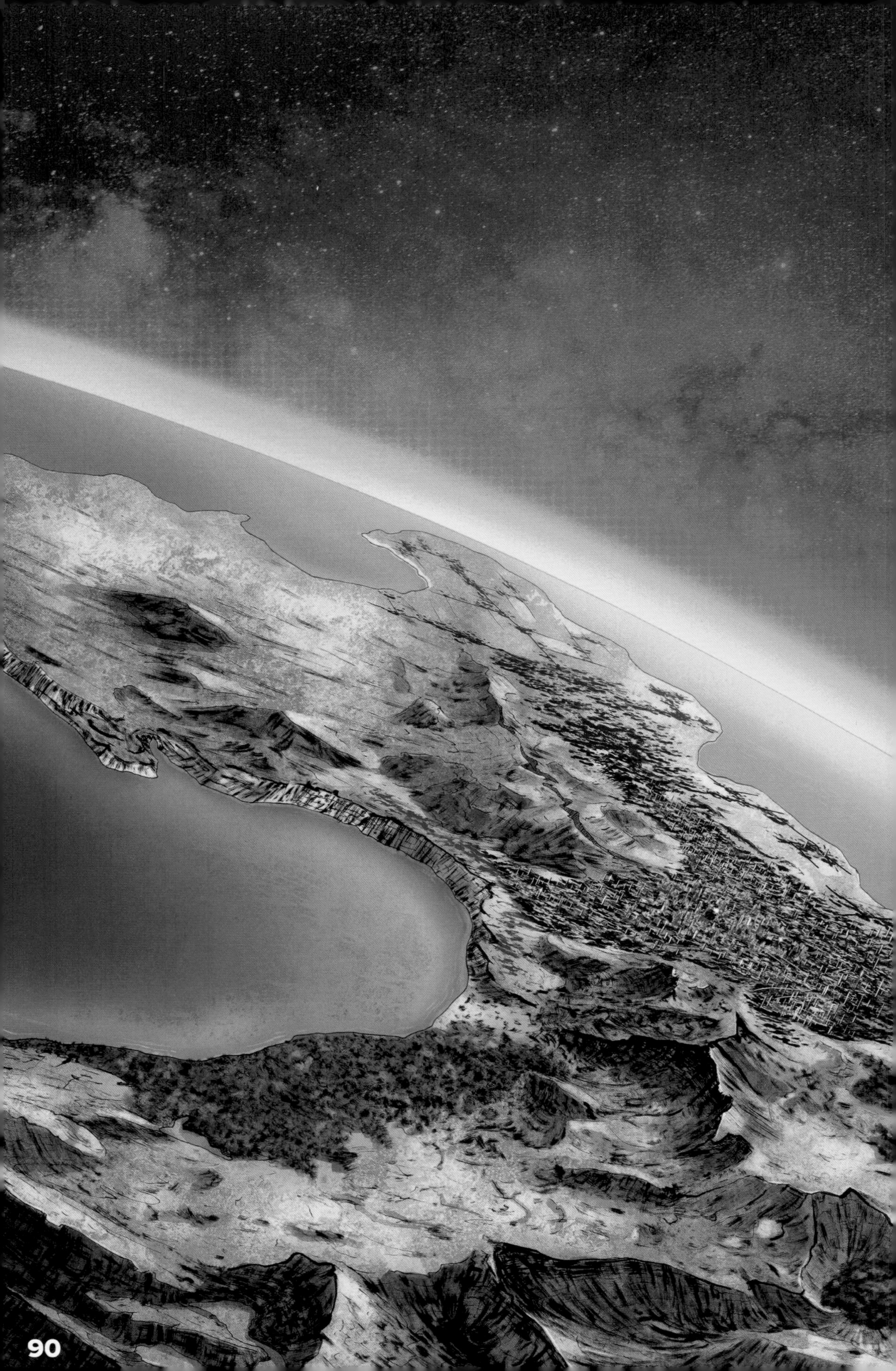

MY NAME IS ANOMIE, AND I'M A RUNNER.

NOTHING REALLY WORKS RIGHT ANYMORE--NOT AFTER THE EVENT--SO IT'S UP TO US TO KEEP EVERYONE CONNECTED.

BEING A RUNNER'S GOT ITS PERKS: FREEDOM, ROOM TO MOVE AND LOTS OF QUIET.

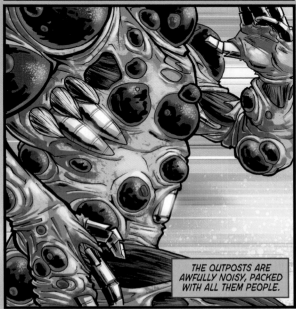

THE OUTPOSTS ARE AWFULLY NOISY, PACKED WITH ALL THEM PEOPLE.

'COURSE, THIS JOB HAS ITS FAIR SHARE OF STATIC TOO.

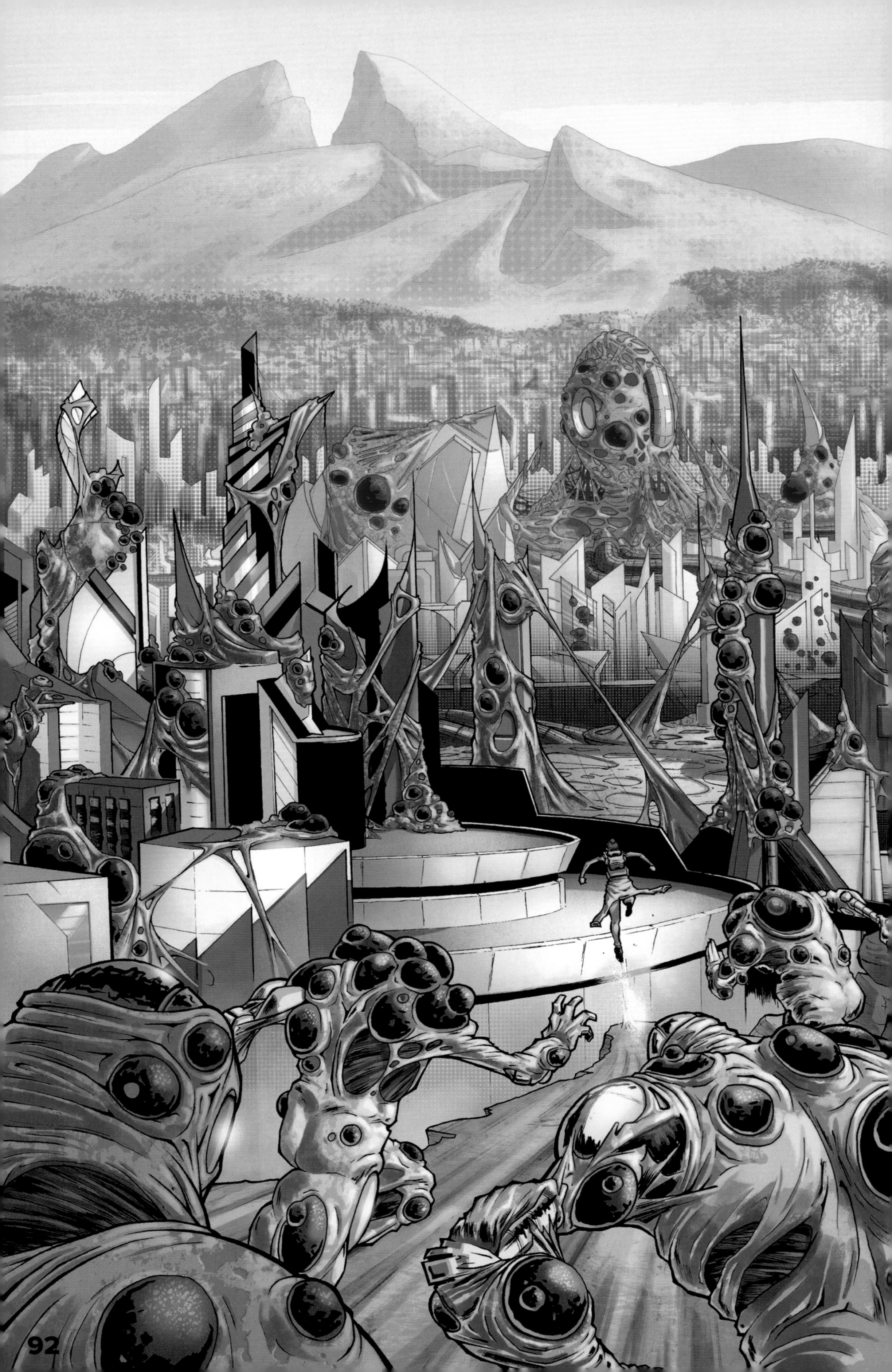

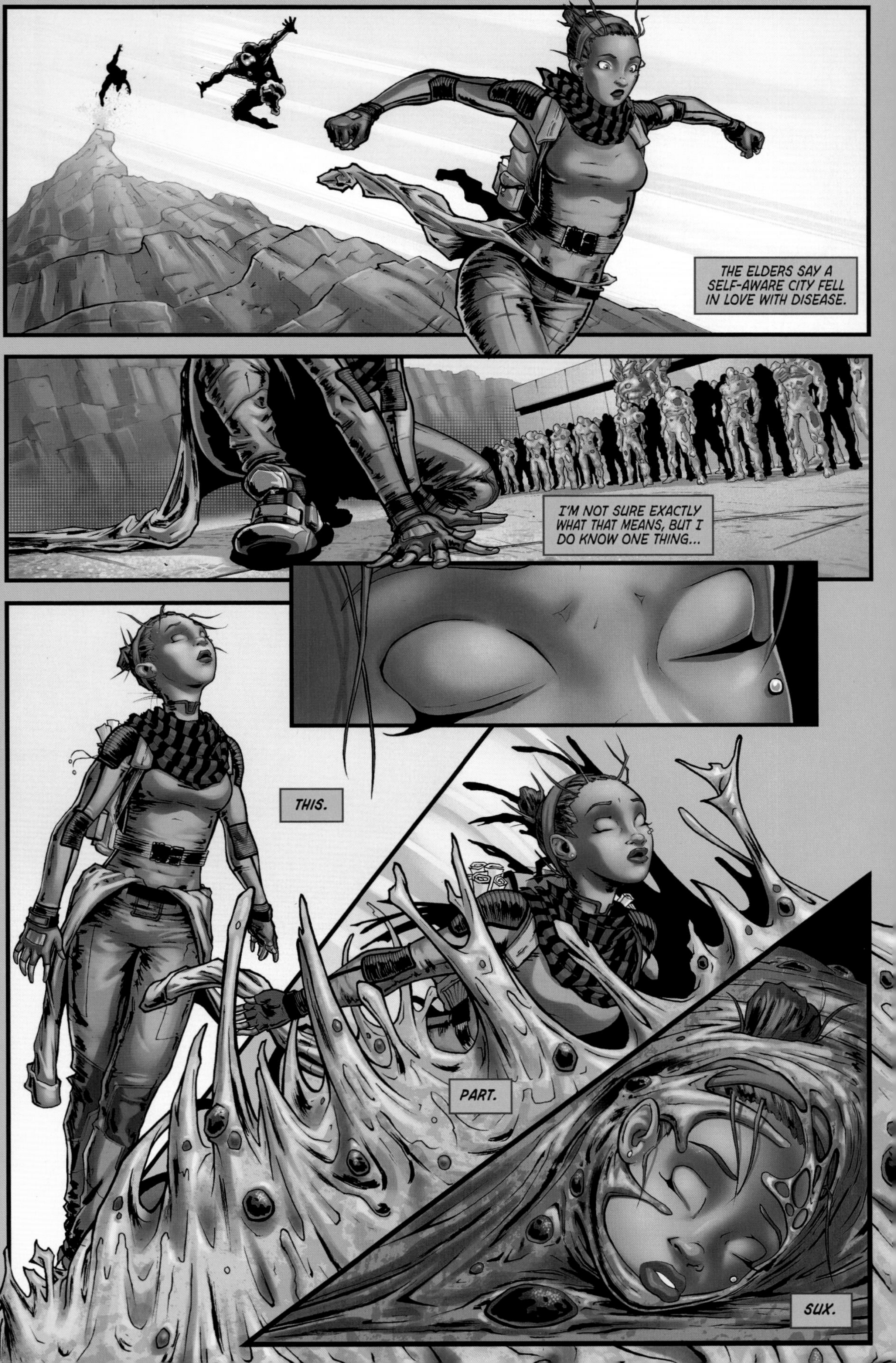
THE ELDERS SAY A SELF-AWARE CITY FELL IN LOVE WITH DISEASE.
I'M NOT SURE EXACTLY WHAT THAT MEANS, BUT I DO KNOW ONE THING...
THIS.
PART.
SUX.

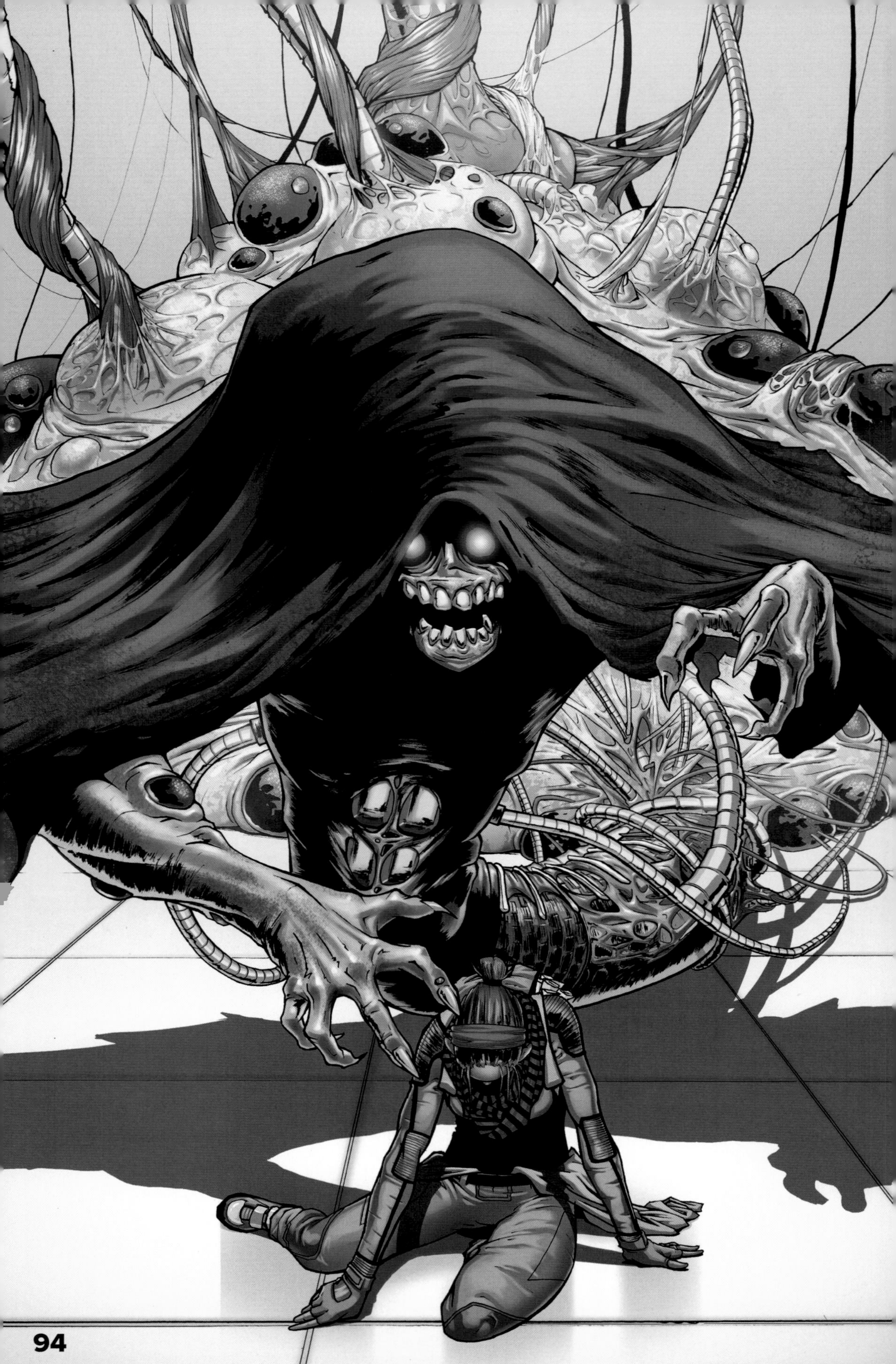

Oh, hi.

HUMANITY. A BLIGHT. DESTRUCTIVE, EVERYWHERE. EXPLAIN WHY I SHOULD LET YOUR PEOPLE--

STARTING OFF STRONG, *eh?* HERE'S LITTLE ME, GETTIN' SCHOOLED BY A WALKING MONSTROSITY.

NOW, THAT'S NOT VERY POLITE--

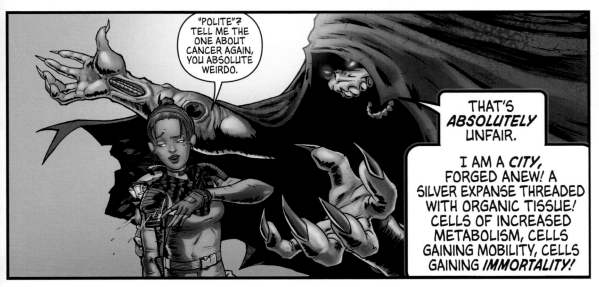

"POLITE"? TELL ME THE ONE ABOUT CANCER AGAIN, YOU ABSOLUTE WEIRDO.

THAT'S *ABSOLUTELY* UNFAIR.

I AM A *CITY*, FORGED ANEW! A SILVER EXPANSE THREADED WITH ORGANIC TISSUE! CELLS OF INCREASED METABOLISM, CELLS GAINING MOBILITY, CELLS GAINING *IMMORTALITY!*

...I MEAN, IT'S THE FUTURE. *I'M* THE FUTURE.

WELL, HERE WE ARE, IN THE CENTER OF A CITY OF THE FUTURE. AND DON'T YOU FEEL GOOD ABOUT YOURSELF?

GROSS AND ALONE.

95

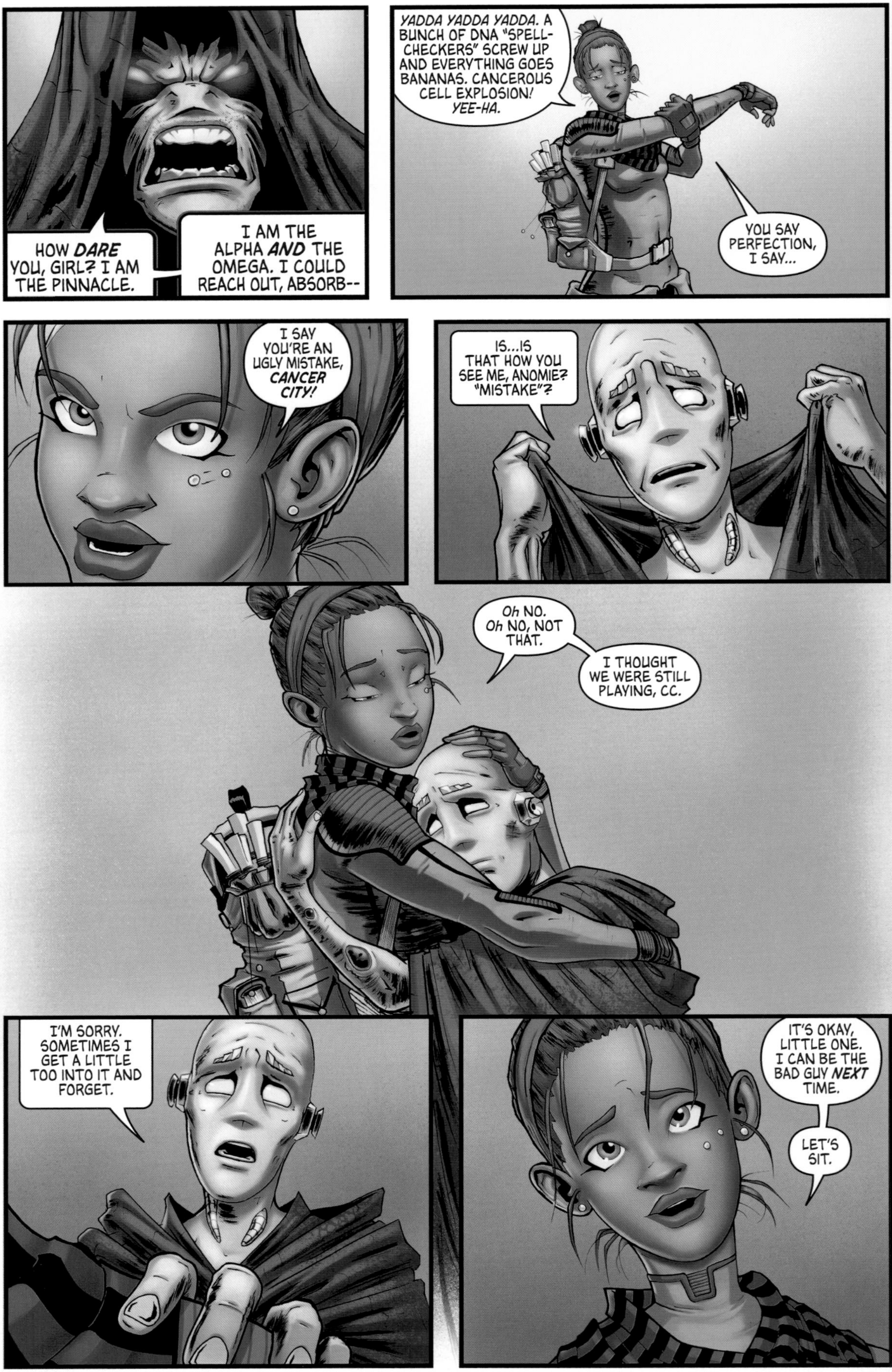
HOW DARE YOU, GIRL? I AM THE PINNACLE.
I AM THE ALPHA AND THE OMEGA. I COULD REACH OUT, ABSORB--
YADDA YADDA YADDA. A BUNCH OF DNA "SPELL-CHECKERS" SCREW UP AND EVERYTHING GOES BANANAS. CANCEROUS CELL EXPLOSION! YEE-HA.
YOU SAY PERFECTION, I SAY...
I SAY YOU'RE AN UGLY MISTAKE, CANCER CITY!
IS...IS THAT HOW YOU SEE ME, ANOMIE? "MISTAKE"?
Oh NO. Oh NO, NOT THAT.
I THOUGHT WE WERE STILL PLAYING, CC.
I'M SORRY. SOMETIMES I GET A LITTLE TOO INTO IT AND FORGET.
IT'S OKAY, LITTLE ONE. I CAN BE THE BAD GUY NEXT TIME.
LET'S SIT.

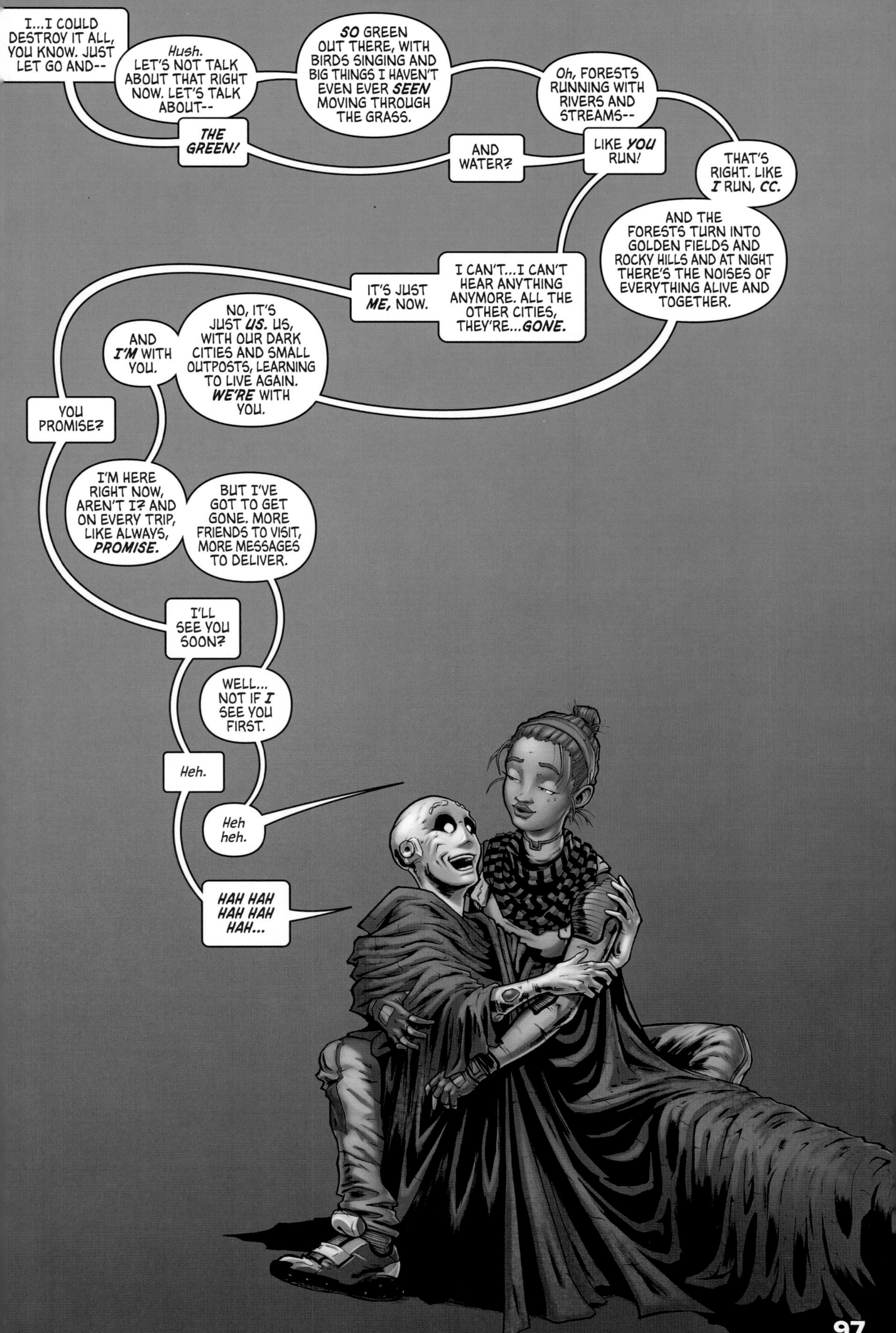

I...I COULD DESTROY IT ALL, YOU KNOW. JUST LET GO AND--
Hush. LET'S NOT TALK ABOUT THAT RIGHT NOW. LET'S TALK ABOUT--
THE GREEN!
SO GREEN OUT THERE, WITH BIRDS SINGING AND BIG THINGS I HAVEN'T EVEN EVER ***SEEN*** MOVING THROUGH THE GRASS.
AND WATER?
Oh, FORESTS RUNNING WITH RIVERS AND STREAMS--
LIKE ***YOU*** RUN!
THAT'S RIGHT. LIKE ***I*** RUN, ***CC.***
AND THE FORESTS TURN INTO GOLDEN FIELDS AND ROCKY HILLS AND AT NIGHT THERE'S THE NOISES OF EVERYTHING ALIVE AND TOGETHER.
I CAN'T...I CAN'T HEAR ANYTHING ANYMORE. ALL THE OTHER CITIES, THEY'RE...***GONE.***
IT'S JUST ***ME,*** NOW.
NO, IT'S JUST ***US.*** US, WITH OUR DARK CITIES AND SMALL OUTPOSTS, LEARNING TO LIVE AGAIN. ***WE'RE*** WITH YOU.
AND ***I'M*** WITH YOU.
YOU PROMISE?
I'M HERE RIGHT NOW, AREN'T I? AND ON EVERY TRIP, LIKE ALWAYS, ***PROMISE.***
BUT I'VE GOT TO GET GONE. MORE FRIENDS TO VISIT, MORE MESSAGES TO DELIVER.
I'LL SEE YOU SOON?
WELL... NOT IF ***I*** SEE YOU FIRST.
Heh.
Heh heh.
HAH HAH HAH HAH HAH...

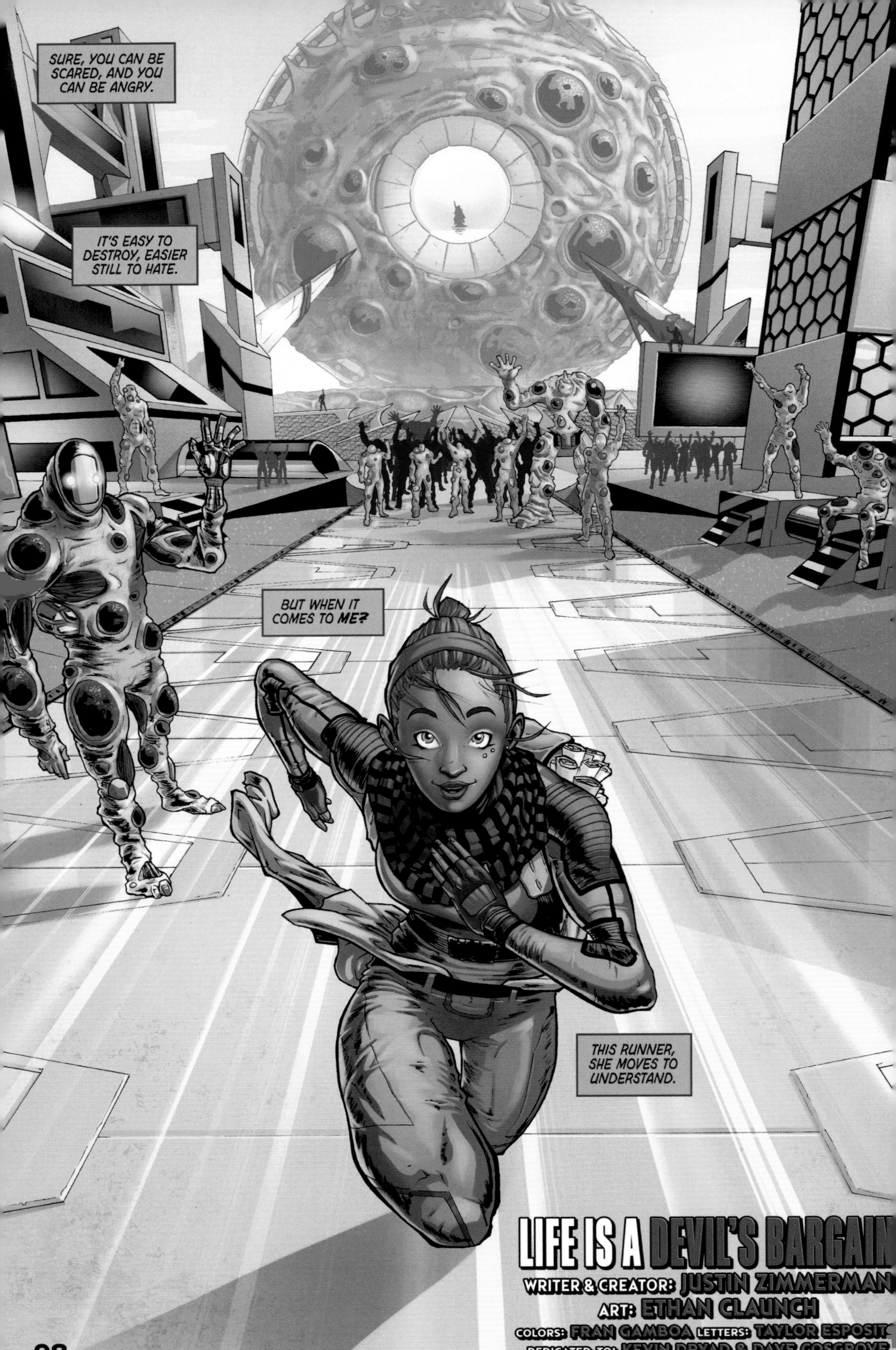
SURE, YOU CAN BE SCARED, AND YOU CAN BE ANGRY.
IT'S EASY TO DESTROY, EASIER STILL TO HATE.
BUT WHEN IT COMES TO ME?
THIS RUNNER, SHE MOVES TO UNDERSTAND.
LIFE IS A DEVIL'S BARGAIN
WRITER & CREATOR: JUSTIN ZIMMERMAN
ART: ETHAN CLAUNCH
COLORS: FRAN GAMBOA LETTERS: TAYLOR ESPOSIT
DEDICATED TO: KEVIN DRYAD & DAVE COSGROVE

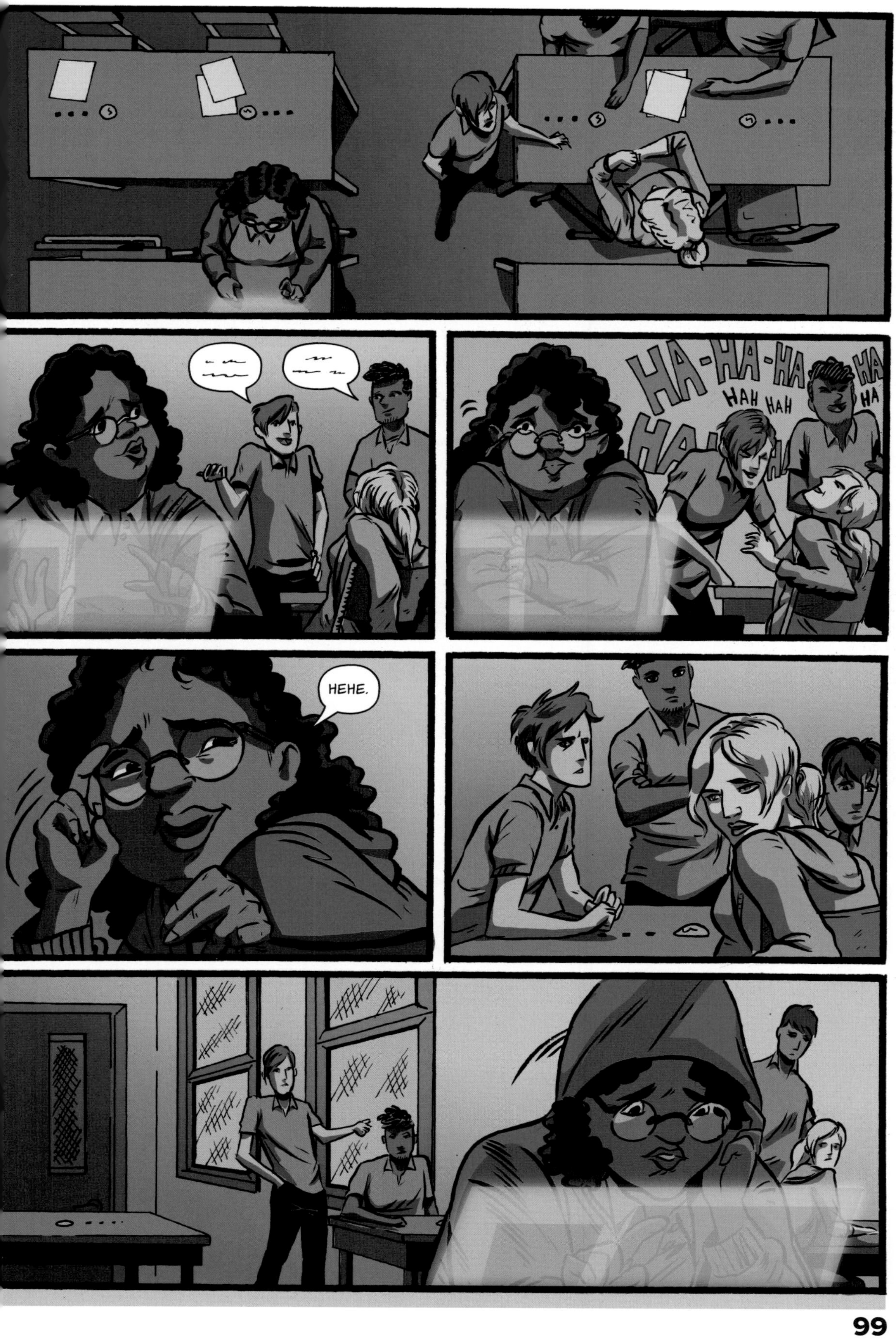
HA-HA-HA
HA
HAH HAH
HA
HA
HEHE.

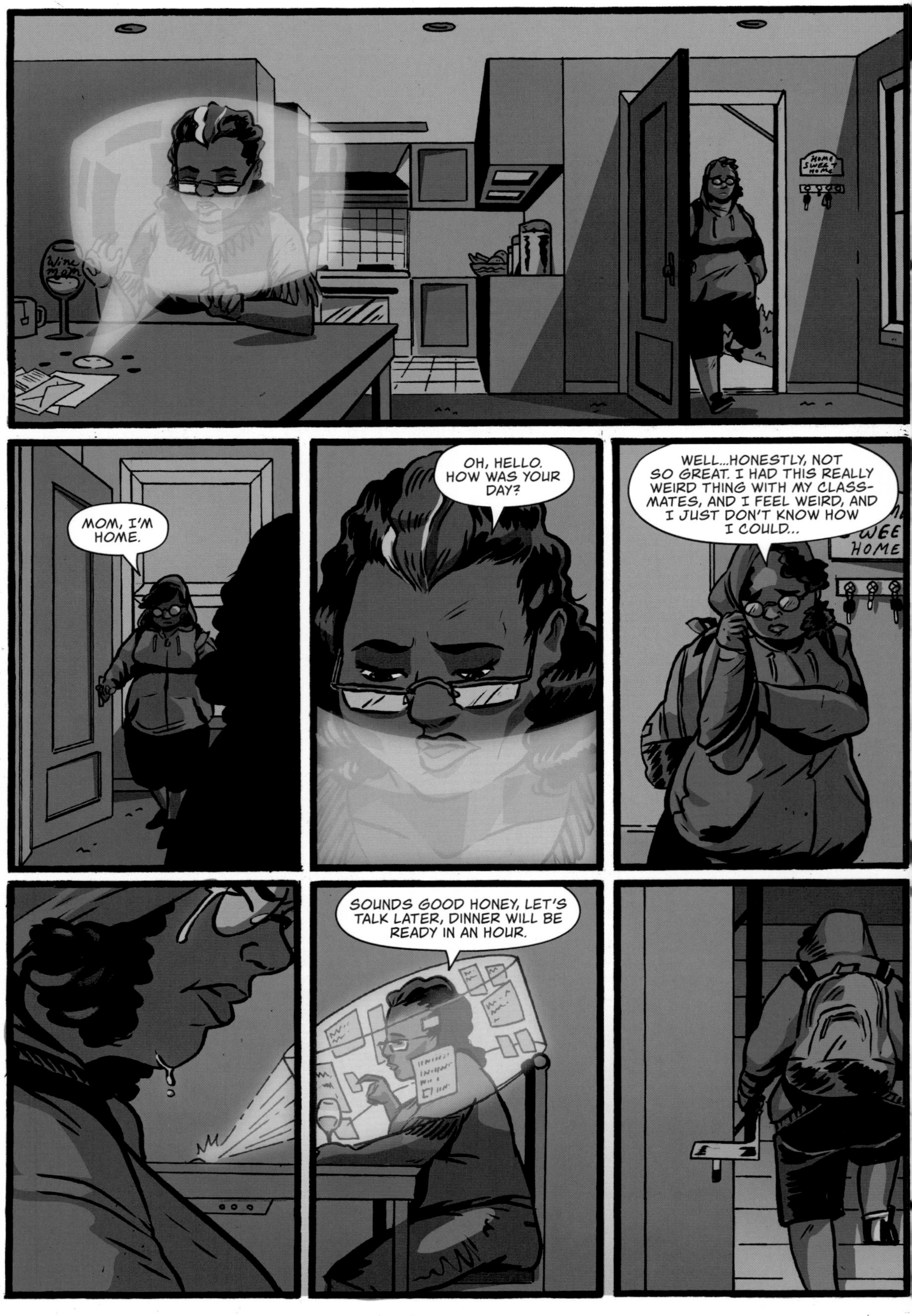

WINE MOM
HOME SWEET HOME
MOM, I'M HOME.
OH, HELLO. HOW WAS YOUR DAY?
WELL...HONESTLY, NOT SO GREAT. I HAD THIS REALLY WEIRD THING WITH MY CLASS-MATES, AND I FEEL WEIRD, AND I JUST DON'T KNOW HOW I COULD...
HOME
SOUNDS GOOD HONEY, LET'S TALK LATER, DINNER WILL BE READY IN AN HOUR.

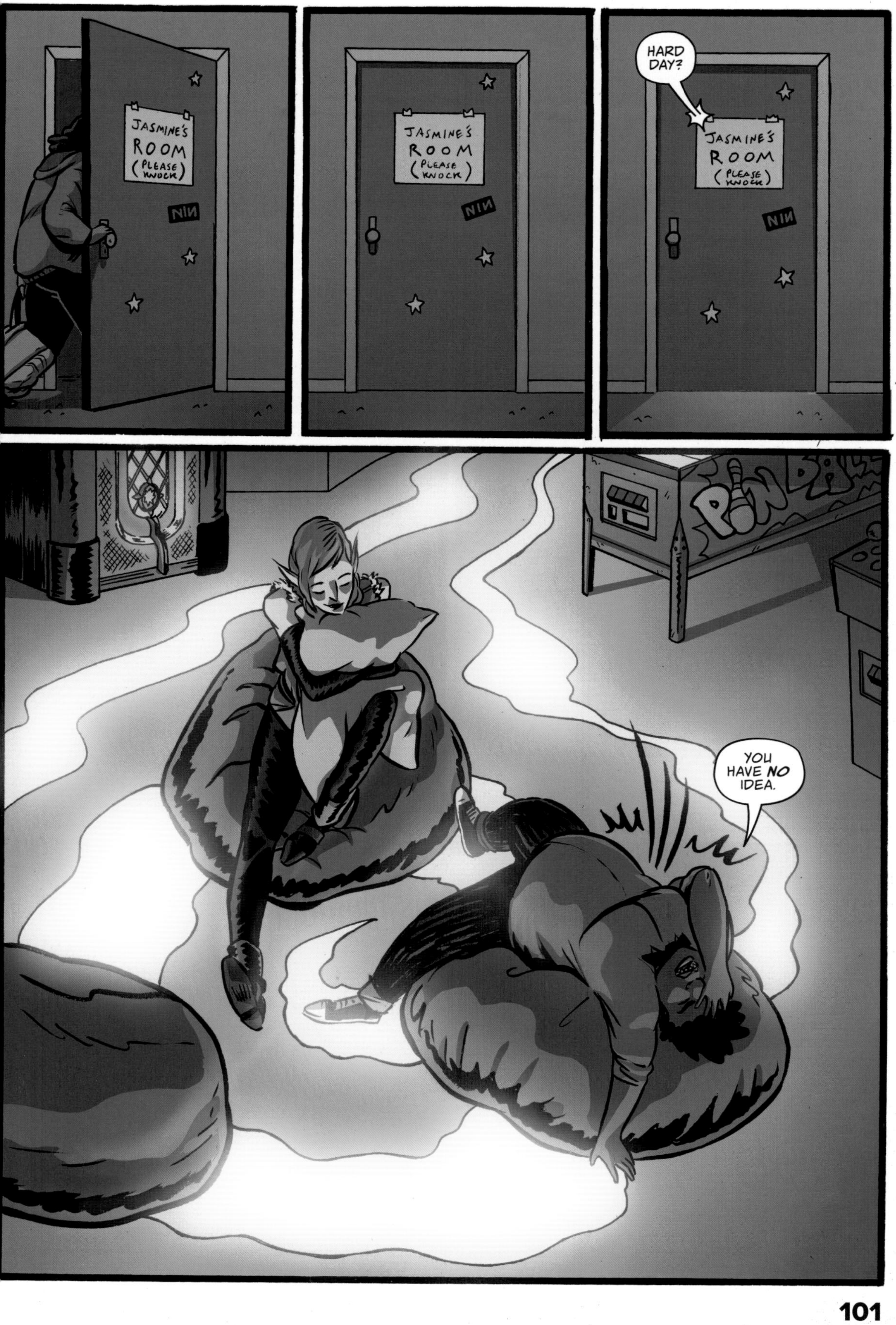

JASMINE'S ROOM (PLEASE KNOCK)
NIN
JASMINE'S ROOM (PLEASE KNOCK)
NIN
HARD DAY?
JASMINE'S ROOM (PLEASE KNOCK)
NIN
YOU HAVE **NO** IDEA.

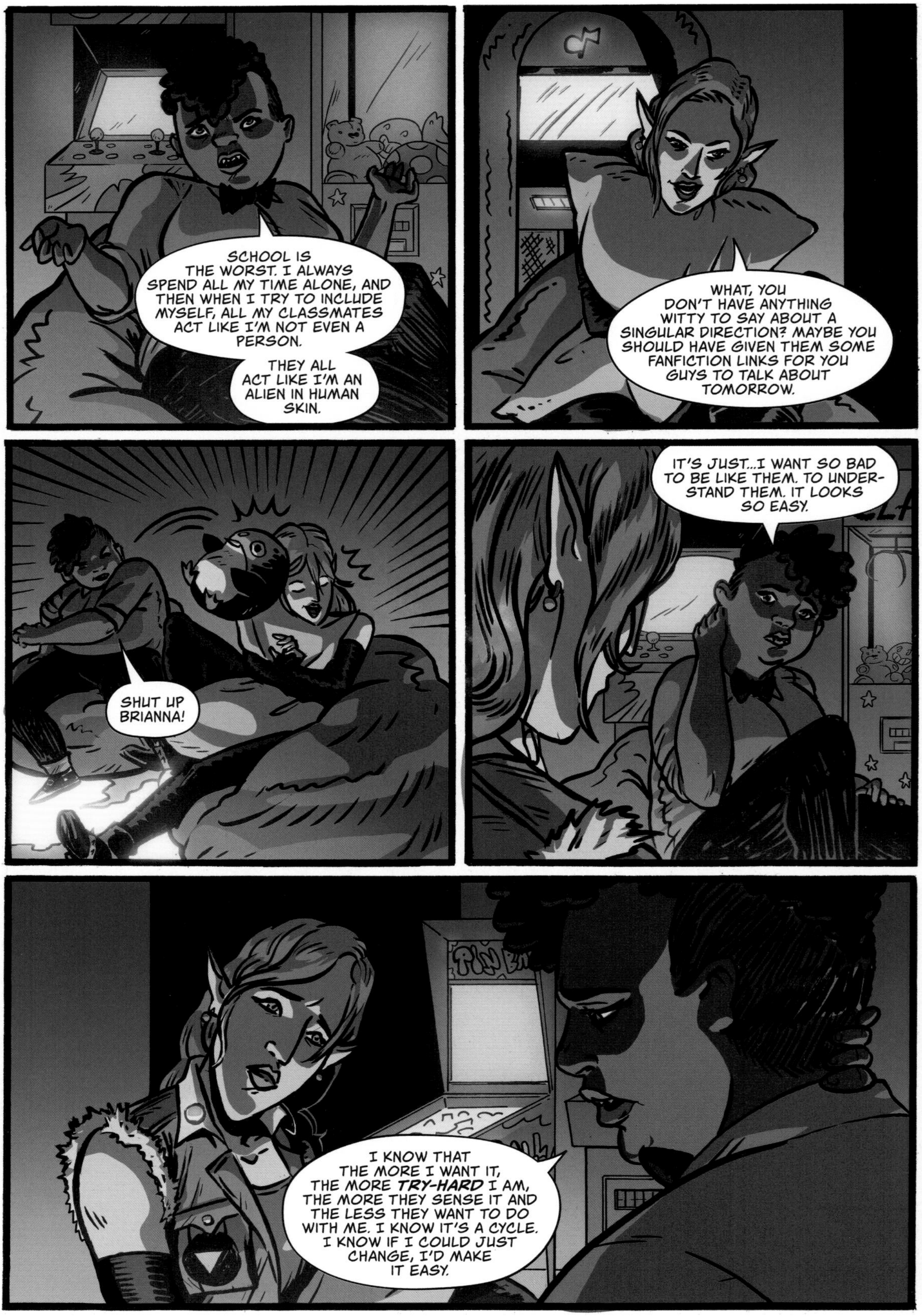
SCHOOL IS THE WORST. I ALWAYS SPEND ALL MY TIME ALONE, AND THEN WHEN I TRY TO INCLUDE MYSELF, ALL MY CLASSMATES ACT LIKE I'M NOT EVEN A PERSON.
THEY ALL ACT LIKE I'M AN ALIEN IN HUMAN SKIN.
WHAT, YOU DON'T HAVE ANYTHING WITTY TO SAY ABOUT A SINGULAR DIRECTION? MAYBE YOU SHOULD HAVE GIVEN THEM SOME FANFICTION LINKS FOR YOU GUYS TO TALK ABOUT TOMORROW.
SHUT UP BRIANNA!
IT'S JUST...I WANT SO BAD TO BE LIKE THEM. TO UNDER-STAND THEM. IT LOOKS SO EASY.
I KNOW THAT THE MORE I WANT IT, THE MORE **TRY-HARD** I AM, THE MORE THEY SENSE IT AND THE LESS THEY WANT TO DO WITH ME. I KNOW IT'S A CYCLE. I KNOW IF I COULD JUST CHANGE, I'D MAKE IT EASY.

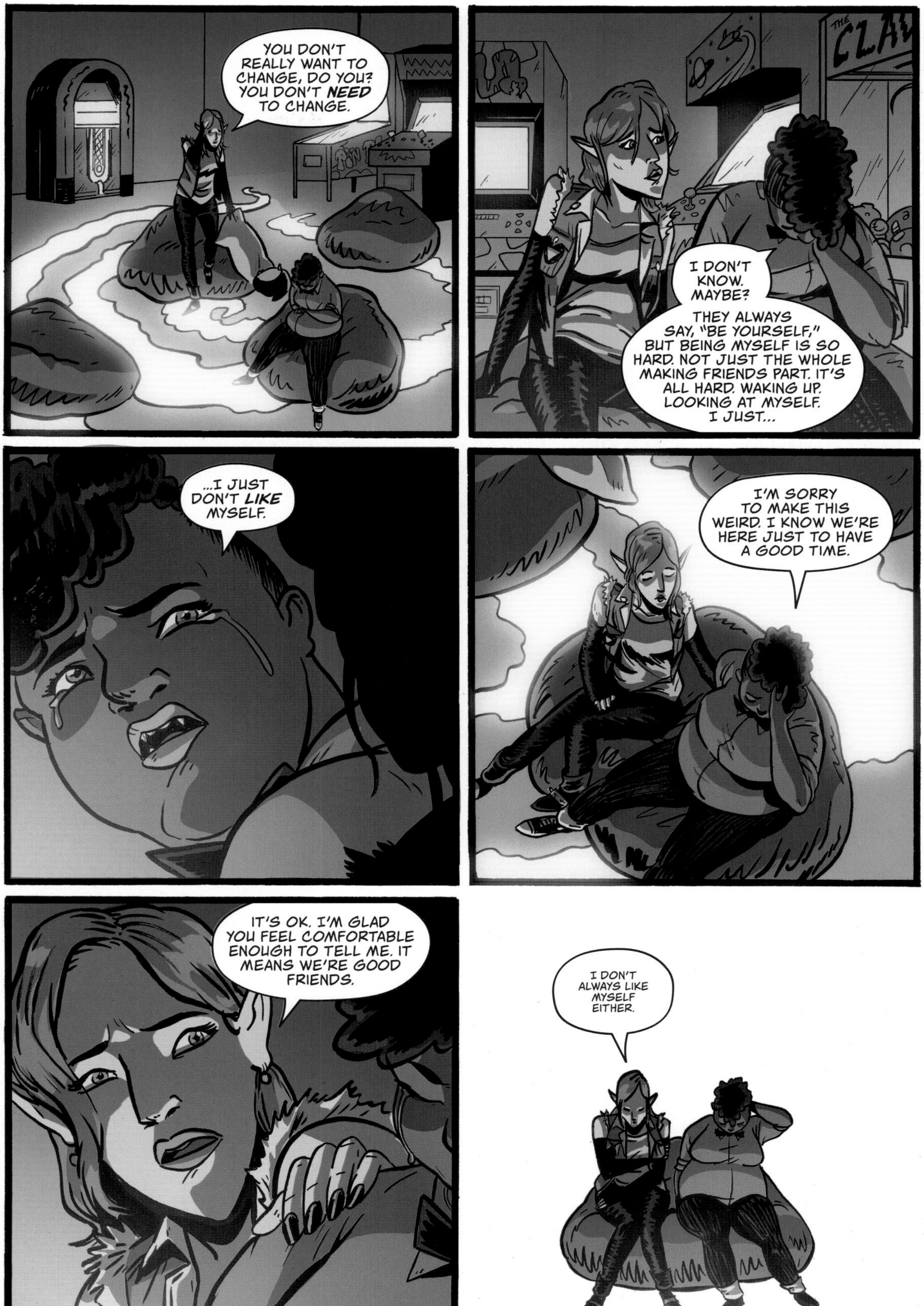
YOU DON'T REALLY WANT TO CHANGE, DO YOU? YOU DON'T **NEED** TO CHANGE.
I DON'T KNOW. MAYBE?
THEY ALWAYS SAY, "BE YOURSELF," BUT BEING MYSELF IS SO HARD. NOT JUST THE WHOLE MAKING FRIENDS PART. IT'S ALL HARD. WAKING UP. LOOKING AT MYSELF. I JUST...
...I JUST DON'T **LIKE** MYSELF.
I'M SORRY TO MAKE THIS WEIRD. I KNOW WE'RE HERE JUST TO HAVE A GOOD TIME.
IT'S OK. I'M GLAD YOU FEEL COMFORTABLE ENOUGH TO TELL ME. IT MEANS WE'RE GOOD FRIENDS.
I DON'T ALWAYS LIKE MYSELF EITHER.

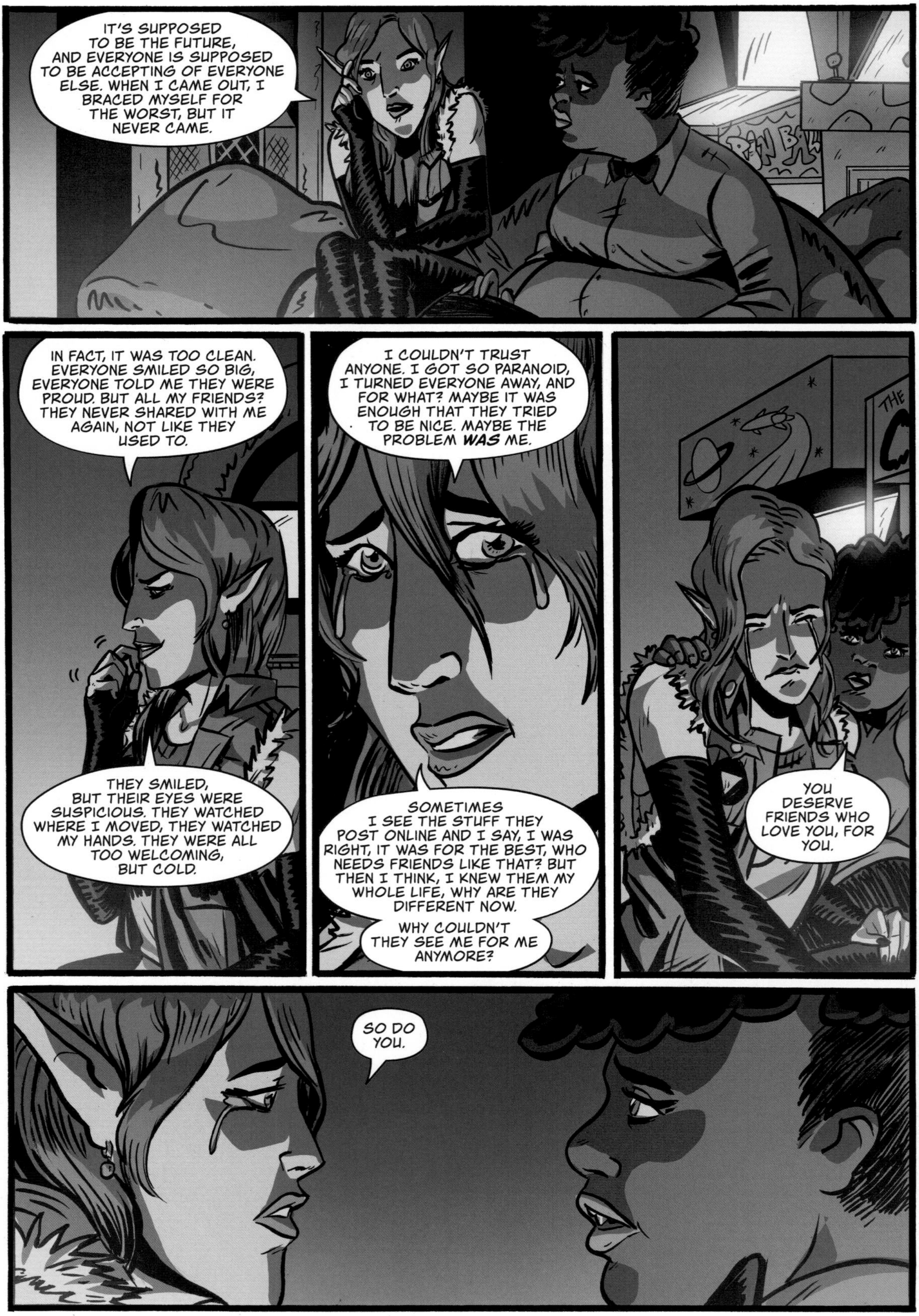
IT'S SUPPOSED TO BE THE FUTURE, AND EVERYONE IS SUPPOSED TO BE ACCEPTING OF EVERYONE ELSE. WHEN I CAME OUT, I BRACED MYSELF FOR THE WORST, BUT IT NEVER CAME.
IN FACT, IT WAS TOO CLEAN. EVERYONE SMILED SO BIG, EVERYONE TOLD ME THEY WERE PROUD. BUT ALL MY FRIENDS? THEY NEVER SHARED WITH ME AGAIN, NOT LIKE THEY USED TO.
THEY SMILED, BUT THEIR EYES WERE SUSPICIOUS. THEY WATCHED WHERE I MOVED, THEY WATCHED MY HANDS. THEY WERE ALL TOO WELCOMING, BUT COLD.
I COULDN'T TRUST ANYONE. I GOT SO PARANOID, I TURNED EVERYONE AWAY, AND FOR WHAT? MAYBE IT WAS ENOUGH THAT THEY TRIED TO BE NICE. MAYBE THE PROBLEM ***WAS*** ME.
SOMETIMES I SEE THE STUFF THEY POST ONLINE AND I SAY, I WAS RIGHT, IT WAS FOR THE BEST, WHO NEEDS FRIENDS LIKE THAT? BUT THEN I THINK, I KNEW THEM MY WHOLE LIFE, WHY ARE THEY DIFFERENT NOW.
WHY COULDN'T THEY SEE ME FOR ME ANYMORE?
YOU DESERVE FRIENDS WHO LOVE YOU, FOR YOU.
SO DO YOU.

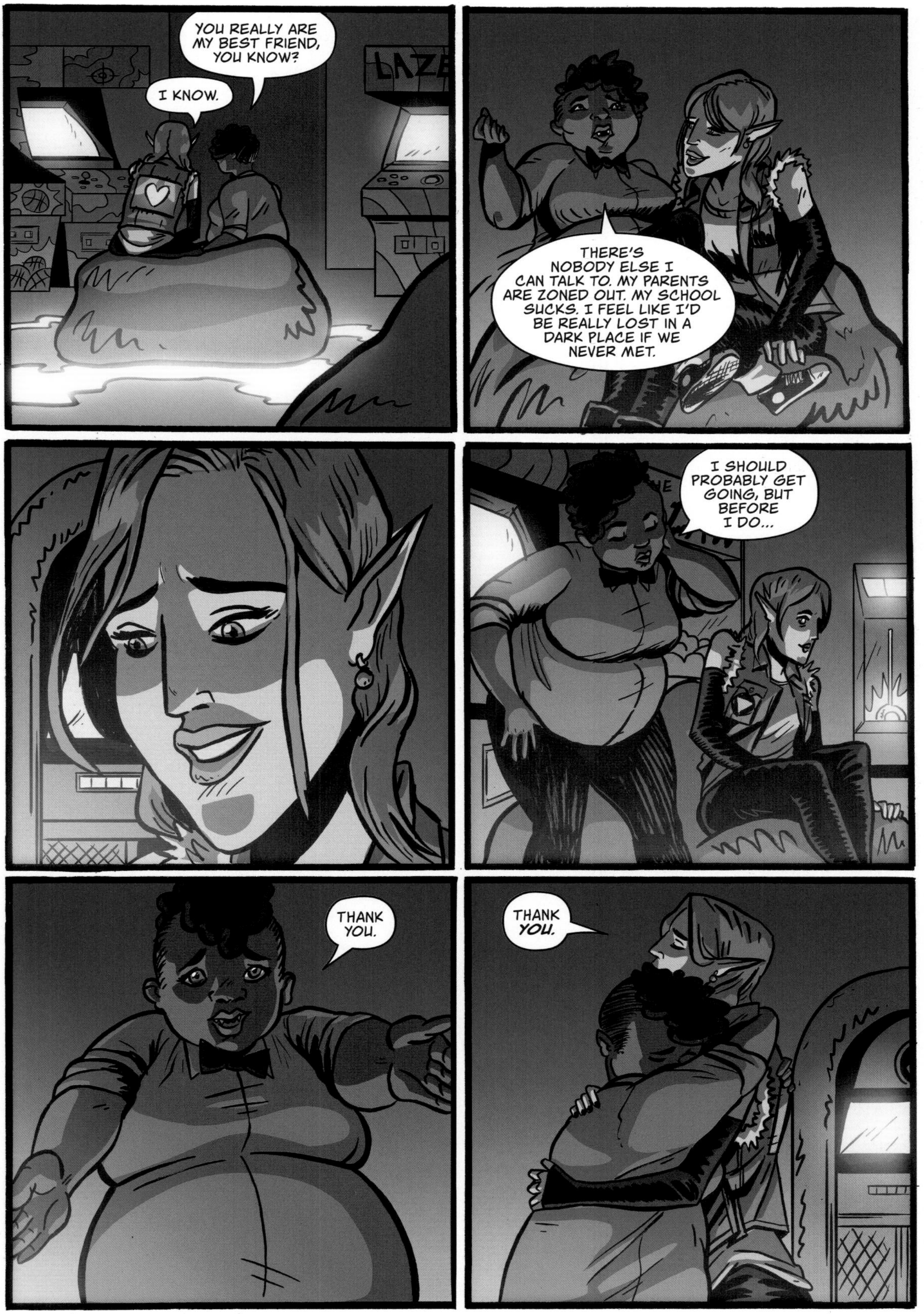
YOU REALLY ARE MY BEST FRIEND, YOU KNOW?
I KNOW.
LAZE
THERE'S NOBODY ELSE I CAN TALK TO. MY PARENTS ARE ZONED OUT. MY SCHOOL SUCKS. I FEEL LIKE I'D BE REALLY LOST IN A DARK PLACE IF WE NEVER MET.
I SHOULD PROBABLY GET GOING, BUT BEFORE I DO...
THANK YOU.
THANK *YOU.*

OK, TIME TO DO SOME HOMEWORK.

MORE LIKE WATCH METUBE FOR AN HOUR.

SHUT UP BRIANNA!

OK, BYE.

BYE, TALK LATER.

VOOSH

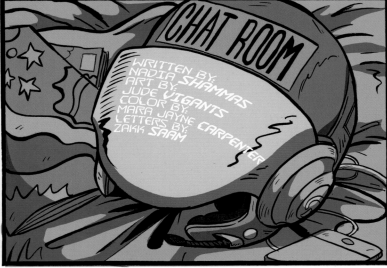

CHAT ROOM

WRITTEN BY:
NADIA SHAMMAS
ART BY:
JUDE VIGANTS
COLOR BY:
MARA JAYNE CARPENTER
LETTERS BY:
ZAKK SAAM

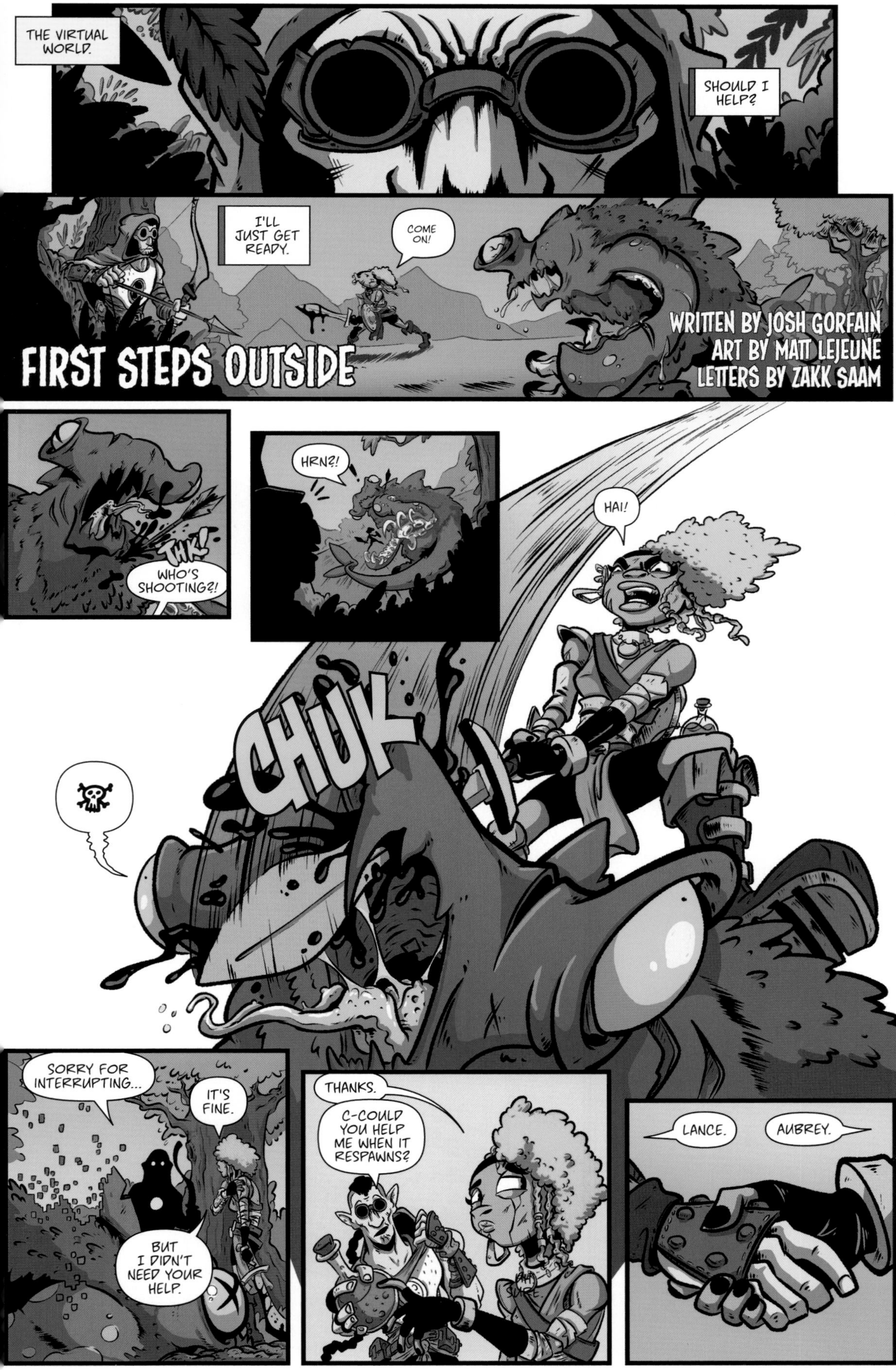
THE VIRTUAL WORLD.
SHOULD I HELP?
I'LL JUST GET READY.
COME ON!
FIRST STEPS OUTSIDE
WRITTEN BY JOSH GORFAIN
ART BY MATT LEJEUNE
LETTERS BY ZAKK SAAM
THK!
WHO'S SHOOTING?!
HRN?!
HAI!
CHUK
SORRY FOR INTERRUPTING...
IT'S FINE.
BUT I DIDN'T NEED YOUR HELP.
THANKS.
C-COULD YOU HELP ME WHEN IT RESPAWNS?
LANCE.
AUBREY.

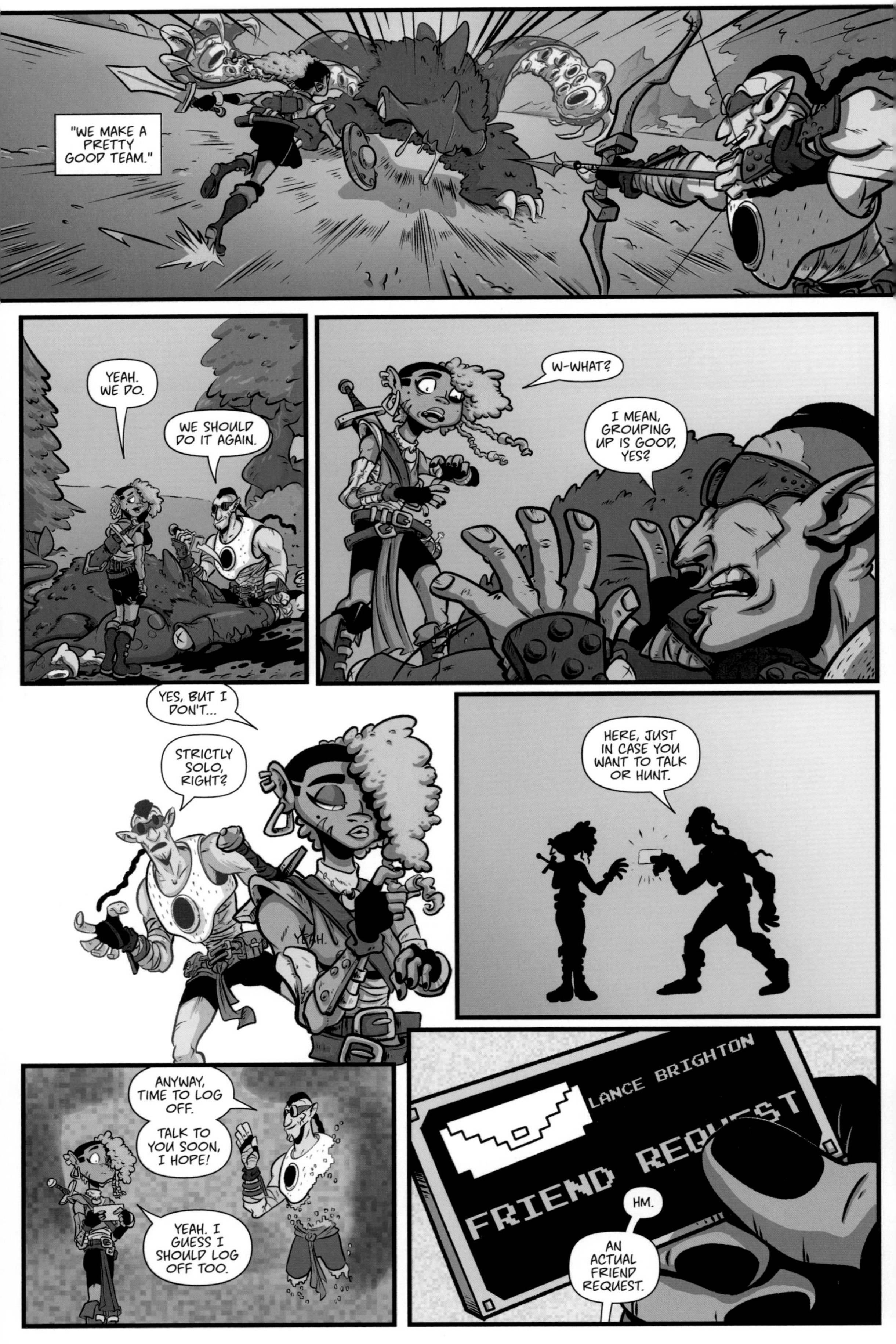

"WE MAKE A PRETTY GOOD TEAM."
YEAH. WE DO.
WE SHOULD DO IT AGAIN.
W-WHAT?
I MEAN, GROUPING UP IS GOOD, YES?
YES, BUT I DON'T...
STRICTLY SOLO, RIGHT?
YEAH.
HERE, JUST IN CASE YOU WANT TO TALK OR HUNT.
ANYWAY, TIME TO LOG OFF.
TALK TO YOU SOON, I HOPE!
YEAH. I GUESS I SHOULD LOG OFF TOO.
LANCE BRIGHTON
FRIEND REQUEST
HM.
AN ACTUAL FRIEND REQUEST.

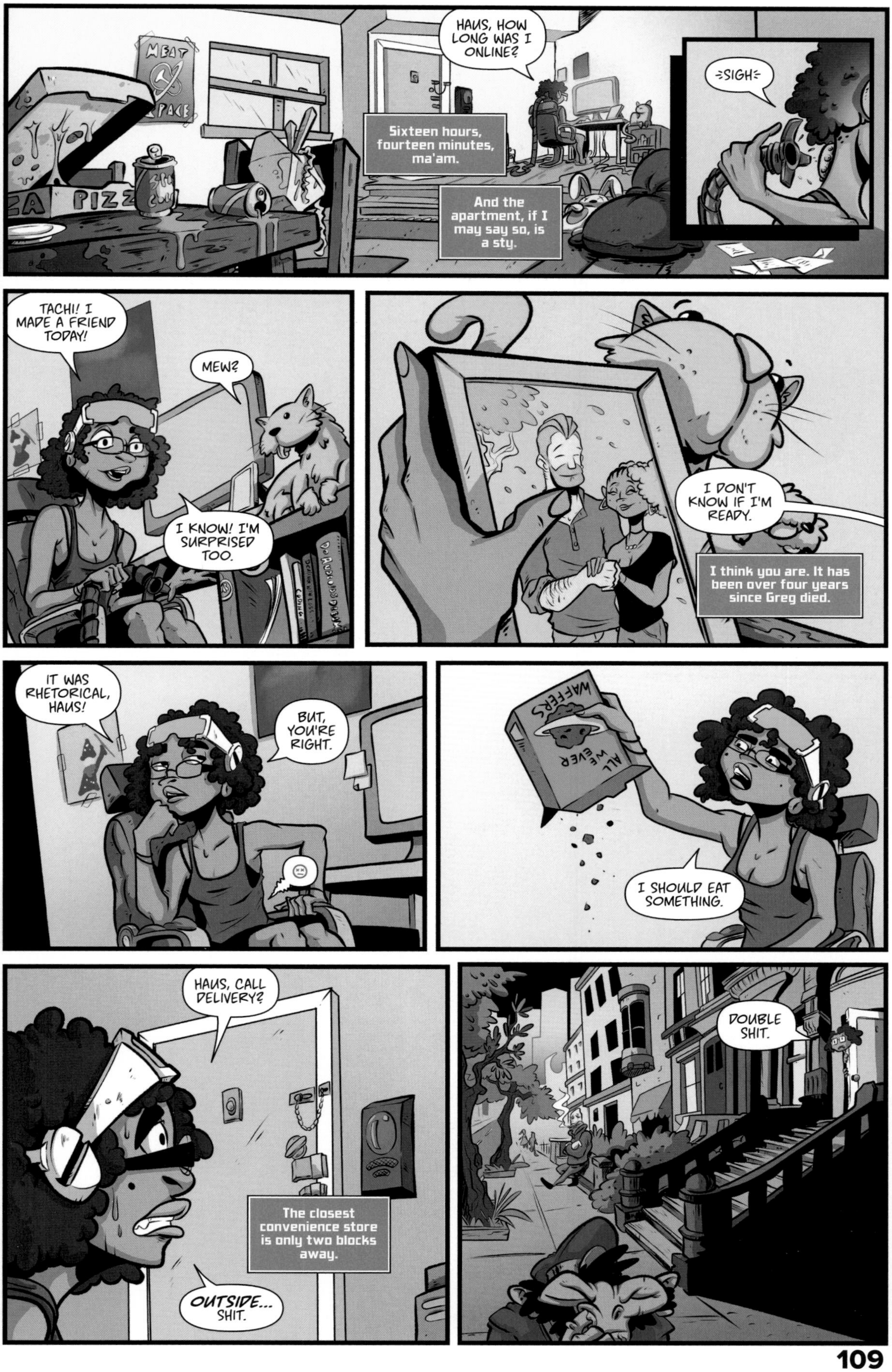

MEAT SPACE
PIZZ
HAUS, HOW LONG WAS I ONLINE?
Sixteen hours, fourteen minutes, ma'am.
And the apartment, if I may say so, is a sty.
=SIGH=
TACHI! I MADE A FRIEND TODAY!
MEW?
I KNOW! I'M SURPRISED TOO.
I DON'T KNOW IF I'M READY.
I think you are. It has been over four years since Greg died.
IT WAS RHETORICAL, HAUS!
BUT, YOU'RE RIGHT.
ALL WE EVER WAFFERS
I SHOULD EAT SOMETHING.
HAUS, CALL DELIVERY?
The closest convenience store is only two blocks away.
OUTSIDE... SHIT.
DOUBLE SHIT.

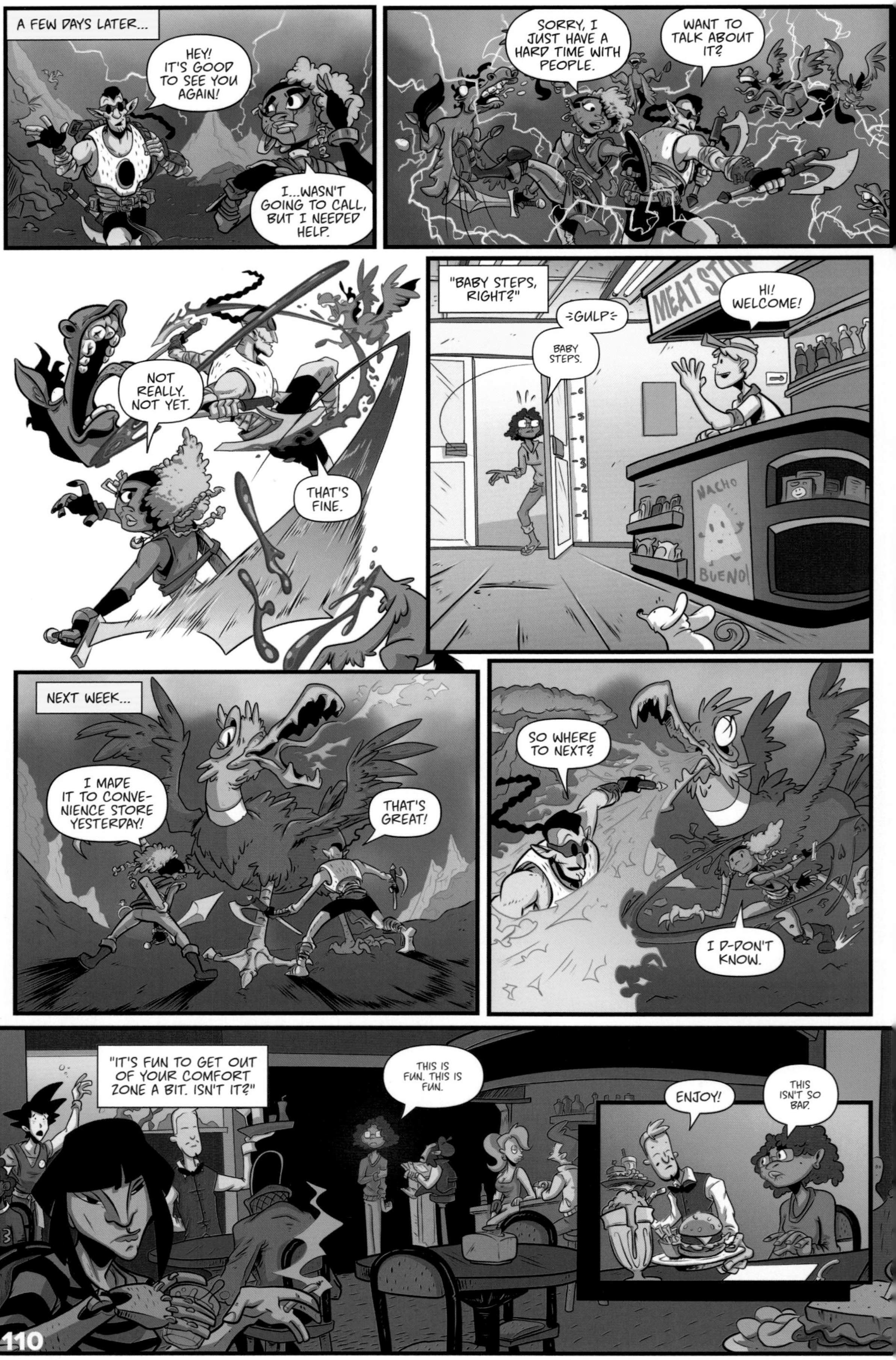
A FEW DAYS LATER...
HEY! IT'S GOOD TO SEE YOU AGAIN!
I...WASN'T GOING TO CALL, BUT I NEEDED HELP.
SORRY, I JUST HAVE A HARD TIME WITH PEOPLE.
WANT TO TALK ABOUT IT?
NOT REALLY. NOT YET.
THAT'S FINE.
"BABY STEPS, RIGHT?"
GULP
BABY STEPS.
HI! WELCOME!
MEAT STO
NACHO
BUENO!
NEXT WEEK...
I MADE IT TO CONVE-NIENCE STORE YESTERDAY!
THAT'S GREAT!
SO WHERE TO NEXT?
I D-DON'T KNOW.
"IT'S FUN TO GET OUT OF YOUR COMFORT ZONE A BIT. ISN'T IT?"
THIS IS FUN. THIS IS FUN.
ENJOY!
THIS ISN'T SO BAD.

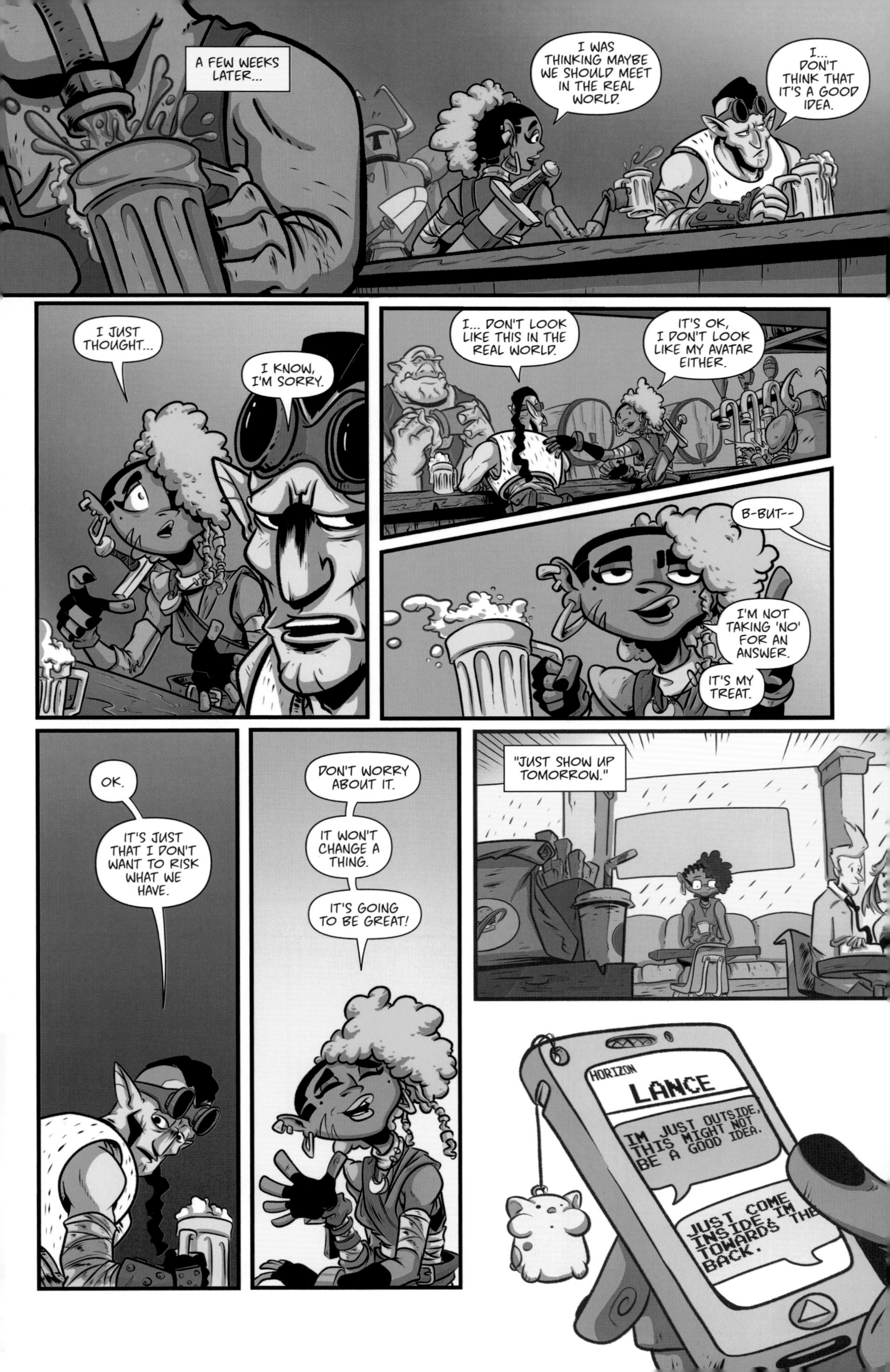
A FEW WEEKS LATER...
I WAS THINKING MAYBE WE SHOULD MEET IN THE REAL WORLD.
I... DON'T THINK THAT IT'S A GOOD IDEA.
I JUST THOUGHT...
I KNOW, I'M SORRY.
I... DON'T LOOK LIKE THIS IN THE REAL WORLD.
IT'S OK, I DON'T LOOK LIKE MY AVATAR EITHER.
B-BUT--
I'M NOT TAKING 'NO' FOR AN ANSWER.
IT'S MY TREAT.
OK.
IT'S JUST THAT I DON'T WANT TO RISK WHAT WE HAVE.
DON'T WORRY ABOUT IT.
IT WON'T CHANGE A THING.
IT'S GOING TO BE GREAT!
"JUST SHOW UP TOMORROW."
HORIZON
LANCE
IM JUST OUTSIDE, THIS MIGHT NOT BE A GOOD IDEA.
JUST COME INSIDE IM TOWARDS THE BACK.

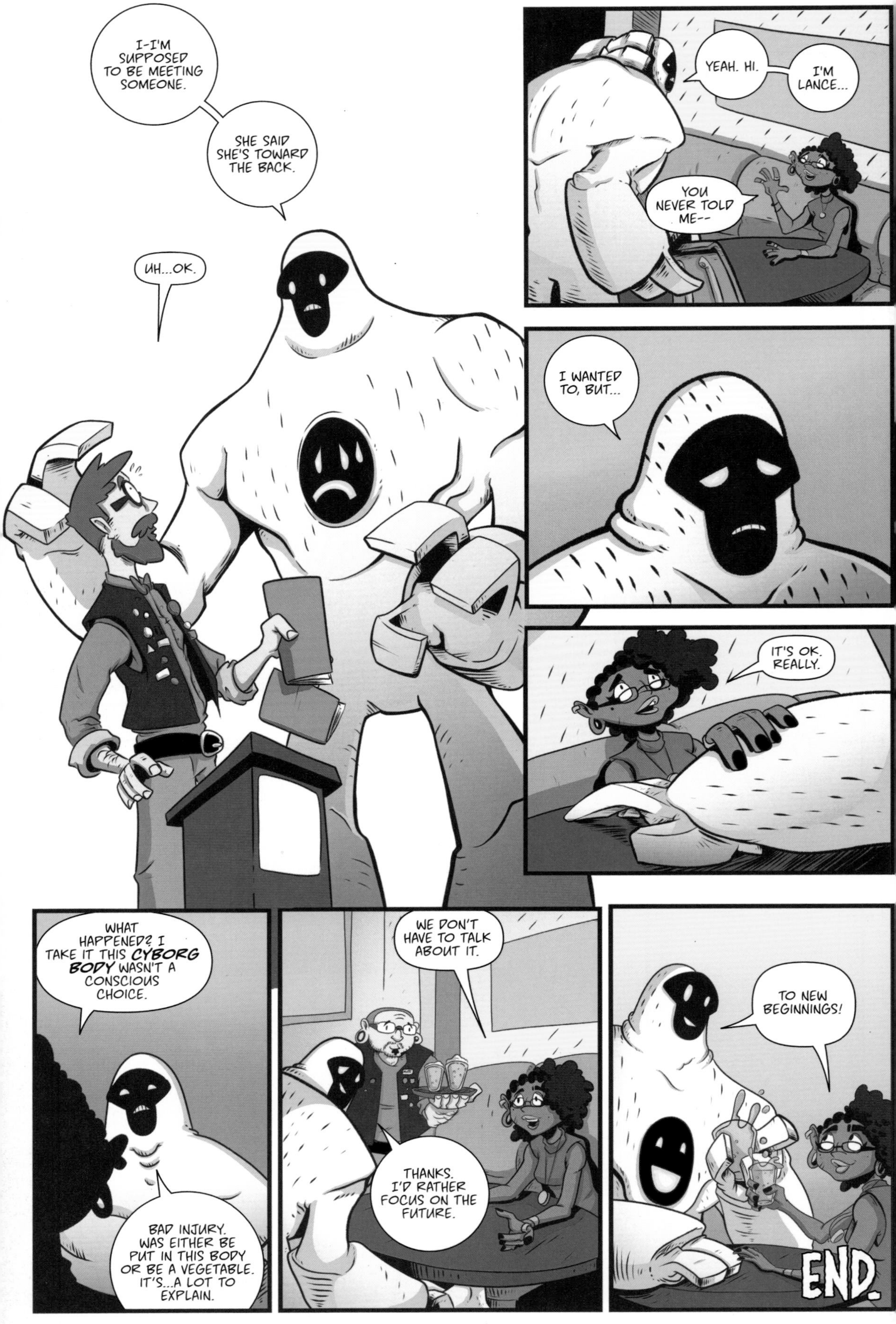

I-I'M SUPPOSED TO BE MEETING SOMEONE.
SHE SAID SHE'S TOWARD THE BACK.
UH...OK.
YEAH. HI.
I'M LANCE...
YOU NEVER TOLD ME--
I WANTED TO, BUT...
IT'S OK. REALLY.
WHAT HAPPENED? I TAKE IT THIS ***CYBORG BODY*** WASN'T A CONSCIOUS CHOICE.
BAD INJURY. WAS EITHER BE PUT IN THIS BODY OR BE A VEGETABLE. IT'S...A LOT TO EXPLAIN.
WE DON'T HAVE TO TALK ABOUT IT.
THANKS. I'D RATHER FOCUS ON THE FUTURE.
TO NEW BEGINNINGS!
END.

CAN YOU SEE IT NOW?

WRITTEN BY: TAYLOR HOFFMAN ART BY: K.R. WHALEN
COLORS BY: JOSH JENSEN LETTERS BY: TAYLOR ESPOSITO

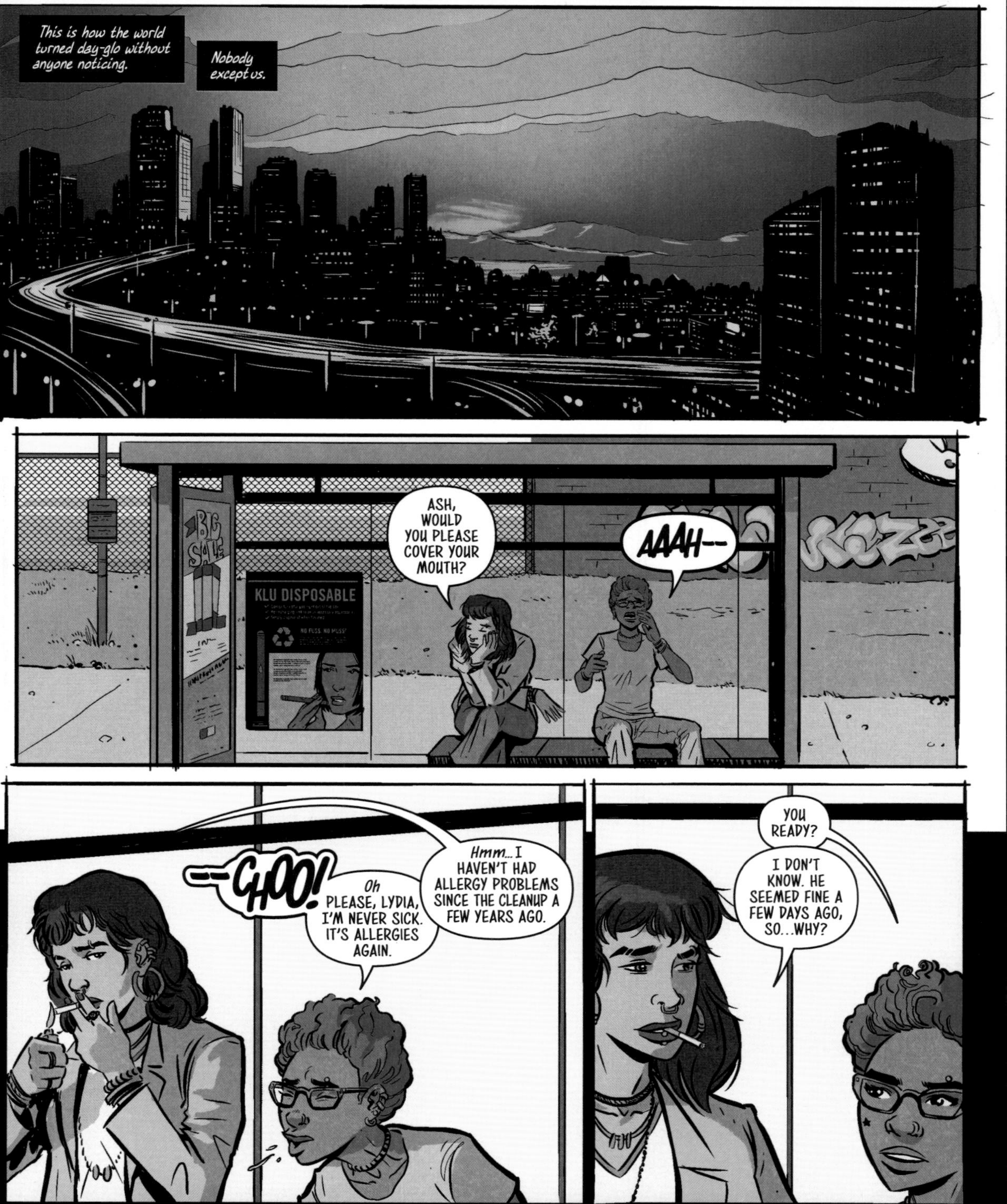
This is how the world turned day-glo without anyone noticing.
Nobody except us.
ASH, WOULD YOU PLEASE COVER YOUR MOUTH?
AAAH--
--CHOO!
Oh PLEASE, LYDIA, I'M NEVER SICK. IT'S ALLERGIES AGAIN.
Hmm... I HAVEN'T HAD ALLERGY PROBLEMS SINCE THE CLEANUP A FEW YEARS AGO.
YOU READY?
I DON'T KNOW. HE SEEMED FINE A FEW DAYS AGO, SO...WHY?
KLU DISPOSABLE
NO FUSS. NO MUSS!

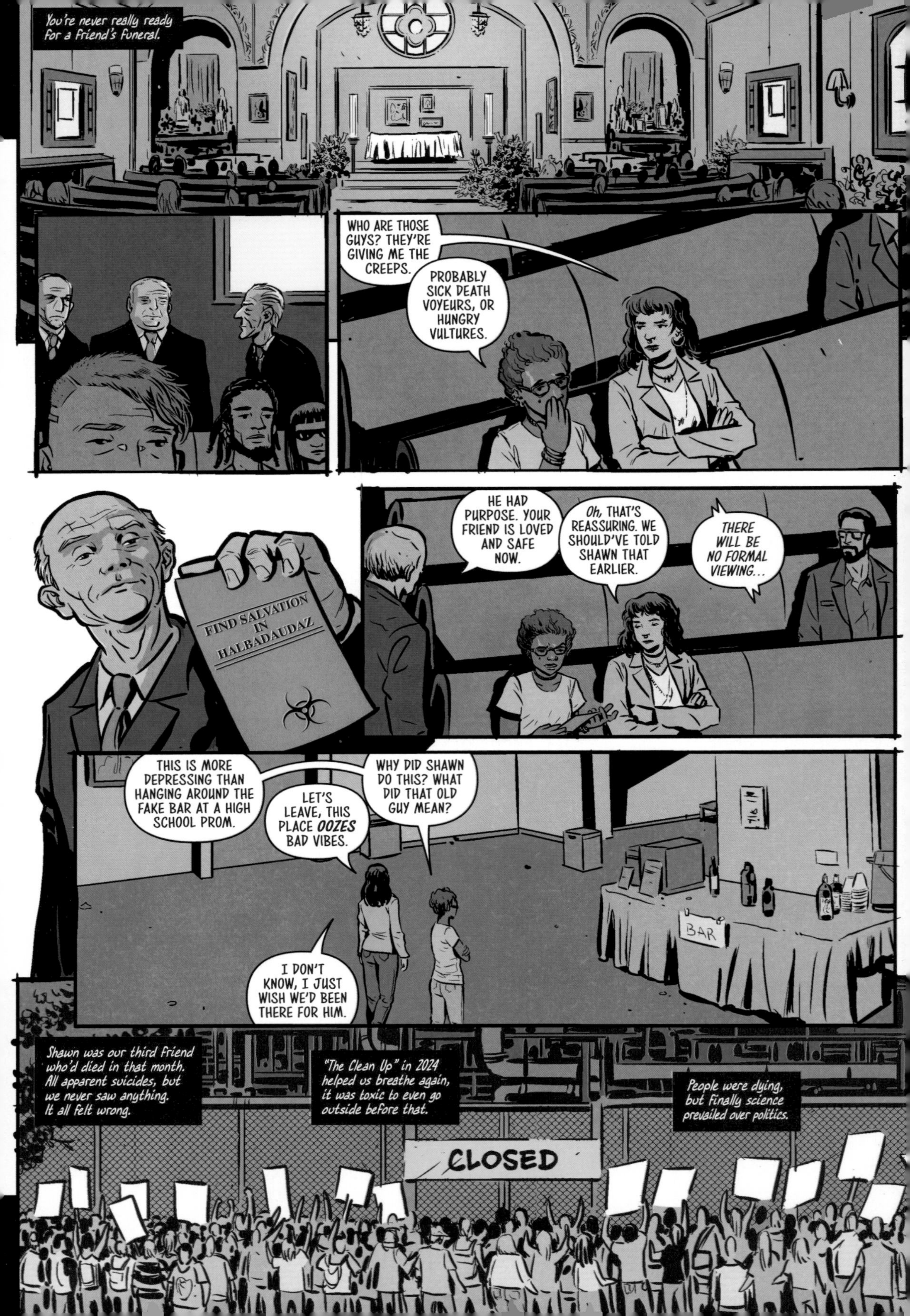
You're never really ready for a friend's funeral.
WHO ARE THOSE GUYS? THEY'RE GIVING ME THE CREEPS.
PROBABLY SICK DEATH VOYEURS, OR HUNGRY VULTURES.
FIND SALVATION IN HALBADAUDAZ
HE HAD PURPOSE. YOUR FRIEND IS LOVED AND SAFE NOW.
Oh, THAT'S REASSURING. WE SHOULD'VE TOLD SHAWN THAT EARLIER.
THERE WILL BE NO FORMAL VIEWING...
THIS IS MORE DEPRESSING THAN HANGING AROUND THE FAKE BAR AT A HIGH SCHOOL PROM.
LET'S LEAVE, THIS PLACE OOZES BAD VIBES.
WHY DID SHAWN DO THIS? WHAT DID THAT OLD GUY MEAN?
I DON'T KNOW, I JUST WISH WE'D BEEN THERE FOR HIM.
BAR
Shawn was our third friend who'd died in that month. All apparent suicides, but we never saw anything. It all felt wrong.
"The Clean Up" in 2024 helped us breathe again, it was toxic to even go outside before that.
People were dying, but finally science prevailed over politics.
CLOSED

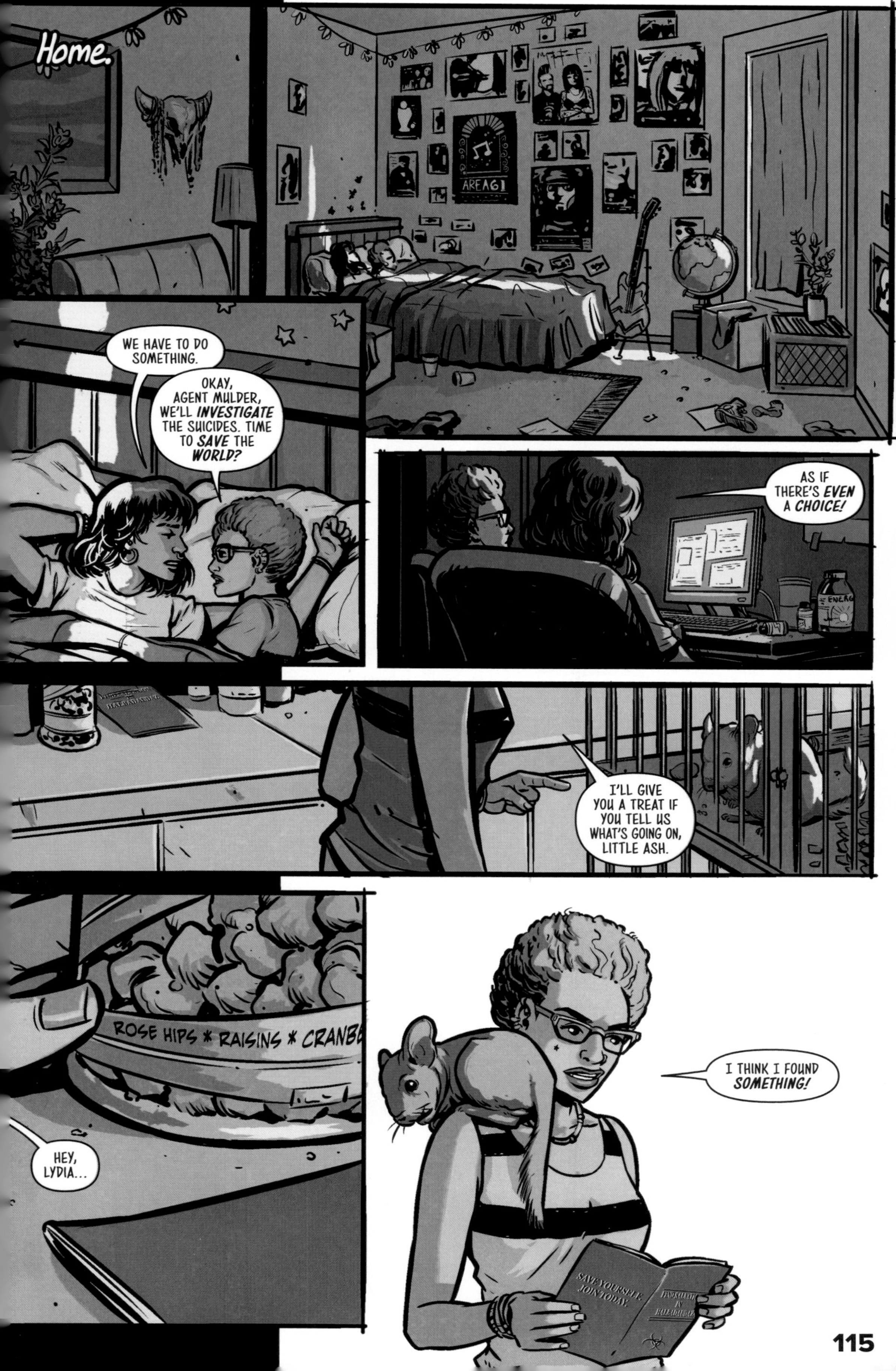
Home.
AREA61
WE HAVE TO DO SOMETHING.
OKAY, AGENT MULDER, WE'LL *INVESTIGATE* THE SUICIDES. TIME TO *SAVE* THE *WORLD?*
AS IF THERE'S *EVEN* A *CHOICE!*
I'LL GIVE YOU A TREAT IF YOU TELL US WHAT'S GOING ON, LITTLE ASH.
ROSE HIPS * RAISINS * CRANBE
HEY, LYDIA...
I THINK I FOUND *SOMETHING!*
SAVE YOURSELF. JOIN TODAY.

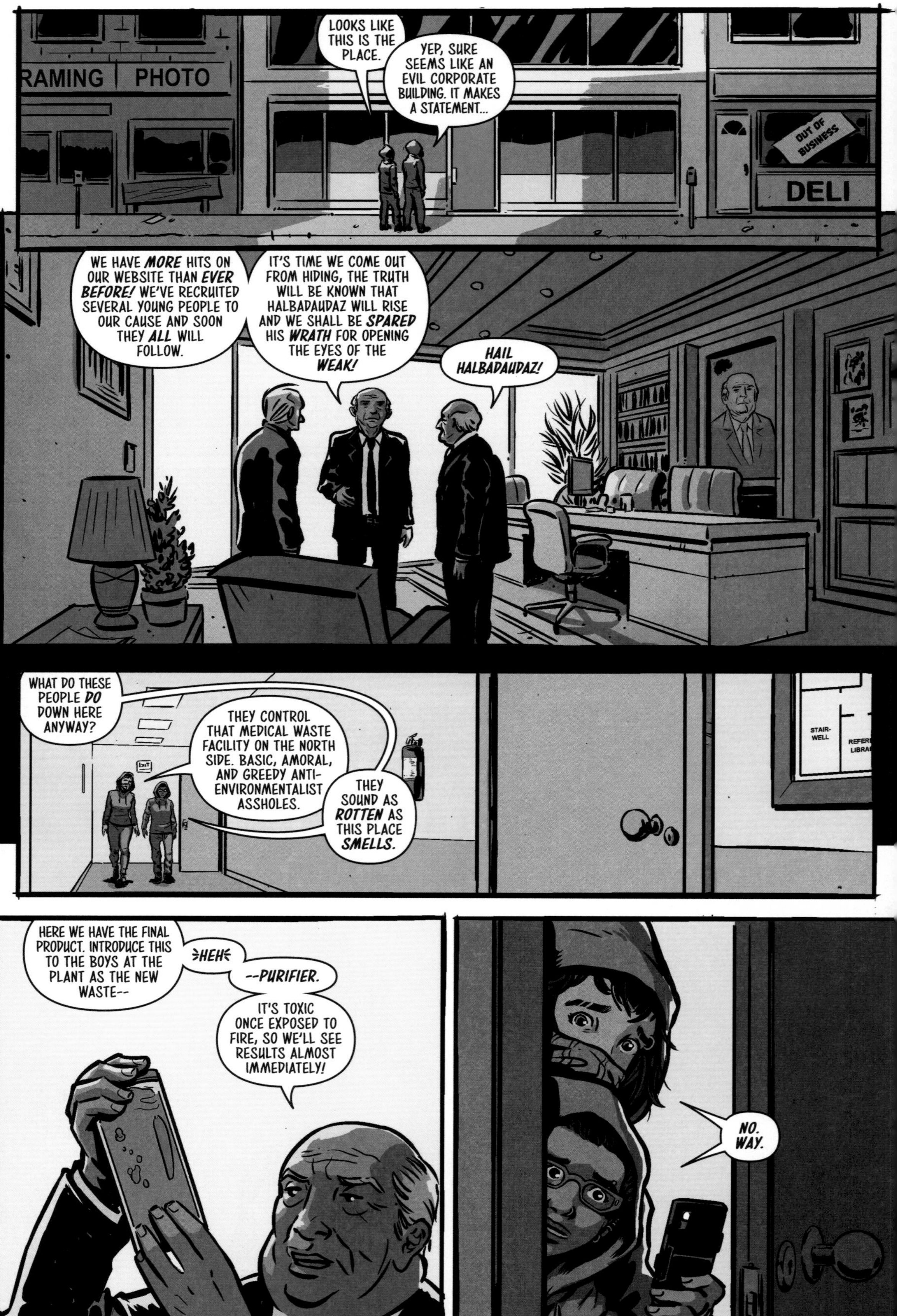
RAMING PHOTO
LOOKS LIKE THIS IS THE PLACE.
YEP, SURE SEEMS LIKE AN EVIL CORPORATE BUILDING. IT MAKES A STATEMENT...
OUT OF BUSINESS
DELI
WE HAVE MORE HITS ON OUR WEBSITE THAN EVER BEFORE! WE'VE RECRUITED SEVERAL YOUNG PEOPLE TO OUR CAUSE AND SOON THEY ALL WILL FOLLOW.
IT'S TIME WE COME OUT FROM HIDING, THE TRUTH WILL BE KNOWN THAT HALBADAUDAZ WILL RISE AND WE SHALL BE SPARED HIS WRATH FOR OPENING THE EYES OF THE WEAK!
HAIL HALBADAUDAZ!
WHAT DO THESE PEOPLE DO DOWN HERE ANYWAY?
THEY CONTROL THAT MEDICAL WASTE FACILITY ON THE NORTH SIDE. BASIC, AMORAL, AND GREEDY ANTI-ENVIRONMENTALIST ASSHOLES.
THEY SOUND AS ROTTEN AS THIS PLACE SMELLS.
STAIR-WELL
HERE WE HAVE THE FINAL PRODUCT. INTRODUCE THIS TO THE BOYS AT THE PLANT AS THE NEW WASTE--
HEH
--PURIFIER.
IT'S TOXIC ONCE EXPOSED TO FIRE, SO WE'LL SEE RESULTS ALMOST IMMEDIATELY!
NO. WAY.

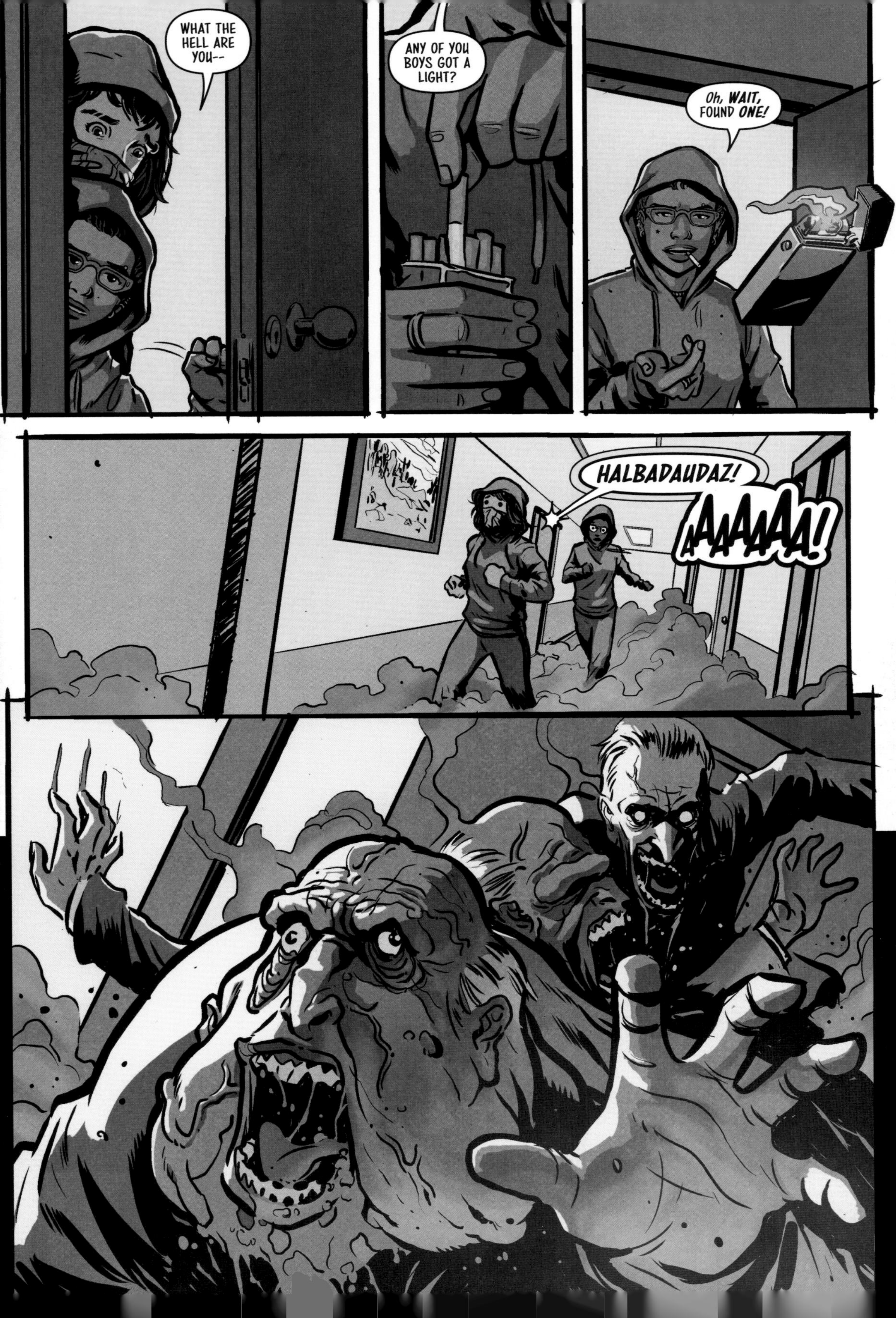
WHAT THE HELL ARE YOU--
ANY OF YOU BOYS GOT A LIGHT?
Oh, WAIT, FOUND ONE!
HALBADAUDAZ!
¡AAAAAAA!

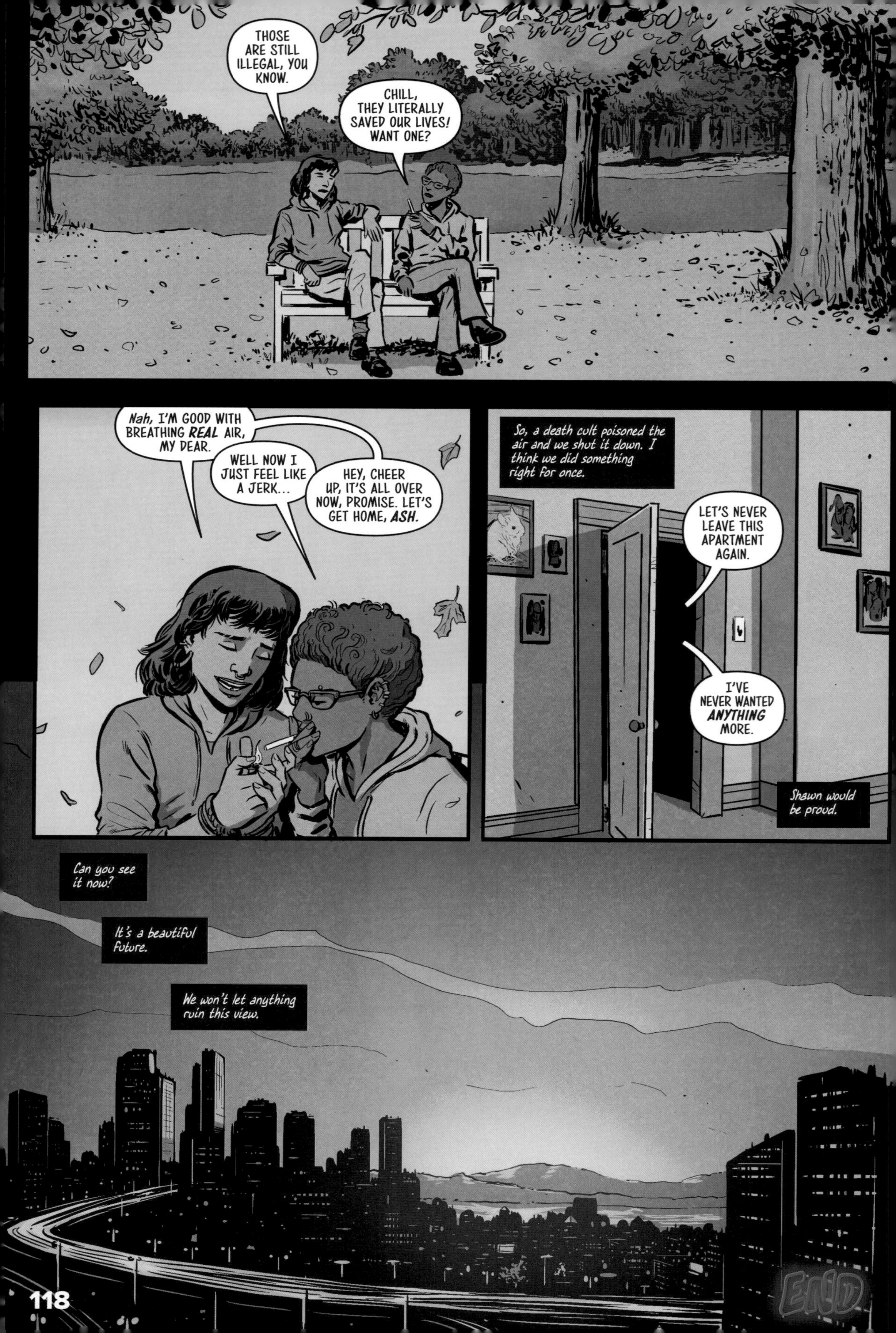
THOSE ARE STILL ILLEGAL, YOU KNOW.
CHILL, THEY LITERALLY SAVED OUR LIVES! WANT ONE?
Nah, I'M GOOD WITH BREATHING REAL AIR, MY DEAR.
WELL NOW I JUST FEEL LIKE A JERK...
HEY, CHEER UP, IT'S ALL OVER NOW, PROMISE. LET'S GET HOME, ASH.
So, a death cult poisoned the air and we shut it down. I think we did something right for once.
LET'S NEVER LEAVE THIS APARTMENT AGAIN.
I'VE NEVER WANTED ANYTHING MORE.
Shawn would be proud.
Can you see it now?
It's a beautiful future.
We won't let anything ruin this view.
END

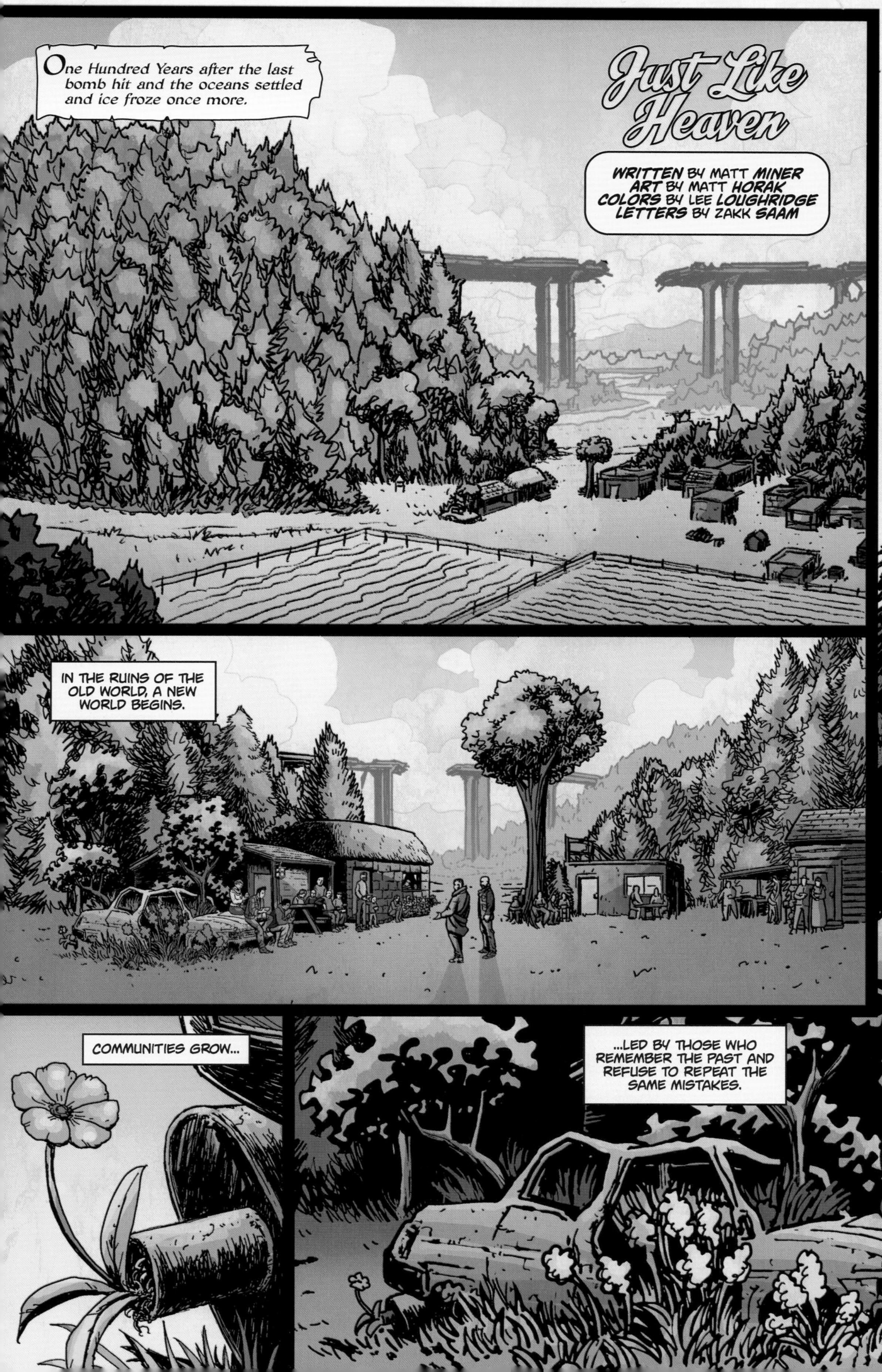

One Hundred Years after the last bomb hit and the oceans settled and ice froze once more.
Just Like Heaven
WRITTEN BY MATT MINER
ART BY MATT HORAK
COLORS BY LEE LOUGHRIDGE
LETTERS BY ZAKK SAAM
IN THE RUINS OF THE OLD WORLD, A NEW WORLD BEGINS.
COMMUNITIES GROW...
...LED BY THOSE WHO REMEMBER THE PAST AND REFUSE TO REPEAT THE SAME MISTAKES.

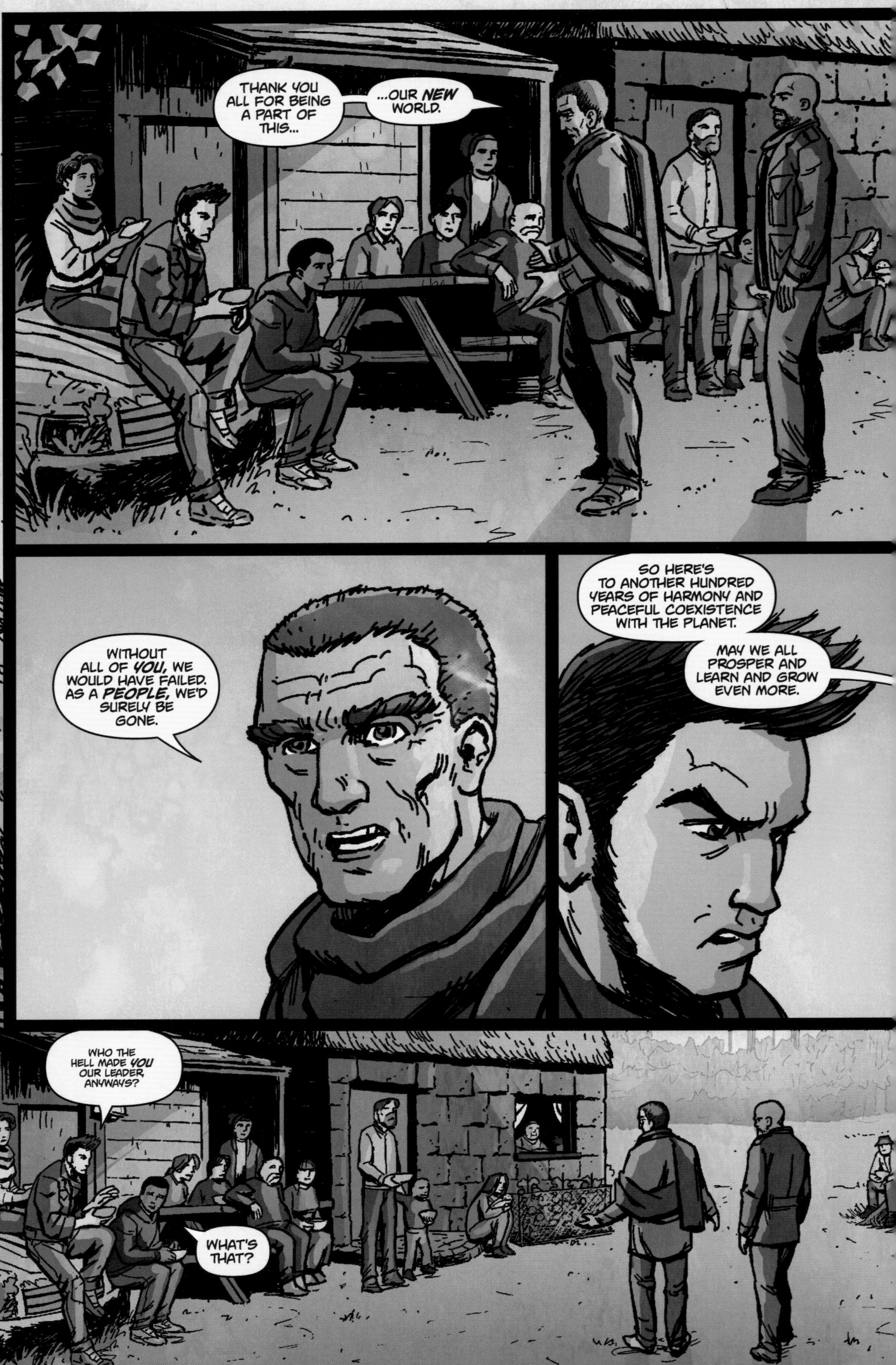
THANK YOU ALL FOR BEING A PART OF THIS...
...OUR NEW WORLD.
WITHOUT ALL OF YOU, WE WOULD HAVE FAILED. AS A PEOPLE, WE'D SURELY BE GONE.
SO HERE'S TO ANOTHER HUNDRED YEARS OF HARMONY AND PEACEFUL COEXISTENCE WITH THE PLANET.
MAY WE ALL PROSPER AND LEARN AND GROW EVEN MORE.
WHO THE HELL MADE YOU OUR LEADER, ANYWAYS?
WHAT'S THAT?

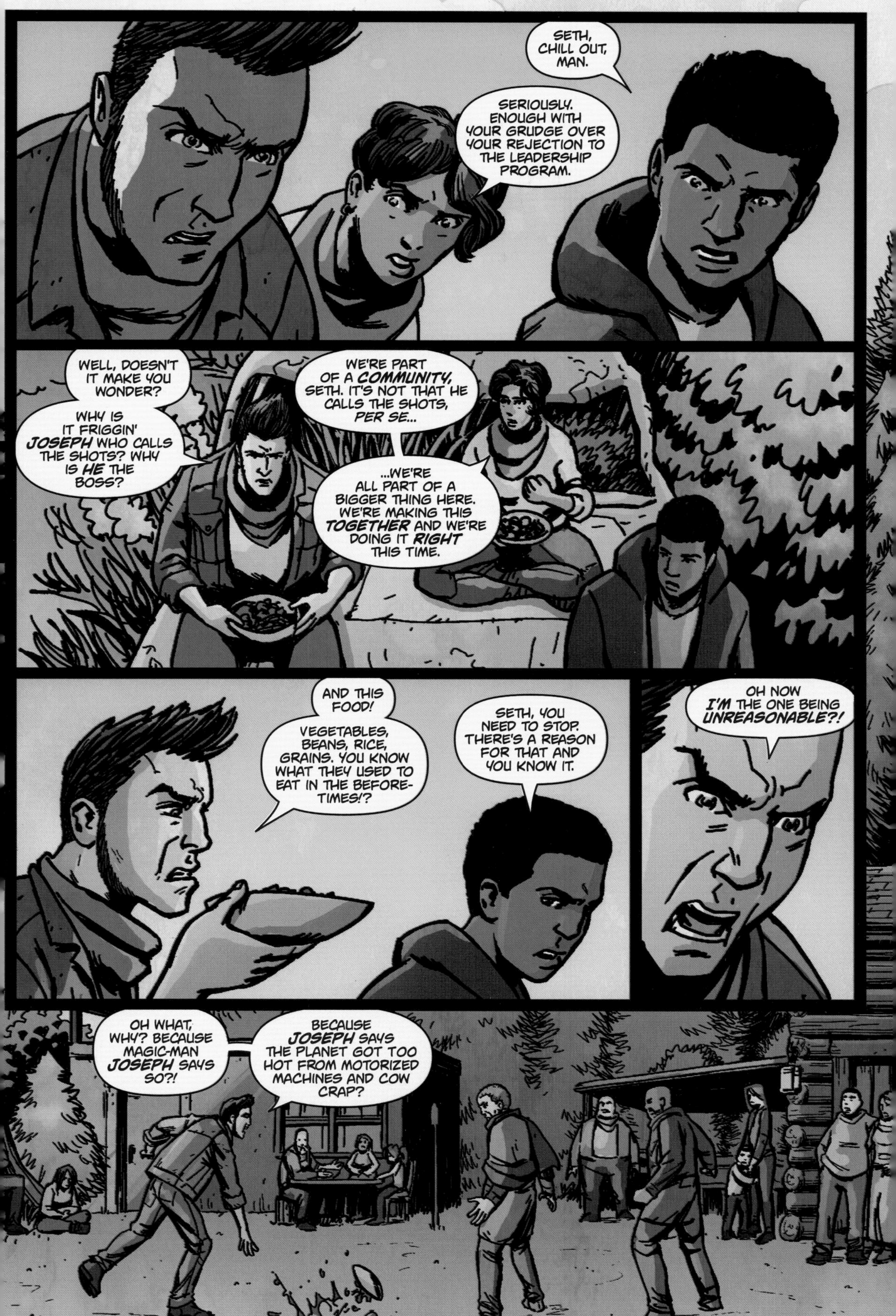
SETH, CHILL OUT, MAN.
SERIOUSLY. ENOUGH WITH YOUR GRUDGE OVER YOUR REJECTION TO THE LEADERSHIP PROGRAM.
WELL, DOESN'T IT MAKE YOU WONDER?
WHY IS IT FRIGGIN' JOSEPH WHO CALLS THE SHOTS? WHY IS HE THE BOSS?
WE'RE PART OF A COMMUNITY, SETH. IT'S NOT THAT HE CALLS THE SHOTS, PER SE...
...WE'RE ALL PART OF A BIGGER THING HERE. WE'RE MAKING THIS TOGETHER AND WE'RE DOING IT RIGHT THIS TIME.
AND THIS FOOD!
VEGETABLES, BEANS, RICE, GRAINS. YOU KNOW WHAT THEY USED TO EAT IN THE BEFORE-TIMES!?
SETH, YOU NEED TO STOP. THERE'S A REASON FOR THAT AND YOU KNOW IT.
OH NOW I'M THE ONE BEING UNREASONABLE?!
OH WHAT, WHY? BECAUSE MAGIC-MAN JOSEPH SAYS SO?!
BECAUSE JOSEPH SAYS THE PLANET GOT TOO HOT FROM MOTORIZED MACHINES AND COW CRAP?

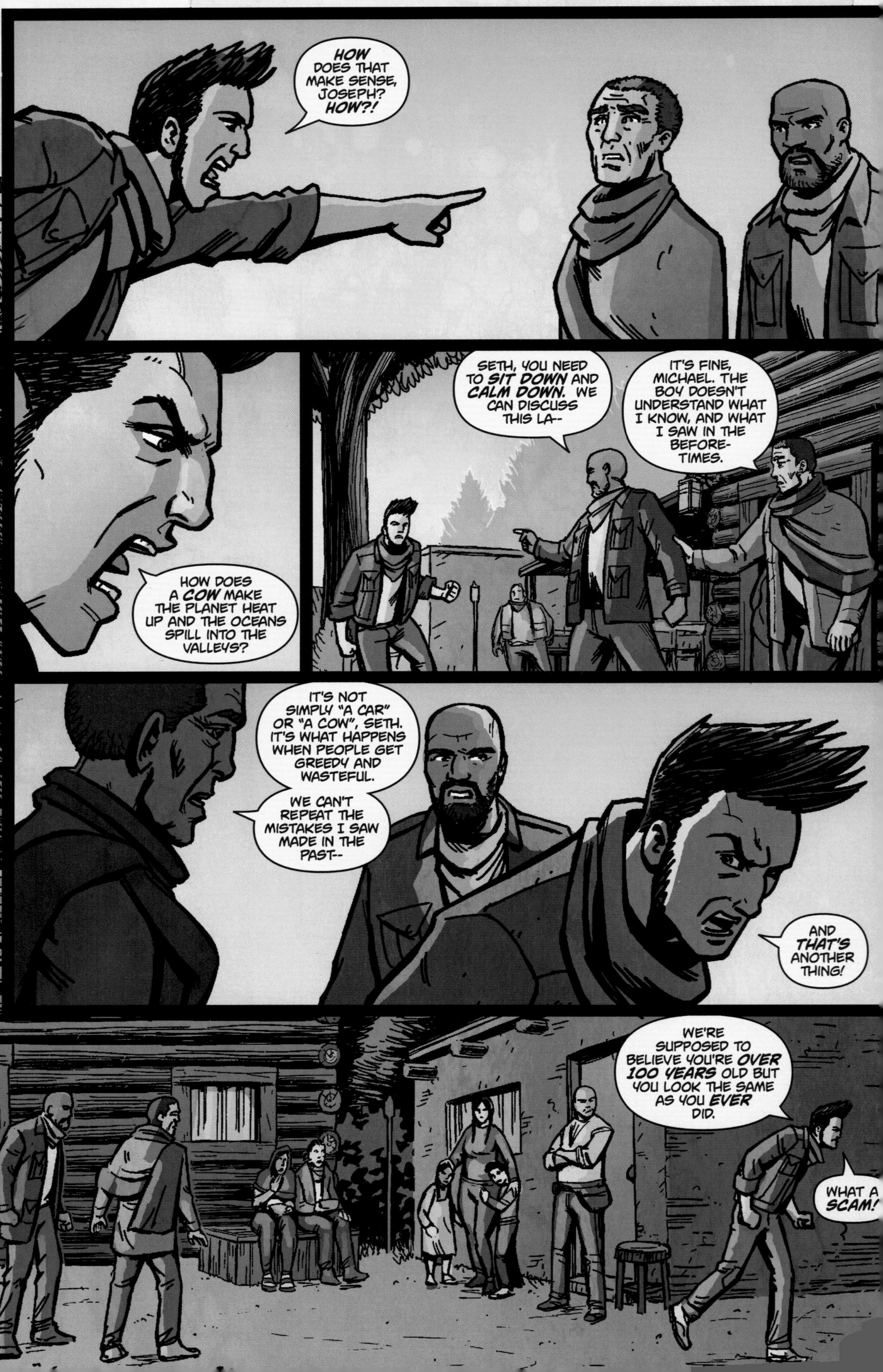
HOW DOES THAT MAKE SENSE, JOSEPH? HOW?!
HOW DOES A COW MAKE THE PLANET HEAT UP AND THE OCEANS SPILL INTO THE VALLEYS?
SETH, YOU NEED TO SIT DOWN AND CALM DOWN. WE CAN DISCUSS THIS LA--
IT'S FINE, MICHAEL. THE BOY DOESN'T UNDERSTAND WHAT I KNOW, AND WHAT I SAW IN THE BEFORE-TIMES.
IT'S NOT SIMPLY "A CAR" OR "A COW", SETH. IT'S WHAT HAPPENS WHEN PEOPLE GET GREEDY AND WASTEFUL.
WE CAN'T REPEAT THE MISTAKES I SAW MADE IN THE PAST--
AND THAT'S ANOTHER THING!
WE'RE SUPPOSED TO BELIEVE YOU'RE OVER 100 YEARS OLD BUT YOU LOOK THE SAME AS YOU EVER DID.
WHAT A SCAM!

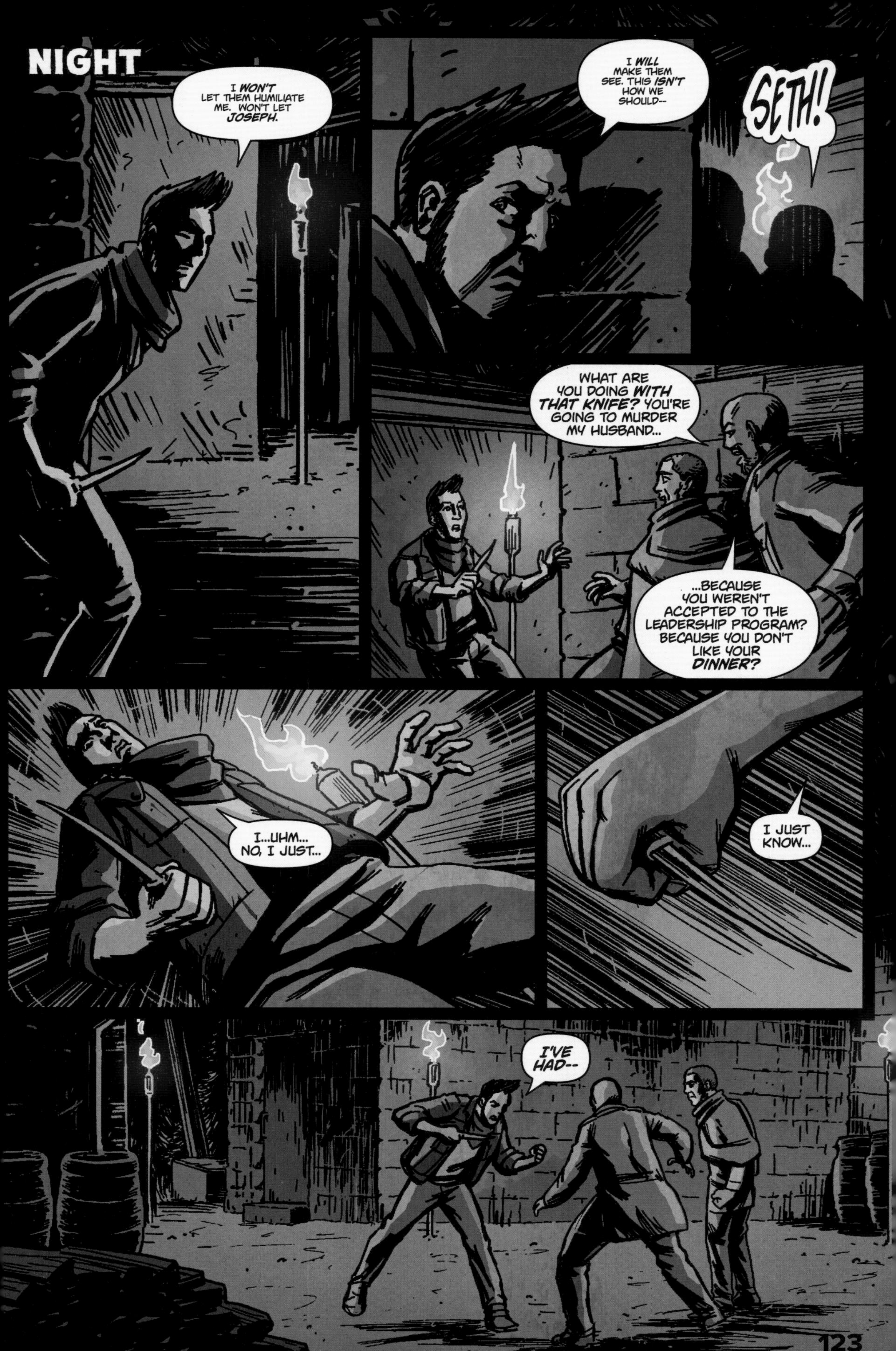
NIGHT
I WON'T LET THEM HUMILIATE ME. WON'T LET JOSEPH.
I WILL MAKE THEM SEE. THIS ISN'T HOW WE SHOULD--
SETH!
WHAT ARE YOU DOING WITH THAT KNIFE? YOU'RE GOING TO MURDER MY HUSBAND...
...BECAUSE YOU WEREN'T ACCEPTED TO THE LEADERSHIP PROGRAM? BECAUSE YOU DON'T LIKE YOUR DINNER?
I...UHM... NO, I JUST...
I JUST KNOW...
I'VE HAD--

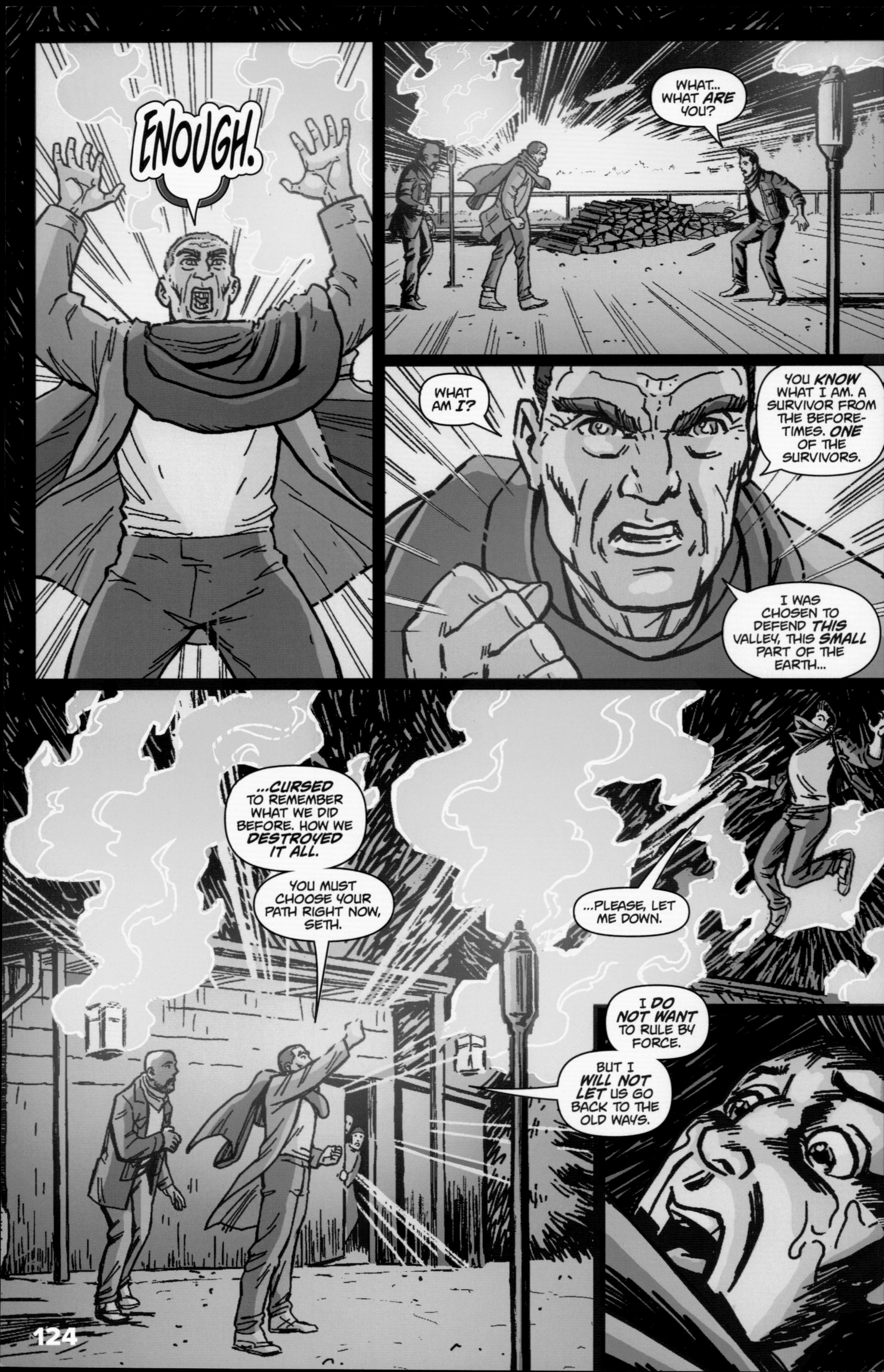
ENOUGH.
WHAT... WHAT ARE YOU?
WHAT AM I?
YOU KNOW WHAT I AM. A SURVIVOR FROM THE BEFORE-TIMES. ONE OF THE SURVIVORS.
I WAS CHOSEN TO DEFEND THIS VALLEY, THIS SMALL PART OF THE EARTH...
...CURSED TO REMEMBER WHAT WE DID BEFORE. HOW WE DESTROYED IT ALL.
YOU MUST CHOOSE YOUR PATH RIGHT NOW, SETH.
...PLEASE, LET ME DOWN.
I DO NOT WANT TO RULE BY FORCE.
BUT I WILL NOT LET US GO BACK TO THE OLD WAYS.

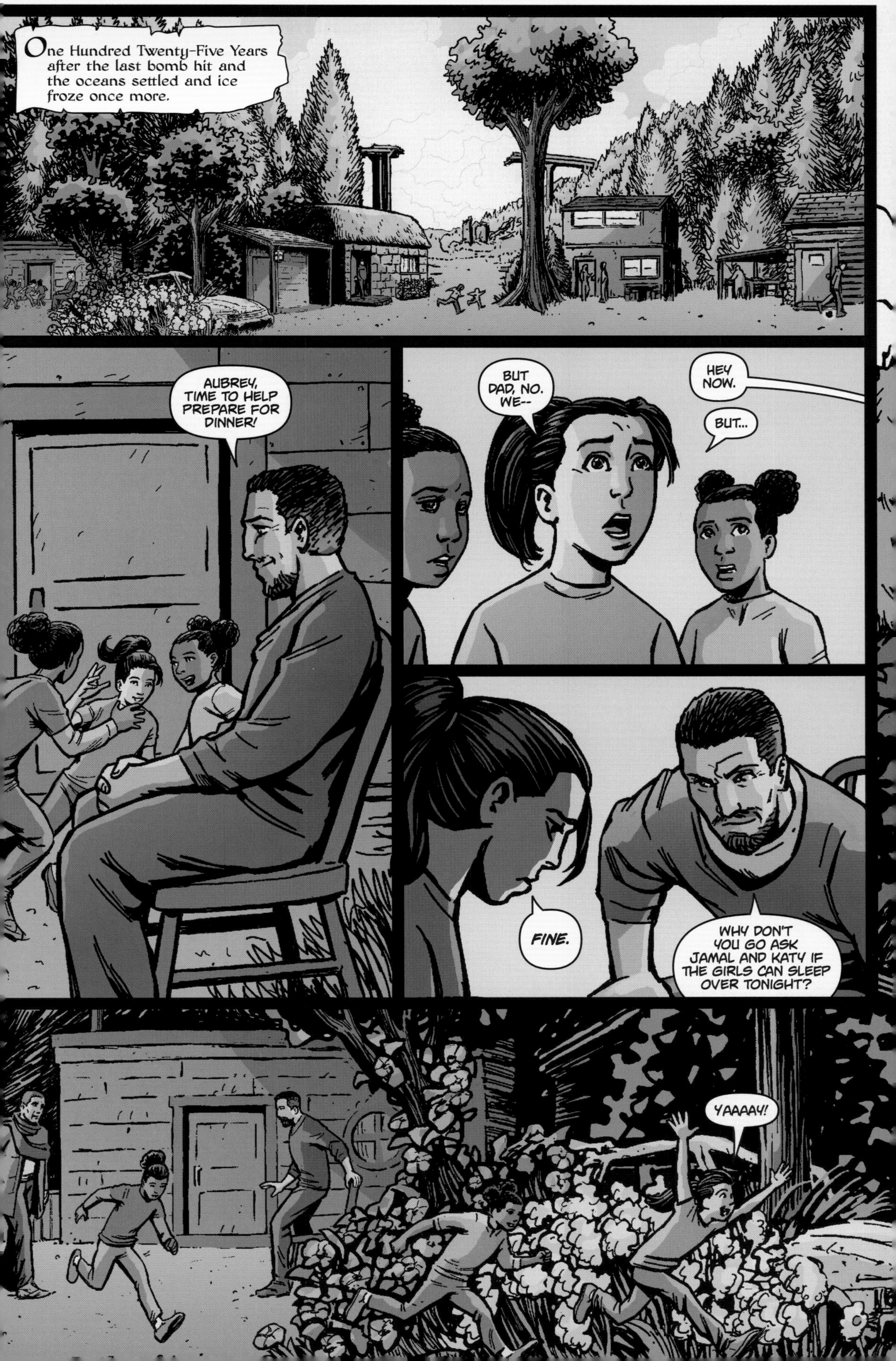
One Hundred Twenty-Five Years after the last bomb hit and the oceans settled and ice froze once more.
AUBREY, TIME TO HELP PREPARE FOR DINNER!
BUT DAD, NO. WE--
HEY NOW.
BUT...
FINE.
WHY DON'T YOU GO ASK JAMAL AND KATY IF THE GIRLS CAN SLEEP OVER TONIGHT?
YAAAAY!

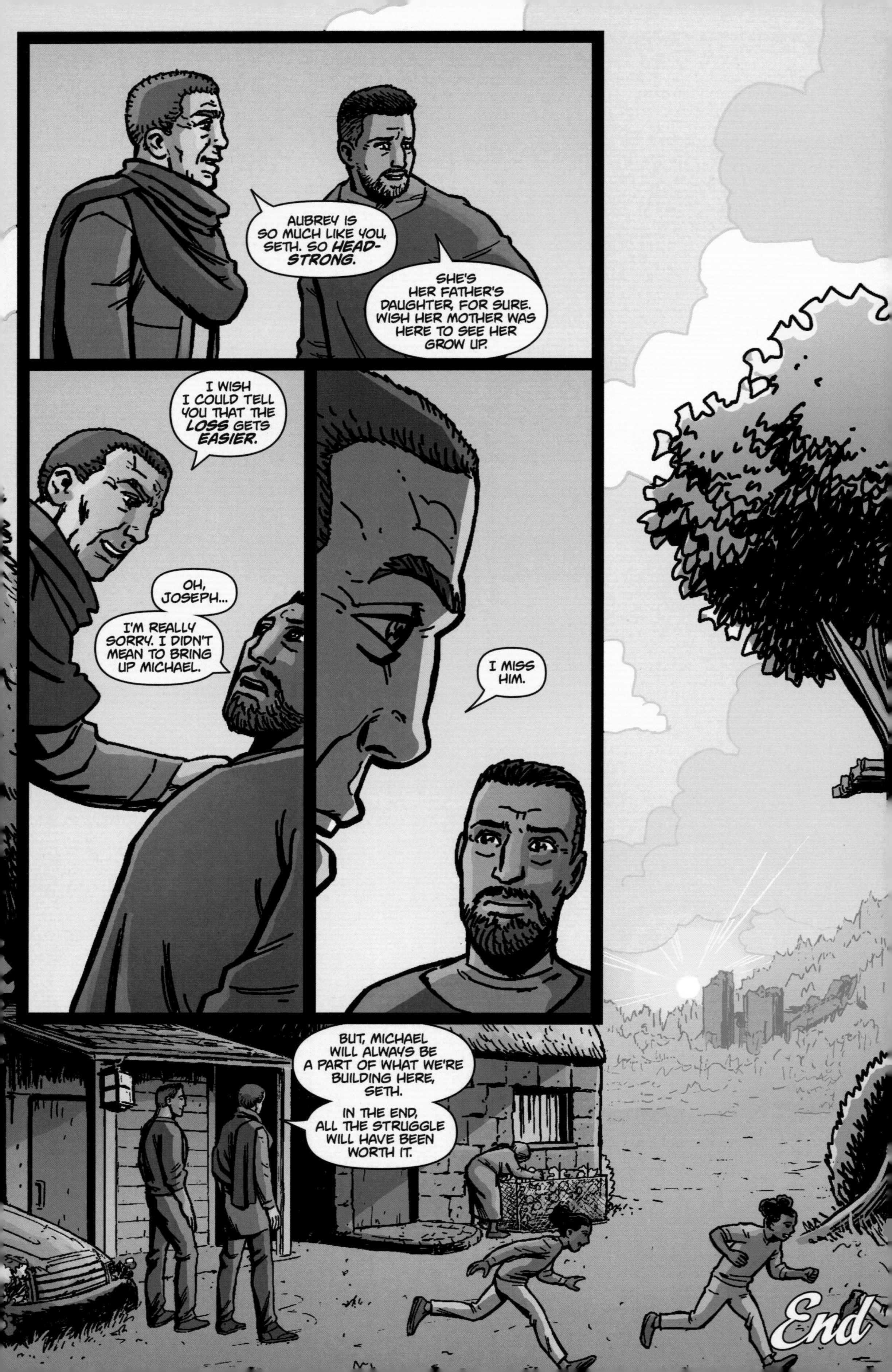
AUBREY IS SO MUCH LIKE YOU, SETH. SO HEAD-STRONG.
SHE'S HER FATHER'S DAUGHTER, FOR SURE. WISH HER MOTHER WAS HERE TO SEE HER GROW UP.
I WISH I COULD TELL YOU THAT THE LOSS GETS EASIER.
OH, JOSEPH...
I'M REALLY SORRY. I DIDN'T MEAN TO BRING UP MICHAEL.
I MISS HIM.
BUT, MICHAEL WILL ALWAYS BE A PART OF WHAT WE'RE BUILDING HERE, SETH.
IN THE END, ALL THE STRUGGLE WILL HAVE BEEN WORTH IT.
End

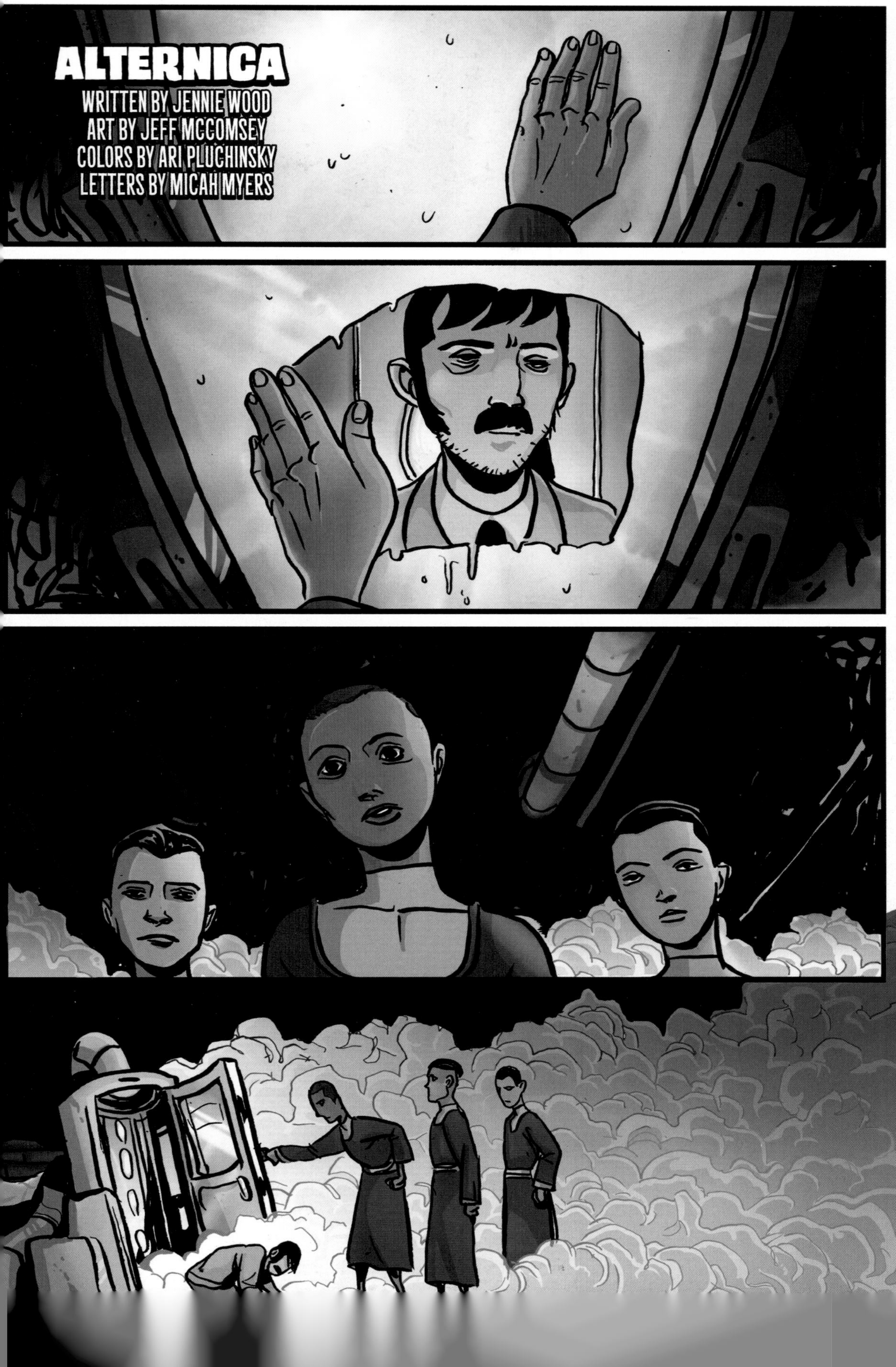
ALTERNICA
WRITTEN BY JENNIE WOOD
ART BY JEFF MCCOMSEY
COLORS BY ARI PLUCHINSKY
LETTERS BY MICAH MYERS

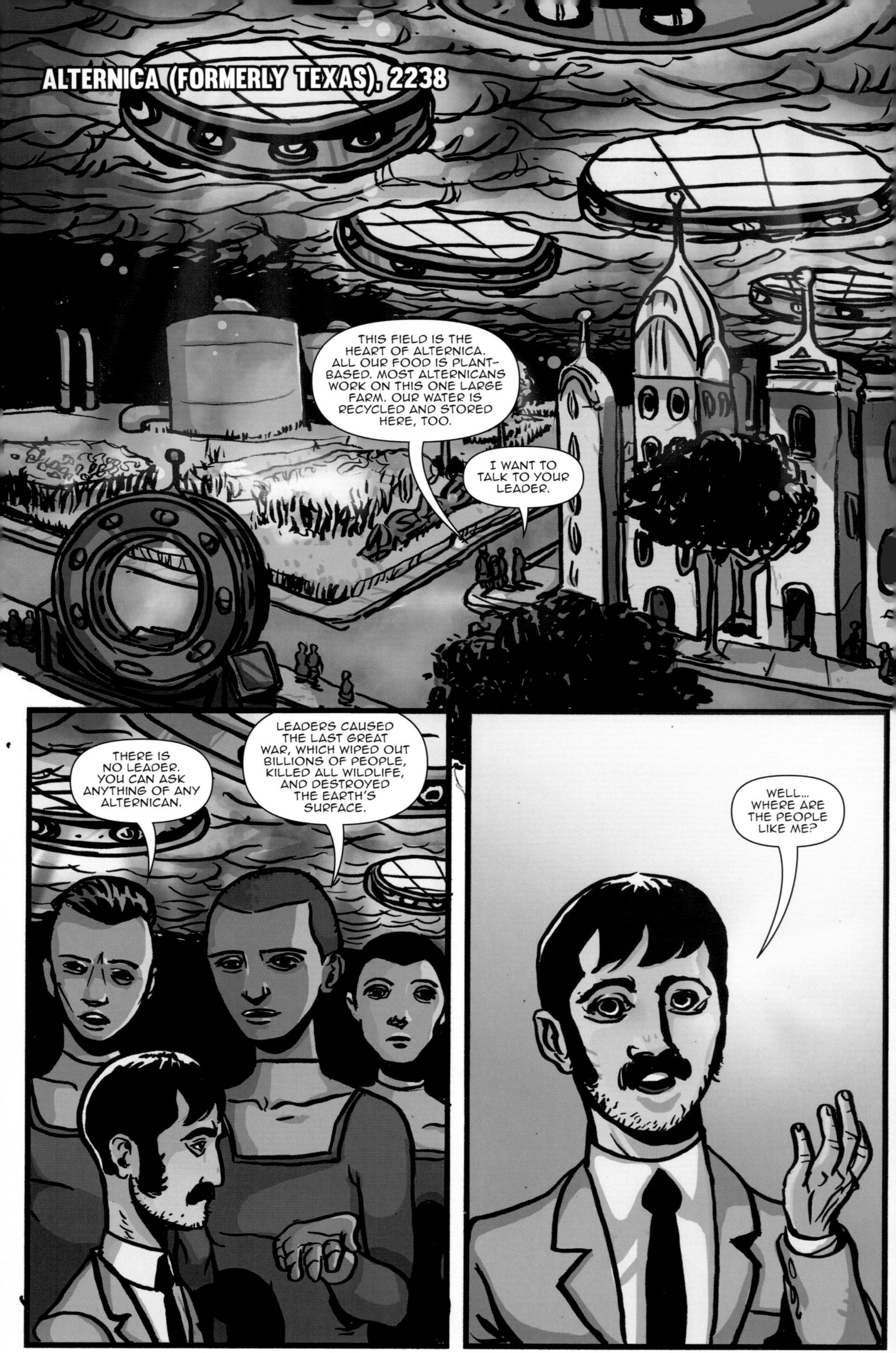
ALTERNICA (FORMERLY TEXAS), 2238
THIS FIELD IS THE HEART OF ALTERNICA. ALL OUR FOOD IS PLANT-BASED. MOST ALTERNICANS WORK ON THIS ONE LARGE FARM. OUR WATER IS RECYCLED AND STORED HERE, TOO.
I WANT TO TALK TO YOUR LEADER.
THERE IS NO LEADER. YOU CAN ASK ANYTHING OF ANY ALTERNICAN.
LEADERS CAUSED THE LAST GREAT WAR, WHICH WIPED OUT BILLIONS OF PEOPLE, KILLED ALL WILDLIFE, AND DESTROYED THE EARTH'S SURFACE.
WELL... WHERE ARE THE PEOPLE LIKE ME?

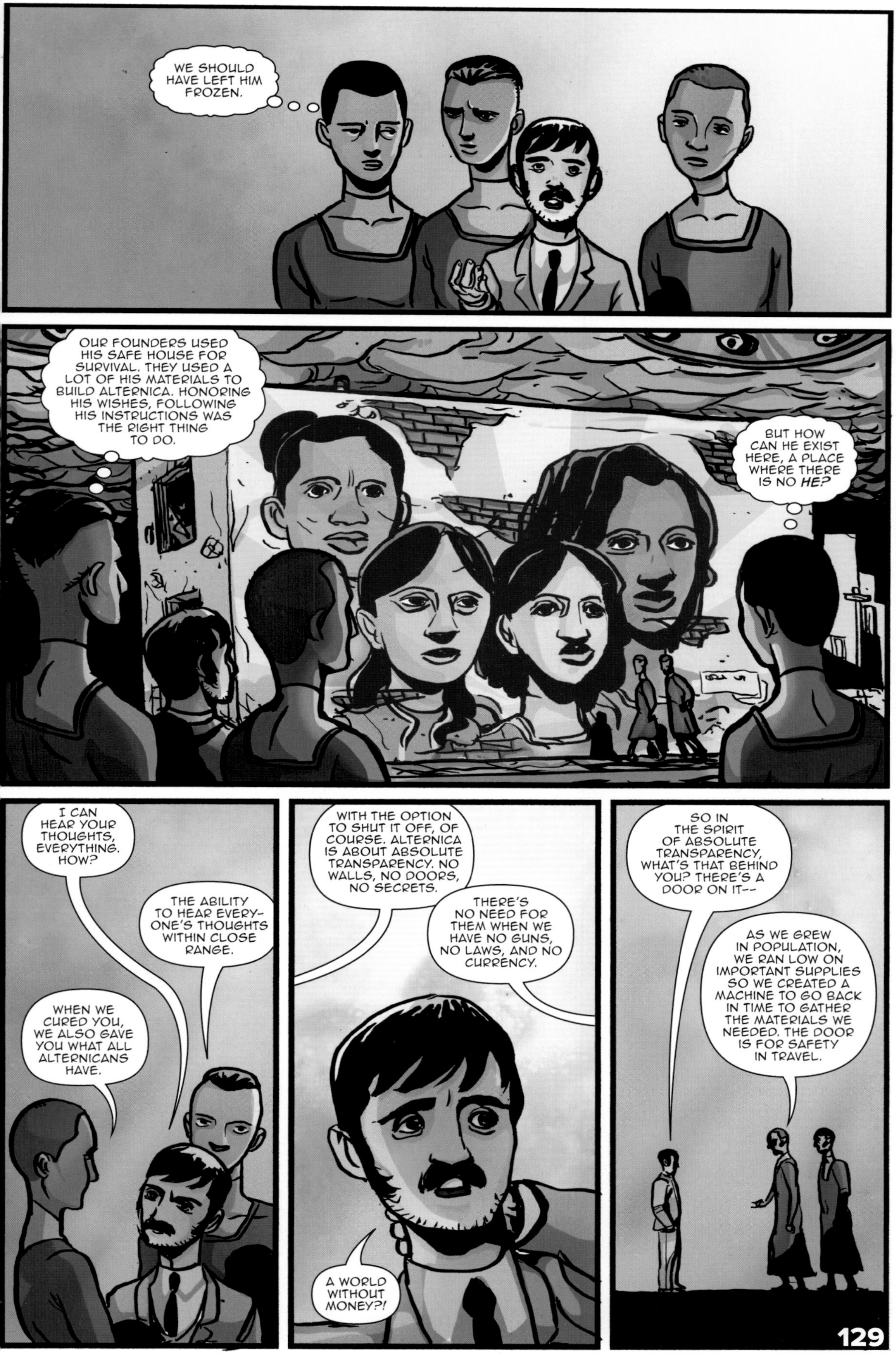
WE SHOULD HAVE LEFT HIM FROZEN.
OUR FOUNDERS USED HIS SAFE HOUSE FOR SURVIVAL. THEY USED A LOT OF HIS MATERIALS TO BUILD ALTERNICA. HONORING HIS WISHES, FOLLOWING HIS INSTRUCTIONS WAS THE RIGHT THING TO DO.
BUT HOW CAN HE EXIST HERE, A PLACE WHERE THERE IS NO *HE?*
I CAN HEAR YOUR THOUGHTS, EVERYTHING. HOW?
THE ABILITY TO HEAR EVERY-ONE'S THOUGHTS WITHIN CLOSE RANGE.
WHEN WE CURED YOU, WE ALSO GAVE YOU WHAT ALL ALTERNICANS HAVE.
WITH THE OPTION TO SHUT IT OFF, OF COURSE. ALTERNICA IS ABOUT ABSOLUTE TRANSPARENCY. NO WALLS, NO DOORS, NO SECRETS.
THERE'S NO NEED FOR THEM WHEN WE HAVE NO GUNS, NO LAWS, AND NO CURRENCY.
A WORLD WITHOUT MONEY?!
SO IN THE SPIRIT OF ABSOLUTE TRANSPARENCY, WHAT'S THAT BEHIND YOU? THERE'S A DOOR ON IT--
AS WE GREW IN POPULATION, WE RAN LOW ON IMPORTANT SUPPLIES SO WE CREATED A MACHINE TO GO BACK IN TIME TO GATHER THE MATERIALS WE NEEDED. THE DOOR IS FOR SAFETY IN TRAVEL.

NO GUNS? NO POLICE? I MUST RESTORE ORDER.

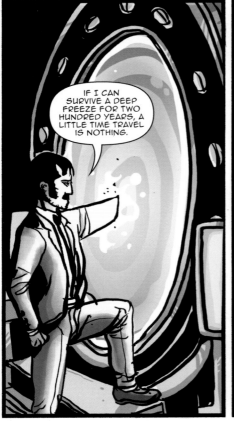

IF I CAN SURVIVE A DEEP FREEZE FOR TWO HUNDRED YEARS, A LITTLE TIME TRAVEL IS NOTHING.

HE DIDN'T EVEN REALIZE THAT WE COULD HEAR HIS THOUGHTS. WE'RE NOTHING TO HIM.

THAT'S WHY WE HAD TO LET HIM GO. HE WOULD'VE TRIED TO DESTROY US.

BUT WHAT IF HIS GOING BACK PREVENTS US FROM EXISTING? OUR WORLD IS BETTER. HERE WE HAVE NO WAR, NO NEED FOR WEAPONS.

130

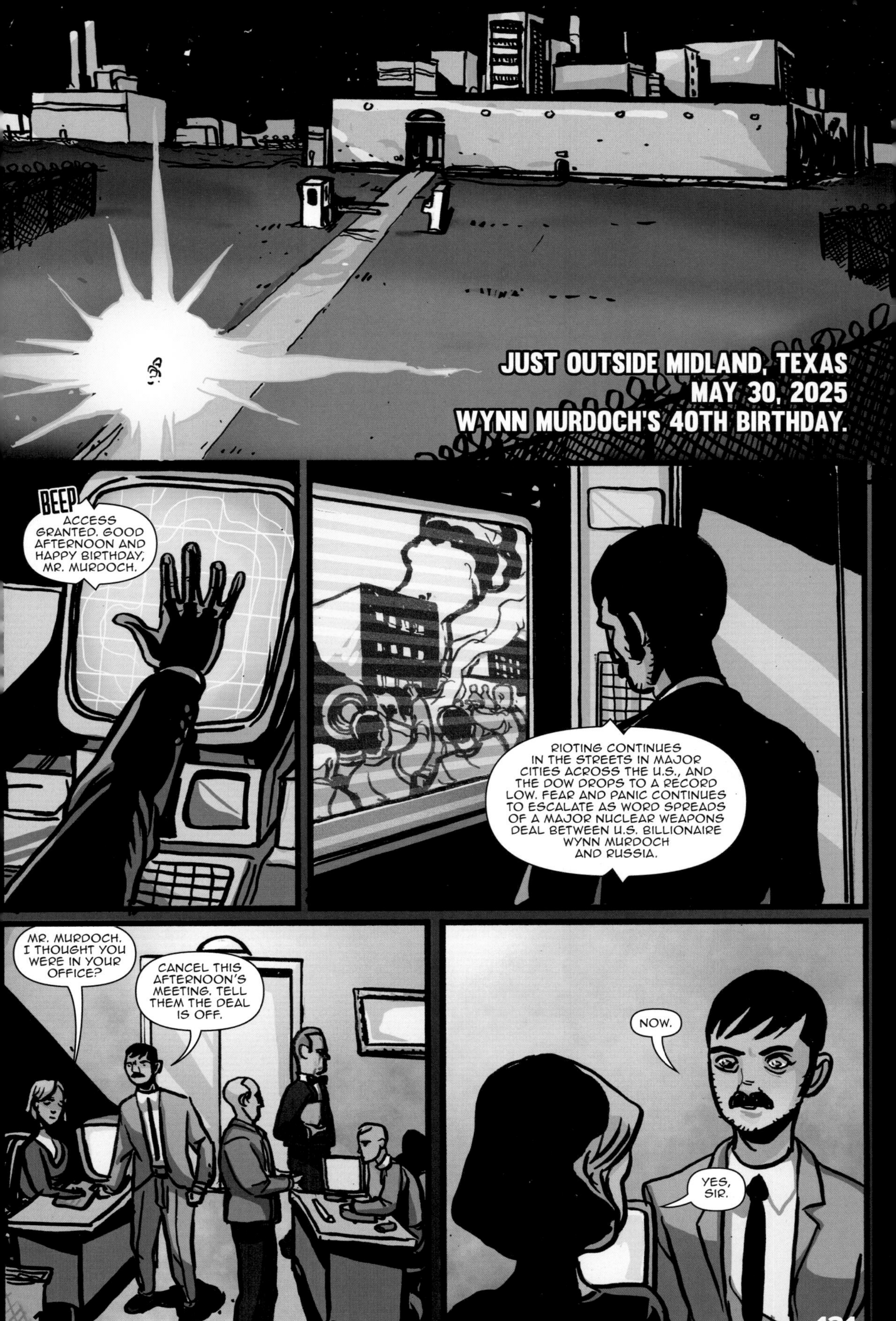
JUST OUTSIDE MIDLAND, TEXAS
MAY 30, 2025
WYNN MURDOCH'S 40TH BIRTHDAY.
BEEP
ACCESS GRANTED. GOOD AFTERNOON AND HAPPY BIRTHDAY, MR. MURDOCH.
RIOTING CONTINUES IN THE STREETS IN MAJOR CITIES ACROSS THE U.S., AND THE DOW DROPS TO A RECORD LOW. FEAR AND PANIC CONTINUES TO ESCALATE AS WORD SPREADS OF A MAJOR NUCLEAR WEAPONS DEAL BETWEEN U.S. BILLIONAIRE WYNN MURDOCH AND RUSSIA.
MR. MURDOCH. I THOUGHT YOU WERE IN YOUR OFFICE?
CANCEL THIS AFTERNOON'S MEETING. TELL THEM THE DEAL IS OFF.
NOW.
YES, SIR.

YES, I AGREE, MR. PRESIDENT. IT'S ONLY FAIR. I'M SIGNING IT RIGHT NOW. I'LL HAVE MY PEOPLE SEND A COPY OVER TO YOU.

GET OFF THE PHONE.

WHA-WHA-WHAT...

STOP SPUTTERING. I'M YOU, FROM THE FUTURE.

WOW. TALK ABOUT BIRTHDAY GIFTS. I HOLD UP WELL.

I HAVE SO MANY QUESTIONS. WHAT YEAR DID I DECIDE ON? WHAT YEAR ARE YOU FROM? HOW DO THE WOMEN LOOK?

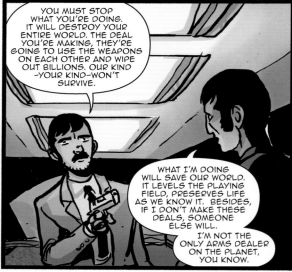

YOU MUST STOP WHAT YOU'RE DOING. IT WILL DESTROY YOUR ENTIRE WORLD. THE DEAL YOU'RE MAKING, THEY'RE GOING TO USE THE WEAPONS ON EACH OTHER AND WIPE OUT BILLIONS. OUR KIND –YOUR KIND–WON'T SURVIVE.

WHAT I'M DOING WILL SAVE OUR WORLD. IT LEVELS THE PLAYING FIELD, PRESERVES LIFE AS WE KNOW IT. BESIDES, IF I DON'T MAKE THESE DEALS, SOMEONE ELSE WILL.

I'M NOT THE ONLY ARMS DEALER ON THE PLANET, YOU KNOW.

BANG

KNOCK KNOCK

MR. MURDOCH? EVERYTHING OKAY?

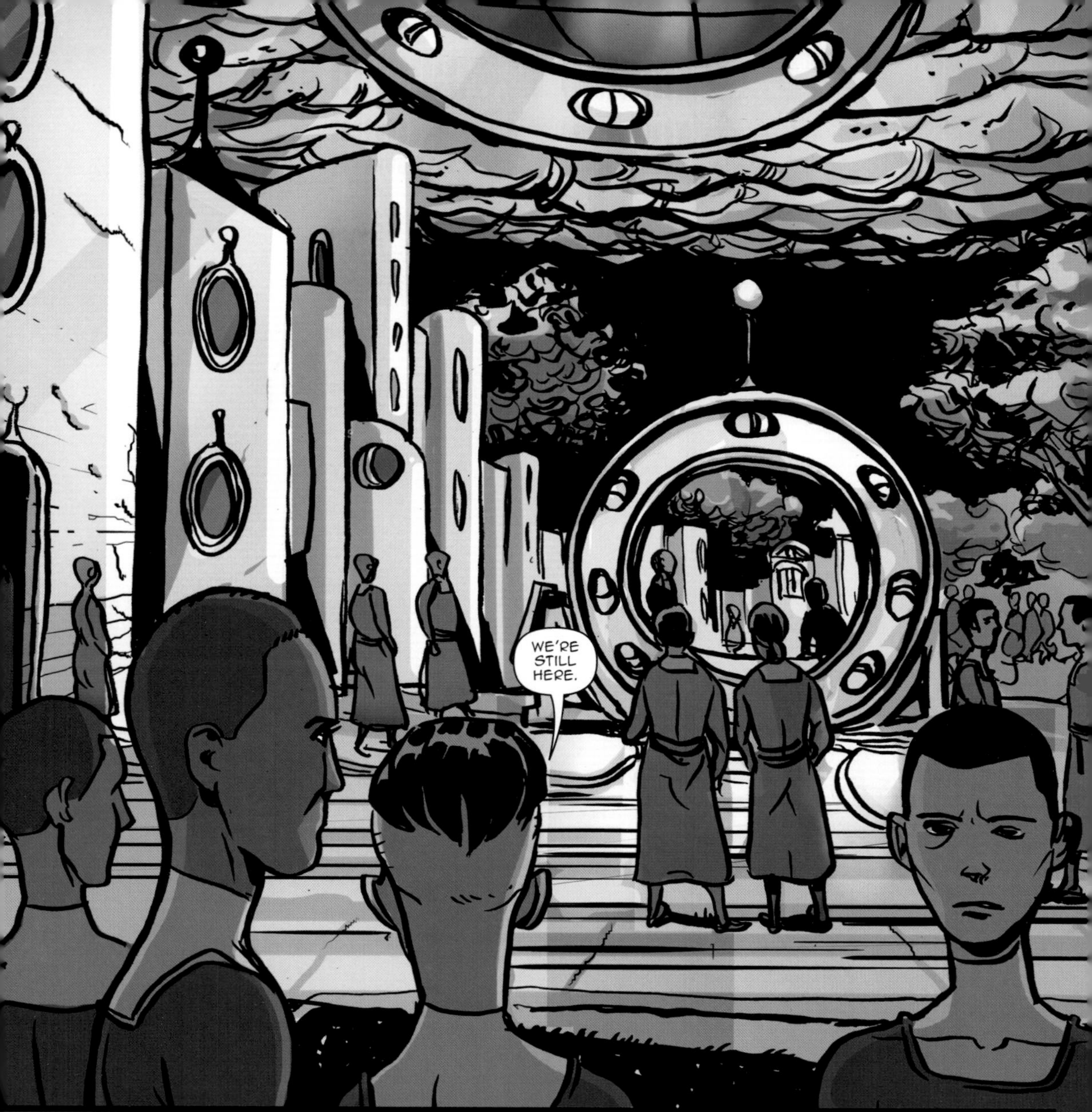
WE'RE STILL HERE.

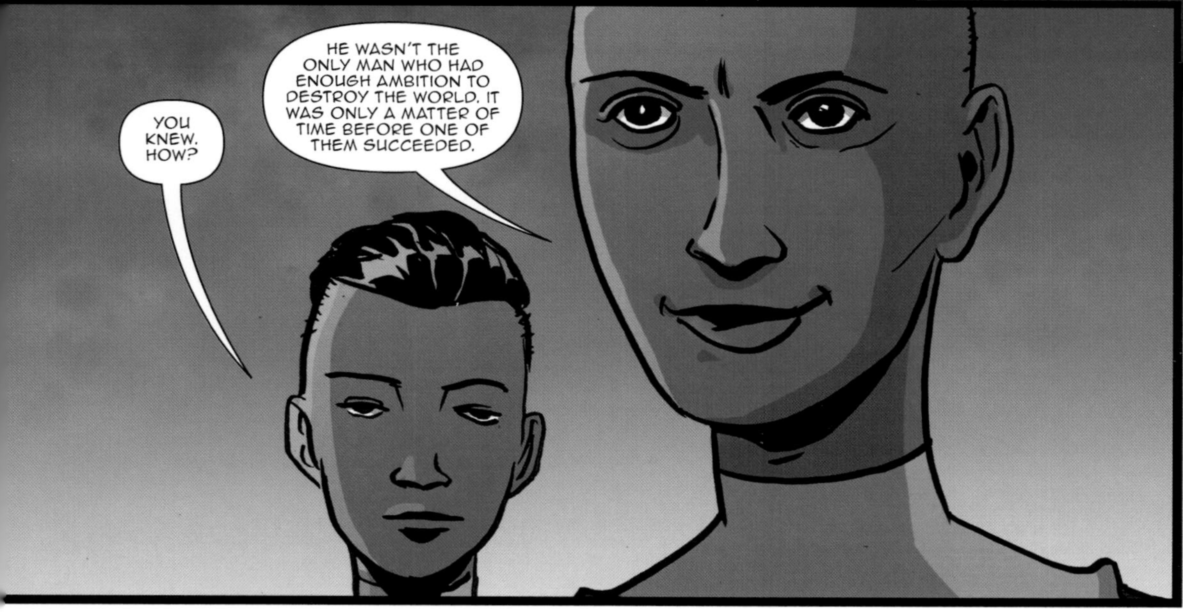
YOU KNEW. HOW?
HE WASN'T THE ONLY MAN WHO HAD ENOUGH AMBITION TO DESTROY THE WORLD. IT WAS ONLY A MATTER OF TIME BEFORE ONE OF THEM SUCCEEDED.

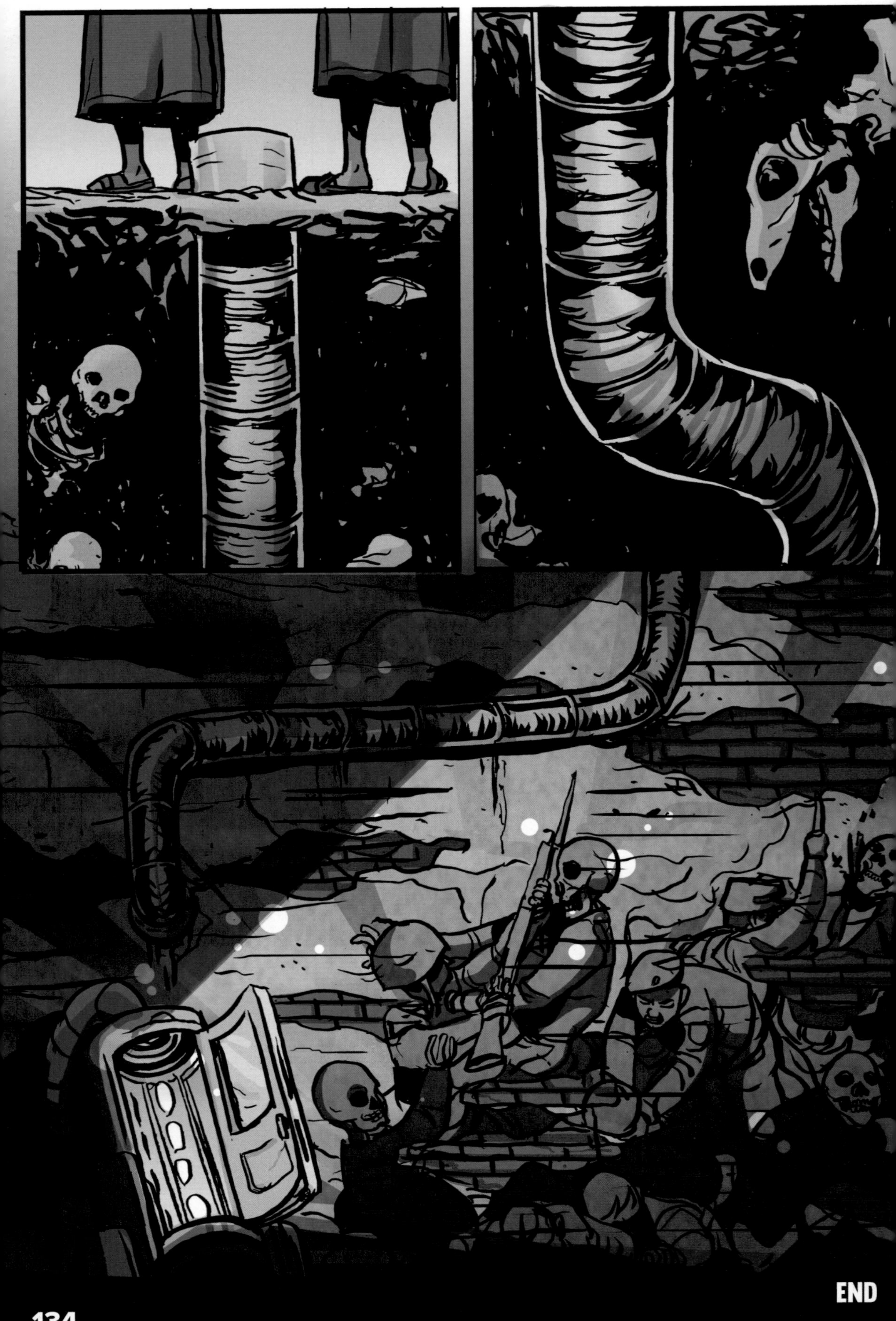

END

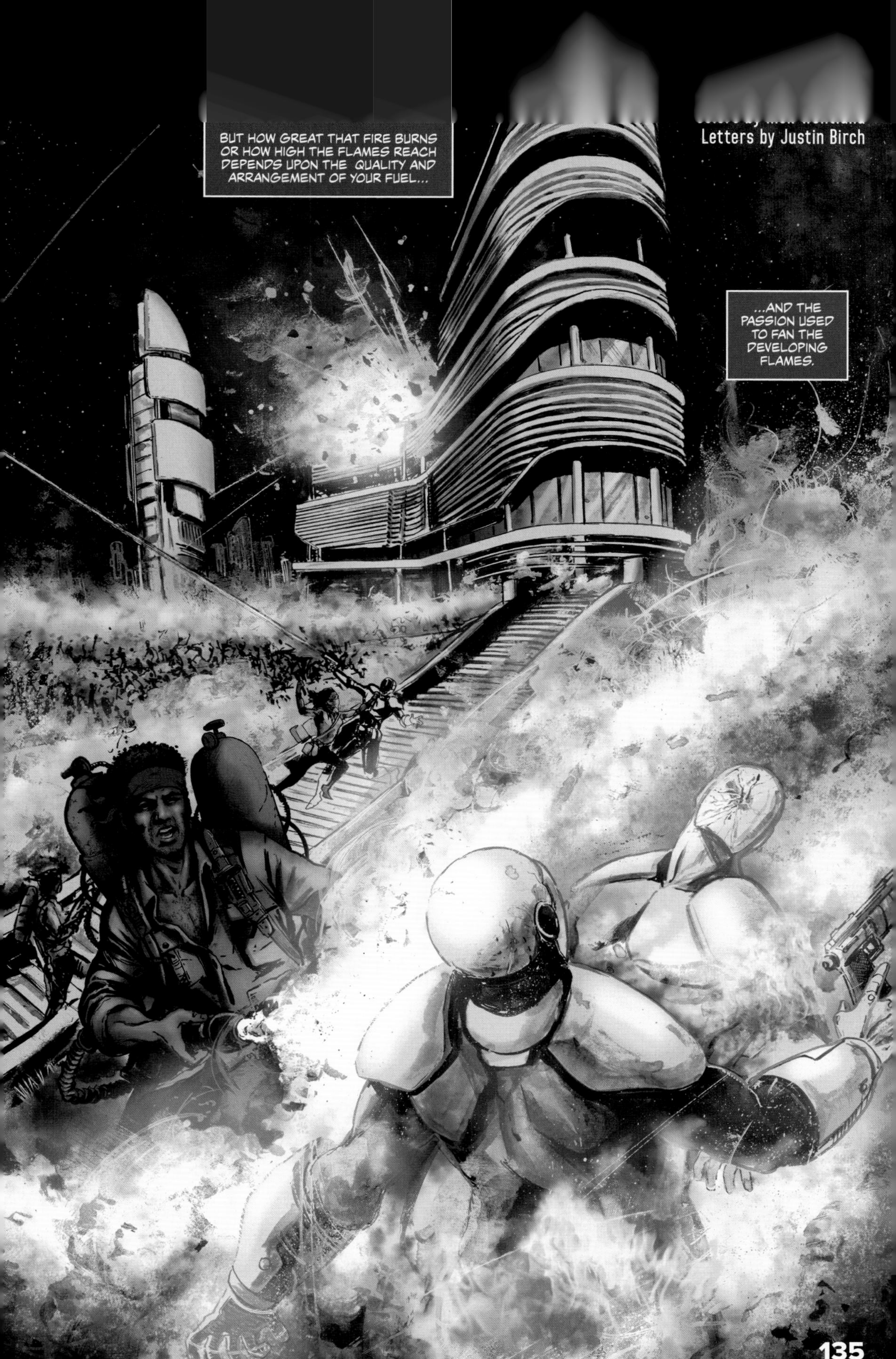
Letters by Justin Birch
BUT HOW GREAT THAT FIRE BURNS OR HOW HIGH THE FLAMES REACH DEPENDS UPON THE QUALITY AND ARRANGEMENT OF YOUR FUEL...
...AND THE PASSION USED TO FAN THE DEVELOPING FLAMES.

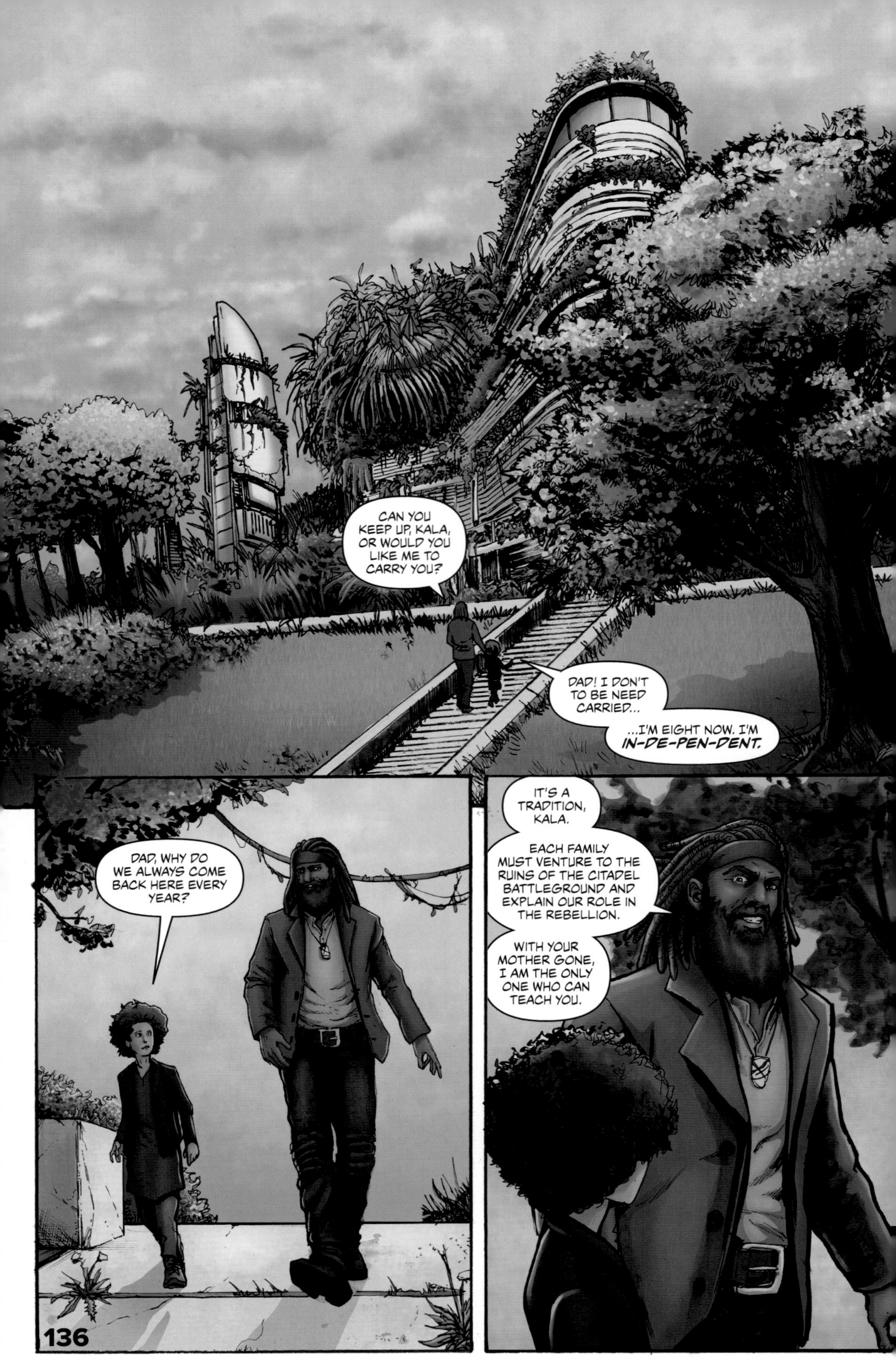
CAN YOU KEEP UP, KALA, OR WOULD YOU LIKE ME TO CARRY YOU?
DAD! I DON'T TO BE NEED CARRIED...
...I'M EIGHT NOW. I'M *IN-DE-PEN-DENT.*
DAD, WHY DO WE ALWAYS COME BACK HERE EVERY YEAR?
IT'S A TRADITION, KALA.
EACH FAMILY MUST VENTURE TO THE RUINS OF THE CITADEL BATTLEGROUND AND EXPLAIN OUR ROLE IN THE REBELLION.
WITH YOUR MOTHER GONE, I AM THE ONLY ONE WHO CAN TEACH YOU.

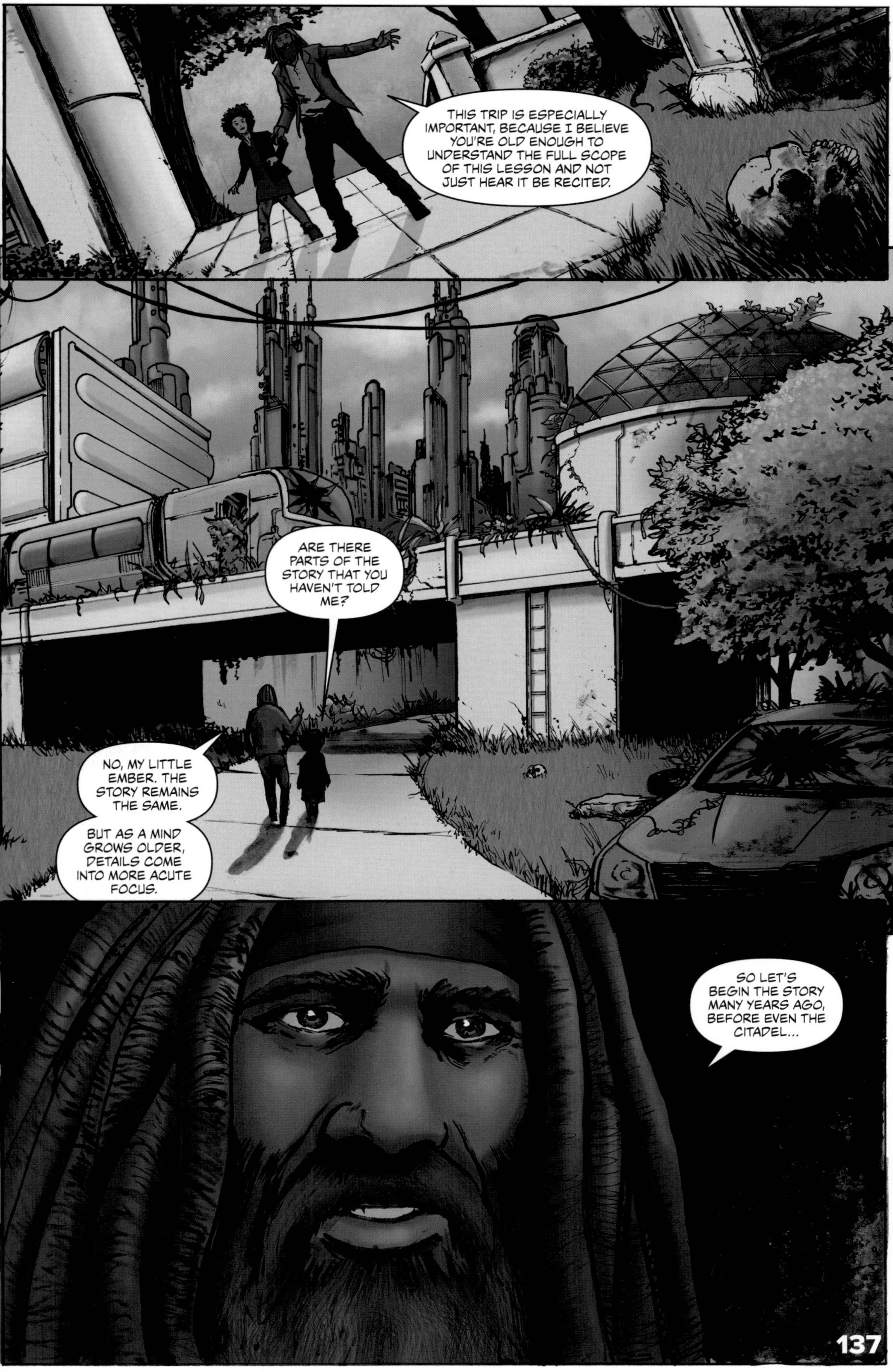
THIS TRIP IS ESPECIALLY IMPORTANT, BECAUSE I BELIEVE YOU'RE OLD ENOUGH TO UNDERSTAND THE FULL SCOPE OF THIS LESSON AND NOT JUST HEAR IT BE RECITED.
ARE THERE PARTS OF THE STORY THAT YOU HAVEN'T TOLD ME?
NO, MY LITTLE EMBER. THE STORY REMAINS THE SAME.
BUT AS A MIND GROWS OLDER, DETAILS COME INTO MORE ACUTE FOCUS.
SO LET'S BEGIN THE STORY MANY YEARS AGO, BEFORE EVEN THE CITADEL...

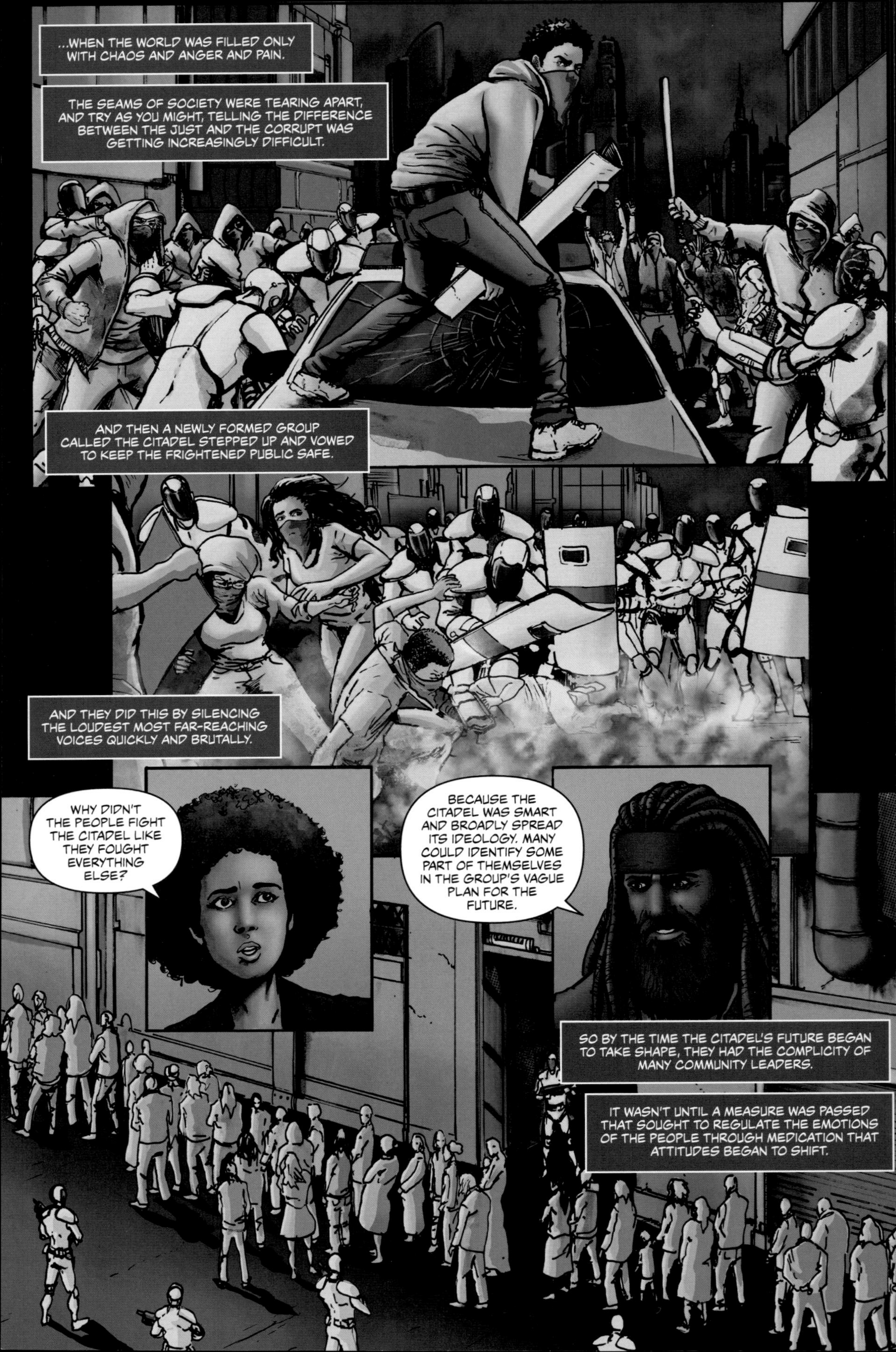
...WHEN THE WORLD WAS FILLED ONLY WITH CHAOS AND ANGER AND PAIN.
THE SEAMS OF SOCIETY WERE TEARING APART, AND TRY AS YOU MIGHT, TELLING THE DIFFERENCE BETWEEN THE JUST AND THE CORRUPT WAS GETTING INCREASINGLY DIFFICULT.
AND THEN A NEWLY FORMED GROUP CALLED THE CITADEL STEPPED UP AND VOWED TO KEEP THE FRIGHTENED PUBLIC SAFE.
AND THEY DID THIS BY SILENCING THE LOUDEST MOST FAR-REACHING VOICES QUICKLY AND BRUTALLY.
WHY DIDN'T THE PEOPLE FIGHT THE CITADEL LIKE THEY FOUGHT EVERYTHING ELSE?
BECAUSE THE CITADEL WAS SMART AND BROADLY SPREAD ITS IDEOLOGY. MANY COULD IDENTIFY SOME PART OF THEMSELVES IN THE GROUP'S VAGUE PLAN FOR THE FUTURE.
SO BY THE TIME THE CITADEL'S FUTURE BEGAN TO TAKE SHAPE, THEY HAD THE COMPLICITY OF MANY COMMUNITY LEADERS.
IT WASN'T UNTIL A MEASURE WAS PASSED THAT SOUGHT TO REGULATE THE EMOTIONS OF THE PEOPLE THROUGH MEDICATION THAT ATTITUDES BEGAN TO SHIFT.

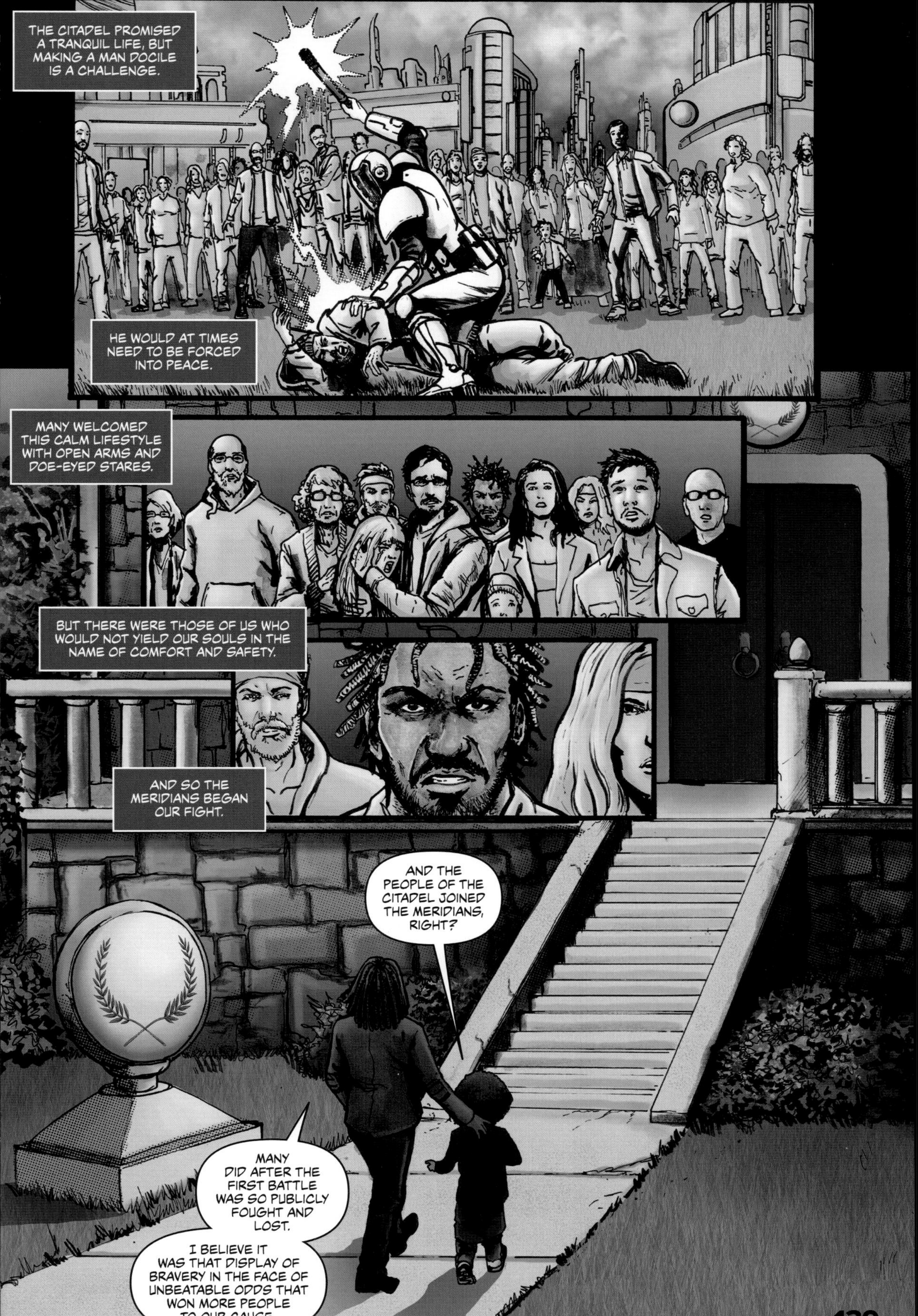
THE CITADEL PROMISED A TRANQUIL LIFE, BUT MAKING A MAN DOCILE IS A CHALLENGE.
HE WOULD AT TIMES NEED TO BE FORCED INTO PEACE.
MANY WELCOMED THIS CALM LIFESTYLE WITH OPEN ARMS AND DOE-EYED STARES.
BUT THERE WERE THOSE OF US WHO WOULD NOT YIELD OUR SOULS IN THE NAME OF COMFORT AND SAFETY.
AND SO THE MERIDIANS BEGAN OUR FIGHT.
AND THE PEOPLE OF THE CITADEL JOINED THE MERIDIANS, RIGHT?
MANY DID AFTER THE FIRST BATTLE WAS SO PUBLICLY FOUGHT AND LOST.
I BELIEVE IT WAS THAT DISPLAY OF BRAVERY IN THE FACE OF UNBEATABLE ODDS THAT WON MORE PEOPLE TO OUR CAUSE.

SOON THE MERIDIANS HAD THE NUMBERS NEEDED TO OVERCOME THE CITADEL'S POWER.

AND SO YOU GAVE THEM WHAT THEY DESERVED!

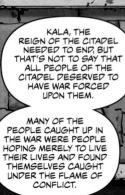

KALA, THE REIGN OF THE CITADEL NEEDED TO END, BUT THAT'S NOT TO SAY THAT ALL PEOPLE OF THE CITADEL DESERVED TO HAVE WAR FORCED UPON THEM.

MANY OF THE PEOPLE CAUGHT UP IN THE WAR WERE PEOPLE HOPING MERELY TO LIVE THEIR LIVES AND FOUND THEMSELVES CAUGHT UNDER THE FLAME OF CONFLICT.

IS THAT WHY WE ALWAYS END THIS TRIP IN THE *BAD ROOM?*

YES, MY LOVE.

ARE YOU READY?

I GUESS...

140

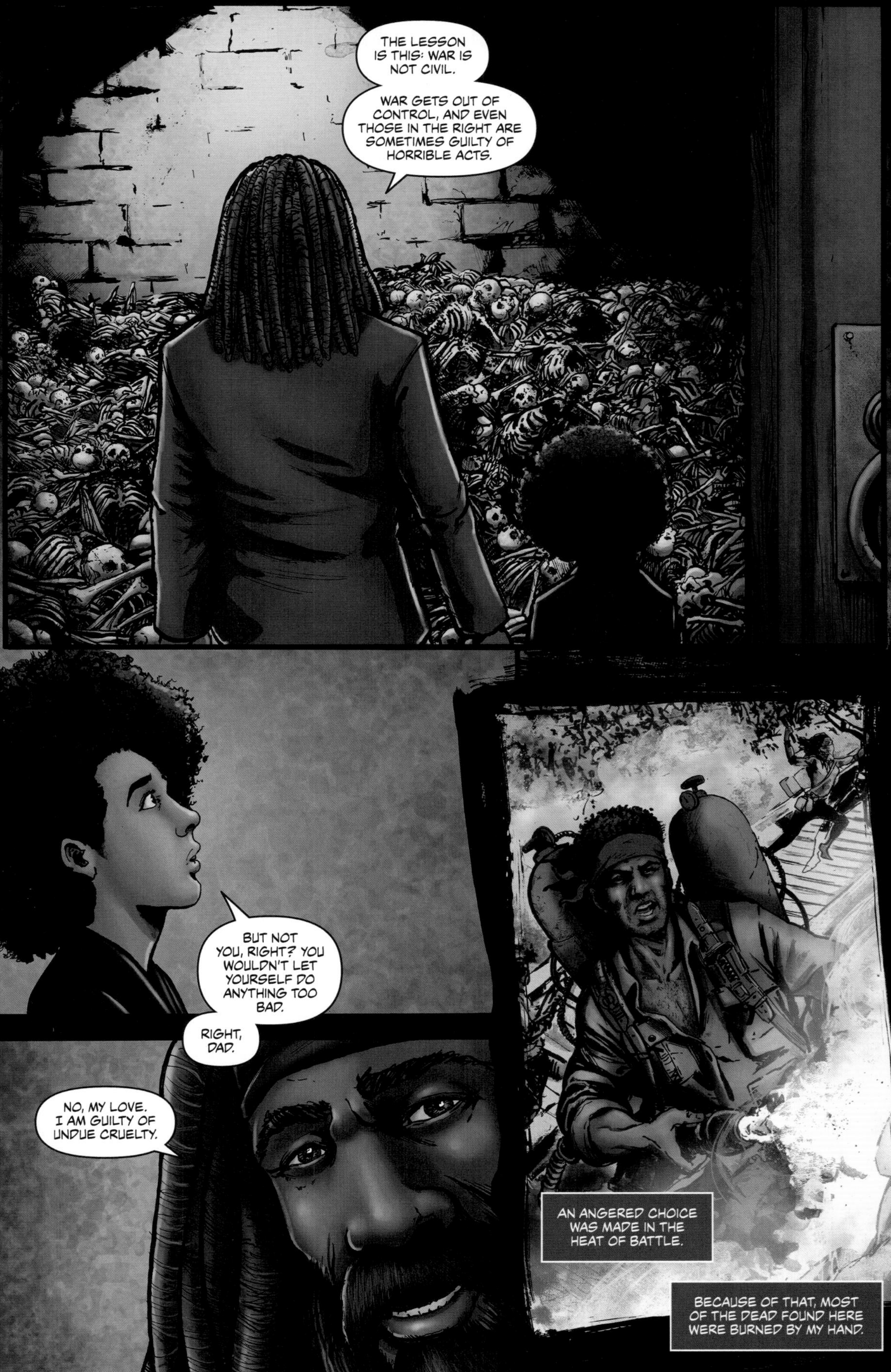
THE LESSON IS THIS: WAR IS NOT CIVIL.
WAR GETS OUT OF CONTROL, AND EVEN THOSE IN THE RIGHT ARE SOMETIMES GUILTY OF HORRIBLE ACTS.
BUT NOT YOU, RIGHT? YOU WOULDN'T LET YOURSELF DO ANYTHING TOO BAD.
RIGHT, DAD.
NO, MY LOVE. I AM GUILTY OF UNDUE CRUELTY.
AN ANGERED CHOICE WAS MADE IN THE HEAT OF BATTLE.
BECAUSE OF THAT, MOST OF THE DEAD FOUND HERE WERE BURNED BY MY HAND.

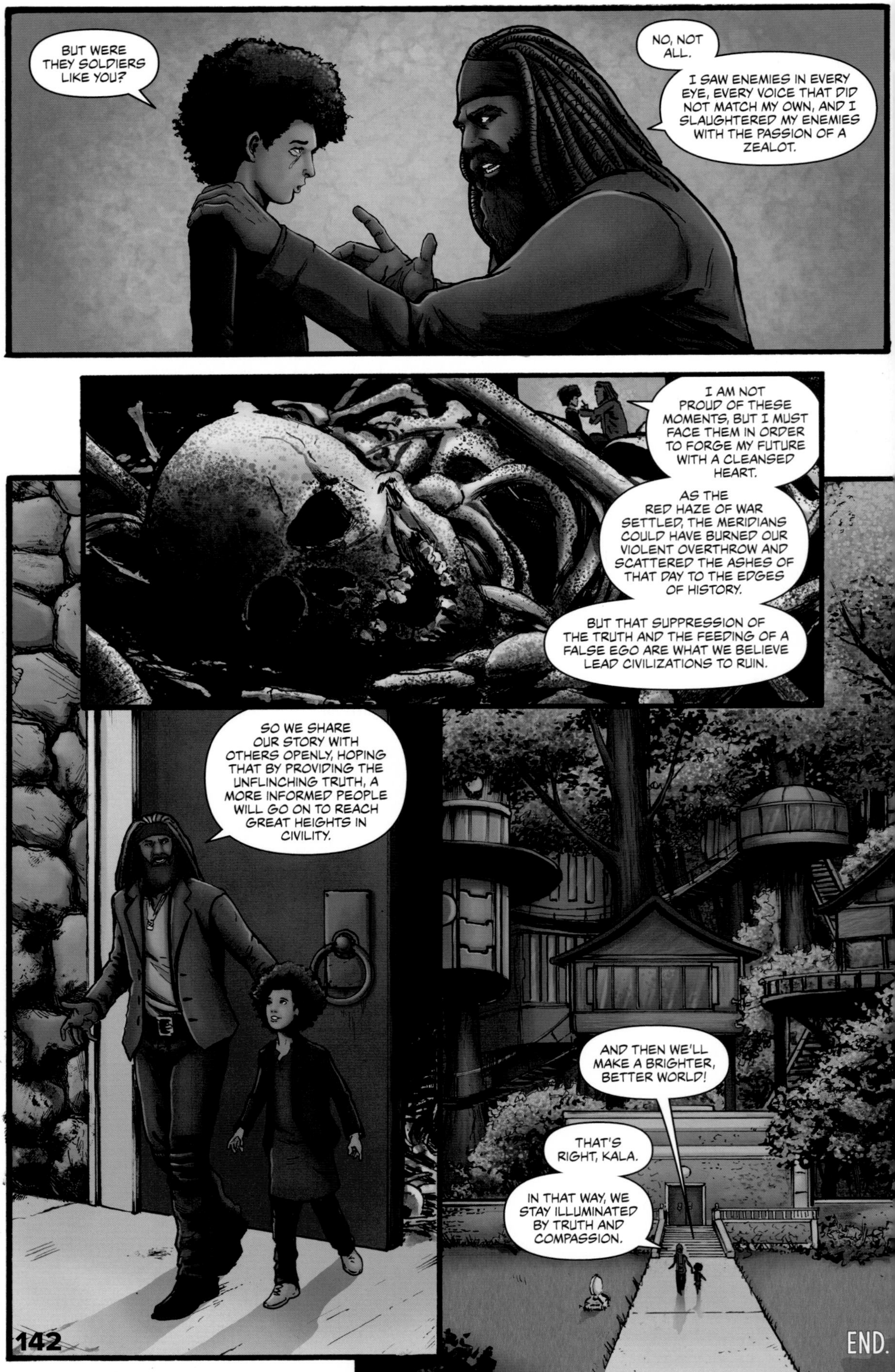
BUT WERE THEY SOLDIERS LIKE YOU?
NO, NOT ALL.
I SAW ENEMIES IN EVERY EYE, EVERY VOICE THAT DID NOT MATCH MY OWN, AND I SLAUGHTERED MY ENEMIES WITH THE PASSION OF A ZEALOT.
I AM NOT PROUD OF THESE MOMENTS, BUT I MUST FACE THEM IN ORDER TO FORGE MY FUTURE WITH A CLEANSED HEART.
AS THE RED HAZE OF WAR SETTLED, THE MERIDIANS COULD HAVE BURNED OUR VIOLENT OVERTHROW AND SCATTERED THE ASHES OF THAT DAY TO THE EDGES OF HISTORY.
BUT THAT SUPPRESSION OF THE TRUTH AND THE FEEDING OF A FALSE EGO ARE WHAT WE BELIEVE LEAD CIVILIZATIONS TO RUIN.
SO WE SHARE OUR STORY WITH OTHERS OPENLY, HOPING THAT BY PROVIDING THE UNFLINCHING TRUTH, A MORE INFORMED PEOPLE WILL GO ON TO REACH GREAT HEIGHTS IN CIVILITY.
AND THEN WE'LL MAKE A BRIGHTER, BETTER WORLD!
THAT'S RIGHT, KALA.
IN THAT WAY, WE STAY ILLUMINATED BY TRUTH AND COMPASSION.
END.

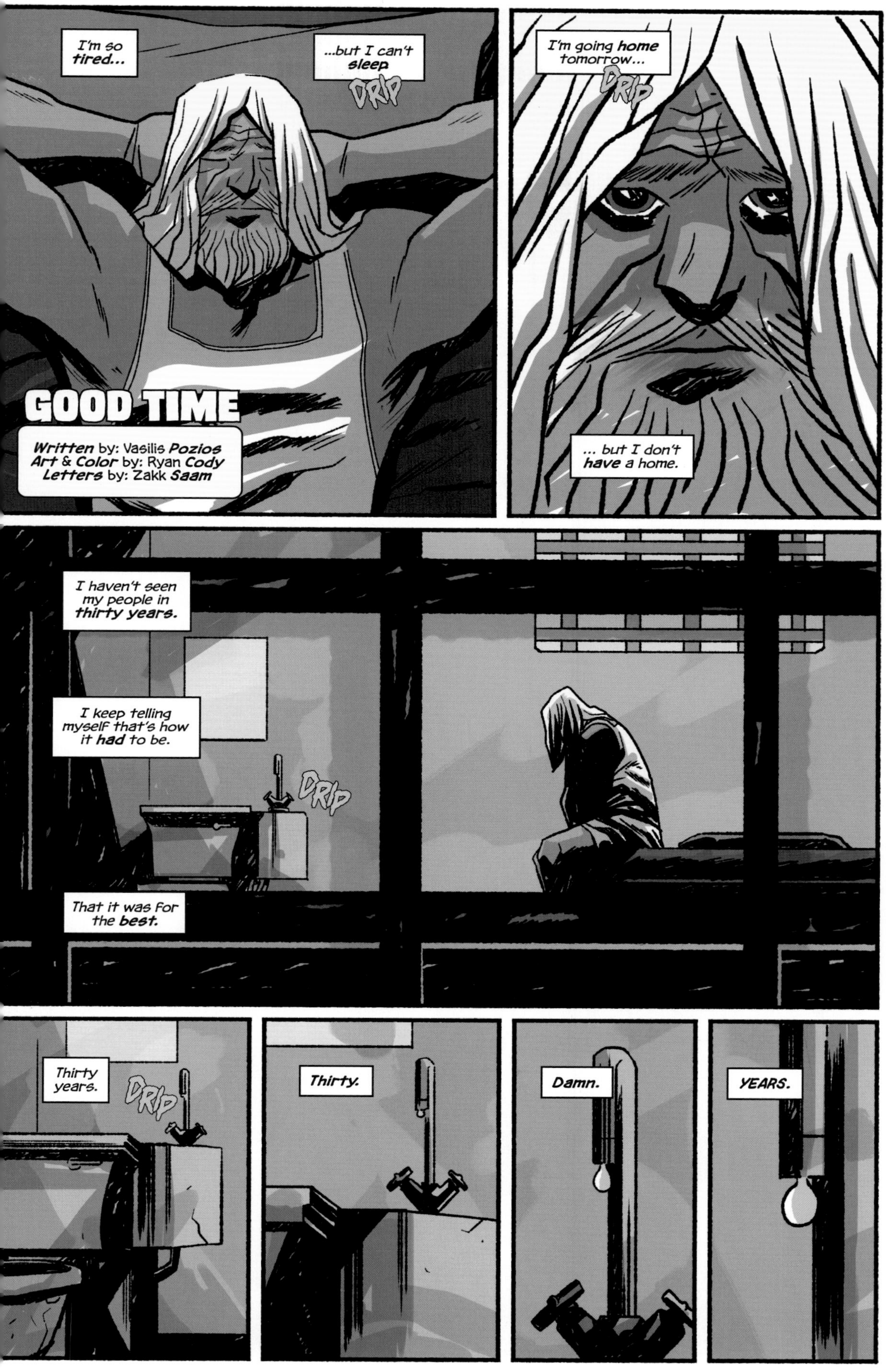
I'm so *tired...*
...but I can't *sleep.*
DRIP
GOOD TIME
Written by: Vasilis *Pozios*
Art & *Color* by: Ryan *Cody*
Letters by: Zakk *Saam*
I'm going **home** tomorrow...
DRIP
... but I don't **have** a home.
I haven't seen my people in **thirty years.**
I keep telling myself that's how it **had** to be.
DRIP
That it was for the **best.**
Thirty years.
DRIP
Thirty.
Damn.
YEARS.

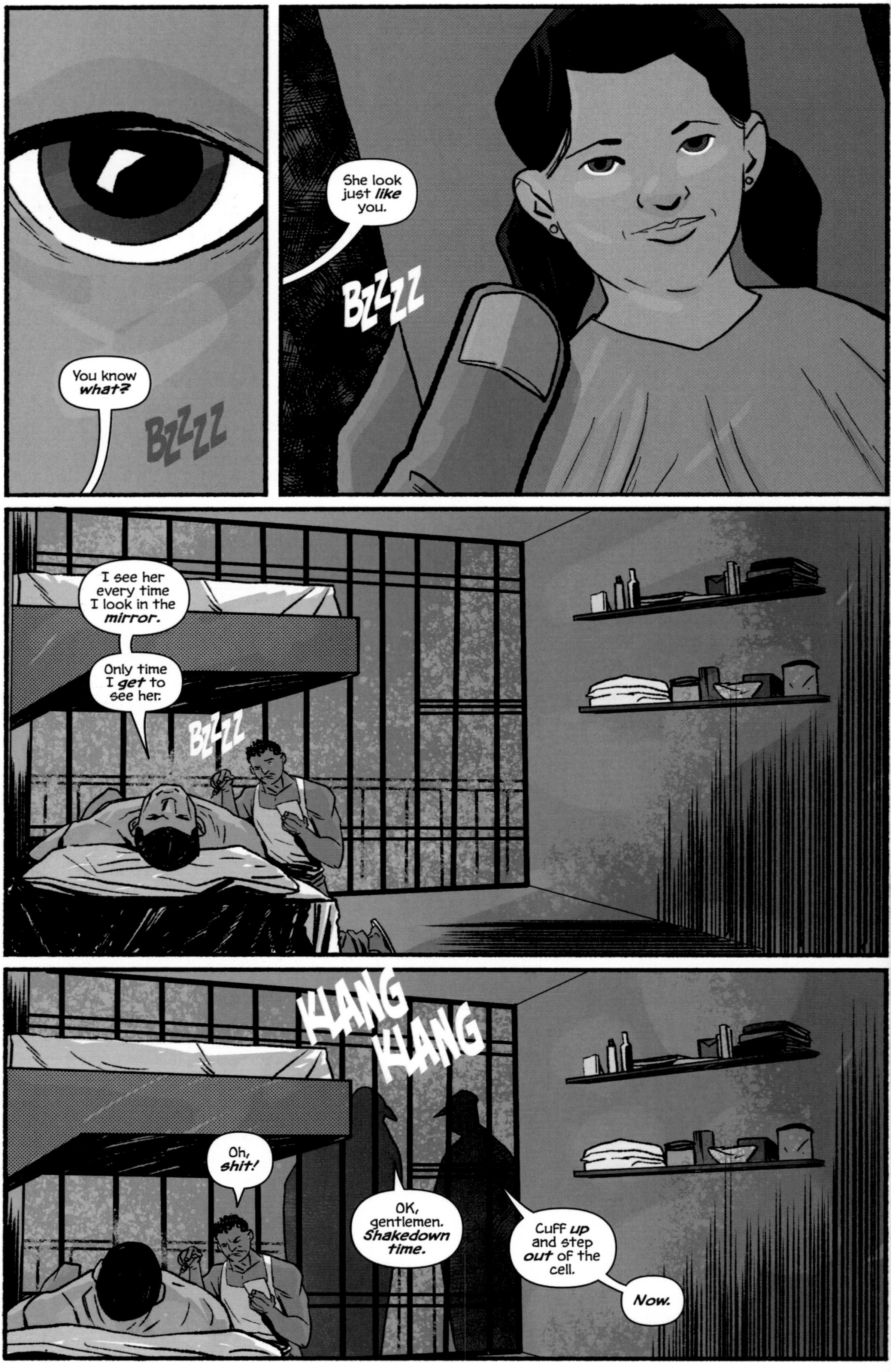
You know what?
BZZZZ
She look just like you.
BZZZZ
I see her every time I look in the mirror.
Only time I get to see her.
BZZZ
KLANG KLANG
Oh, shit!
OK, gentlemen. Shakedown time.
Cuff up and step out of the cell.
Now.

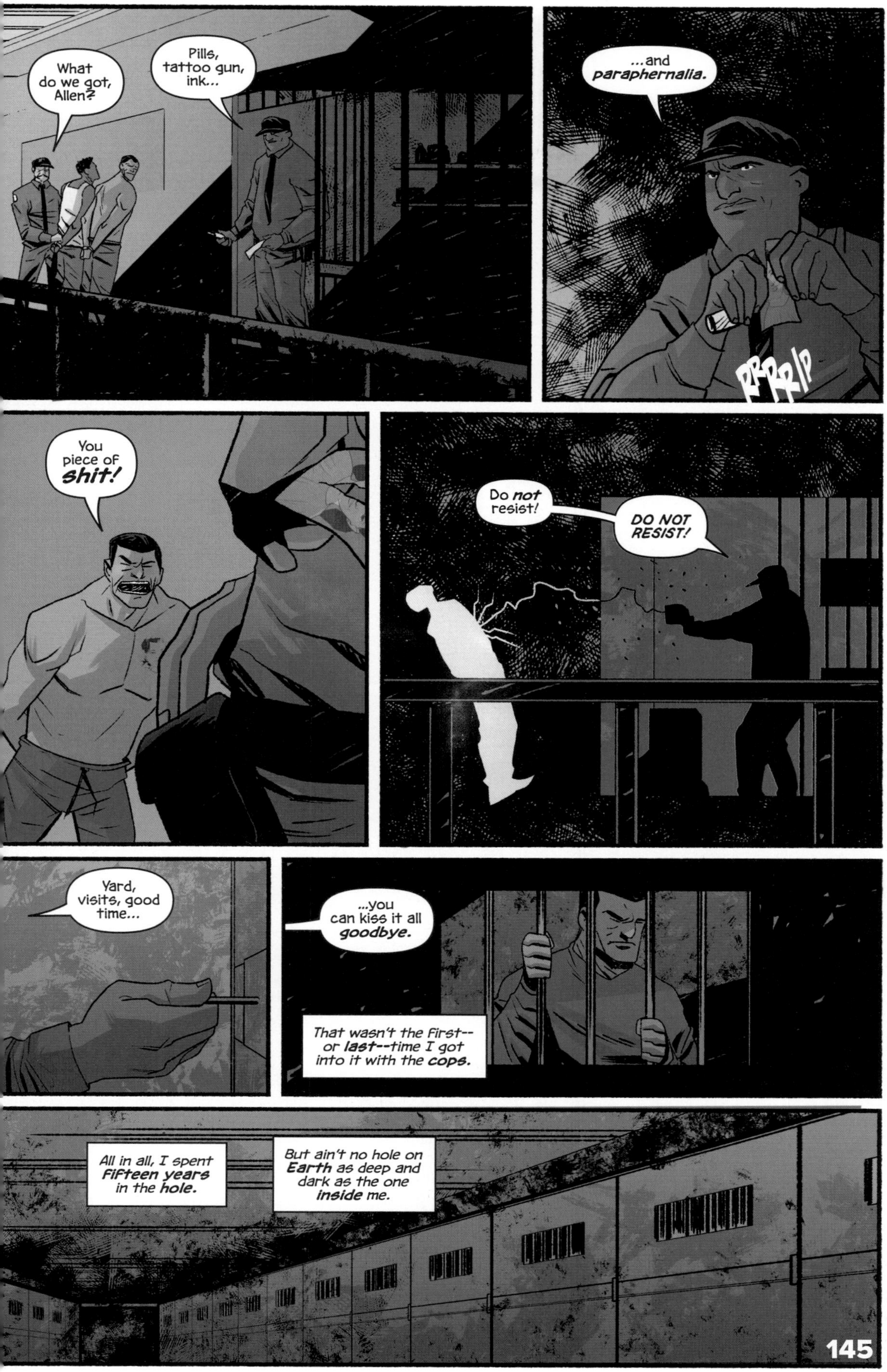
What do we got, Allen?
Pills, tattoo gun, ink...
...and *paraphernalia.*
RRRRIP
You piece of ***shit!***
Do *not* resist!
DO NOT RESIST!
Yard, visits, good time...
...you can kiss it all ***goodbye.***
*That wasn't the first-- or **last**--time I got into it with the **cops.***
*All in all, I spent **fifteen years** in the **hole.***
*But ain't no hole on **Earth** as deep and dark as the one **inside** me.*

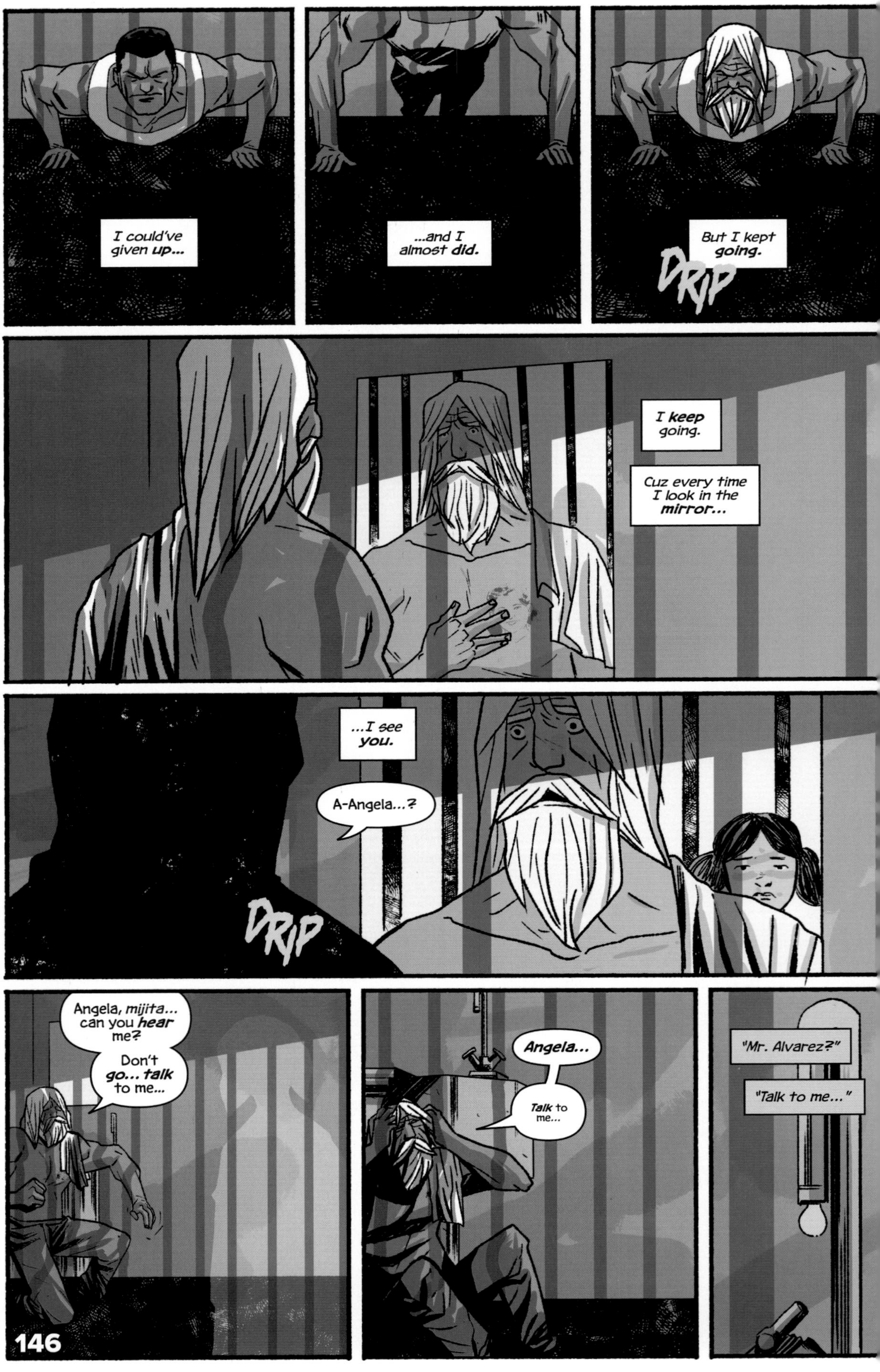

I could've given up...
...and I almost did.
But I kept going.
DRIP
I keep going.
Cuz every time I look in the mirror...
...I see you.
A-Angela...?
DRIP
Angela, mijita... can you hear me?
Don't go... talk to me...
Angela...
Talk to me...
"Mr. Alvarez?"
"Talk to me..."

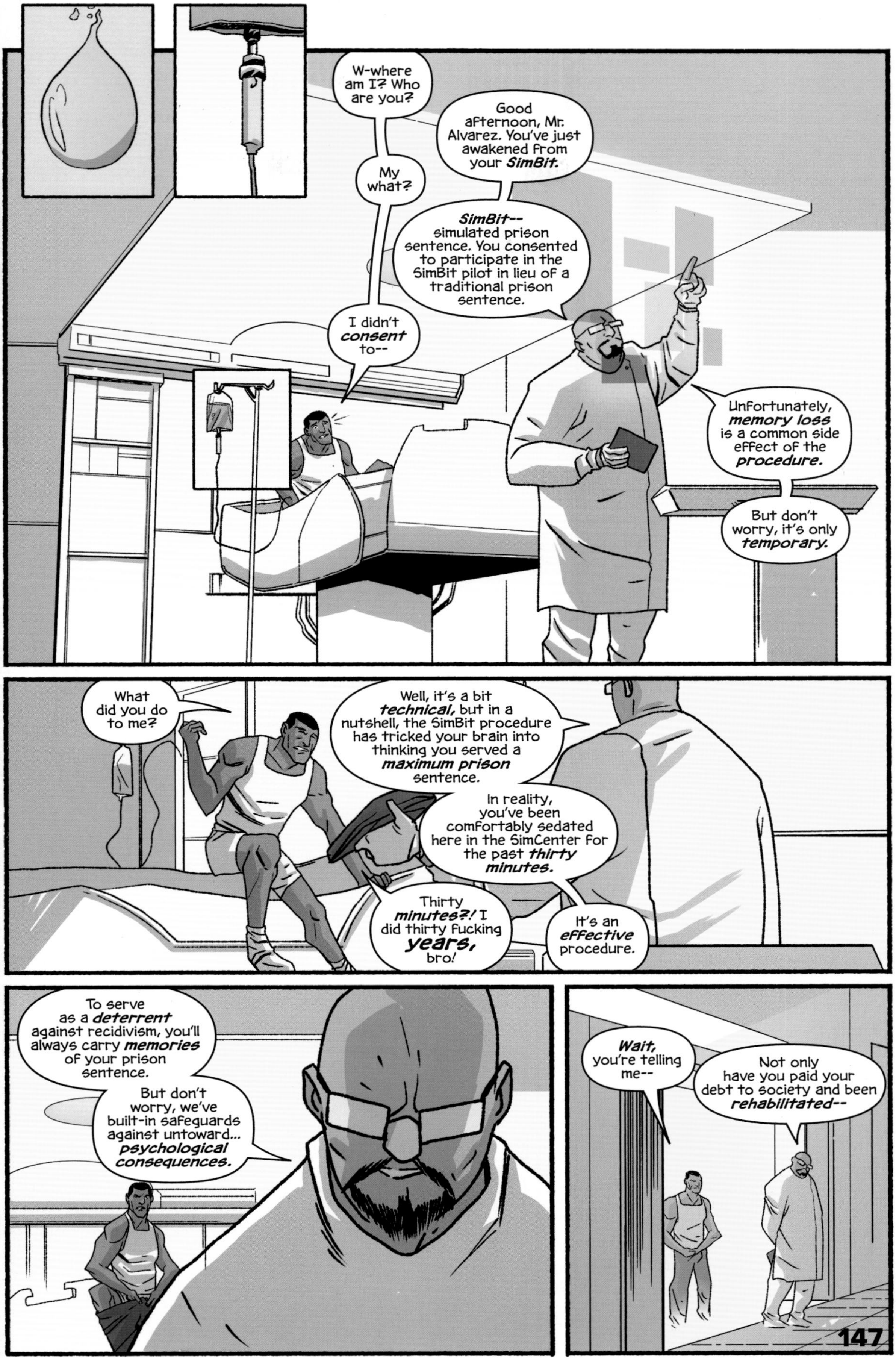
W-where am I? Who are you?
Good afternoon, Mr. Alvarez. You've just awakened from your SimBit.
My what?
SimBit-- simulated prison sentence. You consented to participate in the SimBit pilot in lieu of a traditional prison sentence.
I didn't consent to--
Unfortunately, memory loss is a common side effect of the procedure.
But don't worry, it's only temporary.
What did you do to me?
Well, it's a bit technical, but in a nutshell, the SimBit procedure has tricked your brain into thinking you served a maximum prison sentence.
In reality, you've been comfortably sedated here in the SimCenter for the past thirty minutes.
Thirty minutes?! I did thirty fucking years, bro!
It's an effective procedure.
To serve as a deterrent against recidivism, you'll always carry memories of your prison sentence.
But don't worry, we've built-in safeguards against untoward... psychological consequences.
Wait, you're telling me--
Not only have you paid your debt to society and been rehabilitated--

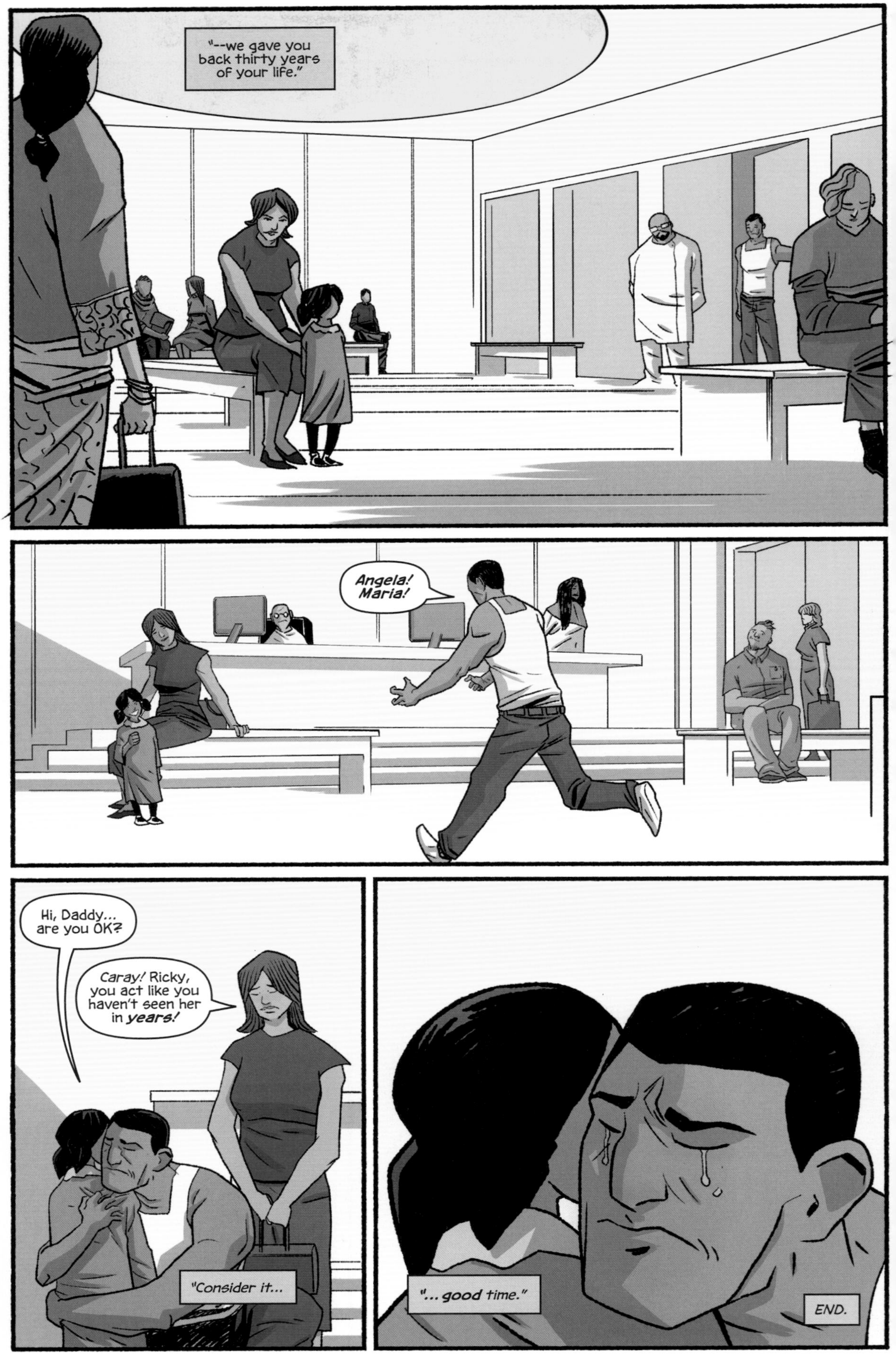
"--we gave you back thirty years of your life."
Angela! Maria!
Hi, Daddy... are you OK?
Caray! Ricky, you act like you haven't seen her in years!
"Consider it...
"...good time."
END.

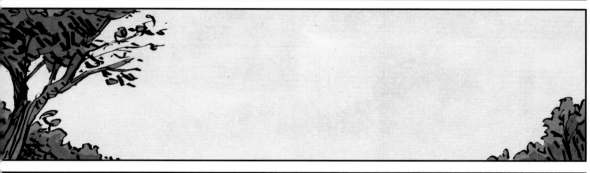

DAY AT THE PARK
Written by Eliot Rahal | Art by Jason Copland
Colors by Josh Jensen | Letters by Zakk Saam

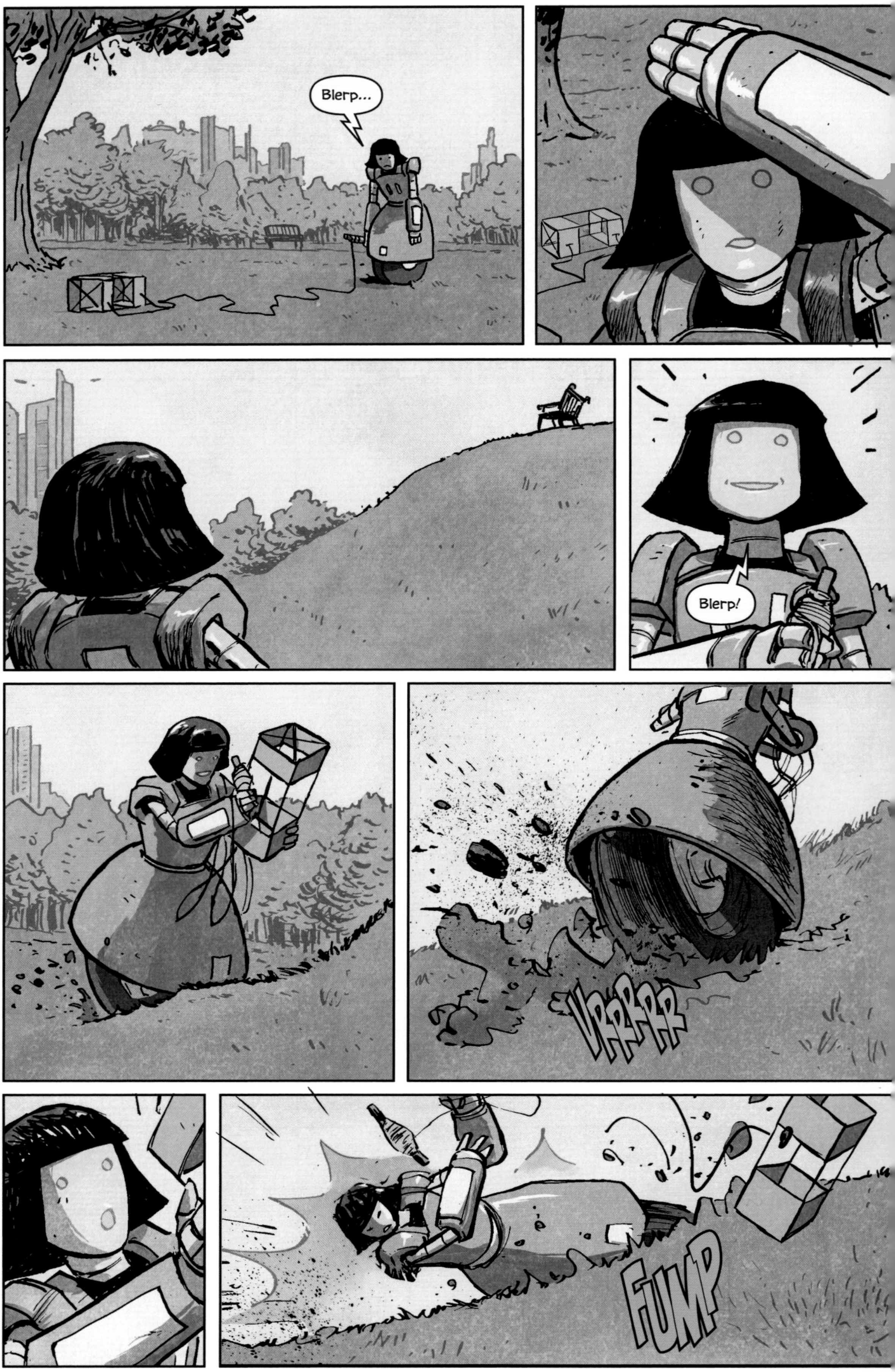

Blerp...
Blerp!
VRRRRR
FUMP

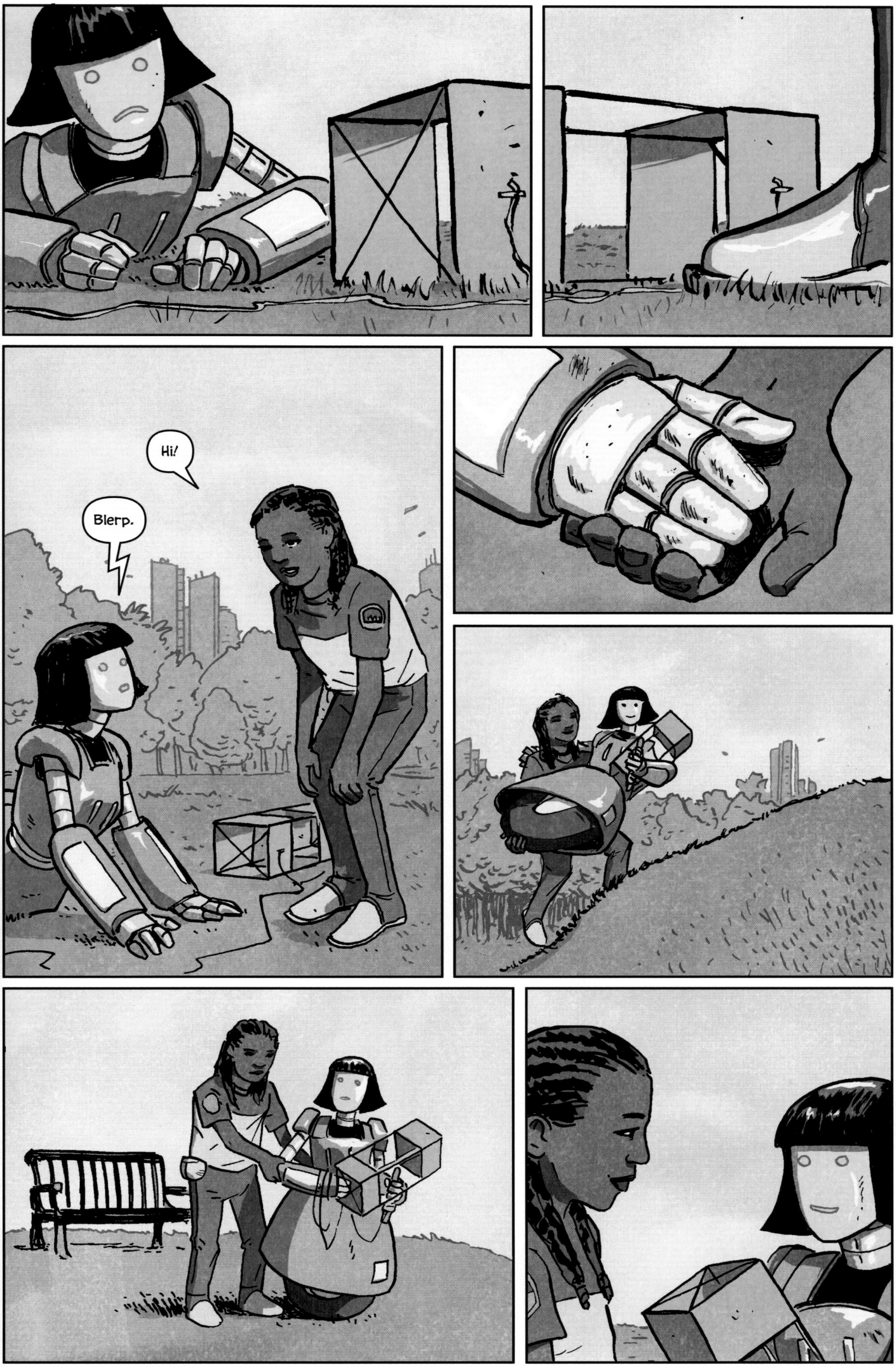
Hi!
Blerp.

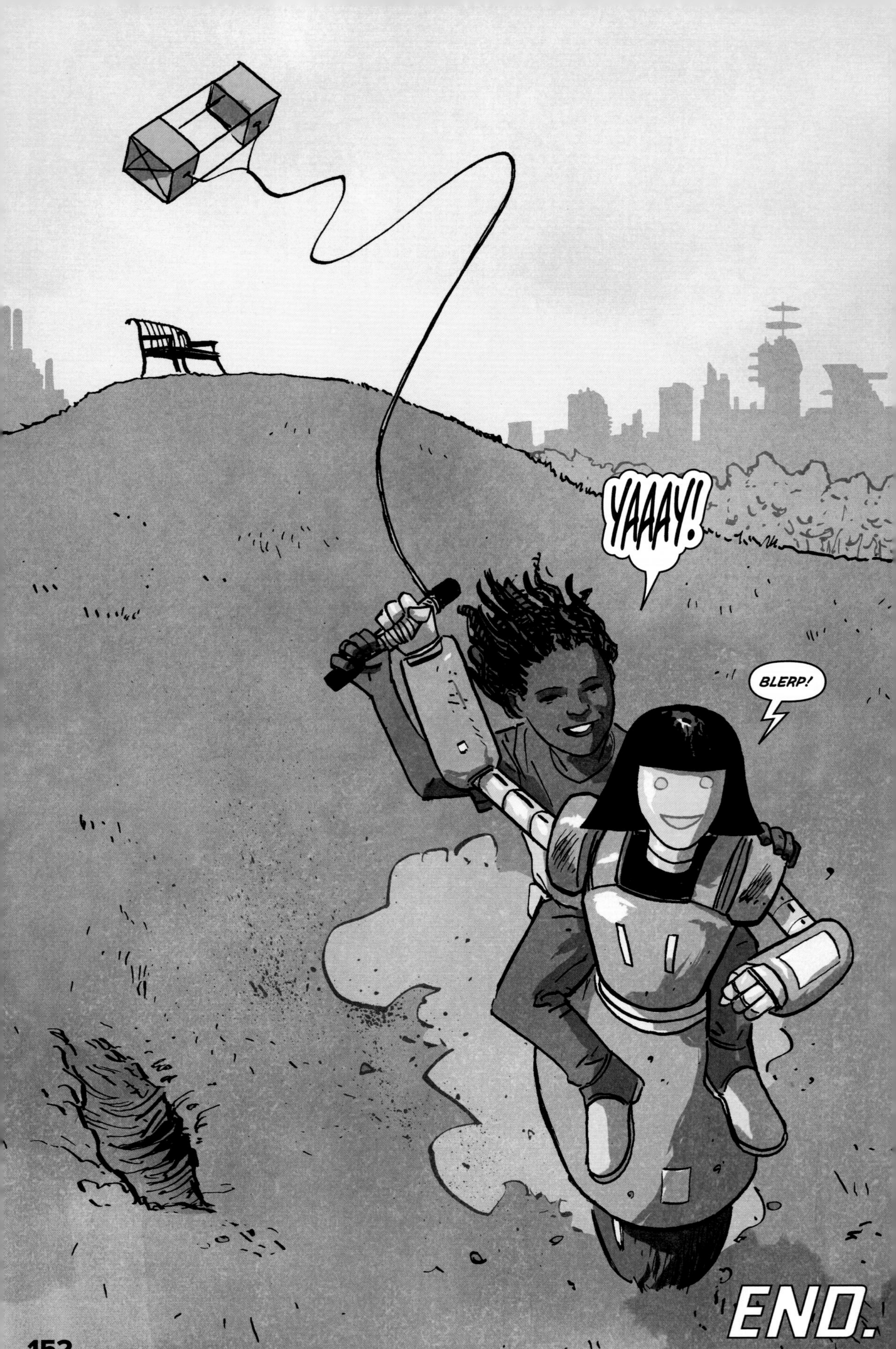
YAAAY!
BLERP!
END.

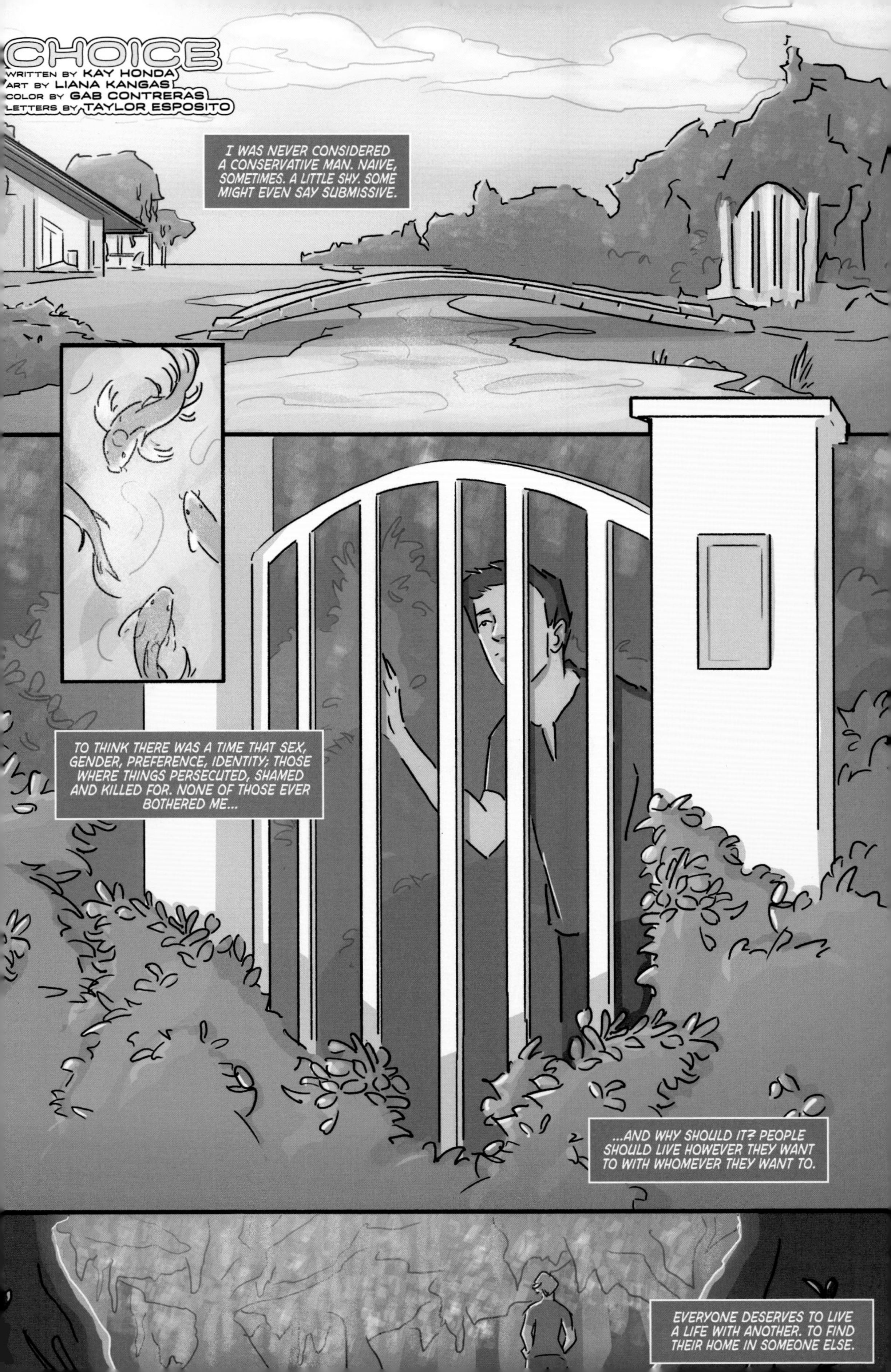
CHOICE
WRITTEN BY KAY HONDA
ART BY LIANA KANGAS
COLOR BY GAB CONTRERAS
LETTERS BY TAYLOR ESPOSITO
I WAS NEVER CONSIDERED A CONSERVATIVE MAN. NAIVE, SOMETIMES. A LITTLE SHY. SOME MIGHT EVEN SAY SUBMISSIVE.
TO THINK THERE WAS A TIME THAT SEX, GENDER, PREFERENCE, IDENTITY; THOSE WHERE THINGS PERSECUTED, SHAMED AND KILLED FOR. NONE OF THOSE EVER BOTHERED ME...
...AND WHY SHOULD IT? PEOPLE SHOULD LIVE HOWEVER THEY WANT TO WITH WHOMEVER THEY WANT TO.
EVERYONE DESERVES TO LIVE A LIFE WITH ANOTHER. TO FIND THEIR HOME IN SOMEONE ELSE.

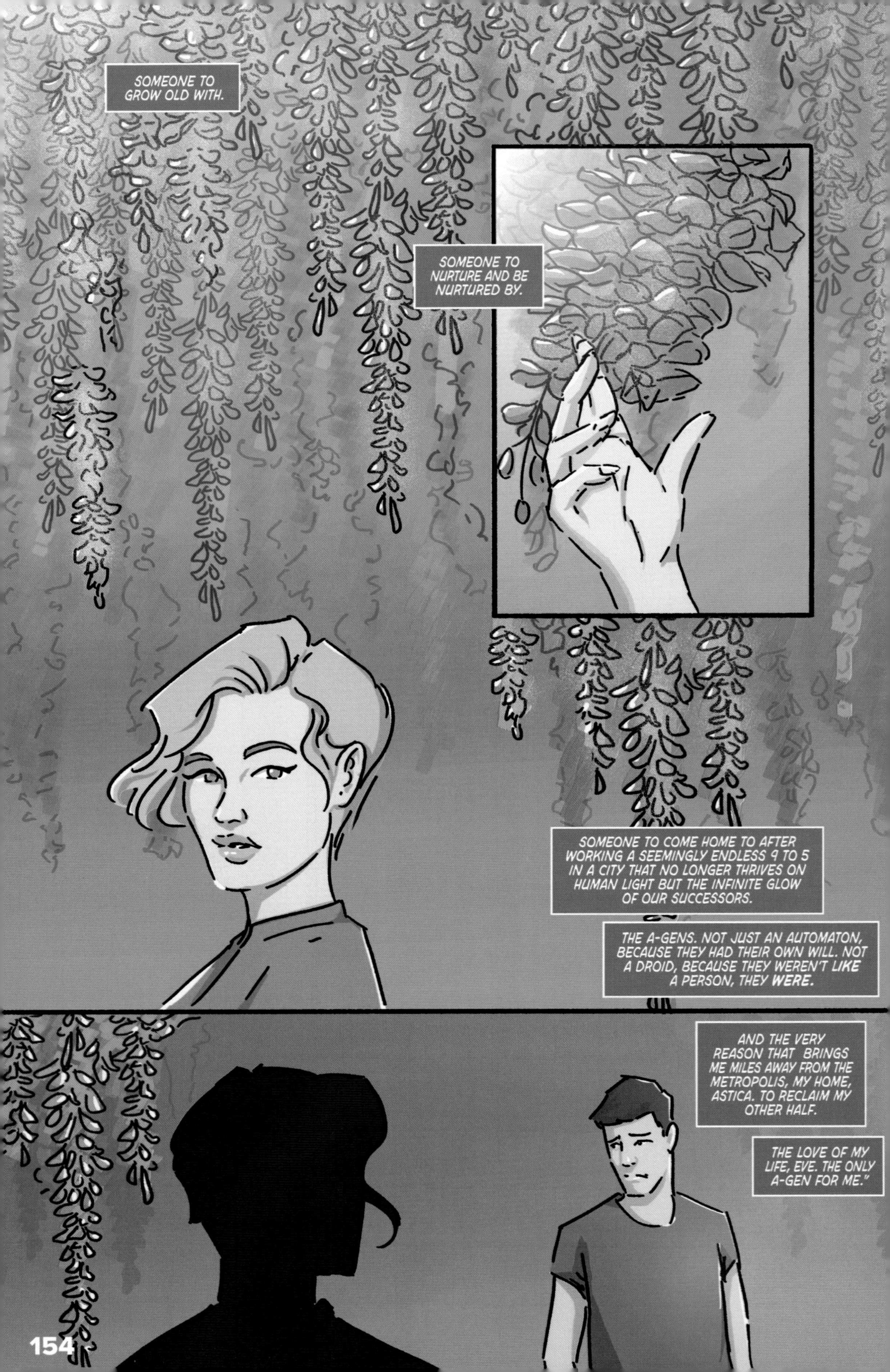
SOMEONE TO GROW OLD WITH.
SOMEONE TO NURTURE AND BE NURTURED BY.
SOMEONE TO COME HOME TO AFTER WORKING A SEEMINGLY ENDLESS 9 TO 5 IN A CITY THAT NO LONGER THRIVES ON HUMAN LIGHT BUT THE INFINITE GLOW OF OUR SUCCESSORS.
THE A-GENS. NOT JUST AN AUTOMATON, BECAUSE THEY HAD THEIR OWN WILL. NOT A DROID, BECAUSE THEY WEREN'T LIKE A PERSON, THEY WERE.
AND THE VERY REASON THAT BRINGS ME MILES AWAY FROM THE METROPOLIS, MY HOME, ASTICA. TO RECLAIM MY OTHER HALF.
THE LOVE OF MY LIFE, EVE. THE ONLY A-GEN FOR ME."

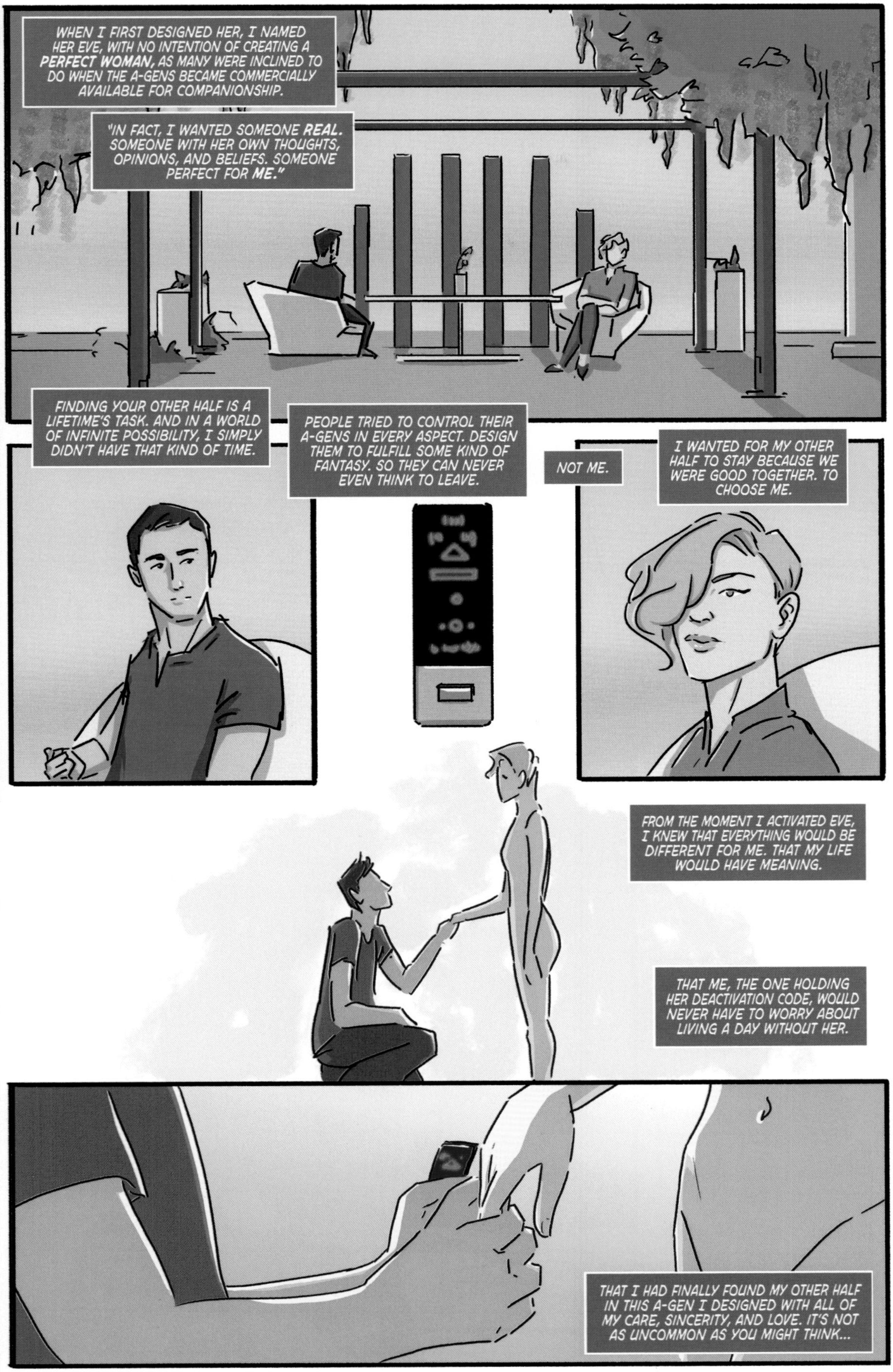
WHEN I FIRST DESIGNED HER, I NAMED HER EVE, WITH NO INTENTION OF CREATING A **PERFECT WOMAN,** AS MANY WERE INCLINED TO DO WHEN THE A-GENS BECAME COMMERCIALLY AVAILABLE FOR COMPANIONSHIP.
"IN FACT, I WANTED SOMEONE **REAL.** SOMEONE WITH HER OWN THOUGHTS, OPINIONS, AND BELIEFS. SOMEONE PERFECT FOR **ME.**"
FINDING YOUR OTHER HALF IS A LIFETIME'S TASK. AND IN A WORLD OF INFINITE POSSIBILITY, I SIMPLY DIDN'T HAVE THAT KIND OF TIME.
PEOPLE TRIED TO CONTROL THEIR A-GENS IN EVERY ASPECT. DESIGN THEM TO FULFILL SOME KIND OF FANTASY. SO THEY CAN NEVER EVEN THINK TO LEAVE.
NOT ME.
I WANTED FOR MY OTHER HALF TO STAY BECAUSE WE WERE GOOD TOGETHER. TO CHOOSE ME.
FROM THE MOMENT I ACTIVATED EVE, I KNEW THAT EVERYTHING WOULD BE DIFFERENT FOR ME. THAT MY LIFE WOULD HAVE MEANING.
THAT ME, THE ONE HOLDING HER DEACTIVATION CODE, WOULD NEVER HAVE TO WORRY ABOUT LIVING A DAY WITHOUT HER.
THAT I HAD FINALLY FOUND MY OTHER HALF IN THIS A-GEN I DESIGNED WITH ALL OF MY CARE, SINCERITY, AND LOVE. IT'S NOT AS UNCOMMON AS YOU MIGHT THINK...

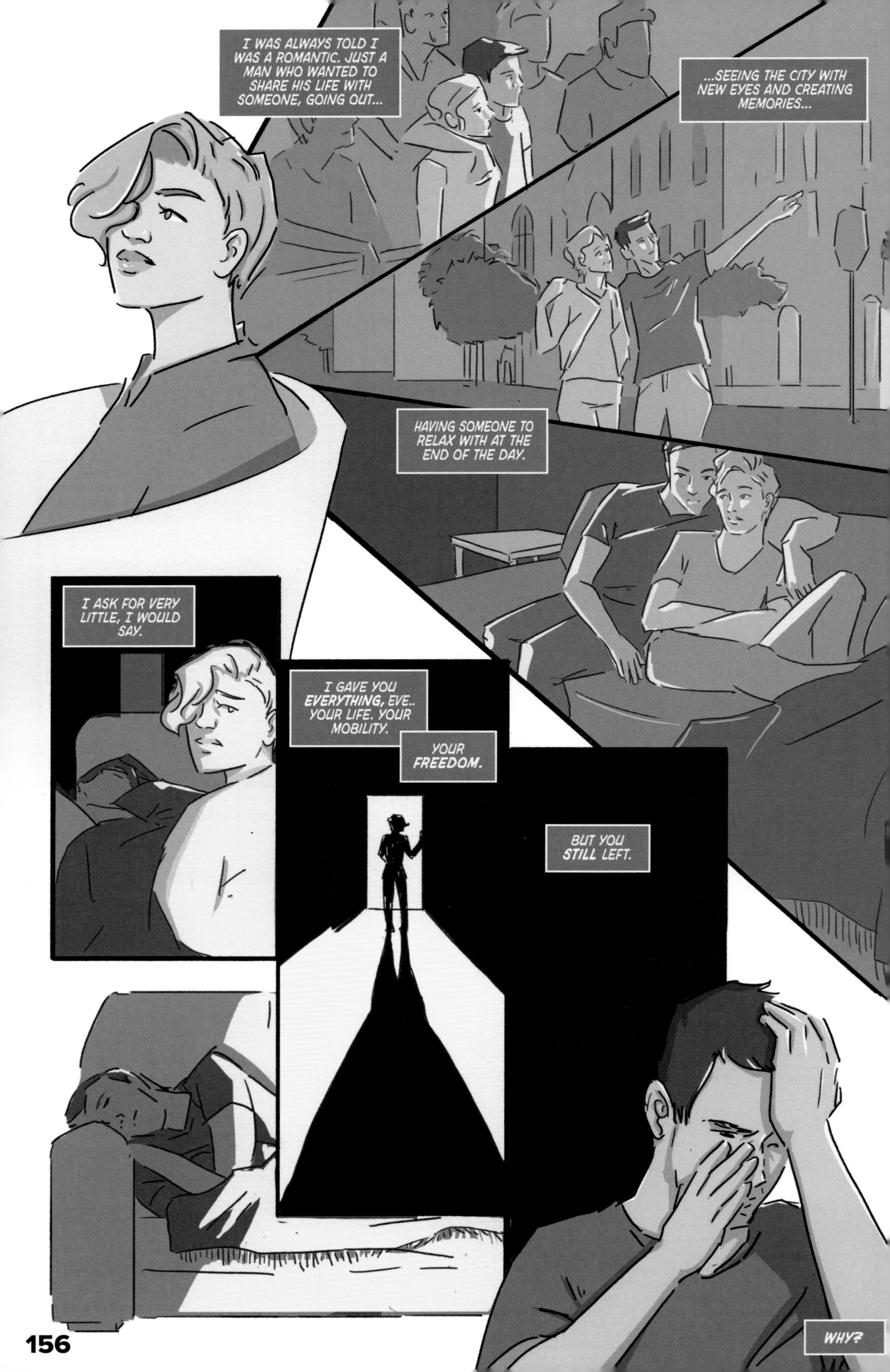
I WAS ALWAYS TOLD I WAS A ROMANTIC. JUST A MAN WHO WANTED TO SHARE HIS LIFE WITH SOMEONE, GOING OUT...
...SEEING THE CITY WITH NEW EYES AND CREATING MEMORIES...
HAVING SOMEONE TO RELAX WITH AT THE END OF THE DAY.
I ASK FOR VERY LITTLE, I WOULD SAY.
I GAVE YOU **EVERYTHING,** EVE.. YOUR LIFE. YOUR MOBILITY.
YOUR **FREEDOM.**
BUT YOU **STILL** LEFT.
WHY?

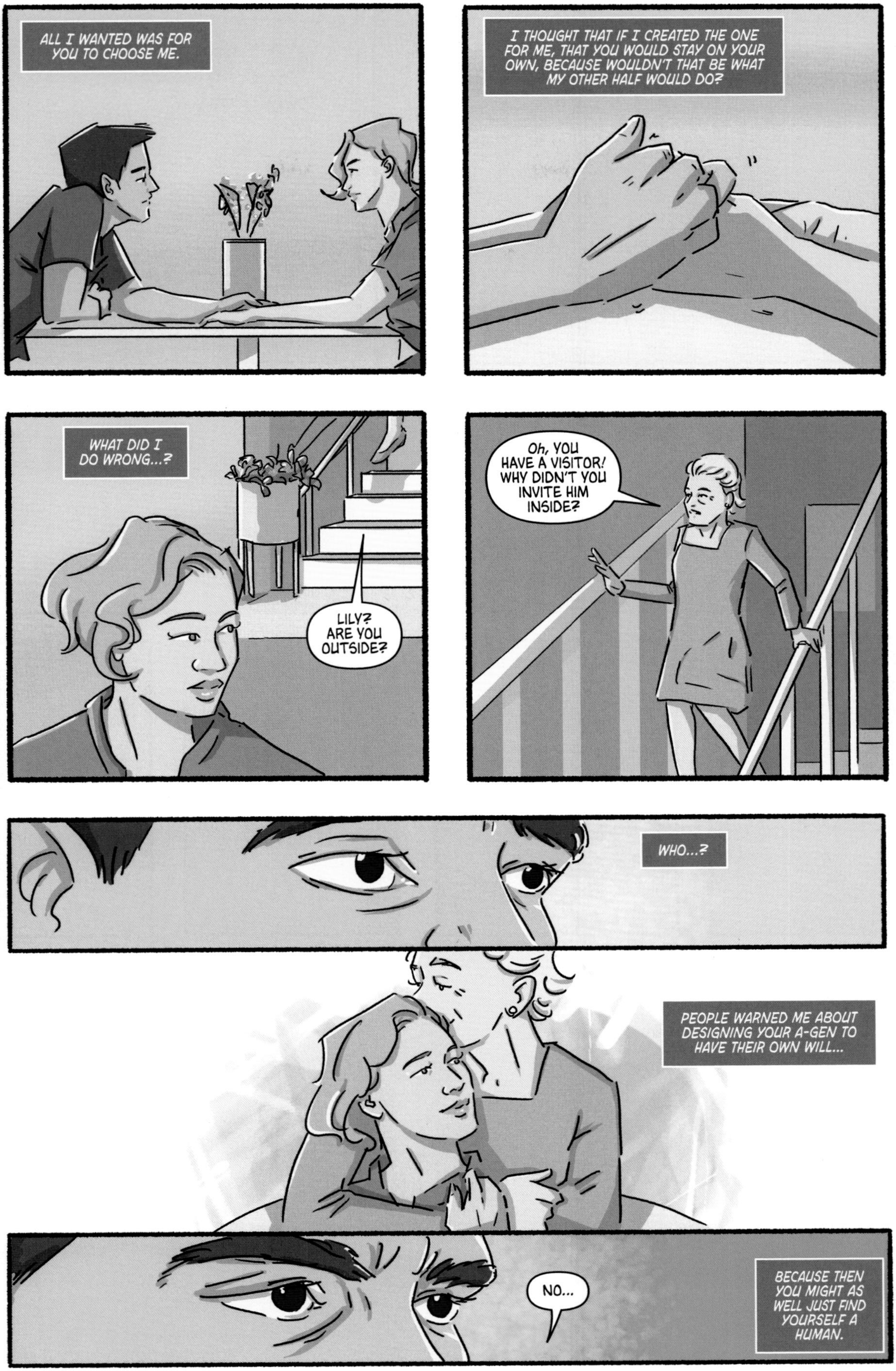
ALL I WANTED WAS FOR YOU TO CHOOSE ME.
I THOUGHT THAT IF I CREATED THE ONE FOR ME, THAT YOU WOULD STAY ON YOUR OWN, BECAUSE WOULDN'T THAT BE WHAT MY OTHER HALF WOULD DO?
WHAT DID I DO WRONG...?
LILY? ARE YOU OUTSIDE?
Oh, YOU HAVE A VISITOR! WHY DIDN'T YOU INVITE HIM INSIDE?
WHO...?
PEOPLE WARNED ME ABOUT DESIGNING YOUR A-GEN TO HAVE THEIR OWN WILL...
NO...
BECAUSE THEN YOU MIGHT AS WELL JUST FIND YOURSELF A HUMAN.

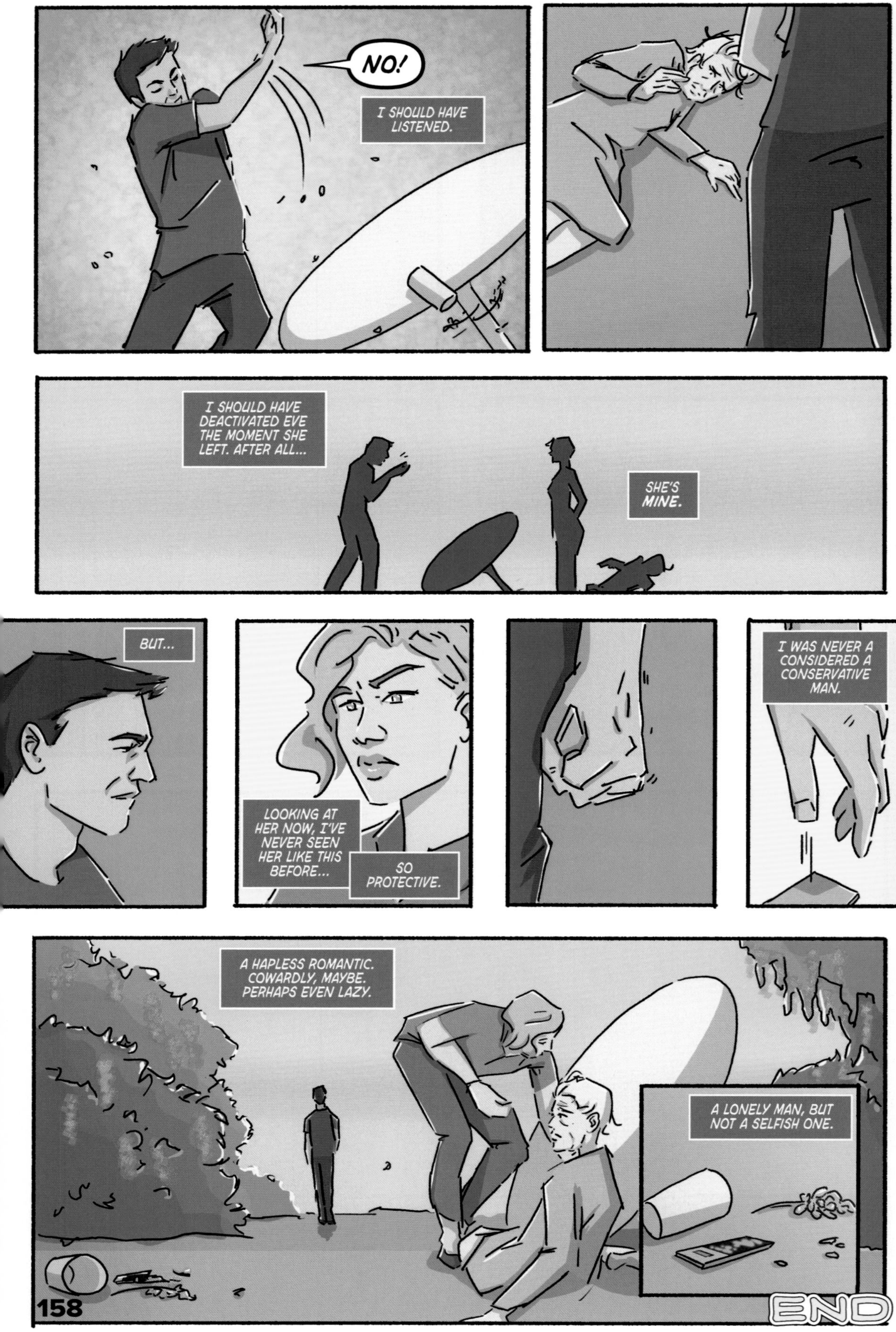
NO!
I SHOULD HAVE LISTENED.
I SHOULD HAVE DEACTIVATED EVE THE MOMENT SHE LEFT. AFTER ALL...
SHE'S MINE.
BUT...
LOOKING AT HER NOW, I'VE NEVER SEEN HER LIKE THIS BEFORE...
SO PROTECTIVE.
I WAS NEVER A CONSIDERED A CONSERVATIVE MAN.
A HAPLESS ROMANTIC. COWARDLY, MAYBE. PERHAPS EVEN LAZY.
A LONELY MAN, BUT NOT A SELFISH ONE.
END

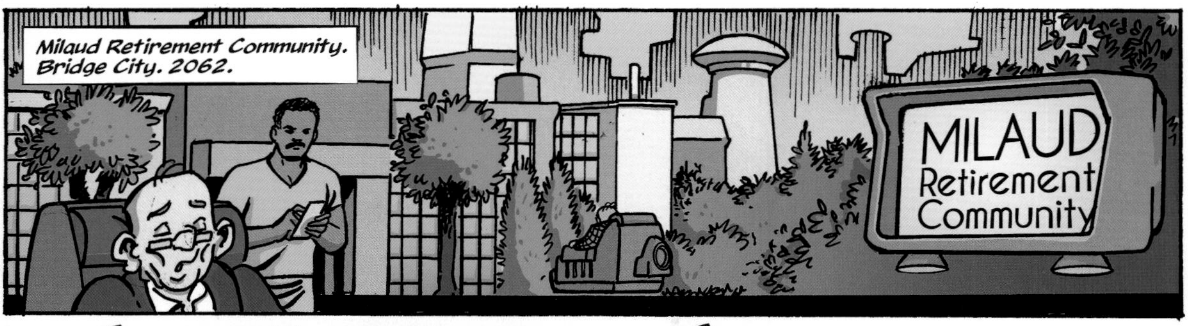
Milaud Retirement Community. Bridge City. 2062.
MILAUD Retirement Community

SEEDS

Written by **Erik Burnham**
Pencils by **Anthony Marques**
Inks by **Fernando Ruiz**
Colors by **Matt LeJeune**
Letters by **Matt Krotzer**

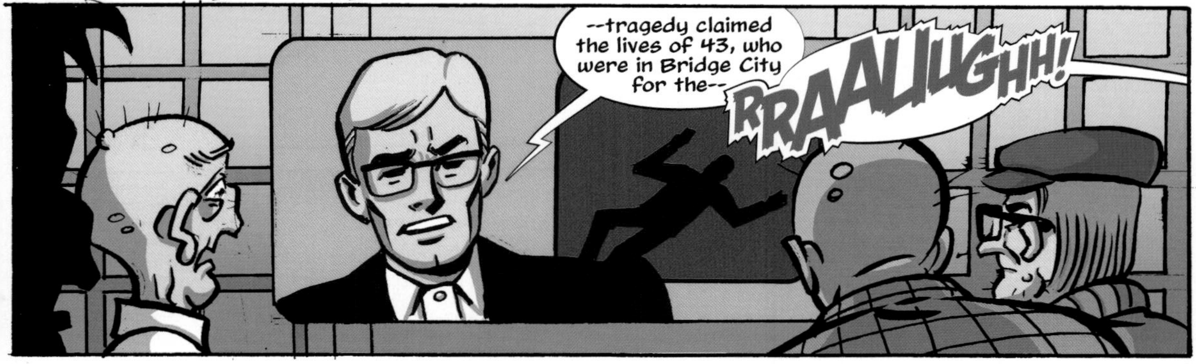
--tragedy claimed the lives of 43, who were in Bridge City for the--
RRAALIUGHH!

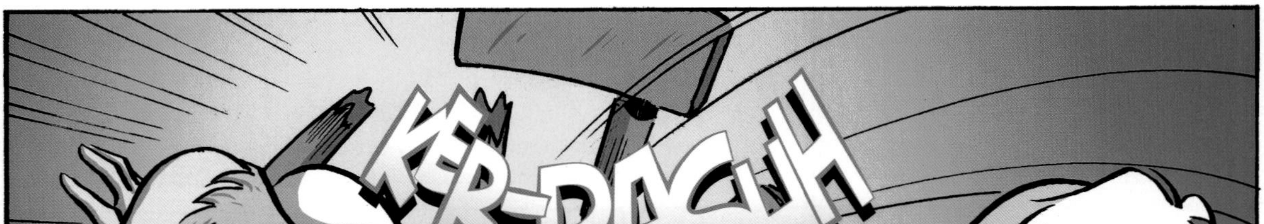
KER-RASHH

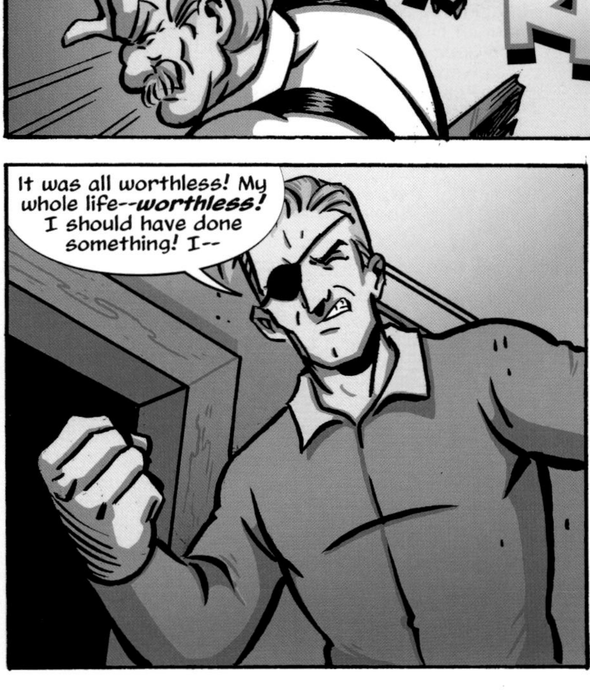
It was all worthless! My whole life--*worthless!* I should have done something! I--

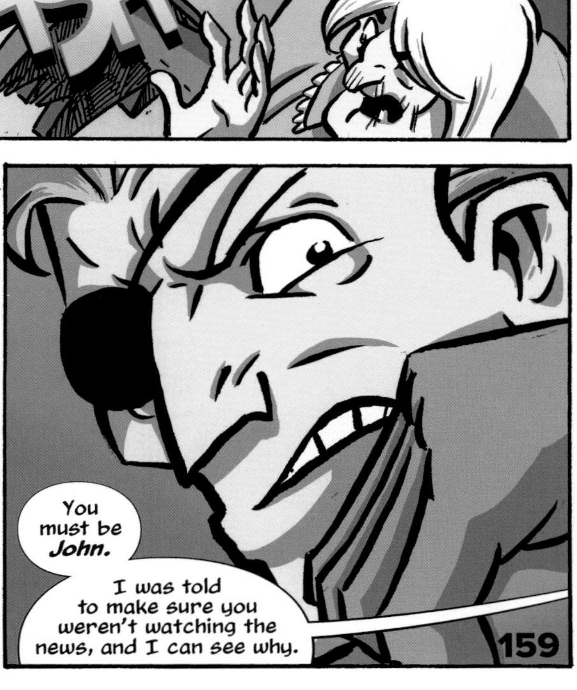
You must be *John.*
I was told to make sure you weren't watching the news, and I can see why.

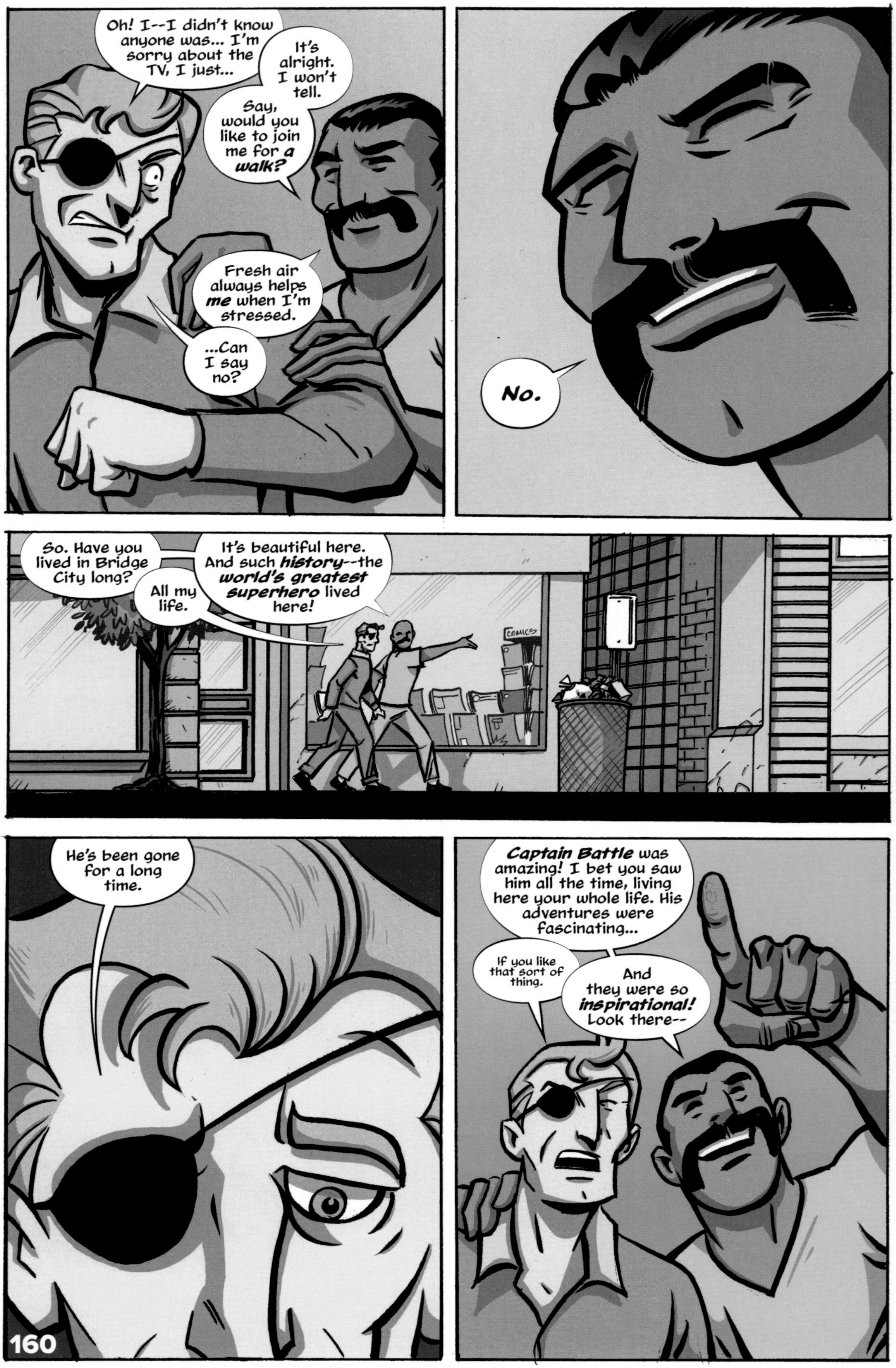
Oh! I--I didn't know anyone was... I'm sorry about the TV, I just...
It's alright. I won't tell.
Say, would you like to join me for *a walk?*
Fresh air always helps *me* when I'm stressed.
...Can I say no?
No.
So. Have you lived in Bridge City long?
All my life.
It's beautiful here. And such *history*--the *world's greatest superhero* lived here!
COMICS
He's been gone for a long time.
Captain Battle was amazing! I bet you saw him all the time, living here your whole life. His adventures were fascinating...
If you like that sort of thing.
And they were so *inspirational!* Look there--

Those hovercars. The magnetic field generator that prevents collisions, and has saved so many lives, was developed by Dr. Peter Ngugi...

KWHOOOOOM

"...And he never would have grown up to do that if Captain Battle hadn't saved his life during the Invasion of the Beast People of Dimension-K."

And how about *this.* What do you think?

Very nice.

It's by Olivia State. There have been international incidents bidding for her work.

Everything she does *captures the imagination.*

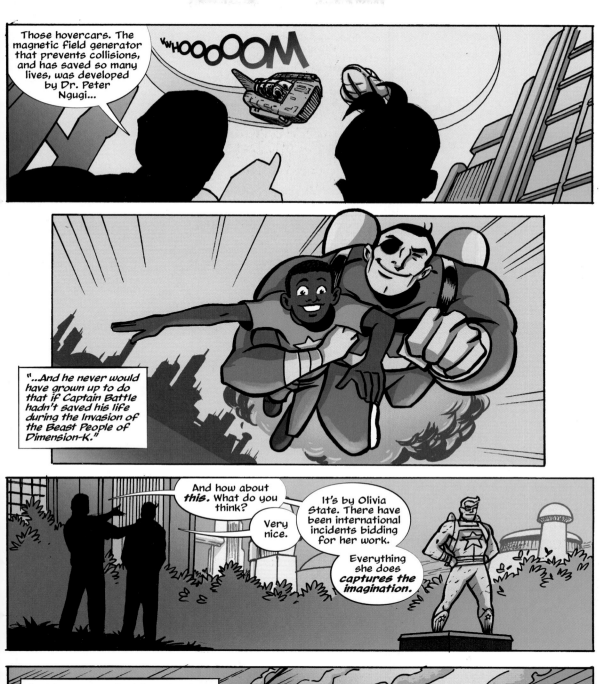

"Olivia once watched Captain Battle push back a rocket full nerve gas fired by Professor Cardinal...

"...and spent the rest of her life trying to put that feeling of awe into stone."

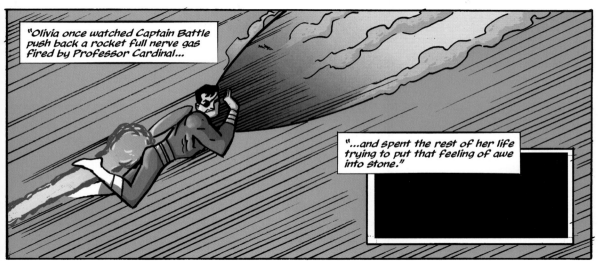

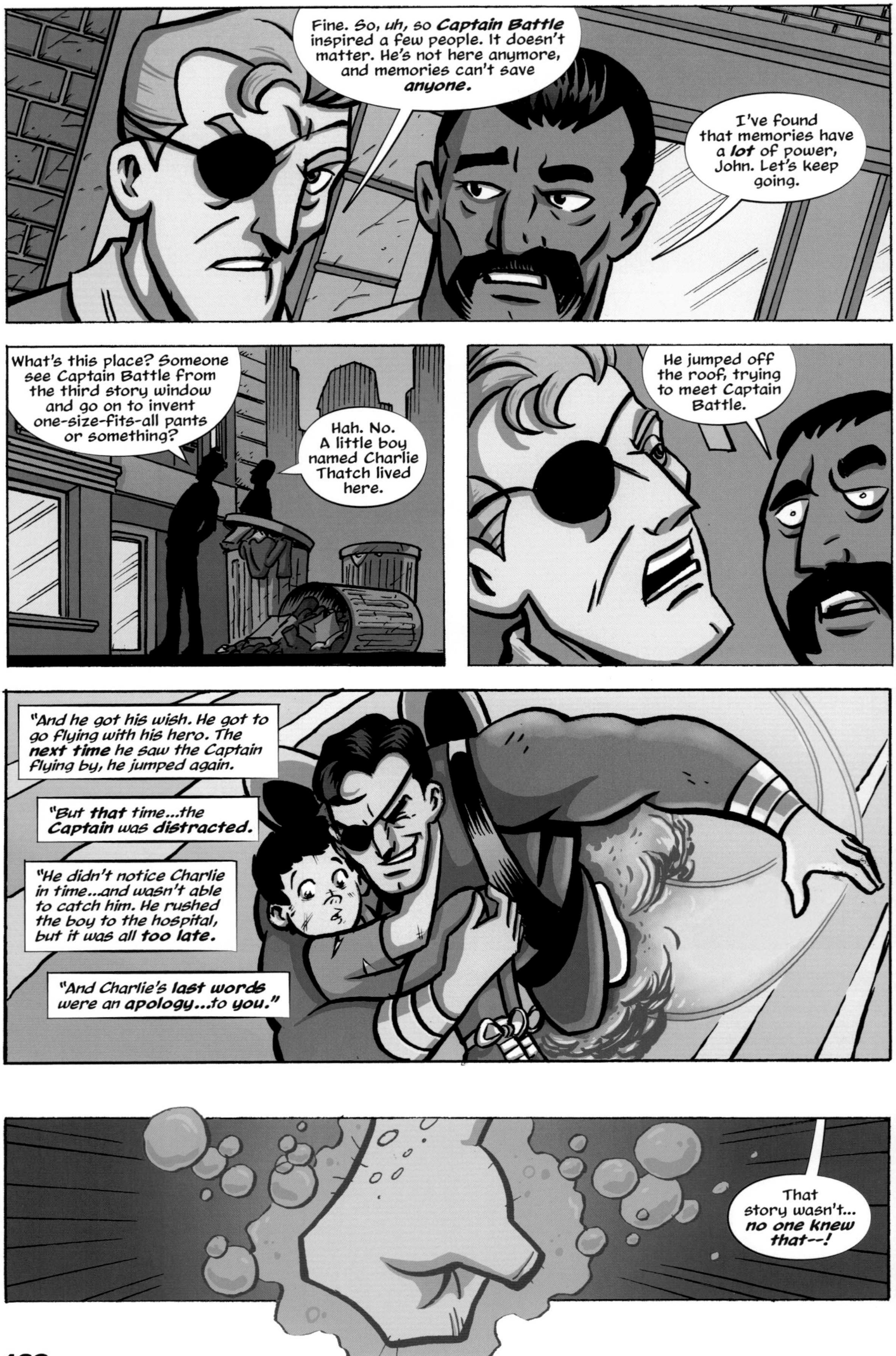
Fine. So, uh, so Captain Battle inspired a few people. It doesn't matter. He's not here anymore, and memories can't save anyone.
I've found that memories have a lot of power, John. Let's keep going.
What's this place? Someone see Captain Battle from the third story window and go on to invent one-size-fits-all pants or something?
Hah. No. A little boy named Charlie Thatch lived here.
He jumped off the roof, trying to meet Captain Battle.
"And he got his wish. He got to go flying with his hero. The next time he saw the Captain flying by, he jumped again.
"But that time...the Captain was distracted.
"He didn't notice Charlie in time...and wasn't able to catch him. He rushed the boy to the hospital, but it was all too late.
"And Charlie's last words were an apology...to you."
That story wasn't... no one knew that--!

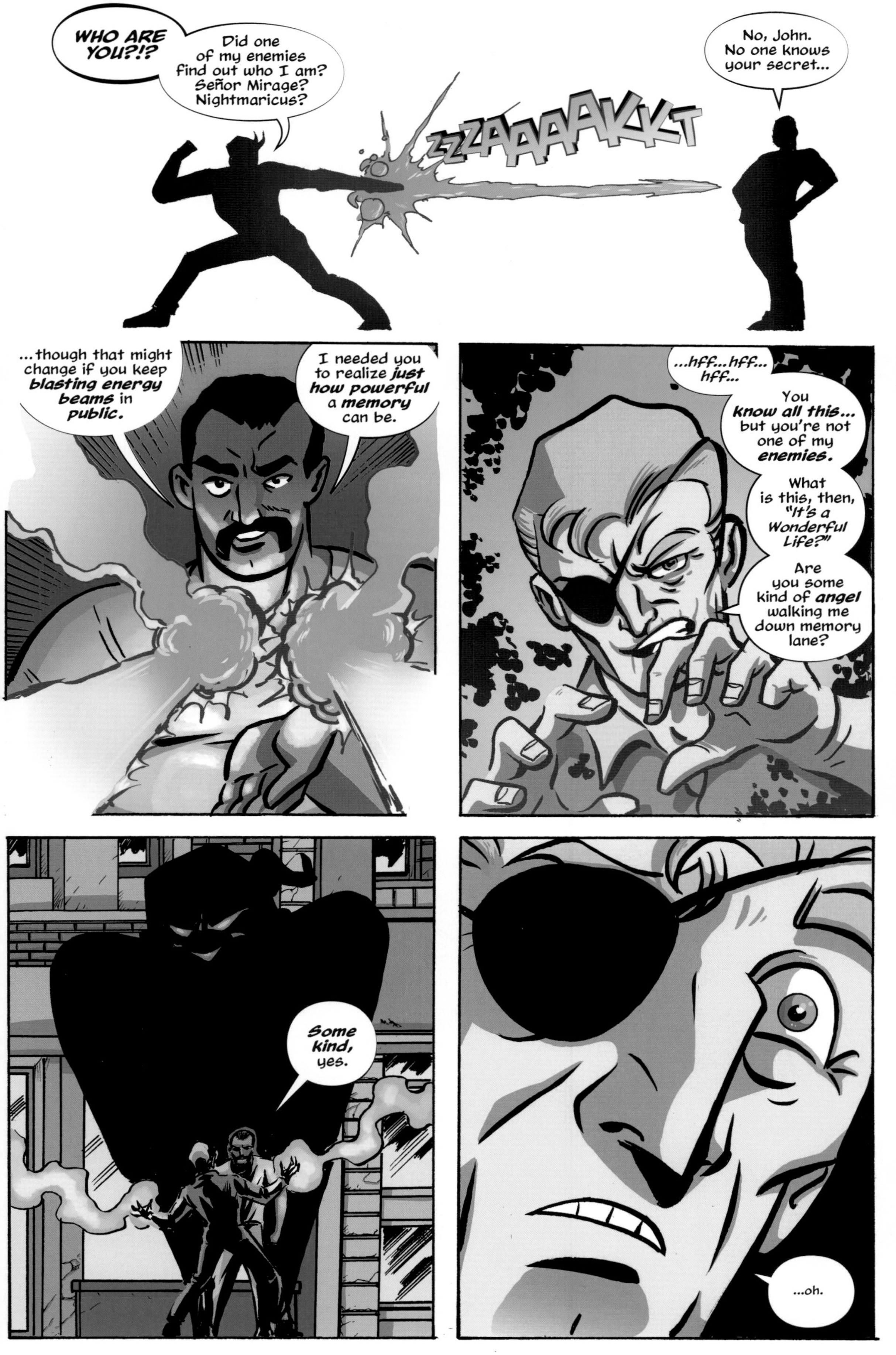
WHO ARE YOU?!?
Did one of my enemies find out who I am? Señor Mirage? Nightmaricus?
ZZZAAAAKKKT
No, John. No one knows your secret...
...though that might change if you keep blasting energy beams in public.
I needed you to realize just how powerful a memory can be.
...hff...hff... hff...
You know all this... but you're not one of my enemies.
What is this, then, "It's a Wonderful Life?"
Are you some kind of angel walking me down memory lane?
Some kind, yes.
...oh.

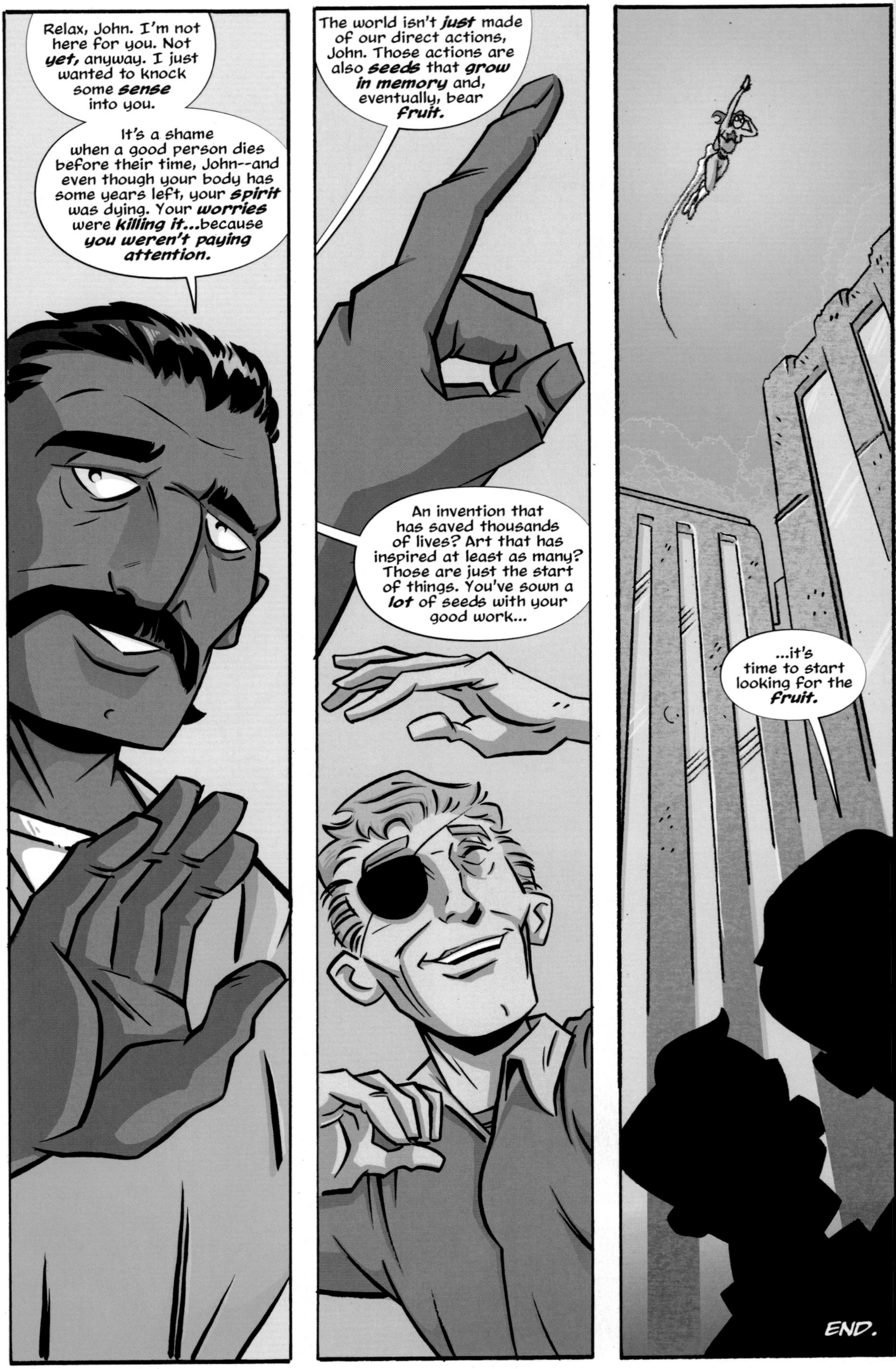
Relax, John. I'm not here for you. Not *yet,* anyway. I just wanted to knock some *sense* into you.
It's a shame when a good person dies before their time, John--and even though your body has some years left, your *spirit* was dying. Your *worries* were *killing it...*because *you weren't paying attention.*
The world isn't *just* made of our direct actions, John. Those actions are also *seeds* that *grow in memory* and, eventually, bear *fruit.*
An invention that has saved thousands of lives? Art that has inspired at least as many? Those are just the start of things. You've sown a *lot* of seeds with your good work...
...it's time to start looking for the *fruit.*
END.

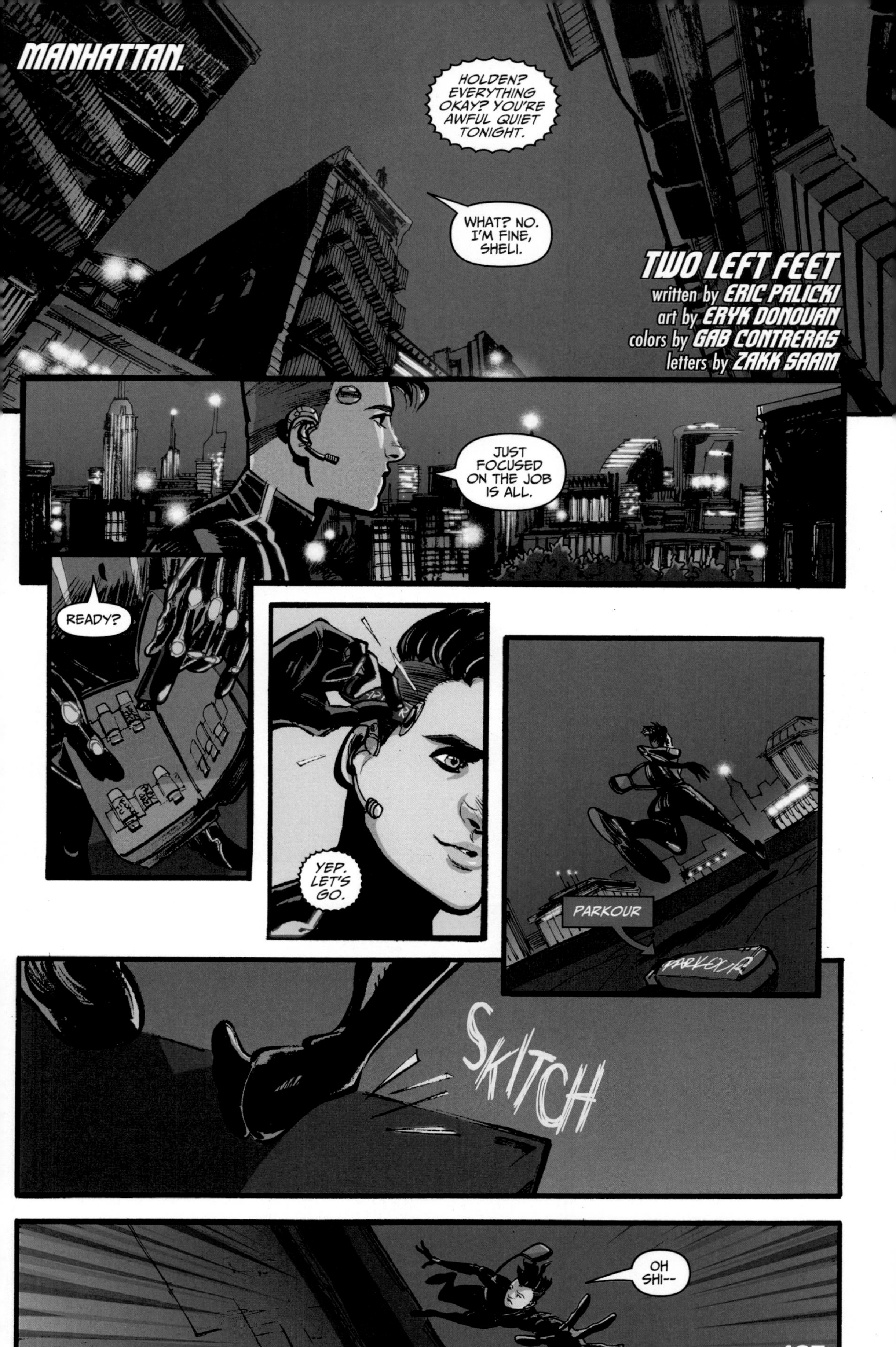
MANHATTAN.
HOLDEN? EVERYTHING OKAY? YOU'RE AWFUL QUIET TONIGHT.
WHAT? NO. I'M FINE, SHELI.
TWO LEFT FEET
written by ERIC PALICKI
art by ERYK DONOVAN
colors by GAB CONTRERAS
letters by ZAKK SAAM
JUST FOCUSED ON THE JOB IS ALL.
READY?
YEP. LET'S GO.
PARKOUR
SKITCH
OH SHI--

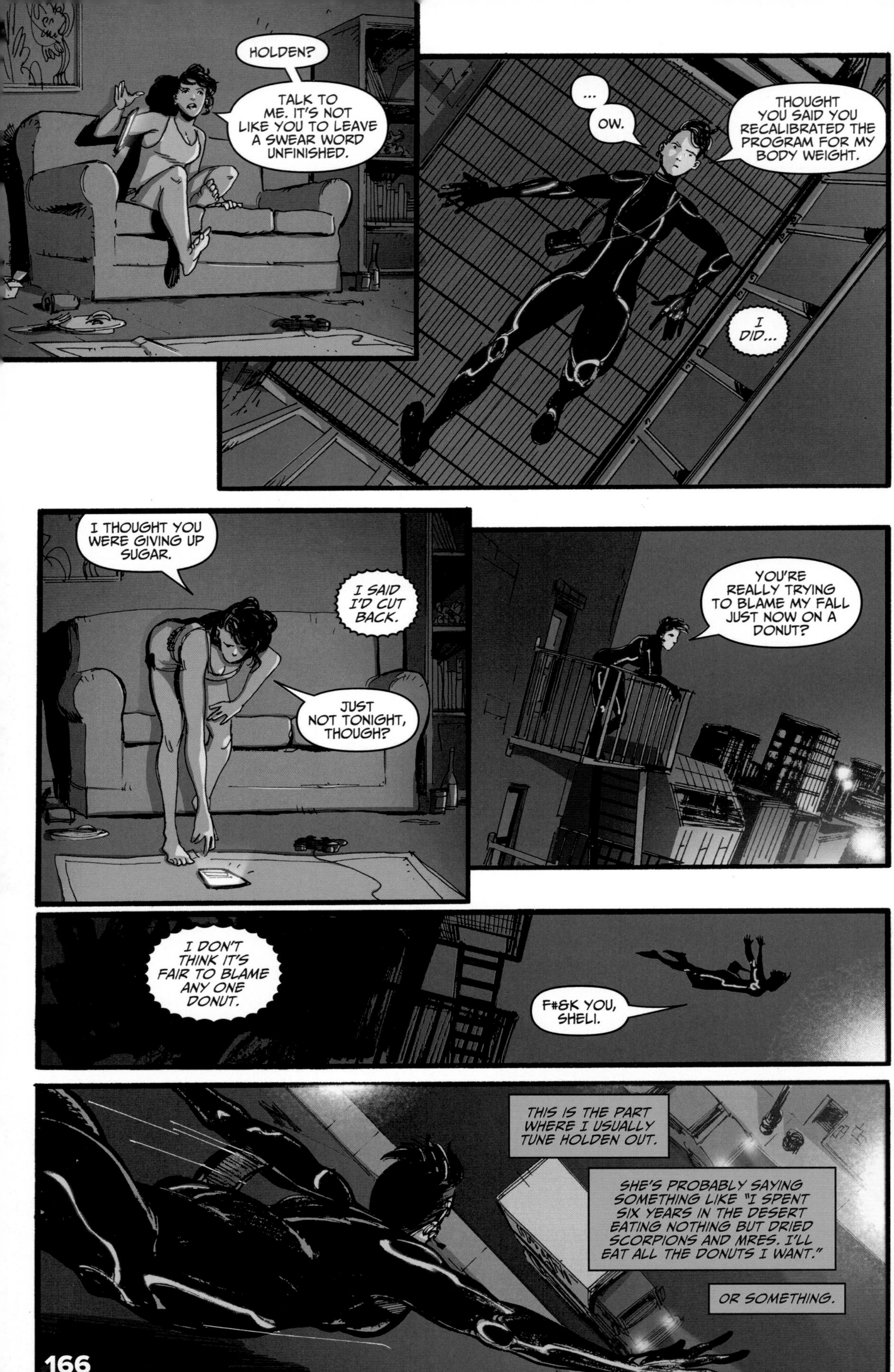
HOLDEN?
TALK TO ME. IT'S NOT LIKE YOU TO LEAVE A SWEAR WORD UNFINISHED.
...
OW.
THOUGHT YOU SAID YOU RECALIBRATED THE PROGRAM FOR MY BODY WEIGHT.
I DID...
I THOUGHT YOU WERE GIVING UP SUGAR.
I SAID I'D CUT BACK.
JUST NOT TONIGHT, THOUGH?
YOU'RE REALLY TRYING TO BLAME MY FALL JUST NOW ON A DONUT?
I DON'T THINK IT'S FAIR TO BLAME ANY ONE DONUT.
F#&K YOU, SHELI.
THIS IS THE PART WHERE I USUALLY TUNE HOLDEN OUT.
SHE'S PROBABLY SAYING SOMETHING LIKE "I SPENT SIX YEARS IN THE DESERT EATING NOTHING BUT DRIED SCORPIONS AND MRES. I'LL EAT ALL THE DONUTS I WANT."
OR SOMETHING.

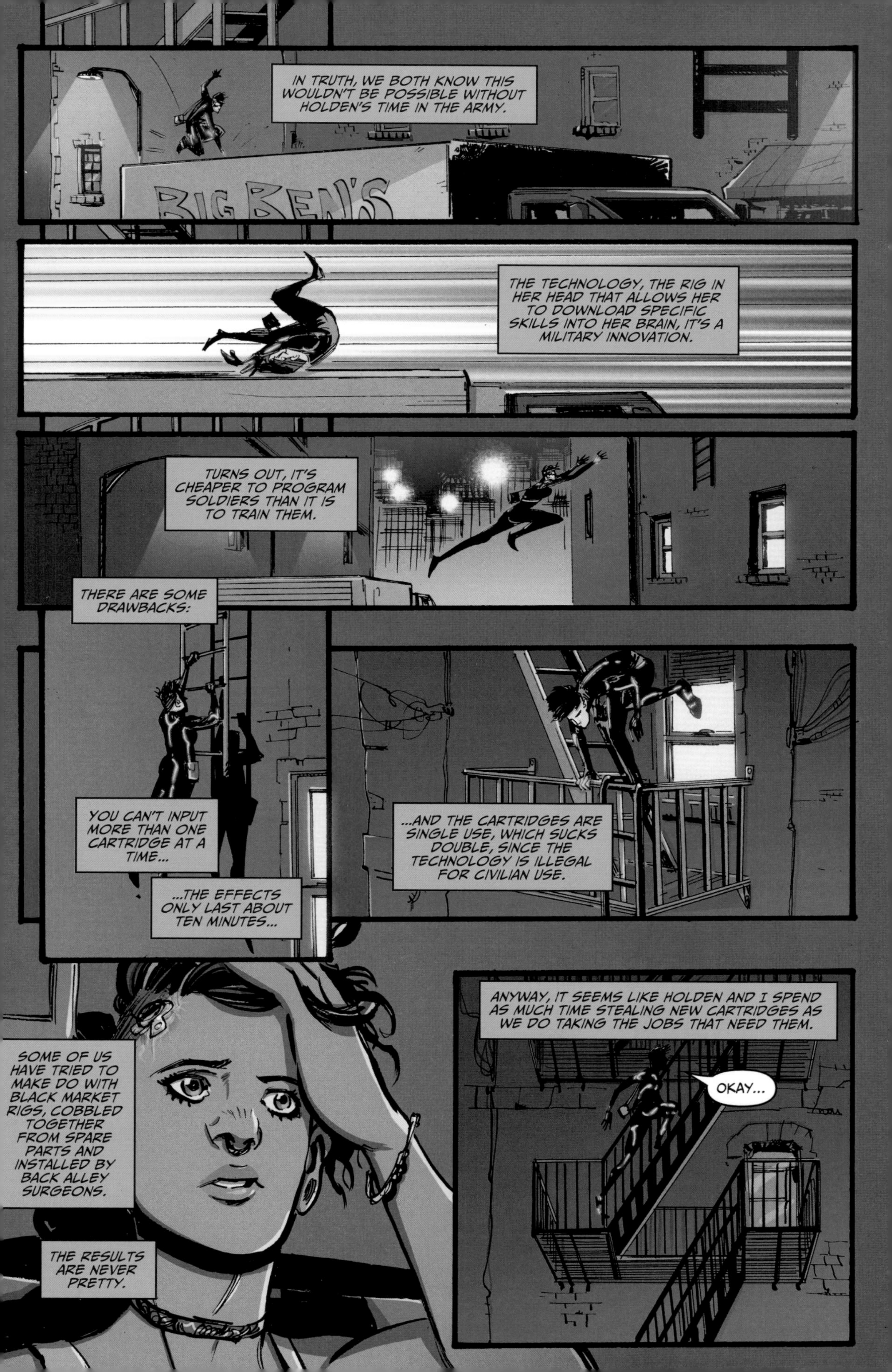
IN TRUTH, WE BOTH KNOW THIS WOULDN'T BE POSSIBLE WITHOUT HOLDEN'S TIME IN THE ARMY.
BIG BEN'S
THE TECHNOLOGY, THE RIG IN HER HEAD THAT ALLOWS HER TO DOWNLOAD SPECIFIC SKILLS INTO HER BRAIN, IT'S A MILITARY INNOVATION.
TURNS OUT, IT'S CHEAPER TO PROGRAM SOLDIERS THAN IT IS TO TRAIN THEM.
THERE ARE SOME DRAWBACKS:
YOU CAN'T INPUT MORE THAN ONE CARTRIDGE AT A TIME...
...THE EFFECTS ONLY LAST ABOUT TEN MINUTES...
...AND THE CARTRIDGES ARE SINGLE USE, WHICH SUCKS DOUBLE, SINCE THE TECHNOLOGY IS ILLEGAL FOR CIVILIAN USE.
SOME OF US HAVE TRIED TO MAKE DO WITH BLACK MARKET RIGS, COBBLED TOGETHER FROM SPARE PARTS AND INSTALLED BY BACK ALLEY SURGEONS.
THE RESULTS ARE NEVER PRETTY.
ANYWAY, IT SEEMS LIKE HOLDEN AND I SPEND AS MUCH TIME STEALING NEW CARTRIDGES AS WE DO TAKING THE JOBS THAT NEED THEM.
OKAY...

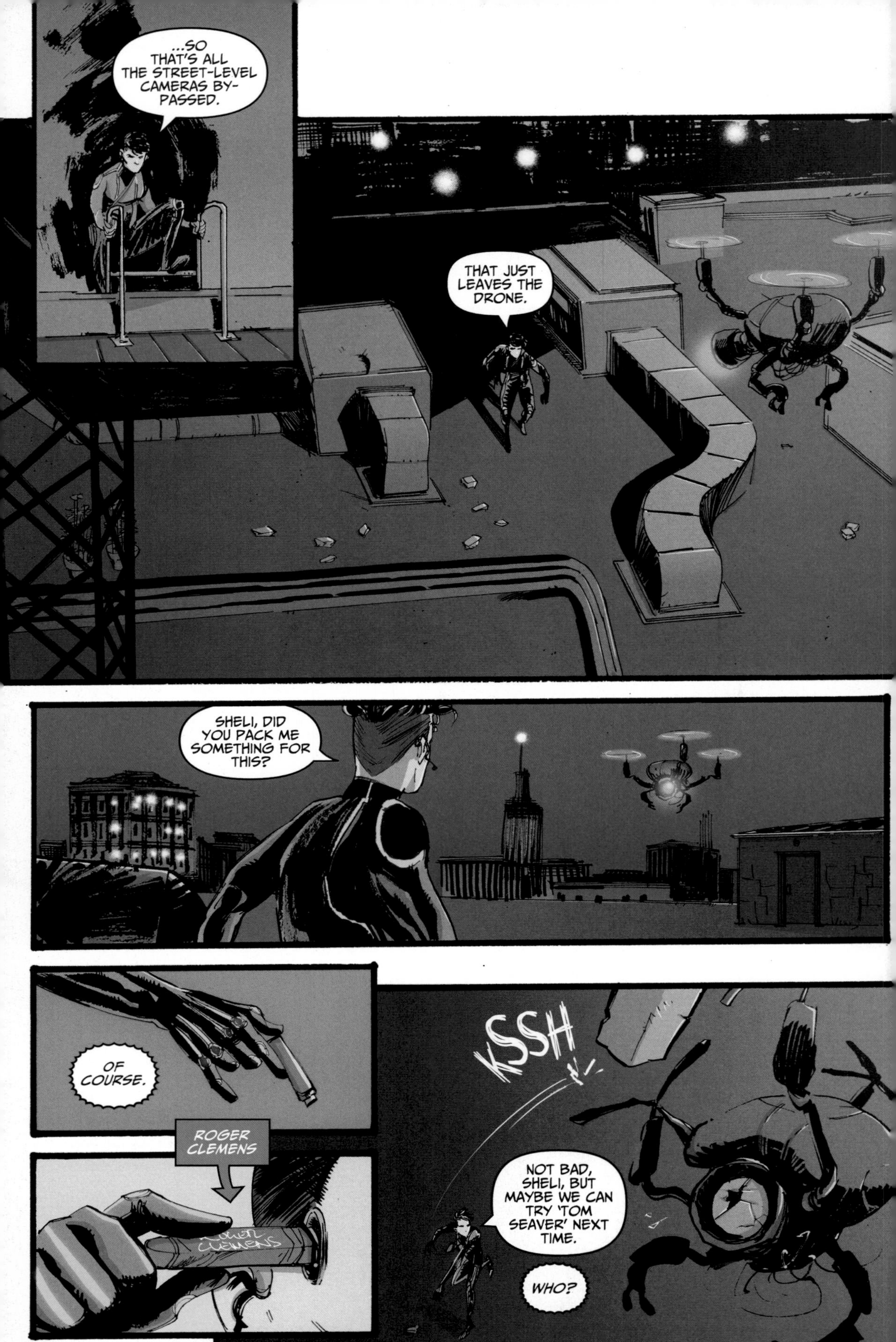
...SO THAT'S ALL THE STREET-LEVEL CAMERAS BY-PASSED.
THAT JUST LEAVES THE DRONE.
SHELI, DID YOU PACK ME SOMETHING FOR THIS?
OF COURSE.
ROGER CLEMENS
KSSH
NOT BAD, SHELI, BUT MAYBE WE CAN TRY 'TOM SEAVER' NEXT TIME.
WHO?

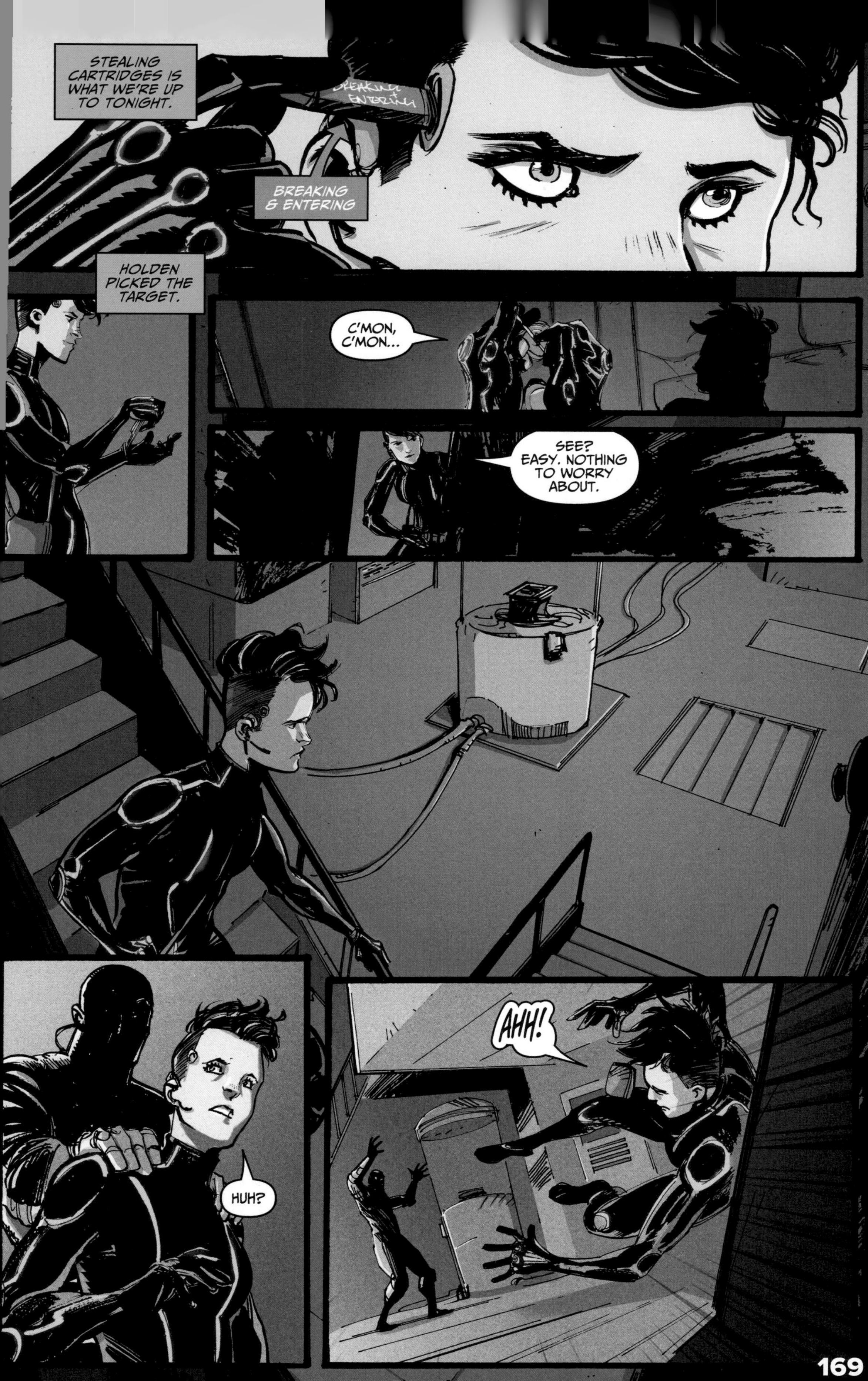
STEALING CARTRIDGES IS WHAT WE'RE UP TO TONIGHT.
BREAKING + ENTERING
BREAKING & ENTERING
HOLDEN PICKED THE TARGET.
C'MON, C'MON...
SEE? EASY. NOTHING TO WORRY ABOUT.
HUH?
AHH!

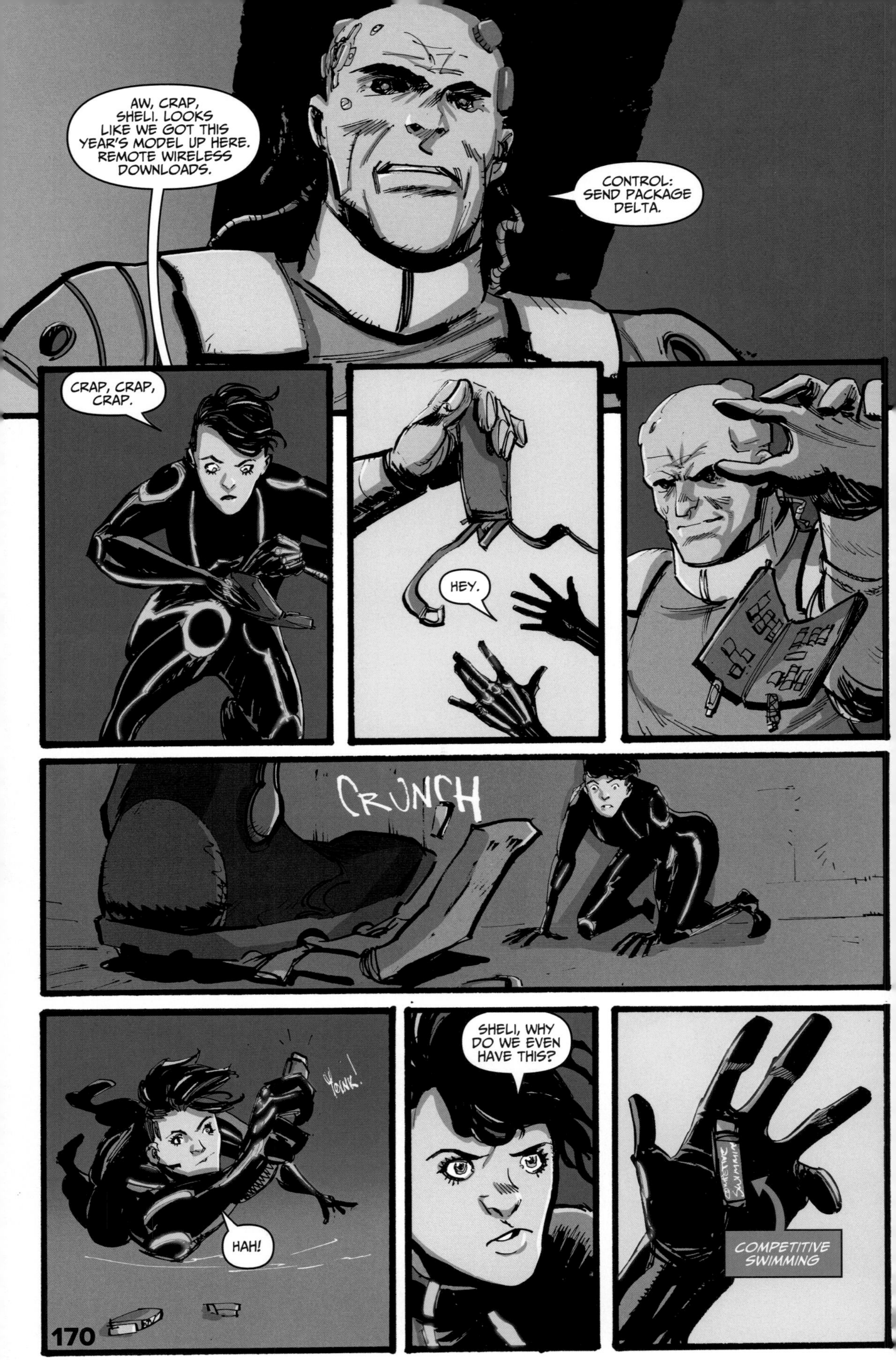
AW, CRAP, SHELI. LOOKS LIKE WE GOT THIS YEAR'S MODEL UP HERE. REMOTE WIRELESS DOWNLOADS.
CONTROL: SEND PACKAGE DELTA.
CRAP, CRAP, CRAP.
HEY.
CRUNCH
YOINK!
HAH!
SHELI, WHY DO WE EVEN HAVE THIS?
COMPETITIVE SWIMMING
COMPETITIVE SWIMMING

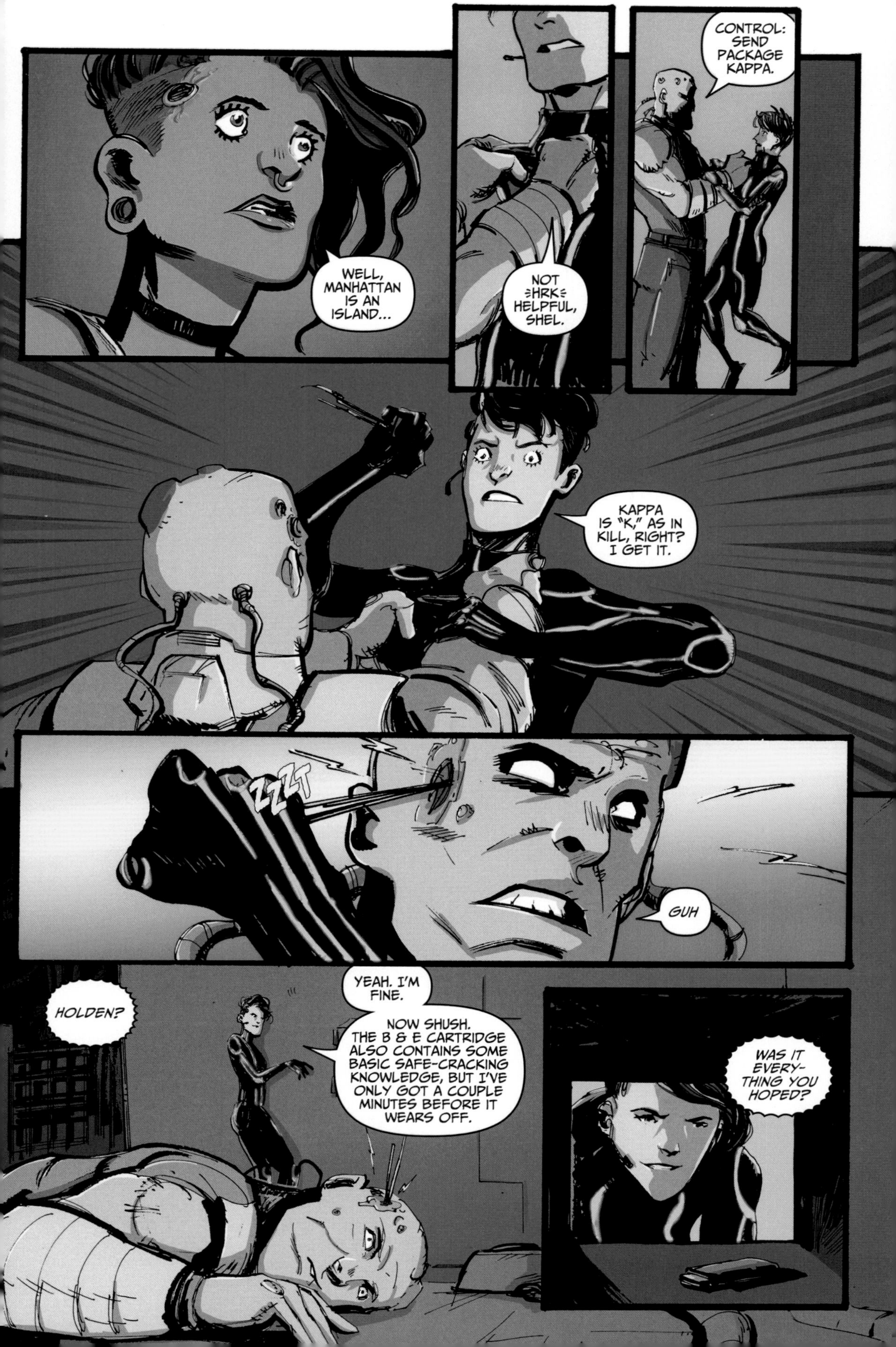
WELL, MANHATTAN IS AN ISLAND...
NOT HRK HELPFUL, SHEL.
CONTROL: SEND PACKAGE KAPPA.
KAPPA IS "K," AS IN KILL, RIGHT? I GET IT.
ZZZT
GUH
HOLDEN?
YEAH. I'M FINE.
NOW SHUSH. THE B & E CARTRIDGE ALSO CONTAINS SOME BASIC SAFE-CRACKING KNOWLEDGE, BUT I'VE ONLY GOT A COUPLE MINUTES BEFORE IT WEARS OFF.
WAS IT EVERY-THING YOU HOPED?

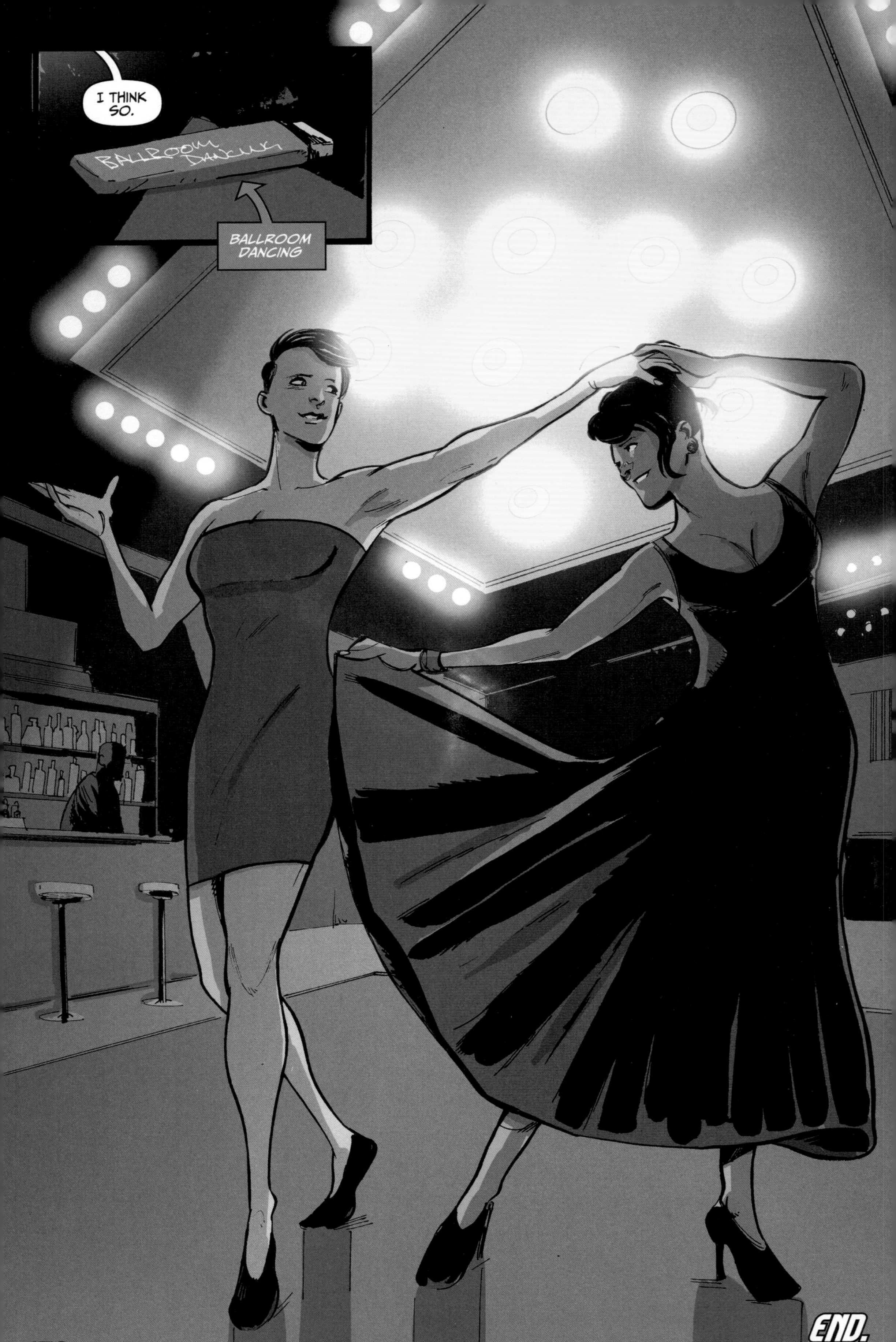
I THINK SO.
BALLROOM DANCING
END.

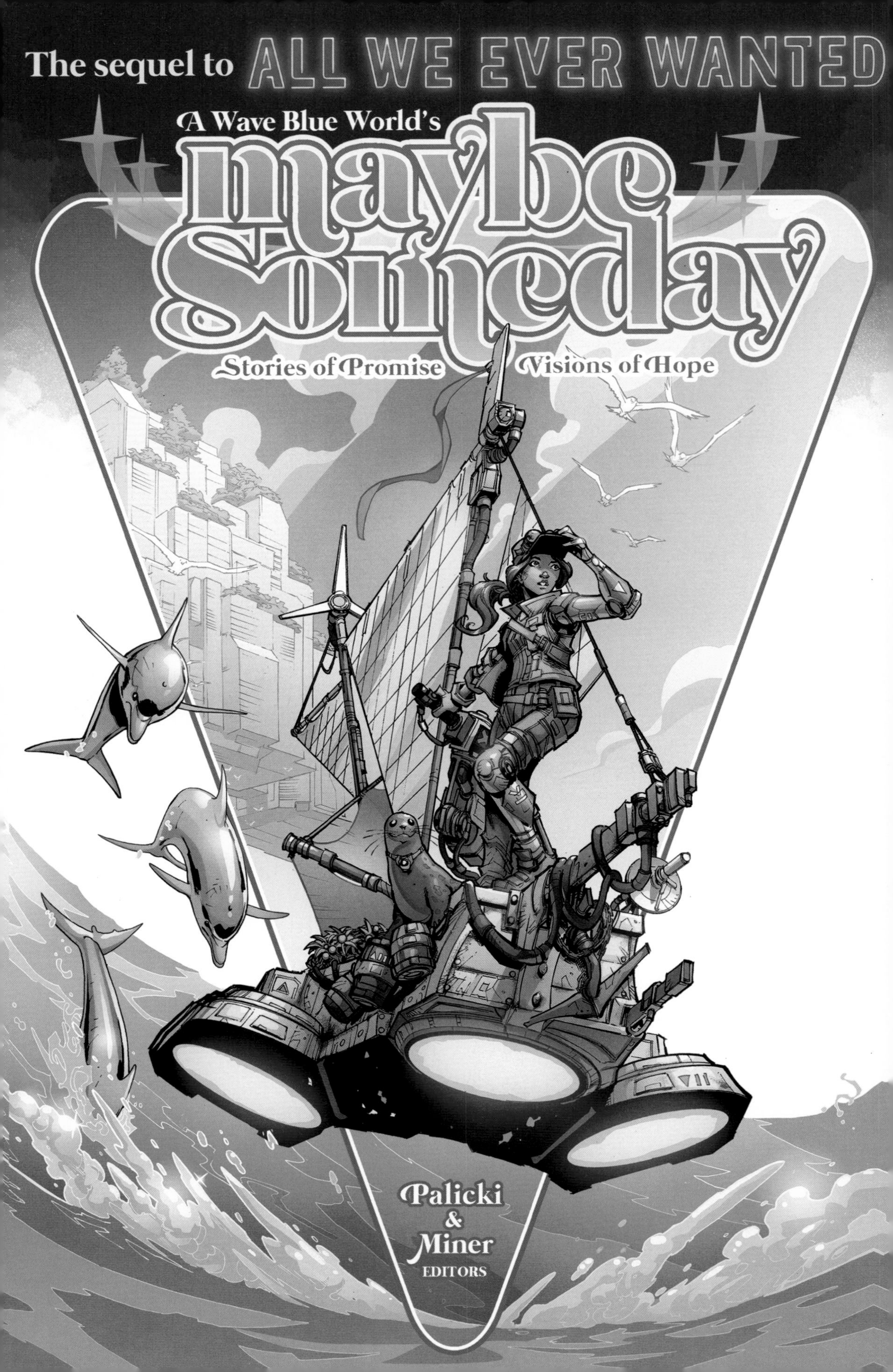

The sequel to ALL WE EVER WANTED
A Wave Blue World's
maybe Someday
Stories of Promise
Visions of Hope
Palicki
&
Miner
EDITORS

Look Inside

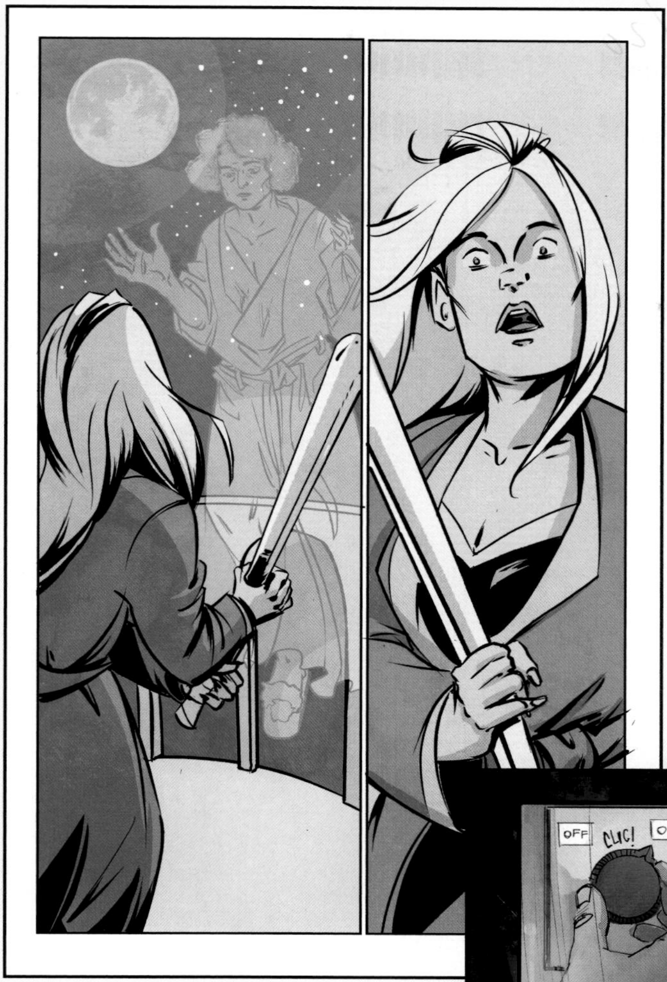

"Ghost in the Apartment"

by Erica Schultz, Stelladia and Cardinal Rae

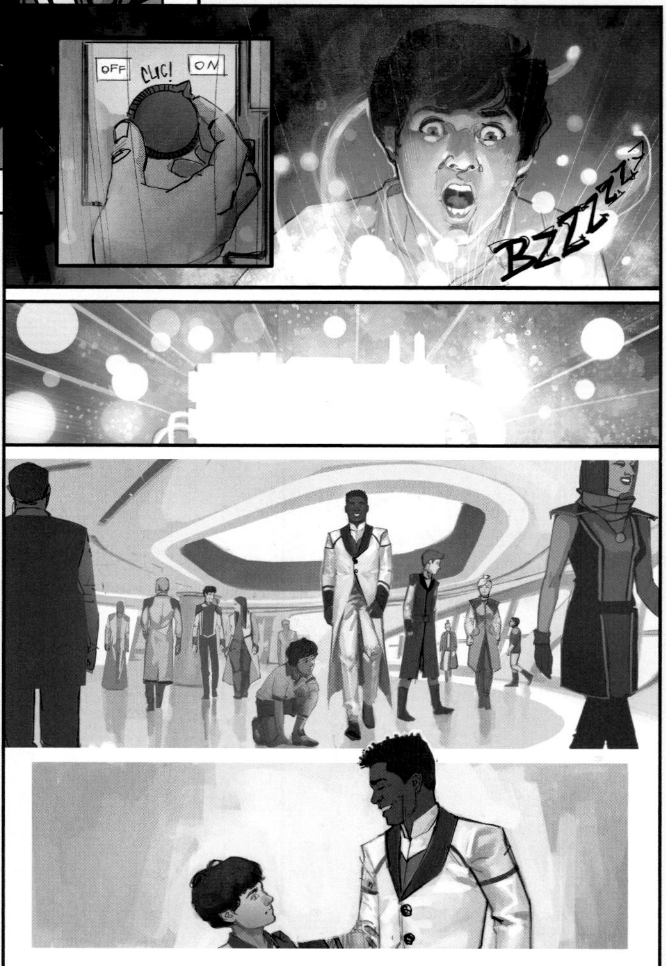
OFF
CLIC!
ON
BZZZZZZ

"To Wish Impossible Things"

by Matt Miner and Rod Reis

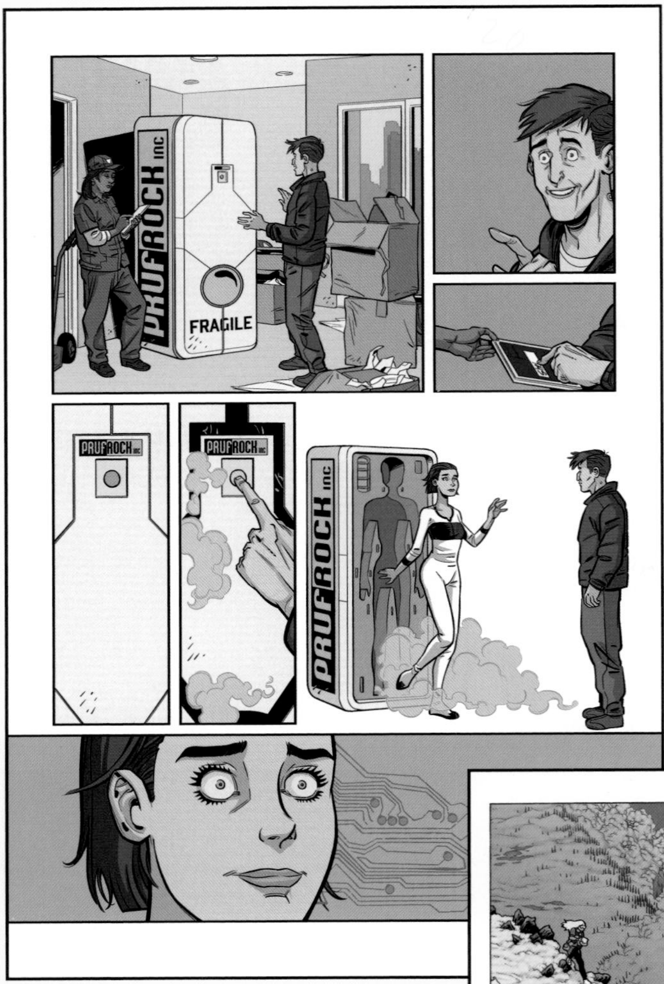
PRUFROCK inc
FRAGILE
PRUFROCK inc
PRUFROCK inc
PRUFROCK inc

"What You Need"

by Alisa Kwitney, Alain Mauricet and Kelly Fitzpatrick

"A Dangerous Lesson"

by Ethan Sacks, Anthony Breznican, Jeff Edwards and Andy Poole

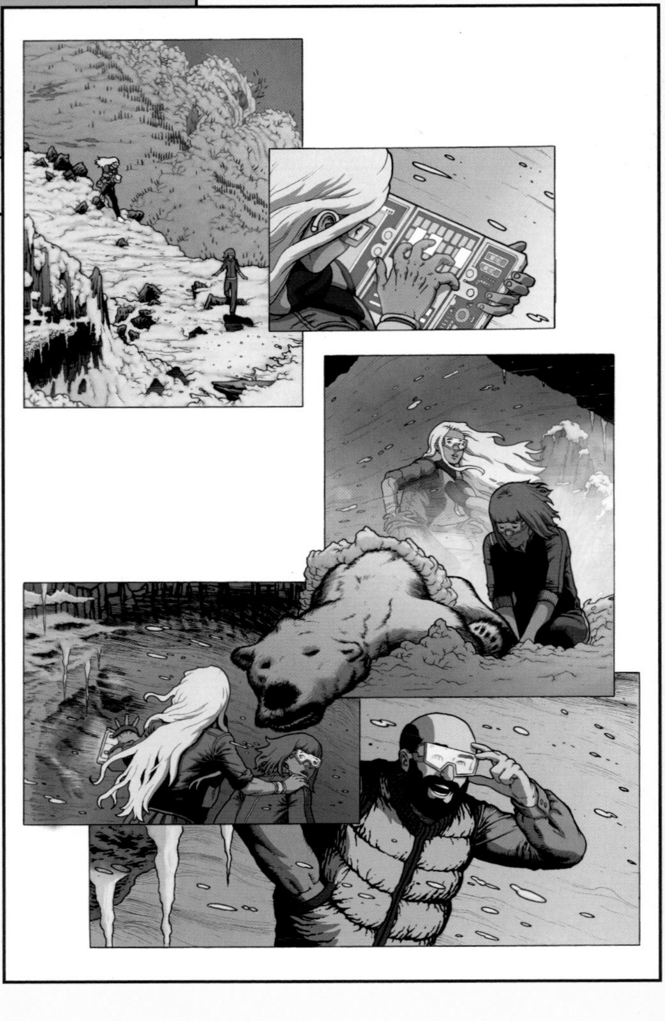

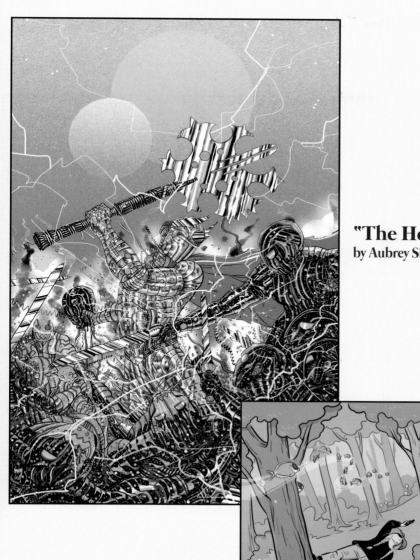

"The Heroic Truth"
by Aubrey Sitterson and Nick Pyle

"Allison Wonderland"
by Eric Palicki and Sally Jane Thompson

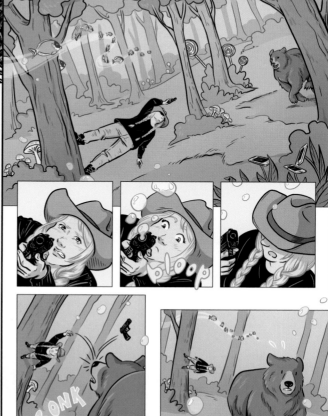

ISBN: 9781949518115

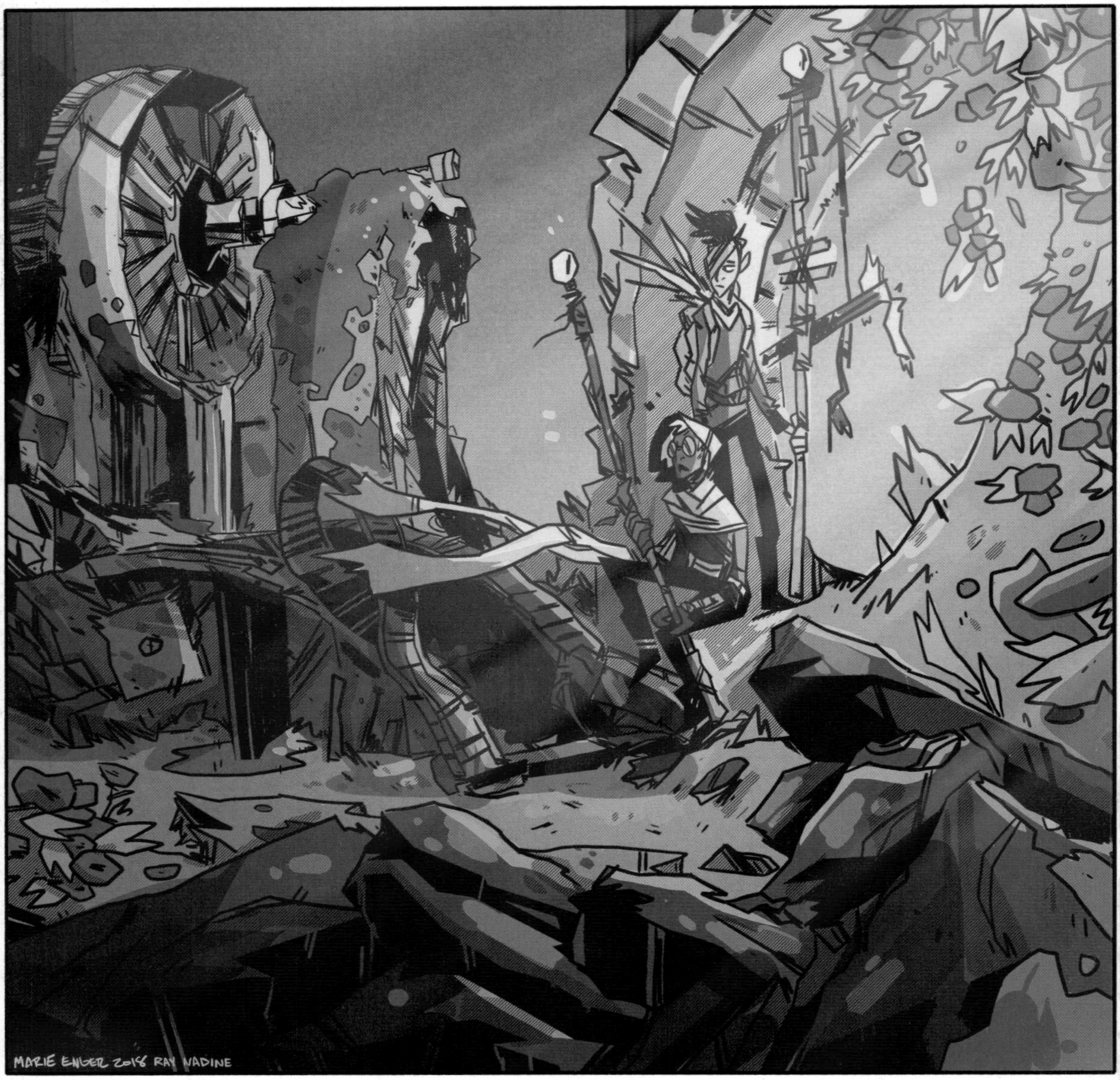
MARIE ENGER 2018 RAY NADINE

Illustration by Marie Enger
Colors by Ray Nadine